No Place to Hide:
The South and Human Rights

No Place to Hide: The South and Human Rights

VOLUME II

by
Ralph McGill
edited with an introduction by
Calvin M. Logue

MERCER
UNIVERSITY PRESS

ISBN 0-86544-109-4 (Volume 2)
ISBN 0-86554-108-6 (Volume 1)

All books published by Mercer University Press
are produced on acid-free paper that exceeds
the minimum standards set by the
National Historical Publications and Records Commission.

Library of Congress Cataloging in Publication Data
McGill, Ralph, 1898–1969.
No place to hide

Includes bibliographical references and index.
1. Afro-Americans—Civil rights—Southern States—
Collected works.   2. Southern States—Race relations—
Collected works.   3. Civil rights—Southern States—
Collected works.   I. Logue, Cal M. (Calvin McLeod),
1935–   II. Title.
E185.61.M477   1984   305.8'96073'075   84-1044
ISBN 0-86554-108-6 (v. 1 : alk. paper)
ISBN 0-86554-109-4 (v. 2 : alk. paper)

Contents

VOLUME I

Editor's Introduction
   Ralph McGill's Moderate Campaign for Racial Reform... xi
Acknowledgments.. xlvii
The World of Ralph McGill in Pictures xlix
1 The Southeast 1
2 Constantine Chapter, C.S.A. 48
3 This Is Our Georgia 54
4 Something of Georgia 59
5 My Georgia 63
6 It Has Happened Here.. 68
7 Hate at Cut Rates 79
8 How it Happened Down in Georgia.................................. 89
9 Will the South Ditch Truman? 96
10 The Housing Challenge... 108
11 Common Sense Can Save Both 118
12 Give Me Georgia 126
13 A Northerner Looks at the South:
    Review of Ray Sprigle's
    In the Land of Jim Crow 131
14 Civil Rights for the Negro...................................... 134

15 Demagoguery State by State:
    Review of V. O. Key's
    Southern Politics.. 141
16 Weighing a Dixie Dilemma:
    Review of Hodding Carter's
    Southern Legacy.. 144
17 The Real Reconstuction Begins................................. 147
18 Why I Live in Atlanta... 156
19 History in a President's Letters:
    Review of *F.D.R.: His Personal Letters, 1929-1945* 161
20 Yellow Fever Experiment.. 165
21 A Word Portrait:
    Review of James Howell Street's Article on Atlanta 168
22 Georgia's Stake in the
    Democratic National Convention, 1952........................ 170
23 Dwight D. Eisenhower 175
24 Report on Adlai E. Stevenson 180
25 How Adlai Stevenson Won Georgia's Heart
    All Over Again 186
26 At the Threshold 188
27 Is the Federal Government Running Our Lives?............... 196
28 New Truth in a New Nation:
    Review of Jay Saunders Redding's
    An American in India.. 211
29 Adlai Stevenson and the Democratic South..................... 214
30 The Angry South, 1956.. 218
31 A Southerner Talks with the South:
    Review of Robert Penn Warren's
    Segregation 228
32 Dwight Eisenhower and the South 232
33 Southern Politics: Won't Gamble Cushy Jobs 235
34 Review of Winston S. Churchill's
    The Age of Revolution.. 238
35 Review of James McBride Dabbs's
    Southern Heritage.. 241
36 The Southern Moderates Are Still There, 1958 244
37 Review of Winston S. Churchill's
    The Great Democracies 254

38 Review of Brainard Cheney's
    This Is Adam 257
39 Speaking for the South—and to It:
    Review of Brooks Hays's
    A Southern Moderate Speaks 260
40 As the South Begins to Put Its Burden Down,
    an Interim Report:
    Review of William Peters's
    Southern Temper 264
41 The Crisis of the City 268
42 If the Southern Negro Got the Vote 274
43 A Changing South as I See It, 1959 282
44 The Agony of the Southern Minister 289
45 She Sifted the Ashes and Built a City 298
46 Saving the Schools 306
47 Foreword to Mildred E. English's
    College in the Country 308
48 Memories of Bellamy and FDR 312
49 Notes for United Negro College Fund Meeting 316

VOLUME II

    Acknowledgments xi
    The World of Ralph McGill in Pictures xiii
50 The State of the South, 1960 323
51 New Law, Old Fears 329
52 South of the Dream:
    Review of C. Vann Woodward's
    The Burden of Southern History 334
53 The Confederates' Torpedoes 339
54 Review of Dan Wakefield's
    Revolt in the South 344
55 What Makes America Great 347
56 The Chattahoochee River 354
57 A Southern Editor Talks with Philadelphia Negroes 362
58 The Road to Southern Maturity Is Long and Bumpy:
    Review of Thomas D. Clark's
    The Emerging South 369

59 The South Will Change, 1961 373
60 Let's Lead Where We Lag.. 382
61 Rebirth of Hope at Ole Miss? 388
62 Chattanooga—
   Where the Mountains Look at Each Other 393
63 Where We Stand: Emancipation 398
64 Television Interview about Africa 402
65 A Sensitive Southerner's View of a Smoking City 413
66 Georgia Tech: Lighthouse to the Postwar South 418
67 An Interview on Race and the Church, 1963 422
68 The South Looks Ahead.. 436
69 Radio "Conversation Piece"................................... 444
70 Hate Knows No Direction 469
71 When a Man Stands Up to Be Counted,
   He May Be Counted Out:
   Review of Charles Morgan's
   A Time to Speak.. 473
72 A Decade of Slow, Painful Progress, 1964..................... 477
73 The Case for the Southern Progressive 482
74 First of All, Georgians Are Americans......................... 492
75 From Atlanta: The Political Assessment, 1964................. 497
76 From Boyhood Onward,
   the Course Was against the Tide:
   Review of Frank E. Smith's
   A Congressman from Mississippi 503
77 Equality on the Firing Line:
   Review of Anthony Lewis's
   Portrait of a Decade: The Second American Revolution 507
78 The Church in a Social Revolution.............................. 511
79 Review of Hubert Humphrey's
   The Cause Is Mankind... 514
80 Race: Results instead of Reasons
   Review of Howard Zinn's
   SNCC: The New Abolitionists and
   The Southern Mystique 517
81 The Clearest Truth Is in Fiction:
   Review of Jesse Hill Ford's
   The Liberation of Lord Byron Jones 520

82 One Magazine Invisible: Review of
    One Hundred Years of the "Nation":
    A Centennial Anthology 525
83 Introduction to Robert McNeill's
    God Wills Us Free 530
84 Statement for Brotherhood Week 533
85 An Interview concerning John F. Kennedy 535
86 Review of C. Vann Woodward's
    Strange Career of Jim Crow 557
87 Radio Program concerning the South, 1966 562
88 Foreword to Hodding Carter's
    Southern Legacy 574
89 Foreword to Margaret Anderson's
    The Children of the South 576
90 Review of William Stringfellow's and Anthony Towne's
    The Bishop Pike Affair 581
91 The American South 588
92 Comment on Pat Watters's and Reese Cleghorn's
    Climbing Jacob's Ladder 591
93 The South's Glowing Horizon—If . . . , 1968 593
94 The New Confederacy:
    Review of Robert Sherrill's
    Gothic Politics in the Deep South 605
95 Review of James G. Maddox's *The Advancing South*,
    and F. Ray Marshall's *Labor in the South* 611
96 Letter to *Center* Magazine 619
97 Foreword to David M. Abshire's
    The South Rejects a Prophet 623
98 We Must Go Along Together for Better or Worse 625
99 Preface to Carl Sandburg's
    Chicago Race Riots 627
100 Introduction to John Osborne's
     The Old South 634
101 The New South and a New America 639
102 A Conversation with Ralph McGill, 1969 648
     Index 661

Acknowledgments

The editor expresses appreciation to the following persons for assistance and support: Ms. Elise Allen, Ms. Robin Gormley, the staff of Mercer University Press, Dr. W. J. Payne, Ms. Diane Hunter, Mr. Harold Buell, Mr. Grant Lamos, Mr. Jim Minter, the University of Georgia Library faculty and staff, Ms. Grace Lundy Tackett, Mrs. Ralph McGill, and Ms. Mary Jo Logue. The *Atlanta Constitution* and Associated Press were generous in providing photographs for the two volumes.

The World
of Ralph McGill
in Pictures

The house of a black family in Ringgold, Georgia, lies in ruins after a bomb exploded in the early hours of 19 May 1960. A 32-year-old mother of four children was killed in the blast; her husband and one of the children were injured. Members of the Ku Klux Klan had recently demonstrated in the area, but police could determine no motive for placing 25 to 30 pounds of dynamite under the bedroom of the house. (Associated Press photo)

*Georgia highway patrolmen carrying clubs watch as black student demonstrators protesting segregation march near the Georgia State Capitol in Atlanta on 17 May 1960. Following the march, Georgia Governor Ernest Vandiver threatened to revoke the tax-exempt status of black colleges that permitted students to demonstrate. (*Atlanta Journal and Constitution *photo by Marion Johnson)*

Dr. Martin Luther King, Jr. (right), accompanied by Lonnie C. King (center), is driven to jail by Atlanta Police Captain R. E. Little, Jr., after being arrested in a civil rights demonstration on 19 October 1960. (Atlanta Journal photo by Charles Jackson)

As the wave of "lunch counter sit-ins" launched by student activists in 1960 reached Atlanta, a Woolworth store closed its lunch counter and stacked merchandise along the counter and on the stools to prevent blacks from occupying the space even as a symbolic gesture. (Associated Press photo)

*Plants, exhibits, and Christmas decorations lie amid the debris of a classroom at English Avenue Elementary School in Atlanta after the school and a dozen houses nearby were shattered by a bomb that exploded at 2:40 a.m. on 12 December 1960. No one was injured, but the school was severely damaged. The bombing appeared to be a reaction to lunch counter sit-ins by college students in Atlanta. Atlanta Mayor William Hartsfield blamed the bombing on an "ignorant rabble, inflamed by political demagogues and encouraged by the silence of most of our substantial civic leaders." (*Atlanta Journal *photo by Bob Dendy)*

Students arrested in a sit-in at The Coffee Shop on Forsyth Street in downtown Atlanta are loaded into a police car to be transported to jail on 12 February 1961. (Atlanta Constitution photo)

xx

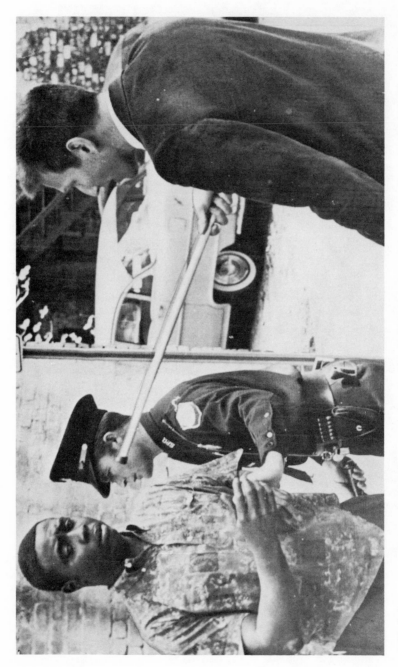

A black demonstrator (left) arrested in Savannah, Georgia, is berated by an angry white participant in a St. Patrick's Day celebration on 17 March 1960. (Associated Press photo)

In a famous photograph President John F. Kennedy and his brother, Attorney General Robert F. Kennedy, confer outside the oval office of the White House as 320 federal marshals escort James Meredith onto the campus of the University of Mississippi on 1 October 1962. After battling a mob of white racists through the night, the marshals and federal troops saw Meredith register as a student the next day. (Associated Press photo)

James Meredith, the first black student formally admitted to the University of Mississippi, meets with Attorney General Robert F. Kennedy at the Justice Department in Washington, D.C. on 27 May 1963. Kennedy arranged the conversation after watching an interview with Meredith on television. Meredith urged the Kennedy administration to pursue stronger civil rights legislation. (Associated Press photo)

*Governor George Wallace of Alabama, "standing in the schoolhouse door" to prevent deseg-
regation of the University of Alabama, is confronted by Brigadier General Henry Graham
of the National Guard. Wallace had earlier refused entry to civilian representatives accompanying two black students, but he stood aside after President John F. Kennedy ordered federal
troops to the scene, and the students were permitted to enroll on 11 June 1963. (Associated
Press photo)*

Blacks march in downtown Savannah, Georgia, during massive demonstrations against segregation in white businesses and denial of voting rights. This march on 11 July 1963 was halted by police, who arrested 48 persons and charged them with "rioting." (Atlanta Constitution *photo*)

Three young blacks attempting to integrate a beach in Savannah, Georgia, on 14 July 1963 are ordered out of the water. All three were arrested after they were forced to stop swimming. (Associated Press photo)

Young black demonstrators protest segregation in Birmingham, Alabama, in the spring of 1963. The "Johannesburg of the South," as blacks called it then, responded to scenes like this with fire hoses, police dogs, and wanton bombings of homes and offices of civil rights leaders. The violent reaction culminated in the bombing of the Sixteenth Street Baptist Church on Sunday, 15 September 1963, just as Sunday School classes were beginning. Four young women were killed and 14 other persons were injured. (Associated Press photo)

Martin Luther King, Jr. (left) listens pensively as Laurie Prichett, the police chief of Albany, Georgia, lectures him at the beginning of the protracted struggle in Albany that lasted for several years. White business and political leaders had vowed massive resistance against the efforts of King and local black leaders to desegregate the city. (Associated Press photo)

As the civil rights movement turned northward, Martin Luther King, Jr., and Ralph Abernathy, one of Dr. King's chief lieutenants in the Southern Christian Leadership Conference, came to Boston to lead a protest march in support of desegregation in schools, jobs, and housing on 23 April 1965. (Associated Press photo)

Ralph McGill (center) poses with Roy Wilkins (left), executive secretary of the National Association for the Advancement of Colored People, and Carl T. Rowan, director of the U.S. Information Agency, after the three received honorary degrees from Atlanta University on 31 May 1965. The citation for McGill's Doctor of Humanities degree lauded him as "a man of keen insight, great moral courage and force, lover of people, prophet and conscience of the new South". (Atlanta Constitution photo by Bob Dendy)

On the march from Selma, Alabama, to the state capitol in Montgomery, in March 1965, Dr. Martin Luther King, Jr. (center) shares a light moment with other black leaders who would eventually establish themselves as the voices of "Black Power." Among them were Hosea Williams (left) and Stokely Carmichael and Willie Ricks (right) of the Student Nonviolent Coordinating Committee. (Atlanta Constitution photo)

Dr. Martin Luther King, Jr. (center), accompanied by Mrs. Coretta King, leads a march on the State Capitol to protest the refusal of the Georgia legislature to seat State Representative Julian Bond. Bond, then a member of the Student Nonviolent Coordinating Committee, had been denied the seat to which he had been elected by voters of the 136th House District ostensibly because of his opposition to the military draft and the war in Vietnam. The march on 14 January 1966 ended in violence when some SNCC members broke from the ranks and rushed at Georgia highway patrolmen standing guard near the capitol. That incident brought relations between SNCC and King's SCLC to the breaking point. (Atlanta Constitution photo by Hugh Stovall)

*Georgia State Representative Julian Bond, who engineered a successful political career on the basis of flamboyant human rights activism. Voter registration campaigns propelled Bond to the Georgia legislature, where he served with distinction despite efforts to deny him his seat because of his political views. Bond led an insurgent delegation to the 1968 Democratic Convention and managed to obtain credentials for half its members; his protest led to important and far-reaching changes in delegate-selection procedures. He was nominated for vice-president from the floor of the 1968 convention, but declined with a smile—he was then too young to serve. (*Atlanta Constitution *photo)*

Ralph McGill greets visitors to his office on 30 January 1969, in the last photograph made before his death. McGill *had joined the* Constitution *as sports editor in 1929; he became executive editor in 1938, editor in 1942, and publisher in 1960. (*Atlanta Constitution *photo by Charles Pugh)*

The State of the South
1960

Acivil rights bill, reduced to near pygmy size by the slimming pills of Senate amendments, has now become law. It is aimed chiefly at establishing voting rights for Negroes long disfranchised in many areas of the South. It will help very little in the counties where disfranchisement is most coercively practiced.

Liberal leaders in the Senate, who sought a much more comprehensive rights bill, said scornfully that the legislative giant labored and brought forth a mouse. Deep South dissenters, though they know better and recognize the bill as moderate, say with anguish that sacred states' rights have suffered a mortal blow in granting a boon to human rights.

Neither of these descriptions fits. The new rights law is a most conservative beginning. The efforts of perhaps two or three more Congresses will be required to strengthen it before it provides adequate protection of the franchise. But an approach has been made. Qualified voters, denied the right to register to vote, may ask the intervention of federal courts. The courts have the power to examine the evidence and, if it indicates the applicants to be qualified, then and there to declare them to be so. But no physical protection will be available for those who try to use this qualification in counties where intimidation and fear have

Reprinted by permission of Mrs. Ralph McGill and the Anti-Defamation League of B'nai B'rith, from the *ADL Bulletin*, May 1960.

heretofore prevented voting. Hence the disappointment of educated, long-denied and frustrated Negroes in the rural South is keen and understandable.

Only a general answer is possible to the question of what the civil rights bill may mean. It should extend registration in the urban communities where a great majority of Negro registrants now are. Perhaps in time the law will produce progress where today a puny percentage of Negro residents are on the clerk's voting lists.[213]

None may honestly guess as to how long that span of time will be. The record of the past is that no state has ever voluntarily made civil rights concessions. The federal courts eliminated the white primaries in 1944-1946. Since the Supreme Court school decision of 1954 the right of franchise has been more grievously restricted than before. But there is today a new strength in the mood of the Negro in the South. It is affected by the South African resistance to discrimination. The appearance of new African nations has influenced it. It is apparent in the student sit-ins. The fact that many white students joined in to sit with them, that many Southern ministers spoke out for their objectives, and that prominent leaders over the nation did the same, has contributed to the new mood.[214]

The Southern picture has been, and is, complex and contradictory. It defies easy analysis. Some idea of why it is difficult to say, in a few simple sentences, what the new act will mean to the Negro voters may be had from a few examples.

There are in the South twenty-nine counties which, the latest available figures show, are without a single Negro registered to vote. Fifteen of these are in Mississippi, four in Louisiana, three in Florida, with two each in Georgia and Alabama. Virginia, Tennessee, and South Carolina each have one such county. There are other counties, of course, which

---

[213]See Steven F. Lawson, *Black Ballots: Voting Rights in the South, 1944-1969* (New York: Columbia University Press, 1976); Chandler Davidson, *Biracial Politics: Conflict and Coalition in the Metropolitan South* (Baton Rouge: Louisiana State University Press, 1972); Numan V. Bartley and Hugh D. Graham, *Southern Elections: County and Precinct Data, 1950-1972* (Baton Rouge: Louisiana State University Press, 1978).

[214]See "Let's Lead Where We Lag," "Church in a Social Revolution," "Southern Moderates are Still There," and "Introduction to Robert McNeill's *God Wills Us Free*," in volumes 1 and 2.

have a token number of registrants, as few as seven or perhaps fifty or one hundred or so. Twelve Alabama counties, for example, have populations over fifty percent Negro. The median percentage of Negro voters is a mere four percent.[215]

A good many Negroes in these populations are qualified. But the facts are that a long time will be needed to raise the total substantially. Most of these overtly restricting counties are in the old-plantation region, or Black Belt, which reaches from Virginia to East Texas. In this area most of the old-plantation-type economy holds on. It still has the highest percentage of Negro population despite immigration to industrial jobs.

The new civil rights law may see the Black Belt counties accept a token few as voters to avoid court action. But it is safe to say that for the foreseeable future there will be but little enfranchisement in them.

It has been these unconscionably repressive counties which have given the South a bad name. And they likely will offer the most flagrant evasions of the new legislation. If so, they will cause additional civil rights actions to be introduced in the Congresses of the future.

What Negro leadership everywhere will be up against as it strives to use the new legislation or to encourage county leaders to open up the books without recourse to it, is a lack of political consciousness on the part of much of the rural Negro population as well as much of the Negro population in cities. This is not just the apathy found among all voters in a nation where only about sixty percent of voters turn out on election days. The Negro was denied the ballot in most of the Southern states until 1944 when the white primary was abolished. (If registered, he could vote in the November general elections. But there were no opposition candidates to those chosen in the white primary in which he could not participate.)

No social-science study exists to give any evaluation of the effect of segregation on the development of political consciousness and civic, or citizenship, responsibility. The Negro has, for generations, been cut off from the ballot, from participation in community policy making, from

---

[215]See Jack Bass and Walter DeVries, *The Transformation of Southern Politics: Social Change and Political Consequences Since 1945* (New York: New American Library, 1977).

libraries, from secondary and college education, and in most places from any real communication with the white community leaders. The process is not calculated to develop a consciousness of political responsibility in politics, or citizenship. The Negro today finds it wryly humorous that after having been refused an opportunity for such development, this lack is now being held against him and he is advised he must demonstrate responsibility before being admitted to citizenship.

Meanwhile, the more thoughtful Southern leadership privately is troubled. It is politically trapped by extremist elements in at least five states and cannot really go to the people with the truth for fear of reprisals by the more demagogic among their number. The change in the congressional attitude was apparent in the Senate filibuster against the rights bill. There were no vulgar speeches of hate and slander such as the late Senators Bilbo and "Cotton Ed" Smith delighted to make. The senators live with great events and they would like to have done with the issue—but they are captives of their constituents. The South is paying a harsh price for listening to those men who told the people the federal courts could be circumscribed.[216]

The South has been in transition since its old social and economic order died at Appomattox. Now there is an acceleration of that process. Abolition of the white primary, the school order of 1954, the court decisions which followed it and the civil rights legislation are examples of this stepped-up pace. The student sit-ins were yet another. These were a real shock to the South. Few Southerners realized, though they had been told, that events were moving so rapidly. And while there were expressions of anger and outrage, there were those on the other side.[217] In North Carolina, where the sit-ins began, a number of white ministers were immediately outspoken in behalf of the student objectives.

[216]See Cal M. Logue and Howard Dorgan, eds. *Oratory of Southern Demagogues* (Baton Rouge: Louisiana State University Press, 1981).

[217]See Monroe Lee Billington, *Political South in the Twentieth Century* (New York: Charles Scribner, 1975); John C. McKinney and Edgar T. Thompson, eds., *South in Continuity and Change* (Durham: Duke University Press, 1965); Thomas H. Naylor and James Clotfelter, *Strategies for Change in the South* (Chapel Hill: University of North Carolina Press, 1975).

Church leaders and publications, particularly the Presbyterian and Episcopalian, also declared the moral issue involved could not be honestly denied. In Florida, Governor LeRoy Collins made a statewide television address in which, while he described the sit-ins as illegal and dangerous, he nonetheless declared them to be morally right. He called on the businesses involved to recognize this moral factor and their own vulnerability. His mail was heavy and overwhelmingly favorable. But what everywhere shocked the South most was that white students from Southern institutions joined the Negro sit-ins as evidence of their own recognition of the moral issue involved. This was a stunner to old traditions.[218]

It is quite possible the net result of the sit-ins will be to allow the moral feature of the whole problem to find expression. Until now the issues of the right to vote, the public schools and use of public facilities have been narrowly confined to politicians, elections, lawyers, and police actions. That it was also a moral issue was obscured. Now, however, a great many persons who are sincerely indignant about the sit-ins nonetheless find themselves admitting, often to their own surprise, it is not "right" to deny the right to vote to a qualified person and not "right" to invite customers into a ten-cent store and deny some of them the sandwich counter. Not until now has the question of what is morally "right" been raised above the dust of legalism and political exploitation. The courts and the Congress will remain the source of solid progress, but the lighting of the lamp of ethical morality was long overdue.

It was inescapable that, as massive resistance to federal law and the Constitution was organized in Virginia and the Deep South, all extremists would have a field day. Anti-Semitic groups were stirred to new life. Most of them were already members of the White Citizens' Councils. A good two-thirds of those chapters are as much anti-Jewish as they are anti-Negro. With the appearance of Sen. John Kennedy, a Roman Catholic, as a possible nominee for the Democratic presidential nomination, they began to use this prejudice as a third dues-getting gadget. The greedy KKK groups could not hold together. They split up into five or

[218]See McGill's "LeRoy Collins: Florida's Nominee for Governor Started Out In a Grocery Store," in *Southern Encounters: Southerners of Note in Ralph McGill's South*, ed. Calvin M. Logue (Macon GA: Mercer University Press, 1983).

six klans, each claiming the greater orthodoxy and each beating the drums for dues from those whom a robe and a mask provide with a feeling of superiority.[219]

The open defiance of courts and processes of law by governors, legislatures, attorneys general, and other leading figures in public and private life encouraged a harvest of lawlessness. Alabama, where one-time Admiral John G. Crommelin has been operating a prolific hate mill for more than a decade, quite naturally is reaping the most tragic harvest, though Georgia, Mississippi and South Carolina all have had their crop of shame.

In these states there is not much middle ground left. But, there is progress in the Southern border states. Since they have not officially encouraged lawlessness, they have had less of it. Their school problem is under control, progress made.

In politics the story is the same. The Deep South states, harried by extremists and propagandized by hate organizations, are in a mood to withhold their electors in November in hopes a close presidential race might give them bargaining power if the decision should be thrown into the House of Representatives. There will be no real decision until after the national conventions.

Meanwhile, the South is beginning to understand that it has been deceived by much of its political leadership about the relative power of state and federal authority. Knowledge that they have been wrong makes present resentment greater. Meanwhile, the processes of law and economics continue. One day common sense and ethical morality will prevail. But when that day will dawn none can say.

---

[219]See Neil R. McMillen, *The Citizens' Council* (Urbana: University of Illinois Press, 1971).

51

New Law, Old Fears

A compromise civil rights bill that pleased nobody has emerged from Congress and is now law. The inevitable question is: What benefits can the Negro citizen, who for so long has been disfranchised in many areas of the South, expect from a bill that was so thoroughtly mutilated and watered down by Congressional conflicts?

Negroes in rural counties where fear and intimidation have long denied them the right to register and vote, or have granted these rights only to a token handful, are far from hopeful. An example of this disillusionment was a letter written to a newspaper by a Negro woman teacher in a rural county in Georgia that had not a single Negro on its voters' list. The letter consisted of two lines from Stephen Vincent Benét's *John Brown's Body*. They were taken from the section that follows immediately after the description of the hanging of the fanatical prophet:

> Slaves will be slaves next year,
>   in spite of the bones,
> Nothing is changed, John Brown,
>   nothing is changed.[220]

Reprinted by permission of Mrs. Ralph McGill and *Reporter* magazine (9 June 1960). Copyright by Reporter Magazine Company.

[220]*John Brown's Body* by Stephen Vincent Benét, from *Selected Works of Stephen Vincent Benét* (New York: Holt, Rinehart and Winston). Copyright renewed 1955, 1956, by Rosemary Carr Benét. Reprinted by permission of Brandt & Brandt Literary Agents, Inc.

Although there was disappointment, there was none of the defeatism that followed earlier disappointments. "I can't tell you what it is," said a young Negro student in Tallahassee, Florida, a participant in the lunch-counter sit-ins.

> I just know how it is with me. My parents learned how to live with seg-regation, to wait, to go to the back of the bus. They saved and sacrificed on a little farm so as to send me here. In times of deep despair I would imagine I could feel the sweat of my father's and mother's hands on the coins in my pocket. I'd like to live long enough and be a part of whatever it takes to see them have a little dignity in their lives. This new civil rights voting law will be used. We'll give it a try.

In South Carolina a Negro farmer said: "My boy is grown and in a job up North. My daughter is a teacher in a state where her job is safe. Now, I think, some of us will be willing to make whatever sacrifice is necessary to use the new voting law."

Southern Negroes are realistic about the sacrifices and risks that lie ahead. A Negro teacher in Alabama said:

> For Negroes in the counties where violence has been the pattern the new act still leaves a man naked. Suppose a federal judge does find, as he can't miss finding in some counties, a pattern of discrimination as the bill specifies must be found? And what if the judge then registers those qualified? The Negro still must take that federal slip of paper and go to the polls with it. And that will be a lonely trip. Yes, sir. Real lonely. He will still find the men there who have refused him before. And they will be hating him. He will still find the black ballot box for segregated voting. Who will protect him or his house? Where will that judge be then?

The question dramatizes the weakness of the bill. In a Mississippi county where no Negroes are registered, a carpenter whose wife teaches school said: "I don't want my job cut off and I don't want my wife's job cut off either. I know the law is passed, but we've got to live here. We own a little house. Who'd buy it if we want to move? It might get burned if we stay and try to vote."

There are still twenty-nine so-called goose-egg counties in which the latest available figures show no Negroes at all registered to vote. Fifteen of these are in Mississippi. Four are in Louisiana. Florida has three. Georgia and Alabama have two each; Virginia, Tennessee, and South

Carolina one each. There are other counties that have only a token number of Negro registrants—less than a hundred and as few as seven.

Most of these counties lie in a rough curve that reaches from southern Virginia to east Texas—the old-plantation region, or Black Belt. (Originally it was so called because of the rich black soil. Today the phrase has meaning in terms of the high percentages of Negro residents rather than the color of soil.) In this area much of the old-plantation-type economy holds on. It still has the highest ratio of Negroes, although that number steadily diminishes by migration to urban areas and industrial jobs, North, East, West, and even in the South.

The politics of all these counties is dominated by agitation over the race issue. They are losing population. Their per capita income is lower than average. Even the white children have never had adequate schools, and until comparatively recent years it was rare to find a high school for Negroes of any sort. The whites in all these counties share an unreasoning fear of the larger Negro population "taking over," and they have, for that reason, created an unwritten but rigidly enforced code. In these counties, for example, the Negro who "dresses up" except on Saturday afternoons and Sundays is made to understand that he is acting "biggity." Most of the Negroes in the Black Belt work as farm laborers or domestic servants. About the only white-collar jobs open for Negroes are in teaching, and few teachers can afford the economic risk inherent in any challenge to the pattern even if they have the courage. Few of the churches have resident ministers. Religion is a weekend or monthly affair, and so there is little if any leadership from churches or schools.

The result is that Negroes of the Black Belt are in general apathetic about the political aspects of citizenship. They know the county is run by a few men. For them there is no real choice of candidates. In each of these counties there are a few qualified men and women who have tried to register, but they know that men have been killed for it. Their homes have been bombed. Still others have lost their jobs, had their credit at the store cut off, or found mortgages on their homes and farms foreclosed. Even relatives have been fired from jobs as a warning against efforts to register. A common saying is that "voting is white folks' business." But there is certainly no reason to conclude, as many white people in these counties do, that this surface apathy means that the Negro is "satisfied" and likes things just as they are. In an attempt to head off increased agitation, there may be some token registration of "trusted" Negroes in these counties.[221]

Outside the Black Belt counties, where repression of voting rights has been most severe, the presence of a Negro population in excess of the white does not always result in disfranchisement. In the coastal county of McIntosh, Georgia, for example, Negroes constitute sixty-one percent of the population; according to the latest available registration lists, there were 1,498 white persons registered and 1,289 Negroes. In five other coastal counties of Georgia, each with large Negro populations, there is a representative number of Negroes registered who vote without overt restrictions. Even in some inland counties a substantial number of Negroes are registered. In other counties with large Negro populations in South Carolina and the other Deep South states, rival factions in county government have registered Negroes in an effort to hold or gain office.[222]

Faced with this immense and complex problem, Negro leaders know they must somehow organize and train their people to earn their rights within the framework of the new legislation. They are up against a lack of political consciousness produced by generations of too little education and even less opportunity to acquire political awareness by practice.

Southern Negro leaders say the Republican party, if it had the vision, could move far toward establishing a two-party competition in the South simply by offering a plan to assist through local organizations the adult education necessary to increase registration in urban areas. The Negro voter in the South, Democratic since the New Deal, will probably not remain so. There is irrefutable logic in this estimate of the possibilities of a quick gain in GOP voting strength. But in most of the Southern states the white Republican organization, though anxious for

---

[221]See John Hope Franklin and Isidore Starr, eds., *The Negro in Twentieth-Century America: A Reader on the Struggle for Civil Rights* (New York: Vintage Books, 1967).

[222]See Jack Bass and Walter DeVries, *The Transformation of Southern Politics: Social Change and Political Consequence Since 1945* (New York: New American Library, 1977); Steven F. Lawson, *Black Ballots: Voting Rights in the South, 1944-1969* (New York: Columbia University Press, 1976).

power, would hesitate to court the Negro vote publicly and thereby incur the hostility of white Democratic neighbors.[223]

But one thing is clear. If Southern leadership is so blind as to try and thwart the intent of the new voting law, the next Congress will surely strengthen it. For the present it may appear that the despairing Negro teacher from Georgia is right: "Nothing is changed, John Brown, nothing is changed."

Not yet, perhaps. But it *is* a beginning.

---

[223]See Paul E. Mertz, *New Deal Policy and Southern Rural Poverty* (Baton Rouge: Louisiana State University Press, 1978); Frank Burt Freidel, *F.D.R. and the South* (Baton Rouge: Louisiana State University Press, 1965); V. O. Key, Jr., *Southern Politics in State and Nation* (New York: Vintage Books, 1949); and Dewey W. Grantham, Jr., *Democratic South* (Athens: University of Georgia Press, 1963).

52

South of the Dream: Review of C. Vann Woodward's *The Burden of Southern History*

Back in 1938 when I sat down to read C. Vann Woodward's *Tom Watson: Agrarian Rebel*, I knew right away that I was reading Southern history and that previously I had wasted too much time on stuff that fitted Henry Ford's definition of history as "bunk." Indeed, I never managed to condemn Mr. Ford for that statement, because there was always the chance he had been reading the more popular Southern historians.[224]

When I had done with the Watson book I was so stirred I went by bus, car, and rail over the old Populist areas of south Georgia hunting up old men who had been fierce Watson adherents and who had seen men killed and beaten for so being. He was a strange and tragic man, Tom Watson, a harsh mixture of good and evil. He left his mark deeply on my region. But, though I had read much, I never had a good window

Reprinted by permission of Mrs. Ralph McGill and *Reporter* magazine (10 November 1960). Copyright by Reporter Magazine Company. Review of C. Vann Woodward, *The Burden of Southern History*, rev. ed. (Baton Rouge: Louisiana State University Press, 1968).

[224]C. Vann Woodward, *Tom Watson: Agrarian Rebel* (New York: Oxford University Press, 1963).

through which to look at him and the Populist period in the South, of which he became a major symbol, until Vann Woodward opened it.[225]

Reunion and Reaction (1951) was light in darkness. *Origins of the New South* (1951) for the first time brought the South fully into focus. *The Strange Career of Jim Crow* (1955) contributed sanity when the White Citizens' Councils and the Southern politicians were strenuously advocating, and practicing, madness. Woodward has never compromised with the racist politicians or apologists for those so-called customs which the Citizens' Councils insist they hold most dear.[226] Nor has he even once been of any comfort to those Southern newspaper editors and columnists whom the novelist James Street once described as "bellhops of Southern reaction." The Southerner who reads Vann Woodward learns what has happened to him and his region, but he does not feel pardoned, and certainly not excused, for what is wrong. He is given a pride in the best of his history and is encouraged through understanding to make no peace with those who strive to keep the South separate from America and her future.

In short, I am a Woodward fan.

His newest book consists of eight essays which, with one exception, have already appeared in various publications during the past eight years. The exception is "A Southern Critique for the Gilded Age," in which Woodward presents Herman Melville, Henry Adams, and Henry James, each in the role of indirect critic of the post-Civil War American society. With artificial nostalgia, they extolled the superiority of the old Southern tradition of leisure based on slavery in literary works featuring a Confederate hero who censured Yankee morals and manners. Adams did so under a pen name, and James was careful to have his hero denounce slavery and the Confederate war policies, but all three mourned, in the manner of Miniver Cheevy, for the perfection of Greek

---

[225]See McGill's essay on Tom Watson in *Southern Encounters: Southerners of Note in Ralph McGill's South*, ed. Calvin M. Logue (Macon GA: Mercer University Press, 1983).

[226]C. Vann Woodward, *Reunion and Reaction: The Compromise of 1877 and the End of Reconstruction* (Boston: Little, Brown, 1966); Woodward, *Origins of the New South, 1877-1913* (Baton Rouge: Louisiana State University Press, 1951); Woodward, *Strange Career of Jim Crow*, 3d rev. ed. (New York: Oxford University Press, 1974).

culture which each wistfully imagined was the hallmark of the old slave South.

In "The Historical Dimension" Woodward takes up the Southern writers who came along beginning about 1929. They had, and most still have after more than three decades, an acute historical consciousness. A great deal of this consciousness, however, is pretty thin stuff. It is often merely narrow partisanship in which a genuine regional consciousness is difficult to identify. This obsession with the past distinguishes many Southern writers, and also can become quite tiresome.

The Southern Agrarians, who in 1930 took their stand on the values of the Old South, along with Melville et al., have long ago departed Vanderbilt University and Nashville. Only Donald Davidson remains on the burned-out deck as a sort of Dixie mullah, daily facing toward John C. Calhoun's grave and calling on all those engaged in trying to grapple with the new problems to repent and pray for a return of the Old South. Dr. Davidson, a deeply sincere man, winces at the phrase "segregated society." The South, he insists, had developed not a segregated but a parallel society which, he seems to believe, has been highly satisfactory in its values to both races.[227]

Now and then one gets the impression that Woodward, too, is disturbed by the sound of bulldozers that are leveling traditions as well as trees, but he is too honest a man and historian to give aid and comfort to the various wistful cultists of the old days, be they Melville or the newer breed.

It is, of course, perfectly true that the South is a distinctive region. This is so not at all because of its myths and ancestor worship; it stems from the collective experience of the Southern people. Generations of scarcity, want, and a lost war do constitute one of the distinctive historical experiences of the Southern people. Americans outside the South have not known the chastening experience of being on the losing side of a war. Success and victory are an American state of mind. That of the South does include large amounts of defeat, frustration, and failure.

---

[227]McGill studied with students later known as the "Fugitives" at Vanderbilt University. See *Ralph McGill: Editor and Publisher*, ed. Calvin McLeod Logue (Durham: Moore Publishing Company, 1969) 1:25-44.

Southerners, says Woodward in the excellent essay "Search for Identity," have lauded the perfection of American institutions since the Declaration of Independence. But for half that time they lived intimately with a great social evil and the other half with its aftermath. Much of the South's intellectual energy went into a desperate effort to convince the world that its peculiar evil was a positive good, but—and here is the point—it failed even to convince itself.

"The South's preoccupation was with guilt," Woodward declares, "not with innocence, with the reality of evil, not with the dream of perfection. Its experience in this respect, as in several others, was on the whole a thoroughly un-American one."

All this is true. And the average Southerner is not yet aware of what his heritage is. Selections from Woodward are not yet required reading in Southern secondary schools. In many of them the old myths, somewhat less iridescent, are still being vended.

I couldn't agree more positively with Woodward's conclusion: "The modern Southerner should be secure enough in his national identity to escape the compulsion of less secure minorities to embrace uncritically all the myths of nationalism." He should, therefore, be ready to become an American national in spirit and mind, without becoming a nationalist.

After all, what really makes the Southerner's heritage "different" is that the South's power structure of 1861 preferred to plunge the nation into a civil war rather than give up the profits obtained from cotton, rice, tobacco, and slavery. This is oversimplified, but it is the nut of the matter. The modern Southerner owes the heritage of that decision no more than understanding. Once he understands, he is freed and an almost literal weight falls from his mind and back.

The unique and lavish good fortune this country has known has isolated it, rather dangerously, from the common experience of the rest of mankind, "all the great peoples of which have without exception known the bitter taste of defeat and humiliation." This good fortune, says Woodward in the essay from which he has taken the title of his book, has fostered the tacit conviction that American ideals, values, and known principles inevitably will prevail in the end. Still, we Americans are exasperated by the incongruities of our position. We have more power than ever before, and enjoy less security.

The South's history presents an ironic contrast. In 1860 the South had grown so sensitive to criticism and the apparent denials of its proclaimed virtues that its exasperations led to disaster.

In 1960 we have shown, according to Woodward, a tendency to allow our whole cause, our traditional values, and our way of life to be identified with one economic institution. We have shown a disposition to suppress criticism and glorify rigidly orthodox capitalistic free enterprise as the sole secret of our superiority. Any and all attempts to change this orthodoxy historically have been met with charges of socialism, creeping and galloping. We have too often sought to impose our form of democracy on all those allied with us or aided by us. Of late many shrill voices demand that we affirm our national perfection.

Today it is America, as once it was the South alone, that stands in great need of understanding its own history. We need leaders, historians, and great writers who will "penetrate the legend" without destroying the ideal. Some of this leadership and those writers may reasonably be expected to rise out of the South.[228]

---

[228]See "Radio Program Concerning the South" in volume 2.

The Confederates' Torpedoes

I t had been a pleasant drive through the sun-drenched Belgian countryside from Brussels to Ostend by the sea. And certainly, waiting for a ceremony to begin, I did not expect to encounter a rare Confederate reminder of the American Civil War.

Before us, hard by the North Sea, was a new building. A ribbon stretched across its open doors. A plaque set in the walls near the entrance identified the structure as "Ecole de Deminage." In it Navy personnel of Belgium and NATO countries will be trained in one of the greatest problems of warfare at sea—mines.

The dignitaries came. A band played. A magnificent philosopher and gentleman, L. J. J. Robins, commodore of the Belgian Navy, whose personality and devotion have created a small, efficient navy where none before existed, spoke. He was followed by Admiral Arleigh Burke, chief of U.S. Naval operations. The American admiral, himself a legend wherever Navy men gather, talked on his favorite subject—sea power. An essential ingredient of it is the mine sweeper.

Admiral Burke made clear the great responsibility which will fall upon the school and the Belgian teaching if war should come. There are seas today which are not safe because of mines laid during the Second

Reprinted from the *Atlanta Journal and Constitution Sunday Magazine*, 4 December 1960, by permission of Mrs. Ralph McGill and Atlanta Newspapers, Inc.

World War and the Korean conflict. Now and then a ship is sunk. Frequently fishermen find one in their great trawler nets in the Atlantic and curse it for the damage it does and the fear it brings. By and large, the mine sweepers are unsung heroes of battle. Theirs is a dirty, tedious business of great and constant danger. Yet it is a service which attracts men and has a high esprit de corps.

The ceremonies done, we entered the school where such men will be trained.

There is a display room of mines from many lands and eras. The oldest is one devised by men of the Confederate States for the defense of Mobile, Alabama, where Admiral Farragut said, "Damn the torpedoes, full speed ahead."[229] Those inventive men had taken a small barrel, or keg, and fitted pointed wooden ends to it. These were to prevent it from tumbling. They had stuffed it with a hundred pounds of gunpowder. At the middle they affixed two crude detonators. The whole thing was heavily coated with pitch. A number of these crude mines were set in the channel at Mobile Bay. They, and others like them, had previously been used in the harbors and rivers of the Confederacy.

Stephen Mallory, secretary of the Confederate Navy department, early turned to what were then called torpedoes in his earnestly pushed program of developing new and secret weapons. (It was not until the launched torpedo began to be developed that the word *marine mine* was given to the fixed, or floating, torpedo.) He set up a special torpedo bureau and plants were organized to produce them.[230]

It was not until after the war was ended that their effectiveness was fully known. It was then revealed by the U.S. Naval Department that more ships had been lost through torpedo blasts than by any other cause.

Matthew F. Maury, one of the famous names in American naval history, went to Great Britain to make a special study of torpedo construc-

---

[229]See Loyall Farragut, *Life of David Glasgow Farragut: First Admiral of the United States Navy, Embodying His Journal and Letters* (New York: D. Appleton & Co., 1879).

[230]See Joseph Thomas Durkin, *Stephen R. Mallory: Confederate Navy Chief* (Chapel Hill: University of North Carolina Press, 1954).

tion.[231] These weapons, used generously in the rivers and harbors likely to be attacked, were very effective. Maury was credited with most of the work done to develop the "spar torpedo." This was a torpedo attached to a long spar projecting from the bow of the ship. This, rammed against a ship, usually produced enough explosive force to destroy the largest of the wooden vessels then in use. The Confederates also used submarines. These, operated by hand cranks, towed a torpedo behind him. The submarine would laboriously dive under an enemy vessel, in a night attack. The towing torpedo would be bashed against its side as the sub reached the theoretical safety of the far side. It rarely worked out. In 1864 the submarine *H. L. Hunley* destroyed the USS *Housatonic* in Charleston harbor, but the resulting concussion also sank the sub with its crew of seven. It was a foredoomed ship. In four trial runs it had also sunk, each time drowning its crew.

The torpedo, or mine, in the Ostend mine-sweeping school, eloquently revealed the ingenuity of the material-scarce Confederates, who transformed barrels, kegs, and whisky demijohns into torpedoes. Given heavy coatings of pitch, many were made really waterproof and protected their mechanisms well despite the crudities of construction.

These torpedoes were of two kinds, the "hunting torpedo" which floated with the currents, and those which were anchored and controlled from the shore. An electric spark was used to set off the latter when an enemy ship was passing over.

Naval, or marine, mines were used as early as 1777. Robert Fulton produced one in 1780 which had a contact explosive mechanism. In 1854 the Russians used mines in the Baltic, but with little success. Electric charges to discharge fixed explosives were used as early as 1839 against sunken wrecks blocking channels in the Thames.

But, the first military use of electrically fired mines was in the American Civil War. From 1805 on, European powers gave top priority

---

[231]See Columbus O'Donnell Iselin, *Matthew Fontaine Maury, 1806-1873, Pathfinder of the Seas: The Development of Oceanography* (New York: Newcomer Society in North America, 1957); Patricia Jahns, *Matthew Fontaine Maury and Joseph Henry: Scientists of the Civil War* (New York: Hastings House, 1961); Frances Leigh Williams, *Matthew Fontaine Maury: Scientist of the Sea* (New Brunswick: Rutgers University Press, 1963).

to their development. They were widely employed, for example in the Franco-Prussian War of 1870.

It was failure of Confederate mines at Mobile which enabled Admiral Farragut to attain a place in history. His phrase, "Damn the torpedoes, go ahead," is one of our more famous slogans.

Farragut had been long-delayed before Mobile in the spring and summer of 1864. The presence there of the iron-clad ram, the *Tennessee*, deterred him. But in July he received a reinforcement of some new iron-clad monitors. He then planned his attack. It was launched on the morn of 5 August with thirteen wooden ships and four monitors. Farragut commanded from the wooden *Hartford*, with his Chief of Staff Fleet Captain Percival Drayton, of South Carolina. (This Southerner had chosen to obey his oath of allegiance to the Union, taken as a cadet and officer at the Naval Academy before the war began.)

Before the heavy guns of Fort Morgan, at the shallow passage of the bar, were two rows of moored torpedoes. These were of the sort to be exploded on contact. They were filled with gunpowder, one hundred pounds of it. On contact a plunger detonated percussion caps or fulminate in priming tubes.

Waiting inside was the Confederate naval force of three gunboats and the most powerful ironclad in the fleet, the *Tennessee*. She had been built the winter before at Selma. She was plated with iron rolled in mills at Atlanta.

As Farragut's ships moved across the bar, under heavy fire from the fort, the *Monitor Tecumseh* struck a torpedo and went down, drowning most of her crew. The *Brooklyn*, leading ship of the wooden line, halted. Farragut, lashed in the rigging of the *Hartford*, ordered full steam ahead, crying, "Damn the torpedoes!" His ships moved ahead. Crewmen actually felt the bumps as they moved over the torpedoes. Not another one fired. Apparently some had leaked. Others may have had faulty plungers. Whatever it was, Farragut's gamble paid off. Only the *Tecumseh* was torpedoed.

The *Tennessee* fought with great gallantry, engaging the entire fleet for more than an hour. She was terribly battered, but surrendered only when her exposed steering gear was shot away, leaving her helpless.

It was one of the Confederate Mobile Bay-type mines which was there in the Belgian mine-sweeping school. Alongside the more deadly mines of later years, and the technologically advanced terrors of our time, the pitch-smeared old keg, with her pointed, wooden ends, attached by nails, caulked and tarred, looked primitive indeed. But, in 1861-1865 they were new and terrorized naval commanders.

Basically, mines have not changed since that time. But they reflect man's continued technical advance. They remain an explosive set off by a mechanism. Some are magnetic, and mine sweepers which seek them out must be expensively built of nonmagnetic materials. The cost for one such average-sized ship runs well above a million dollars.

There is one mine which is a horror. It was used in small numbers by the Germans in the concluding months of World War II. To this date, no nation has devised a way to sweep it. It is the most fiendish of all such hidden weapons. It is the pressure mine. It is set off when the passage of a ship changes the water pressure about it.

It is the more a terror because it can be set to blow at any given number of pressures. It can, for example, be set to explode when the fifth ship passes over, or the eighth or twelfth. Sweepers may wear themselves out and think the area clean. And then, the mine blows. To date, the experts have not found an answer. They will. But for the time being, those who man the mine sweepers shake their heads, and the look on their faces is grim.

Divers are today being trained to go down to look for mines. In the school I talked with a young officer who takes this training. The new equipment frees men and enables them to walk about like skin divers. But these men hunt a deadly fish and the waters in which they work are rarely warm and lambent. One always is somehow surprised, and pleased, to meet men who seek out very dangerous things to do. Because, let it not go unnoted that there will be many dangerous things to do in the future. And mine sweeping is but one of them.[232]

And, in thinking how there are always brave and daring men, one remembers the Confederates who, in a hand-cranked submarine, took the great chance and died.[233]

---

[232]See Emory M. Thomas, *The American War and Peace, 1860-1877* (Englewood Cliffs NJ: Prentice Hall, 1973); Thomas, *The Confederate Nation, 1861-1865* (New York: Harper & Row, 1979).

[233]See McGill's "Constantine Chapters, C.S.A.," in volume 1.

Review of Dan Wakefield's
Revolt in the South

S omehow, along the way, I have never met with Dan Wakefield, but after reading his *Revolt in the South* I know him to be an honest reporter whose instincts are true and who is given to few errors of fact and judgment.

Mr. Wakefield properly describes his work as a report, rather than a book. It is a collection, with generous amplification, of articles written for the *Nation* during five journeys into the South following the 1954 decision by the United States Supreme Court outlawing school segregation. His concluding chapters discuss the sit-ins, a pacific policy of protest which, temporarily, at least, has made the school issue a secondary one in the South's conversation. The report is largely anecdotal, which is a part of its charm and value. The anecdotes are all relevant and serve to tell the story so that it can be seen and, in a sense, felt. Any sensitive Southerner, on reading the book, will feel as if he is again

Apparently written for *Saturday Review*, 11 February 1961 but not found in that source. Published by permission of Mrs. Ralph McGill and *Saturday Review*. Copyright 1961, *Saturday Review*. Manuscript provided by Mrs. Ralph McGill from the McGill papers, now at Emory University, Atlanta. Review of Dan Wakefield, *Revolt in the South* (New York: Grove Press, 1960).

seeing a horror movie, for the reason that the narrative is replete with horror and incredibility.[234]

Mr. Wakefield also does a helpful thing by setting this report in perspective. Too many persons outside the South have watched the struggle for human rights in a way that this country looked at the revolt in Hungary—as though it were highly significant, but distant. His report, then, is about the South because the South is the center of the revolution, the focus, too, of the efforts of the federal courts to end segregation among citizens of this country, and of the new tactics of the sit-ins as a weapon of the struggle. The hopes in the South, as well as its tragedies, are national properties, not regional.

This report is a valuable primer for those who wish to know the story. The old story of the White Citizens' Councils and their contributions to our national sickness, and of the various demagogues who preached and wrought defiance of law and courts, is here. New Orleans has followed it. But one can substitute Little Rock and there is not much difference. New Orleans did make plainer the fact that for all their protests, the Citizens' Councils are largely anti-Semitic and anti-Catholic as well.[235]

The story of the sit-ins is the newer one. They are, I think, more important. They have done what the school decision was not able to do. They have revealed the preposterousness of the segregation position. Even the most segregation-minded Southerner now sees that it is not possible seriously to defend a system which will sell everything in the store to a colored person right up to the chair or stool at the lunch counter. The fact that a hot dog, hamburger, and a cup of coffee have become symbols of freedom may not be too farfetched. During the Second World War we were repeatedly assured we were fighting for the right to buy a hot dog and root for the Brooklyn Dodgers. The Dodgers are gone, but the hot dog remains.

---

[234]See Numan V. Bartley and Hugh D. Graham, *Southern Politics and the Second Reconstruction* (Baltimore: Johns Hopkins University Press, 1975); John Hope Franklin and Isidore Starr, eds., *The Negro in Twentieth-Century America: A Reader on the Struggle for Civil Rights* (New York: Vintage Books, 1967).

[235]See Neil R. McMillen, *The Citizens' Council* (Urbana: University of Illinois Press, 1971); Cal M. Logue and Howard Dorgan, eds., *Oratory of Southern Demagogues* (Baton Rouge: Louisiana State University Press, 1981).

Gov. LeRoy Collins of Florida, in an early television speech on the sit-ins, placed them in proper perspective. He said it was immoral to invite in customers and then refuse the colored ones the full service. This is why the sit-ins have proved increasingly effective. Moral power goes with them.[236]

Mr. Wakefield has told the story well. He is not pious about it. Indeed, he maintains an excellent perspective. It would have been helpful if he had more clearly differentiated between the Deep South and the rest of it. The major issue is in the old cotton South. For those who need a primer, this is it.

---

[236]See McGill's essay on LeRoy Collins in *Southern Encounters: Southerners of Note in Ralph McGill's South*, ed. Calvin M. Logue (Macon GA: Mercer University Press, 1983).

What Makes America Great

L ast February, on the opening day of the annual Georgia Press
Institute at Athens, a member of the University of Georgia's
faculty told me that Miss Charlayne Hunter likely would be
among a number of students who would attend the third lecture of the
day, since it came at an hour when most of those in journalism classes
would have a free period.

I had not met Miss Hunter, but she had earned my respectful, un-
stinted admiration for her courage and consistent poise in the face of the
violent riot, threats, and court hearings which grew out of her admission
and that of Hamilton Holmes to the University of Georgia on 9 January
1961. They were the first two Negro students to be accepted at the oldest
chartered state university. Both had conducted themselves admirably
and in such marked contrast to the vulgar boorishness of the relatively
few students, adults, and teenagers who made up the White-Citizens'-
Council-inspired riot, that even occasional segregationists had been
moved to grudging respect.

A handful of journalism students were already present, and they
asked me to wait with them, as one of their members in the same class
was driving her over. Within a few minutes the car pulled into the drive

---

Manuscript mailed to *McCall's* magazine 6 March 1961 but not published by that
periodical. Text provided by Mrs. Ralph McGill from the McGill papers.

of the university's handsome Center for Continuing Education, a gift to the university by the Kellogg Foundation. We went out to meet them and walked, talking the while, back into the long, crowded lobby and through it to the auditorium. All save one of the students, a coed reporter for the University's weekly, the *Red and Black*, and a stringer for a state daily, went in to the lecture. The reporter and I found chairs for a talk. I had been deeply moved by the sight of the few students who had so naturally and quietly accompanied the young girl who was so much a living part of an important and unexpected chapter in their state and their lives. They were all from small Georgia cities and rural county seats. Yet each had risen above the majority view in those areas. There was not the slightest sign of exhibitionism or defiance in their presence. Yet, the very fact of their being there very eloquently was saying to the whole university, "She is not alone." They were an effective rebuke to the conformity of fear and prejudice.

"She is so obviously a nice and intelligent girl," I said, "that even though the riot was not too long ago, I am somehow surprised that even more have not become her friends."

"It is mostly the sororities," the young reporter said, with an understanding pity, well-laced with calm contempt. "A number of them want to get to know her, but they are afraid the social status of their chapters will be damaged if they do it. Each sorority is fearful that if any of its members make the break the others will not do so and will use it against them in next year's rushing. But slowly, more students are beginning to speak, to be friendly. It takes a little time."

That many wanted to enrich their lives by participating personally in the development of what suddenly had become the central drama of their college years, had been demonstrated on the first night the new student had spent in the dormitory, the evening before the adult-incited riot. Some fifty girls in the dormitory had more or less spontaneously gone to her room to greet her and make her welcome. Later, calls and letters from parents, prejudice, and conformity each held up their warning fingers, and the natural impulse was curbed. Looking at the assured, sufficient young staff member of the college newspaper, and thinking of the conformists, a small, light verse from Edna St. Vincent Millay's "A Few Figs from Thistles," learned in my own college days, came to mind:

All right,
Go ahead!
What's in a name?
I guess I'll be locked into
As much as I'm locked out of![237]

"I am glad there are persons like you and your friends," I said. "What a lot you are learning that could not be had from books!" She nodded. I had no need to tell her so. She knew. That was why she was there. It was why the first Negro girl ever normally to attend a Deep South university was even then sitting quietly in the auditorium, flanked by fellow students.

Talking with other student reporters, I began to comprehend that the whole story of the admission of Charlayne Hunter and Hamilton Holmes at Georgia's state university had been much more than simply an end to segregation in a Deep South college. It also was a moving portrayal of what makes America great. It was something which could be viewed and emotionally experienced as can the scenes in a stage or screen play. In time of crisis, large or small, there always are those who will not conform and thus endure wrong because of fear or coercive influence. A Joe McCarthy is tumbled down from his highest peak by a gentle lawyer from New England. A mob and a hard core of extremist students, hied on by their elders of like mentality, are put to shame and silence by students and faculty members in a Deep South university who resisted the conformist pressures.

The students, their parents, and, for that matter, the whole nation, had seen the Bill of Rights transformed, in the fast-driven drama of court tests, from printed words to action. The whole process of how our system works to protect and delineate the rights of the citizen was exposed in the swift series of events.

On Friday, 6 January, the Georgia legislature, gathering in Atlanta for its annual session to begin on the following Monday, had no idea of any emergency. It believed that the severely restrictive segregation statutes enacted by previous legislatures made any new action unnecessary. Had any person in the hours before mid-afternoon of that day suggested

---

[237]From "The Prisoner" by Edna St. Vincent Millay (New York: Harper & Row). Copyright 1922, 1950 by Edna St. Vincent Millay and Norma Millay Ellis.

that before the next week was out two young, superiorly qualified Negro students would have been sitting in classes at the university, he would have dismissed it as preposterous. Had it been further predicted that all segregation laws would be removed from the books and legislation enacted allowing local boards to desegregate or close schools, such a prophet would have been waved aside as mentally unbalanced.

But even as the assembly leaders were being interviewed and expressing the views that the upcoming session would be a quiet one, a court case, long under consideration, was ready for decision. At just after 3 o'clock that afternoon a law clerk in the district court at Macon, Georgia, routinely released a court order. An excited reporter telephoned his newspaper. Bells soon began to ring in Atlanta at hotels where legislative leaders were registered and at the governor's office.

The order declared that Charlayne Hunter and Hamilton Holmes were qualified and were being deprived of their constitutional rights by being denied admission. They were, therefore, to be admitted at 9 o'clock on Monday, 9 January, when the new term began.

A shocked and somewhat awed legislature had little to say. There privately was general acknowledgement that an era had ended. Members talked in official and unofficial caucuses. Save for a few diehards, all accepted the fact they were up against the Constitution of their country and its guarantee of equal rights before the law for all citizens. There was nothing to do but wait, to play it, from then on, by ear. For them, too, the Constitution had ceased to become words and was present in the form of physical action.

So it was that on Monday morning the two students were admitted. But at the same time two automobiles hurried toward Macon. There the state, making one last effort, sought time in the district court for an appeal. The Negro attorney opposed. The district court reflected and then granted a delay.

The two cars moved again. In Atlanta, a hundred miles north of Macon, an appeals judge heard the Constitutional arguments. He ruled there was no Constitutional basis for a delay. The students remained in school.

The next night the "bad guys" had their inning. Extremist adults urged students to riot. They did. But of 7,500 enrolled, less than 500 participated. Among the mob were Klansmen, seven of whom were arrested. When order finally was obtained, the two students were suspended because of the threat to law and order. But by morning the drama was back in the courtroom. The Constitution was there, too. It spoke and said that the rights of individuals could not be denied because of the threat of disorder. The Constitution presumed the law enforcement agency would prevent violence. And, said the Constitution, the rights of some could not be suspended while the rights of others were maintained.

So Charlayne Hunter and Hamilton Holmes went back to Athens and to classes. And there they remain.

The journey from court to court, the solemn arguments, the decisions based on the equality of citizenship, the acceptance of court order by the Georgia legislature and the elimination of state segregation laws, all combined to reveal what makes this country great.

There are checks and balances between the executive, the legislative and the judicial. We Americans sit, a wise man said, on a neat, well-balanced three-legged stool. And if ever one leg gets shorter than the other two, or longer, we won't sit comfortably again. And all that is true. But above this process of checks and balances is the Constitution and its guarantee of human rights so early added to that original document.

It is the Constitution which has made us Americans and enabled us to achieve national greatness. It explains that quality of independence, of stubborn individualism, of irreverence and a lack of awe in the presence of the powerful. Europeans, looking at the American soldiers in World War I, noted they had about them an assurance which some said was cockiness. In the countries of Asia, of Africa, and Europe, in the Second World War, observers made the same notes—the American soldier was a confident man—too damned much so, said some. Some critics found him naive, ignorant, uninformed, immature, often sadly lacking in knowledge about paintings, books, music, and sculpture. But all had that indefinable quality—of assurance. Men who have never had to worry about liberty, or individual rights, grow up with a unique psychology. They may not be able to explain it. They may not even know they possess it. But they have it. They take it in with their mother's milk. It is a part of the national environment.

For three quarters of a century the Negro was shut out of the inspiring, developing forces of American life. In the South the exclusion was greatest, though it existed everywhere. He was never really permitted a full part in the political developments. The unions closed most of their doors. It is not a story we like to remember.

But the Constitution was there. And since it was, the Negro kept trying to be more American—not less. He did not seek, like some European minority, such as the Sudeten Germans, for example, to obtain special rights and a separate national identity.

It is this which makes the developing story in the South one which illustrates the greatness of what we rather glibly call the American dream. Because they have so long been excluded, many Negroes, especially in the rural South and those who have gone from the land, unskilled and untaught, are not, as their critics say, ready to move into the mainstream of American life. But this is part of the cost of exclusion, and what rarely is said is that the cost was great, too, in white persons who also are not fully prepared to join in the tremendous decision, the new knowledge, to cope with the vast complexity of their lives.

There is a long way yet to go. But the processes of law continue, and today it is a rare thing to find a person who will say that we should make America mean one thing for some Americans and still another, and lesser thing, for others. There is, for example, no Bilbo in the U.S. Senate today. Only a few brief years have passed since he was there condemning the Negro as unfit for equal citizenship. Yet, already he, and others like him, seem like museum pieces. We make progress.

The American is not, by nature, a conformist. The hidden persuaders work on him. He seeks status. Suburbia enfolds him. But he has a comforting habit of rebelling. He can utterly confound the persuaders by abandoning the long sleek chariots with fins and putting the automobile makers furiously to work building compacts. Just when the takers of polls believe they have him neatly filed and cross-indexed, he gets out of pocket. He makes up his mind to elect a rich young Roman Catholic as president of his country and does so when most of the experts are agreed it can't be done. He becomes more politically sophisticated just when the experts feared he was too apathetic.

The American, like his country, has growing pains. And presently, the Southerner feels most of the stresses of growth and change. But he will grow. History and the economics of cotton and tobacco have tended to keep him out of the psychological processes of national life and development. But the South has never lost its best human qualities. Possessing these and rid, one of these days, of the old fears, myths, and outworn and unworthy customs, it and all its people will match the dream of its most hopeful prophets.

One thought of those things while watching the Constitution and Bill of Rights cease to be words and take on literal meaning and application in the lives of two young Negro students in a Deep South crisis. And one thought of the greatness of our country, too, while sitting and talking with Southern students who were waiting to go to a journalism lecture with a classmate named Charlayne Hunter.

The Chattahoochee River

U p above Poplar Stump Gap, where the great rock rim of the Blue Ridges marks the southwestern border of the huge Highland area, a small trickle of water spills from the rocks. It splashes down to form a small pool. Two small streams not more than two or three inches wide flow from it, splashing down into the laurel thickets. Thus begins the Chattahoochee River.

Once in the thickets others join the source of streams, and soon there is what might be called a small mountain creek. Others hurry to merge with it. In Habersham, Rabun, White, Towns, Union, and Lumpkin [Georgia counties], there are waters which flow into it.

In the mountains it is a river for poets. Sidney Lanier, ill and slowly wasting away with tuberculosis, sat by its banks near Helen. He saw it in his mind's eye all the way to the sea, and gave it literary immortality.

Out of the hills of Habersham,
Down the valleys of Hall,
I hurry amain to reach the plain,
Run the rapid and leap the fall,
Split at the rock and together again,
Accept my bed, or narrow or wide,

Reprinted from the *Atlanta Journal and Constitution Sunday Magazine*, 20 August 1961 by permission of Mrs. Ralph McGill and the Atlanta Newspapers, Inc.

And flee from folly on every side
With a lover's pain to attain the plain
Far from the hills of Habersham,
Far from the valleys of Hall.[238]

The river did turn many wheels. It gave the state its first complex of industry at Columbus. It still is a river for the poets. The Cherokees put the name on it which the English spelled phonetically Chat-Cho-chee, Chat-a-Hotchee, or in some approximation of the Indian words. The phrase meant, in a free translation, "river of the painted rock," a nice name, with poetry in it. There were rocks in the upper reaches stained red and pink by nature. If the Cherokee believed this to be the work of the gods they may not have been wrong.

From its beginnings in the Appalachian Blue Ridges until it reaches Columbus, the Chattahoochee is one of the oldest rivers in the Southeast. From the old Coweta Falls (near Columbus) close by which was the old war town of the Creeks, the river is younger, geologists say, by many hundreds of thousands of years.

In the dim geologic ages rivers "pirated" one another with frequency. They would do so today, if man did not impose dams and controls.

Once upon a time, say geologists, the Chattahoochee was a mighty river, indeed. It included what is now the Chattooga and the Tallapoosa. The drainage changes took place a million years or so ago, but geologists are reasonably sure of what happened. The Atlantic coastline was then at the approximate position of Montgomery, Columbus, Macon, and Augusta. The huge river at that time would have entered the sea at a point not far northeast of Montgomery. With the new sea at this level, the tributaries flowing from the north began to cut their beds in a manner best illustrated by the formation of a gully in a field. It is cut backward, so to speak, and deepest, where the water is strongest, just as gullies are deeper where the heaviest surge of collected rain water flows. As the new ocean receded toward the present Atlantic and Gulf coasts, the rivers cut easily into the softer soils of the coastal plains, making

---

[238]*Poems of Sidney Lanier,* ed. Mary Day Lanier (Athens: University of Georgia Press, 1981) 24.

wide valley courses. Shorter streams, not as sluggish as the larger and
longer Chattahoochee, of course, cut deeper and more swiftly.

One such stream, geologists say, cut into the valley of the Chattahoochee above West Point, diverting the Chattahoochee into the Gulf by
way of what is called the Apalachicola. The Flint, Ocmulgee, Oconee,
and Savannah, a millions years or so before they had names, were likewise busy with their own evolutionary struggles. The Savannah, called
the Tugaloo in its upper reaches, intercepted the Chattahoochee somewhere around the Habersham-Stephens County line, taking these headwaters into what became the Tugaloo-Savannah system.

Geologists like to think what a vast roaring there must have been,
and what a spectacular sight it was, when in those early days of our part
of the New World, a small tributary of what is called the Tugaloo inter-
sected the Tallulah and set it to cutting the Tallulah gorge in its rush into
the Tugaloo system. Once upon a time the Tallulah flowed down past the
present gorge and falls and turned southwest, going then down to the
valley of Deep Creek and Soque River where it became the leading tributary to the Chattahoochee. To this day, between Atlanta and Gainesville, some of the headwaters of seaward-flowing streams are close to the
Chattahoochee, but dams and modern engineering prevent any "piracy"
of interception.

So it is, as geologists construct the ancient evidence, that the oldest
part of the Chattahoochee remains in Georgia, its channel following the
narrow Gulf-Atlantic divide. It flows first through the pleasant and
beautiful valley of Nacoochee, where most historians agree DeSoto
halted after he had at last found what we call Rabun Gap and emerged
from his long, arduous passage through the seemingly endless folds of
the Appalachians into the Piedmont region. From there the river sets out
on its peculiar, unorthodox course, southwest across the state.

From Nacoochee the river flows to Clarksville and there steps down
in swift cascades to the Atlanta plateau. Nowhere is this plateau more
than 50 miles wide. In places it is as narrow as 35. Yet, it stretches for
about 100 miles, composed of two fairly distinct levels, or benches, with
about 250 feet difference in elevation. The plateau's terrain is pleasant.
It bears the principal railways and highways. It is dotted with attractive
cities—Gainesville, Atlanta, Carrollton, Newnan, and West Point
being the better known.

The most striking feature of this plateau is the great trench which the river cut in the dim and distant past. This trench ranges from 150 to 400 or more feet in depth and from two to five miles in width from rim to rim. For a short distance below Roswell the trench is almost a gorge. There is some evidence that the trench, or valley, is a double one with a deeper, more narrow river course cut into the floor of a wider one which dates back to the ages when the Chattahoochee was a mighty river.

Below Franklin, in Heard County, where once the slave-poled barges came for cotton and people dreamed of its becoming a river port, the Chattahoochee begins its cross swing and steps down to the Greenville Plateau, so-called after the seat of Meriwether County. This plateau extends well into Alabama. The river flows across it as far south as Columbus.

It there nears the Flint, which rises in College Park. The Flint cuts through the Pine Mountain ridges near Woodbury, Georgia. It had a great struggle in the ancient days when it was becoming a river. Within the space of six miles the Flint had to slash three gorges through the complicated low loops of the rocky ridges. But though near, it has miles to go before it joins the Chattahoochee. At Columbus is the fall line. For years the steamboats came there in considerable numbers. The writer has talked with men who worked on them. They recalled the difficult channel, the several boats sunk by running on hidden snags. They remembered the fine meals and how, in the autumn and winter, hunters would come to the landings and sell hundreds of quail at a cent apiece and offer choice cuts of deer meat at low prices.

The first steamer to make the long journey from the Gulf to Columbus was the *Fannie* in 1828. The *Stubenville* came the same year. In 1829 the *Virginia* appeared and set a record by making the trip from Apalachicola to Columbus in thirty-eight hours. In December of 1829 she took 400 bales of cotton from Columbus to New Orleans. In 1834 there were six steamers on the river from Columbus to the sea.

The Civil War saw federal gunboats on the lower stretches of the river. They operated frequently to Eufaula, Alabama. The Confederate gunboat *Chattahoochee* was built at Columbus. She was blown up in April 1865 by the Federals.[239] Steamboating slowly died out and by 1921

---

[239]See McGill's "Confederates' Torpedoes," in this volume.

was ended. But in February of 1939, a tug towed a barge containing 150,000 gallons of gasoline to Columbus. In the years ahead, as dams are built, ocean barges will come to Atlanta. Until then, Columbus will remain the head of navigation.

Below Columbus, the Chattahoochee flows into the flat of the coastal plain. It moves by Ft. Benning, where thousands of troops trained for the Second World War and where Gen. George Patton formed his tank battalions. The first test of rubber tank pontoons was on the Chattahoochee.

Flowing on, the Chattahoochee goes past historic Eufaula [Alabama] in old Barbour County, Fort Gaines, and Columbus, the latter now well back from the river, and so on until its union with the Flint at the southwest corner of Georgia.

In Florida the river flows past the town of Chattahoochee, where the swamps begin along the river, flows by Blountstown, and finally, by the mouth of Brothers River. There the river slows for the bay, where the town of Apalachicola still holds to the old dream of becoming a great seaport.

Early Spanish explorers fixed the name Apalachicola on the lower stretch of the river. French explorers also paddled canoes up it to the Indian towns at Coweta and Cusseta. But the Spanish made the most persistent effort to get their foot in the Creek-nation door and extend their bases up from St. Augustine. In 1679, Friar Juan Ocon attempted to set up a mission near Coweta. He was ordered out. In March of 1681 two Franciscans and seven soldiers rowed up the Chattahoochee to the Cowetas. It was the first armed expedition to use the river. The mission was ordered out in May.

In 1670 the British founded Charleston and the great wrestling match for the New World was begun in earnest with France, Britain, and Spain as major contestants. By 1686 the Spanish and their missions were gone from the Georgia coast. But later, Indian wars brought the Spanish back to Coweta on the Chattahoochee. In London, decision was reached to establish a buffer colony against the Spanish. Georgia was founded.

History has it that southeast America was saved for the British by General Oglethorpe's defeat of the Spanish at Bloody Marsh. But the battle could not have been won without a heroic journey to the Cowetas

on the Chattahoochee by General Oglethorpe three years before the battle at Bloody Marsh.

One is awed today in thinking of that long 300-mile trip through
heat, swamps, unexplored wilderness, and rivers. At Coweta Town—in
what is now Russell County, Alabama—General Oglethorpe met with
the leaders of some twenty thousand Indians. The general attended their
ceremonies, drank "the Black Drink" and won them over. He then visited other towns on and near the Chattahoochee. A treaty was made. It
endured all through the "War of Jenkins Ear," or King George's War,
that followed. Without these friendly Indians, Georgia, and perhaps
Carolina, might have been lost.

The destiny of the new colony was determined at Coweta Town on
the Chattahoochee in August 1739.

There are many stories of the Chattahoochee's past.

There are others to come when the dams are built and the ocean
barges come to docks at cities along the way. She is not a large river, nor
a great one, if we think of the Mississippi, the Ohio, or the Tennessee,
but she nonetheless is a river for poets, for recreation, for providing Atlanta and other cities with water, and for the economic, utilitarian plans
of the future.

There is plenty of length to her, if there is not great width and depth.
She stretches 436 miles in a series of sinuous curves, tumbled rapids,
placid meanderings. No other river in the state is as long.

It is anticipated that the Walter F. George and Columbia dams will
be completed as a sort of Christmas present in 1962. This will bring
navigation to Columbus. This will mean that ocean barges and the
tough, fast tugs will be tying up the docks with heavy goods and, in
time, oil.

There are eleven major dams on the river or under construction.

Navigation to Atlanta is practical—but at considerable cost. Burton
Bell, information specialist for the U.S. Army Corps of Engineers, and
Caughey Culpepper, general manager of the Atlanta Freight Bureau,
predict Atlanta one day will be an inland port. The fact that it is already
one of the nation's major distribution cities will in time make it so.

The problem is a simple, if costly, one, best illustrated by arithme-
tic. At Columbus the river is 190 feet above sea level. West Point, only
25 miles upriver but up a steep slope, is 372 feet higher. From there the
rise is only 174 feet to Atlanta, where the waterworks intake pipe is 736

feet above sea level. Expensive dams and locks will be needed to care for the difference in elevation.[240]

But, already there is a compelling necessity to construct one or more dams between West Point and Atlanta to care for the flood-provision problem. When these are built, and studies are being made, they will make Atlanta a port.

Opposition to Chattahoochee River navigation from the Gulf to Atlanta stems from the shortsighted who think in narrow terms of the cost for such transport. River barges are really one of the by-products of the chief need for the dams. The Buford Dam affords ample illustration. Completion of that dam gave to the state its finest playground in Lake Lanier. Last year it attracted 5,119,000 visitors—all of whom spent money. There is nothing intangible about the economic benefits in cold cash from recreation areas. In addition, Lake Lanier has revolutionized the area about it. It has brought hundreds of new businesses into being. It has stimulated a building boom. The sale, maintenance and service of boats is a multimillion-dollar business. This alone will pay for the dam. But, in addition, we must include the value of land protected from floods. Until it is so protected, that land cannot be put to use for farming, homes, or industry.

Nor is this all. All cities are growing. This steadily increases the water demand. Industries require huge amounts of water. The dams which store and conserve water will, in time, pay for themselves by retaining water.

It is neither honest nor constructive to think of river transport as bearing the whole cost of the necessary dams. If there were to be no barges the dams would be a requirement of the future.

If it were not for the Chattahoochee River and its dams the state of Georgia would be much poorer and its future less bright. Atlanta long ago would have been in serious difficulty because of water shortages.

Eight Georgia Power Company plants on the river now produce more than five billion kilowatts per year. Two new plants are being built.

---

[240]See McGill's "Introduction to *The Old South*," "My Georgia," and "Give Me Georgia," in volumes 1 and 2; also Kenneth Coleman, *American Revolution in Georgia, 1763-1789* (Athens: University of Georgia Press, 1958); and Kenneth Coleman, ed., *A History of Georgia* (Athens: University of Georgia Press, 1977).

They will produce more than four billion kilowatts annually. The total output will be in the neighborhood of ten billion kilowatts. What this means to industry and to cities of the state is obvious.

The Atlanta Water Works takes an average of 74,000,000 gallons of water per day from the Chattahoochee. On peak days in summer it has run as high as 110,000,000 gallons daily. The waterworks now serves, according to General Manager Paul Weir, six hundred thousand persons. It can supply two million, so well have the plans been made and executed. Intake of Atlanta's water is at Bolton, on the west side of Atlanta, near Ridgewood and DeFoor roads. Bolton was the old gateway to the Cherokee nation. During the Civil War a boatyard did business there.[241]

In addition to Atlanta, waterworks systems taking water from it are Gainesville, Buford, DeKalb, Gwinnett, Cobb, West Point, and Columbus.

Some years ago, former Mayor James Nichols, of Apalachicola, gave Atlanta a one-thousand-pound anchor, inscribed "The Port of Apalachicola salutes the Port of Atlanta." On the day the ocean tugs and barges come it will be a part of the celebration. And that day is a part of the river's future.

---

[241]See McGill's "Why I Live in Atlanta," "The Housing Challenge," "Georgia Tech: Lighthouse to the Postwar South," and "She Sifted the Ashes and Built a City," in volumes 1 and 2.

57

A Southern Editor Talks
with Philadelphia Negroes

A visitor from the South walks in Eastwick and West Philadelphia: "I have been here before," the mind says as the eyes look
at an old woman sitting on the stone stoop of a scabrous slum
house.

"I have seen her in maybe a hundred places. When I was a boy I saw
her sitting on the wooden steps of sharecroppers' cabins in south Georgia. I have seen her on the porches of narrow, shotgun houses in the
slums of a dozen Southern cities. She looks always the same, immobile,
lost to the world about her with memory reaching back into God-knows-
what—a loved child who died young, a dead husband, a sorrow, a joy, a
grief.

"Ask her what she is thinking," the mind suggests. But one does not.
She is many women. She has lived in many places. She has done many
chores—washing, cooking, sewing, tending babies, laying out the dead.
She has done without, made out, hoped, despaired.

And that man—the short, thickset one coming toward me on the
sidewalk; he is a mule man. I can tell by his walk. I have seen him with
his mule going out to the field where the plow was left last night. I have
heard him singing as he went in the early morning.

Reprinted from the *Philadelphia Sunday Bulletin Magazine,* 17 September 1961, by
permission of Mrs. Ralph McGill and the *Philadelphia Bulletin.*

Day, oh day,
Yonder comes day,
Day done broke into my soul,
Yonder comes day—

I have seen him, too, in many places, and I do not have to ask why he is here in a harsh corner of a large city.

There are many like him in all our cities—the men who knew and loved mules, who could chop cotton and plow. They are here because of many things.[242]

One would say the boll weevil came and the man quit growing cotton. Another would say with a bitterness on his tongue, "They got tractors. And they got machines to pick. They didn't need me or the children. They don't even use mules now. . . ."

What few comprehend is that a way of life is gone; that the South they knew is changed.

The southern farms, towns, cities, have for years been pouring them out of a great cornucopia of a changing economy, of too-few jobs, of prejudice and discrimination.

It began long ago. The first mass exodus came when an unprepared nation began to gear up for the First World War and there were good-paying jobs in the eastern industrial cities.

The boll weevil reached the South's old cotton states about 1919-1920. Within a few years hundreds of cabins of white and Negro tenants and sharecroppers were empty, their doors sagging or broken off, the shingles sliding from the roof.

The people, with no training save what a farm worker knows, went to Dee-troit, to Chicago, to Pittsburgh, to Akron, to Philly—wherever the word said jobs waited.

The depression came and the out-migration slowed. Some came back, but by 1938 the tide of men and women, colored and white, was

---

[242]See Edgar Streeter Dunn, *Recent Southern Economic Development as Revealed by the Changing Structure of Employment* (Gainesville: University of Florida Press, 1962); Timothy Thomas Fortune, *Black and White: Land, Labor, and Politics in the South* (Chicago: Johnson Publishing Co., 1970); Jay R. Mandle, *Roots of Black Poverty: The Southern Plantation Economy After the Civil War* (Durham: Duke University Press, 1978).

flowing out again. It has never stopped. In 1961 the industrial growth in the South has reduced the total. But it continues. Most of the Southern rural counties are losing population.

It is these that provide most of today's migration.

Four men stood in front of a corner-tavern door. One man held a child about a year old—a very good baby too. It peered at us with grave, brown eyes as the talk went on.

"I got a good job," said the man with the child. He was medium height, slender, but not thin. His face had a severe cast. "I cut meat. I had learned it some down South in Kentucky before I came here, cutting up hogs and the like. But times is hard on folks as hasn't got a trade. It's hard on some as has, too."

The other three nodded. They seemed to be around fifty or so years of age. They did not have regular jobs. Nor did they have a skill. They let the man with the job be their spokesman.

"You ask me about here and the South. Well, I'll tell you. It's better here. The cops here is bad. They arrest you for nothing. But it ain't like down there with those sheriffs and deputies. Not like that. Here, there ain't nobody calling you boy or making you do this and that because of your color. It's better. But it ain't all it should be.

"You take the government surplus now. Mr. Kennedy he put meat back on the list. Mr. Eisenhower he took it off. There is more to eat now."

The three men nodded solemnly.

"Yes, sir," said one, "It's better with some meat in the surplus."

It was plain that they had been in a near-destitute situation for so long that the surplus food was an accepted routine feature of their lives.

"The main thing is," he said, "there has to be jobs. There ain't a thing for a lot of people to do."

I thought about the coal miners I'd seen in West Virginia and Kentucky, who were about fifty or sixty years of age, and who had only the skill of digging coal. Machines had replaced that. Mines were closed and would never open again.

I remembered, too, the small farmers I'd seen in the South, renters, and tenants, who had not moved North, pulled by the magnet of jobs. They would never again be able to use their simple, agrarian skills.

In every city there are men who will have to be retrained if they are again to have gainful employment. Many of these, when retraining is attempted, prove to have too little education to "take" instruction.[243]

The plight of the migrant Negro is complicated by urban life. Until recently most of the Negro population was in the South. And most of it was in the rural areas. Segregated school systems were below the national standards, even for white children. The U.S. Supreme Court never said a truer thing than in 1954 when it ruled that segregated education was not, in fact, equal.[244]

With few exceptions the educational opportunities for the Negro child in small towns and farm communities was, from every viewpoint, grievously inadequate and inequitable.

So what we have—and what Americans have not yet quite understood—is a generation with a high percentage of economic obsolescence.

Some can be trained for other jobs. But not too many. A packing house closed a little more than a year ago in a state which borders on the South. Management and the union worked out a retraining program. Both were shocked when a whopping fifty percent turned out to be too illiterate to be retrained.

So it is in the mining towns where the mines are closed, in farm areas where the machines have come, in the slum areas of industrial cities, North and West, there are men who are economically obsolete. A few can be trained. Some will do odd jobs, pick vegetables in season, work as "helpers" or at the temporary tasks which still call for hand labor or semiskilled work. This is something we need to know—the fact of obsolescent men.

And all who move North, or to the cities of the South, for that matter, take with them their rural fears and prejudices, their folkways and a cultural experience which does not fit them for urban life.

And their children?

---

[243]Brian Rungeling et al., *Employment, Income, and Welfare in the Rural South* (New York: Praeger, 1977); Harriet Laura Herring, *Passing of the Mill Village: Revolution in a Southern Institution* (Chapel Hill: University of North Carolina Press, 1949).

[244]See C. Vann Woodward, *Burden of Southern History* (Baton Rouge: Louisiana State University Press, 1960).

It was that time of afternoon when school children were on the way home. Three girls came along with the laughter and talk of the young. They were, as it turned out, fourteen, fourteen, and fifteen. They were neatly clad, if shabbily. Two of their families had come from the South, Virginia and Louisiana. The other said her family "had always" lived in Philadelphia.

There is always a spokesman. For this group it was the fifteen-year-old, a somewhat stocky girl, assured, poised and articulate.

"Yes, sir. I like it better here. We been living here three years. Yes, sir, I like school. We got good teachers. Yes, sir, I feel like I am learning.

"Yes, sir, I remember the South. It's better here. My mother says you move away from being afraid. You have rights here. The law protects you. You can go to the law. Do we learn about civil rights in school? Oh, yes, sir. We learn that. We talk about it. Up here you learn you are an American."

They went on, heads close, whispering, and giggling a bit.

Professor LaFayette Powell, senior psychologist for the Philadelphia school system, is a quiet, impressive man whose excellent training and sensitive awareness of the tremendous responsibility of his job were somehow reassuring. He and his associate psychologists deal exclusively with the problem of young minds—many needing only a little help to bloom and learn, some requiring long, tedious, hard-to-give assistance. And some hopeless or nearly so.

He said what I had heard from deans of admissions in Ivy League universities and in other institutions around the country: in general, with the usual exceptions, the pupils from the South are not as well prepared as children from other areas.

"Here I find the most apparent deficiencies in reading and mathematics," he said. "This applies to both white and Negro children of parents who move here from the South. The slums are, of course, the major problem.

"Many of the parents are totally unfitted to cope with competitive urban life," he said. "Some run away from it, abandoning their families. In the worst of the crowded slums a man can disappear by moving to another street. The corner taverns too often become the recreation place for those crowded into one room.

"The sudden feeling of being free of fears and restraints of a segregated society causes some of the younger ones to run wild, to get into trouble.

"But we have learned that the children can be rescued by remedial work, by psychological testing. Many who seemed retarded suddenly begin to bloom. We cannot always neglect the deeper, more meaningful facts of slums—and the distressing cost in human resources."

In Eastwick, where one of Philadelphia's bold imaginative renewal programs is in progress, one can see the eagerness of some of the southern Negroes to hold on to a small piece of ground, to have a patch of collards, a row or so of onions and cabbage.

In another area a woman sat in a straight chair before a small, sparsely stocked grocery store. Two stood talking with her.

The question was put. There was silence. Then one of those standing said, "Sure, I'll talk about what it feels like to move here from the South."

Almost immediately the others who stood drifted away. The woman who had begun to speak did not seem to notice.

"I'm doing domestic work," she said. "I came here from a South Carolina plantation 'cross the river from Augusta, Georgia. My daddy was killed, shot down at night. You know why? He could read and write. He could figure. He helped the others figure the padded costs at the commissary and the high interest on the crop loans.[245]

"One night they killed him. My mother stayed on a few years and then moved us up here where we had kinfolks.

"I went back once a few years ago. I rode the dirty day coach for colored. I rode the back of the bus. I kept the place they assign to colored people. I saw what they have to take, every day of their lives. When I got out of there I looked up at the sky and said, 'Oh Lord, write it in the sky. I'm never going back.'[246]

---

[245]See Jay R. Mandle, *Roots of Black Poverty: The Southern Plantation Economy After the Civil War* (Durham: Duke University Press, 1978).

[246]See C. Vann Woodward, *The Strange Career of Jim Crow*, 3d rev. ed. (New York: Oxford University Press, 1974); Robert Haws, *Age of Segregation: Race Relations in the South, 1890-1945* (Jackson: University Press of Mississippi, 1978).

"We have segregation here. But it isn't the law. I am not afraid a deputy sheriff will come and arrest me just for being a Negro.

"You read about crime here. We got it. Lots of it. Let me tell you something. You ever see colts and mules let out into the lot? You know how they run and leap and cut up? Young people and some of the old do that when they are let out of those Southern towns. Up here you get a feeling of release and being free. You don't have that down South."

"We are on the way," said the visitor from the South. "It's coming."

"You reckon?" she said, cocking her head to one side, a quizzical grin on her face.

"Yes, the trumpets are sounding around the walls. They are crumbling," answered the visitor.

"That'll be the day," she said.

And it will—and it is coming.

58

The Road
to Southern Maturity
Is Long and Bumpy:
Review of Thomas D. Clark's
The Emerging South

I n this book Thomas Dionysius Clark takes the year 1920 as mark-
ing the beginning of the South's emergence from the corrosive effect of civil war, reconstruction, and a long, bitter agricultural
depression in which the thunder and lightning flashes of the Populist rebellion played so great a part. He is right in that it was the coming of
the boll weevil that brought down the cotton kingdom and its serfdom
of tenants and croppers. The nation largely has fogotten, if indeed it
ever clearly comprehended, that the cotton South was economically pros-
trate and in the hands of receivers by the mid-1920s. The depression of
the 1930s was to be piled on top of that.

The Southern revolution, therefore, may well be said to have begun
with the end of the crop year of 1920, though there were areas where it
arrived the year before. This reviewer recalls being shown one Georgia
cotton plantation which, in 1919, had produced 2,110 bales, and in 1920,

Thomas Dionysius Clark, *The Emerging South* (New York: Oxford University
Press, 1961). Review reprinted with permission from the *New York Times Book Re-
view,* and Mrs. Ralph McGill, 17 September 1961. Copyright 1961, by the New York
Times Company. An earlier draft of this review is in the McGill papers, now at Emory
University, Atlanta.

on the same number of acres, with like seed, fertilizer and plows, offered a mere 270 bales.[247]

Mr. Clark, whose life began on a Southern farm, and who presently is chairman of the department of history at the University of Kentucky, has organized his book with thoroughness and clarity. It will be associated, I am sure, with Howard Odum's *Southern Regions of the United States* and W. J. Cash's *Mind of the South* as providing a comprehensive, lucid, factual look at the American South.[248] It is not a duplication of either, or a supplement, but an updating of both. It stands by itself as a very real, solid study.

All the necessary data is in it, but one must hasten to say that the book also is most readable, and, once begun, is not easily put down. The author's use of an appropriate paragraph from Frederick Law Olmsted at the beginning of each of his chapters provides an added interest. Olmsted traveled in the South prior to the Civil War, reporting for the *New York Times*. The books based on his dispatches are still required reading for any who would have a clear picture of the Old South.[249]

Mr. Clark's book is an attempt to assess the present state of the South and the changes which have taken place there during the last forty years. Although he neglects the political events, he considers in detail the changes and the progress which have resulted from the availability of cheap electrical power, the agricultural revolution, the expansion of industry, the impact of population shifts, the move toward racial integration and the improvements in public health and education.

This reviewer does not believe any writer on the South has done, for example, so revealing a chapter as Mr. Clark's titled "The Burden Grows Lighter." It is an examination into the devastating effect on the South of the afflictions of hookworm and malaria. These two killers did

---

[247]For McGill's explanation of historical causes of present conditions see the editor's introduction.

[248]Howard W. Odum, *Southern Regions of the United States* (Chapel Hill: University of North Carolina Press, 1936); W. J. Cash, *Mind of the South* (New York: A. A. Knopf, 1941).

[249]Frederick Law Olmsted, *The Cotton Kingdom: A Traveller's Observations on Cotton and Slavery in the American Slave States*, 1861, ed. Arthur M. Schlesinger (New York: A. A. Knopf, 1963).

so much damage "as to make General Sherman appear to have been a casual visitor." A single malarial death was officially reported by a state director of health as representing "a background loss of 2,000 to 4,000 days of labor due to illness."

Mr. Clark estimates that the cost to the South of malaria since the coming of the English to Jamestown would have built and supported an outstanding university in every Southern state. Vast fortunes were made on "chill tonics." It was not until the 1940s that public health finally brought malaria under control in the more affected rural areas of the South and, in time, virtually eliminated it.

Hookworm was also a killer, though an indirect one. It set up the image of the lazy, shiftless, poor-white-trash Southerner. Southerners were lazy and shiftless from anemia. Being so weakened, they died of tuberculosis and of any serious infection which felled them. Southern editors and the more oratorical politicians were, of course, insulted and outraged at the findings, as early as 1894, that rural Southerners were heavily infested with this unpleasant parasite. There was a mighty defense of Southern health. Yet, hookworm has not been completely eradicated to this day, though rural electrification and a more sanitary, informed rural population have accomplished much.

Mr. Clark's analysis of the Negro's emergence is thorough and lucid. There was, and is, a revolution in the Negro's way of life, as well as in the life of his region. He is changing his image of himself. It is no longer politically profitable, save in a few of the more backward, feudally controlled areas of the old cotton states, for political candidates to cry, "Nigger, Nigger!" And even in those the end is in sight. The old wool-hat politician is, as Mr. Clark says, speaking more and more in a vacuum. Law is officially on the side of the Negro, as he seeks what has so long been wickedly and needlessly denied him—the right to an equal share in American citizenship and all that it means. Morality is on his side, too. It will be a stronger, better, happier South when this transition to full citizenship is completed.

The truth is the majority of Southern people are not as stubbornly prejudiced as they have been made to appear. History surely will deal severely with their political leaders when it examines their deceit of their own people. The senators and congressmen, the governors, mayors, and state legislative leaders who encouraged their people to defiance of law, who told them the Supreme Court had acted illegally in the school desegregation decision and that their government was simply trying to "ram something down their throats," have not yet been judged—but in God's good time, they will be.[250]

There are signs of the emergence of new leadership. Business has ceased listening to the falsehoods and folly of the White Citizens' Councils. The tie between education and progress is more and more recognized. There are still two voices in the South, but, as Mr. Clark says, that of the extremist no longer is heeded as it was.

It may be that the South will, in time, be able to get on with industrialization. Substantial progress has been made. In some few areas it is spectacular. Overall, the South has passed through the initial stages of industrialization. What the future holds depends on what the emerging South does with itself. There are states that offer special inducements to industry: free rents, low taxes, etcetera; but the thinking Southerner knows that his region cannot attain its magnificent potential unless it cleans up its problems. Its political system is grossly inequitable, being overweighted in favor of the rural areas, which are fiercely anti-urban. An end to racial chaos also is an imperative requirement.

The reader of this book will learn much. The South stands, as the author says, "astride the Great Divide." Behind it lies "both the nineteenth century and the first half of the twentieth, eras marked by crisis and frustration." The emerging South, therefore, is seeking new values, creating new images. In his last sentence Mr. Clark writes, "How much of the past the South of the future preserves will depend on what standard of values it adopts in this period of change."

We must wait a while and see. This is not yet a New South—but an emerging one.

---

[250]See Numan V. Bartley, *The Rise of Massive Resistance: Race and Politics in the South During the 1950's* (Baton Rouge: Louisiana State University Press, 1969).

59

The South Will Change
1961

I n the long years of the Negro's discouragingly slow advance against his country's long-entrenched practices of segregation, the historically unique feature of this struggle has been largely unnoted. It is that the Negro, a distinct racial minority, was trying to become more American—not less. He was not, like some of the minorities of Europe, seeking to be set apart, to be recognized as a separate race with special privileges and status. He had already experienced being excluded from the national life, and he did not like it. He wanted to be accepted as a citizen, which the Constitution said he was, and to have the privileges accorded to other citizens—no more, no less.[251]

Nor was this all the story. Despite rejections and exploitations, often cunning, cruel, and ruthless, the Negro stubbornly identified himself with America and its promise. He persisted in this, even though his denials often have been stupid and stultifying in coarseness and violence.[252]

Reprinted from the *Saturday Evening Post* 234 (30 September 1961), by permission of Mrs. Ralph McGill and the *Saturday Evening Post*. The essay was reprinted in Hoke Norris, ed., *We Dissent* (New York: St. Martin's Press, 1962).

[251]See C. Vann Woodward, *Burden of Southern History* (Baton Rouge: Louisiana State University Press, 1960).

[252]See Howard N. Barinowitz, *Race Relations in the Urban South, 1865-1890* (New York: Oxford University Press, 1978); Robert Haws, *Age of Segregation: Race Relations in the South, 1890-1945* (Jackson: University Press of Mississippi, 1978).

When the wars came in 1898, 1917, 1941, and later in Korea, he served as he was permitted. It was experiences of the Korean conflict which precipitated the decision to integrate military services. Morale in the segregated units understandably was low. The all-Negro companies became an embarrassment as we emphasized our principles of democracy in the bloody campaign to stop Communist aggression. Jim Crow was cawing raucously and mockingly all the while.

At the conclusion of the Korean armistice, there were twenty-one American G.I.'s who refused exchange and announced they were indorsing Communism and going to Red China. Only three were Negroes. Studies of the twenty-one who stayed revealed some with backgrounds of inadequacies and educational lacks. Yet none of the white soldiers had case histories of discrimination and psychological pressures to match that of the average Negro G.I. It also is true that, despite a consistent campaign by the Communist party to convince the Negro that Marxism is his most logical political faith, the percentage of Negroes so persuaded is smaller than that of white Americans who have embraced it.

In the face of the whole record it is ironic that the canons of conformity are so fixed, so sicklied o'er with the pale cast of myth and the hypocrisy and falsehood of a separate but equal status, that the Negro's effort to become more American is attacked by extremist opposition as an un-American Communist plot.[253]

Until very recent years the Negro's total identity was with America. But once African ambassadors began to be heard in the United Nations and political leaders of the new nations began to appear in world conferences, a great many Negroes, especially the more aggressively committed students, began to feel an identification with Africa and its emerging nationalisms. This was, in a sense, healthy. It can become dangerous only if the white-supremacy extremists are permitted to filibuster legitimate civil rights bills in the Congress and if the states continue to deny the simple uncomplicated rights of equal citizenship.[254]

---

[253]See Paul M. Gaston, *New South Creed: A Study in Southern Mythmaking* (New York: Vintage Books, 1970). For McGill's analysis of false myths relating to blacks see the editor's introduction.

[254]See Alfred O. Hero, *Southern and World Affairs* (Baton Rouge: Louisiana State University Press, 1965).

The familiar rationalizations against doing what is, after all, a necessary and decent thing required by—in addition to the Constitution—the ethics of Judaism, Christianity, and Western civilization, long ago lost whatever dubious relevance they may have had. Yet they continue to be repeated by those whose emotional involvement prevents perspective. These irrelevancies are the essential ingredient of the White Citizens' Councils' speeches and printed propaganda.[255]

After the 1954 school decision, for example, one began to read statements by leaders of massive-defiance groups to the effect that "To admit Negro children to school would pull down the level of classroom performance. They aren't ready for it yet."[256]

Now the irony of this rationalization was that it was, with some notable exceptions, true. What the rationalists did not realize they were doing was indicting the system of segregated education. It had been separate. It had never been equal. It had been callously, heartlessly maintained in a most unequal manner. The white schools of the South were much inferior to the national averages, but they were far better than those for Negroes. The major inequities are familiar. The amount spent per Negro student was substantially less than that per white student. Later years have seen most urban pay scales equalized, but not all are, and for many years Negro teachers have suffered serious discrimination in salaries.

In myriad other ways Negro children in the South were deprived of opportunity to participate in the race of life. In a number of Southern states, as late as 1957, sums as low as two dollars or three dollars per pupil were being spent for libraries for white pupils while a few cents, or nothing at all, was being spent for Negro children.

For years after the development of school-bus transportation, seventy or eighty percent of the white children of the Deep South states re-

---

[255]See Neil R. McMillen, *The Citizens' Council* (Urbana: University of Illinois Press, 1971); William J. Simmons, *The Mid-West Hears the South's Story* (Greenwood MS: The Citizens' Councils, 1958); Thomas P. Brady, *A Review of Black Monday* (Winona MS: Association of Citizens' Councils of Mississippi, 1954).

[256]See Numan V. Bartley, *The Rise of Massive Resistance: Race and Politics in the South During the 1950's* (Baton Rouge: Louisiana State University Press, 1969).

quiring such service were provided it. But in some states not more than ten percent of the Negro children were so served.

It was a common practice in a number of Southern states to supply Negro schools with used or outdated textbooks discarded by white students. Negro schools were more crowded and had more double sessions. Vocational training was rarely first class for either race.

Advanced training in medicine, dentistry, law, nursing, architecture, electrical, mechanical and textile engineering in Southern state institutions was open to Negro students only after court decisions began to crack a few doors.

Southern politicians and a dismaying number of businessmen have been heard to say that the Negro can't learn, that he is inherently incapable of achievement. For this to be said, in the face of the educational discrimination which historically has existed, reveals either an unworthy ignorance of the facts or a deliberate distortion of them.

School superintendents, psychologists, truancy supervisors, and juvenile-court officers in the Eastern and Western states know the lacks of both white and Negro children who have come out of the average Southern school—especially those of rural areas. The level of work in many classrooms has been reduced. Desegregated schools are faced with the need to create remedial classes and to screen newcomers carefully to determine the grade for which they are prepared.

This background helps explain other things too—all very well known to sociologists and social caseworkers.

The Negro children who had no access to libraries, whose classroom instruction was poor, who had little home incentive to go to school, who had to walk long distances, who had little or no access to vocational skills, are the Negro adults of today—thousands of them in big-city slums, struggling in marginal jobs, or picking up what work they can find in unskilled capacities. And always there are the white products of the same system, the cruel cost of which, in human and dollar loss, daily becomes more apparent.

There is another rationalization which is an inevitable feature of the talks and writings of the prosegregationist politicians and apologists. It runs like this: "Let the Negro show some responsibility of citizenship before he is given the ballot. Let him prove himself ready to assume some of the burdens of civic life."

That this sort of nonsense should be written and spoken in heat and anger and received with applause by Klan-type mentalities is fantastic. It is even more preposterous than the arguments that the Negro is not capable of learning. After all, there were some schools. More often than not they were a disgrace to the flag that flew over them, but there were schools. But, in voting, there are to this day many rural areas where no Negro votes at all. There are others where a few are registered. And there are cities in at least four Southern states where the most qualified Negro finds it extremely difficult to be registered. The depths of this deprivation lend eloquence to statistics. As late as midsummer of 1961 only twenty-five percent of the Negroes in the Southern states who had reached voting age were registered to vote.

During the past summer, for example, civil rights cases were filed by the United States Department of Justice in Clarke and Forrest counties, Mississippi. Clarke County, in the east-central area, had more than fifty percent of her white citizens registered. A disputed total of not more than 6 of the 2,988 eligible Negroes was on the registration books. In Forrest County, in southeast Mississippi, about half the 22,431 eligible whites were registered. Only 25 of the 7,495 Negroes had been able to become qualified. There was, in the Justice Department files, a long record of attempted registrations that failed.[257]

In filing suit, Attorney General Robert Kennedy said, "Negroes in those two counties still are being deprived of the right to vote, the fundamental right of all American citizens. It is our responsibility under law to guarantee this right, and we will meet the responsibility. . . ."

The reply of Mississippi's Gov. Ross Barnett will almost certainly be at least a footnote in the history of the time. "I don't understand why they want to interfere with local self-government," he said. "Local government is the thing that has made this country great."

It is not comforting to know that there are those who feel so alien to the United States and its principles that the fundamental rights of citizens have so little meaning.

This inability to vote has inevitable side effects. The Negro in the South has not been permitted to participate in community discussions

---

[257]See Margaret Price, *Negro Voter in the South* (Atlanta: Southern Regional Council, 1957).

about the problems of schools or of other civic affairs. It is only in the last few years that an occasional Negro has been elected to a school board in some of the larger cities.

Not only was the Negro barred from any opportunity to gain understanding of local government; he had to listen in public and on radio and television to demagogic speakers who tried to outdo one another in their pledges to keep the Nigger (or Nigra) in his place. Nor was this all. The Negro was confronted daily with a picture of government which plainly and officially, through state statutes and municipal ordinances, gave him an inferior position as a human being. It was not logical to expect him to acquire any competence or interest in civic responsibilities. Yet there are Southerners today who, in the face of the record, say that the Negro isn't ready to participate in government. Let him earn the right "by demonstrating his responsibility as a citizen," they say.

That all of this is a costly piece of business to us as a country is plain. The South will pay the heaviest price. But in these days when population is used to mobility, an illiterate, untrained white or Negro boy or girl from Alabama or Georgia can quickly become a hoodlum in Illinois or California, a social-welfare statistic in Philadelphia or Milwaukee. A national responsibility for an end to discriminations in the rights of citizens and for equitable public education is inescapable. We already have a problem of two generations, adult and young, which have filled the slums of our industrial cities.

Another oft-repeated argument against citizenship rights for the Negro is based on irrational intermarriage fears, stemming from God-knows-what Freudian experiences and guilts. This is a real puzzler.

Do those who use the argument mean to imply that, of the 180,000,000 Americans, only Southerners need segregation laws to protect them from such marriages? Questions like this bring only recriminations, some vile and violent, never a logical discussion.

A question automatically poses itself when morality, law, and economics begin to make themselves felt.

What are our chances of avoiding a continuance of irrational processes? The answer is that the chances are good. There will be much resistance to desegregation and some of it will be violent. But there are new conditions. We are not, to be honest, having too much success changing the hearts and minds of men, as President Eisenhower suggested be done to solve the problem. But we are moving. Attorney General Kennedy saved the lives of perhaps a hundred or more persons by dispatching United States marshals to Montgomery, Alabama, where a federal judge, native of the state, later severely reprimanded the police department for its failure to be on hand in enough numbers to cope with the mob during the Freedom Rider troubles. The attorney general also made it plain that no community may support its own peculiar customs by attempts to maim or kill other citizens. The people of Alabama already are beginning to be grateful to the attorney general for saving their state from an even more shocking excess in lawlessness. In time, they may thank him publicly.

There are no evidences of wholesale integration, but this has not been the objective. Negro leadership has sought to make the Negro a citizen in the full sense of the word. Whatever integration takes place in the private sectors of life is for persons privately to determine. But if we begin with a date as late as May 1954, when the school decision was published, we can see how vast has been the change in the legal status of the Negro.

Laws and courts have declared and defined the Negro's equal citizenship. What the nation is just beginning to understand is that the Negro's efforts at citizenship now are being officially opposed only by those who are defying law, or clinging to contradictory state laws which have been declared unconstitutional.[258]

That desegregation will for some time be a process confined largely to the urban complexes of the South and the nation is plain. The rural areas have not yet been affected directly, although all feel the heat of change. But these eddies of semifeudal ruralism are dying. Their people are leaving to go to the cities—where resolution will be had.

The businessmen of most Southern cities now understand that they cannot have lawlessness, violence and closed or crippled schools—and progress. They already are looking with questioning eyes at the blatant White Citizens' Councils' leadership and at the bull-like antics of police staffs which have been party to violence.[259]

-----

[258]See Francis M. Wilhoit, *Politics of Massive Resistance* (New York: George Braziller, 1973).

[259]See Timothy Thomas Fortune, *Black and White: Land, Labor, and Politics in the South* (Chicago: John Publishing Co., 1970); Raymond W. Mack, ed., *Changing South* (Chicago: Aldine Publishing Co., 1970).

So, as 1961 moves toward the exit, it can be said that the status of desegregation now is at the point where all who oppose it are in defiance or technical evasion of law. And room for evasive maneuver is about used up.[260]

A lot of persons, mostly in trade, are not really concerned with the principles involved. But they are increasingly interested in a climate of law and order in which business and community life may flourish.

But while this force is most influential, it cannot be said that the moral influence is absent. All Southerners, save the most obtuse and insensitive, have long carried a private weight of guilt about the inequities of segregation. This weight now tilts many over to the side of justice and humanity.

Prejudice, bigotry, and defiance remain. But this is still a nation which understands it must live by law. It is no longer lawful to deprive any citizen of his rights to vote and to attend the public schools, parks, auditoriums, and concerts. The sit-ins and the freedom riders spotlighted economic injustice.

The excitement and challenge of the Negro's determined drive to become more American increasingly outweigh the forces which seek to influence him to abandon his identity as an American. The Black Muslims represent a religion alien to the American traditions. Christianity and the Bible have more appeal than Mohammed and the Koran. In addition, the Muslims propose a number of ghetto states. Only the most despairing and neurotic are likely to be attracted by such principles. Nor is there any sign that Communism is becoming more persuasive.

Dr. Martin Luther King, the student sit-in leaders, the Freedom Riders, the intelligent and able leaders of the NAACP, the Urban League, and other organizations joined in common cause might well be called the abolitionist force of 1960-1961. They are giving the South and the nation a new image of the Negro. And, perhaps even more important, they have made it possible for the Southern Negro to change his own image. In time, the South, which has been deceived by its local politicians into damning and fearing the NAACP and Martin Luther King, will come to appreciate the beneficial Americanism of this Negro

---

[260]Thomas Jackson Woofter, *Southern Race Progress: The Wavering Color Line* (Washington DC: Public Affairs Press, 1957).

leadership. They will come to see, as some already do, that Dr. King and the NAACP acted always from a basis of law, not violence or defiance of law. This could not be said of all the White Citizens' Councils, the Klans and the zoo-like lesser organizations which sprang up to incite lawlessness. Had the Negro leadership also used violence, instead of passive resistance and the processes of law, the results would have been dreadful.[261]

Nothing in the South is left unchanged by the changes which are occurring. And for the overwhelming majority of Negroes there is a pioneering determination to become more American, not less. The Negro also will always be a part of the South. Millions feel themselves Southerners as well as Americans. And as growing numbers of white Southerners learn to appreciate the new image of the Negro as a citizen, the South will accept him as such.

Day by day, opposition to the Negro's rights to equal citizenship finds itself more and more in the position of opposing the law and the Constitution. Tactics of delay and defiance cannot long sustain themselves, particularly in the urban communities, where the total of qualified Negro voters grows larger and larger. The depressed rural defiance will, in good time, fall of its own weight. The end is not yet in sight—but it is there.

---

[261]See John Hope Franklin and Isidore Starr, eds., *The Negro in Twentieth-Century America: A Reader on the Struggle for Civil Rights* (New York: Vintage Books, 1967).

60

Let's Lead Where We Lag

On the Sunday following the brutal mob actions at the bus depots in Anniston and Birmingham, Alabama, a dispirited Episcopal communicant of the latter city wrote:

There is no condemnation of the riots from our pulpit today. There was no moral guidance in a time when the eyes of the world were focused on our state and nation. Our churches really have become gymnasiums where we exercise with the reading of the Book of Common Prayer, neither sweating nor breathing hard in the stuffy air of sanctity.[262]

In an eastern city last summer I had a pleasant visit with an able young newspaperman, a Negro and an Episcopal communicant. It developed that later in the afternoon he was meeting his son who was coming home from camp via bus.

"You might be interested to know," I said, "that the Diocese of Atlanta has just had its first integrated camp. One Negro boy, aged eleven, applied and promptly was accepted. He proved to be a popular camper and had no difficulty at all. His personality was such that he did not feel

Reprinted from the *Episcopalian*, March 1962, by permission of Mrs. Ralph McGill and the *Episcopalian*. Copyright 1962, The Episcopalian, Inc. Also reprinted in *Negro Digest*, August 1962.

[262]For significant insight into McGill's position, see "An Interview on Race and the Church,"in this volume.

alone or an outsider. And, of course, this personality was precisely why the other boys did not think of him in such terms."

The young newspaperman's eyes widened.

"You did that in Georgia?"

I nodded affirmatively.

"We couldn't do that here, he said. "I am grieved to say that here we do not have a very happy relationship between the white and Negro Episcopal churches. There is little communication between us. Some feel there is a drawing apart. There is a need for some positive action. How did the Atlanta Diocese manage the camp?"

It was explained that when the youngster applied for camp, and was accepted, the clergy and laymen on the camp committee informed by letter all parents of other boys who had been accepted. They were told they could withdraw their son, or sons, if they wished, but earnest hope was expressed they would not. None did. Officials in the small city near the camp (Mikel) quietly were informed. The teenage counselors were briefed on their practical and Christian duties. All went well. It was a happy, rewarding experience.

Each of us recognized the jarring contradictions in the drama of race. In Alabama brutal mobs were for some time unchecked by police. In that time there were inflicted severe injuries to many for the crime of having ridden on a bus to which they had been sold a ticket. In Mississippi the jails were being filled with white and colored travelers, young and middle-aged, who were testing what is an incredible denial in this last half of the twentieth century—the right of a citizen of the United States freely to travel on common carriers and to use the public services in the depots.[263]

It is a sad commentary that the Episcopal churches in these states were largely Sunday gymnasiums insofar as any leadership in the tremendous moral problem of our time was concerned. Nor were they alone. The silence of all the churches was inescapable. Later there was a mild protest by some minister against the inactivity of police. But still there is no action—only silence. In Georgia one small boy makes Episcopal camping history by being accepted at the camp maintained by the

---

[263]See Numan V. Bartley, *Rise of Massive Resistance: Race and Politics in the South During the 1950's* (Baton Rouge: Louisiana State University Press, 1969).

diocese for the summer recreation and instruction of its young people. In an eastern state a young Negro doubted this could have been done in his diocese.

There is a third illustration—and a more damning one. There came to Atlanta University two brilliant young Negro students, graduates of mission schools in their native country maintained by one of the larger Protestant Southern denominations. Neither was ever called upon by members or officers of that denomination. A distinguished member of Nigeria's high court, who had been educated in elementary and secondary schools and colleges all maintained by one of the largest of United States denominations, visited four Southern cities and four in the North and was never approached by any representative of the church which had given him all but his graduate education.

Still another African visitor, whose youth had been spent in schools supported by American missions, had a similar experience.

"I am glad I was ignored," he said. I have heard your joke about the African visitor who was finally admitted to a restaurant with the apology of the manager—'You see, I thought you were one of these American Negroes.' I am afraid I would not have been happy talking with a pastor who would not admit American Negroes to worship in his church—even though the same church educated me."[264]

There is more than one reason why Christianity is not more of a force in the newly emerged—and emerging—countries of Africa. But one of them is this inescapable gulf which the African intellectual quickly sees, even though he has never been out of Africa. A visitor here, of course, experiences the harsh irony of it.[265]

The Episcopal Church in America suffers equally with the others. All are afflicted by those callous persons of Christian affiliation who insist that the Negro is an inferior person and that segregation is decreed by God. Nor may we Episcopalians play the Pharisee and "pass on the other side" from these. The ugly, distorted, even vicious publications of the more fanatic White Citizens' Councils, and the hate-organization

---

[264]See C. Vann Woodward, *Strange Career of Jim Crow*, 3d rev. ed. (New York: Oxford University Press, 1974); Woodward, *Burden of Southern History*, rev. ed. (Baton Rouge: Louisiana State University Press, 1968).

[265]See "Television Interview about Africa" in volume 2.

pamphlets, delight in printing sermons and statements from the three or four Episcopal rectors in the Southern states who lend their names and positions to the prejudices and passions of the extremists.[266]

Certain questions are posed. Is there any thoughtful person who does not understand why communism, which also claims it can redeem and change the world, is able to attract so much dedicated service, especially, though not exclusively, in so many depressed areas of the world? One must ask what sort of examples, or alternatives, are offered them. Missionaries all over the world have sent urgent pleas to their churches in America to put Christianity to work in America's problem of race. Some churches, clergymen, and laymen have acted with vigor and courage. But it still is true that 11:00 A.M. on Sunday is the most segregated hour of all the week.

That Christianity in America cannot go on with this without disastrous results must be plain to all save the most stubbornly obtuse.[267]

It is not easy—and yet, in fact, it is if there is a will to act. That we think in terms of images has become almost a trite truth. But truth it is. When confronted with something which radically alters the status quo, we invent mental images to help us rationalize resistance to change. In Southern school cases, the extremists—too often assisted by the daily press, members of the clergy, the bar, and the politicians—invariably conjured up two false ones. They first rubber-stamped every Negro as dirty, illiterate, criminal, or dishonest. (That this reflected one of the worst evils of segregation—a separation from truth and fact and acquaintance with the great body of educated, cultured Negroes—never occurred to these makers of false images.) They then pictured the chil-

---

[266]See William J. Simmons, *The Mid-West Hears the South's Story* (Greenwood MS: The Citizens' Councils, 1958); Thomas P. Brady, *A Review of Black Monday* (Winona MS: Association of Citizens' Councils of Mississippi, 1954); James O. Eastland, *We've Reached Era of Judicial Tyranny* (Greenwood MS: Association of Citizens' Councils of Mississippi, 1955).

[267]For more by McGill on religion and race, see: "Interview on Race and Church," "Southern Moderates are Still There," "Church in a Social Revolution," and "Introduction to *God Wills Us Free*," in volumes 1 and 2. See Charles Reagan Wilson, *Baptized in Blood: The Religion of the Lost Cause, 1865-1920* (Athens: University of Georgia Press, 1980); Samuel S. Hill, *Religion and the Solid South* (Nashville: Abingdon Press, 1972).

dren of such persons as overrunning the schools. And then, paradoxically, they expressed unreasoned fear about intermarriage and the loss of racial purity.

That the United States Supreme Court decisions plainly had said this overrunning was not the intent of the rulings, and had declared placement laws to be constitutional when not used to discriminate, was blithely ignored in a campaign to deceive people and create resistance, defiance, and mobs. That most of the nation's population had for a long time been operating without laws requiring segregation and without signs of the much feared race-ruin also was bypassed. The extremists were, in fact, insulting their own people by implying that only they, of all Americans, were in need of such laws.

This obsession with false images can be as harmful to Christianity as false gods. Common sense somehow becomes paralyzed. It is utterly preposterous that in this period of history millions of Americans should be most concerned with where a colored child shall sit in school and whether colored persons shall be welcomed to worship.

Christianity cannot afford to be made to appear ridiculous—and yet it is. Even Christians must agree that the long history of foreign missions and the opposition of Christians to acceptance of colored persons in their churches would be the subject of loud, coarse laughter were it not for the by-product of it.

A number of Christian and Judaic leaders, in individual sermons in the past several months, seriously have suggested that fewer and fewer persons are using religion as a yardstick for determining values. All the evidence tends to sustain them.

The Episcopal Church, which sensibly avoided any rupture at the time of the American Civil War, should be better able to act with common sense and Christian conviction than those denominations which divided in acrimony and prejudice.

A decision to accept Negro worshipers which results in years of budgets being unmet and building programs bankrupted is perhaps valid in a temporary and superficial manner. It is unlikely that any diocese which planned, prayed, and educated its communicants would suffer any real losses. But it may be that the Christian church—not merely the Episcopal—is at the point where it must face up to losing those persons who cannot entertain the idea of being in the same sanctuary or at the same Communion rail with a colored person. To compromise almost surely means a slow death, as communicants with a prodding sense of conscience and morality drop out. This would certainly be true of the young communicants.

The problem of race is not, of course, the only one facing Christianity today. There is the complex problem of growing urban populations, the shifts to suburbs, the abandonment of many city churches, and the urgent need for Christian leadership in the so-called asphalt jungles of the large cities. But that of race is the most pressing of all.

Many voices ask, "Where is the Church going?" Only the Church can answer.

61

Rebirth of Hope at Ole Miss?

"I trust it will not be misunderstood," wrote a member of the faculty at the University of Mississippi, "if I say that every time I see James Meredith on our campus the tune and words of an old spiritual run through my head: 'Swing Low, Sweet Chariot, coming for to carry me home.' Some of us here see in him, and the slow evolving meaning of his entrance and presence, a destiny-sent chariot, swung low, to lift this university and all who love it and hope for it out of the morass of fear, educational inadequacies, and make-believe in which it has so long lived.

"To speak in the vernacular of the times," he continued, "we are freedom riders riding the hope symbolized by Meredith's presence. Through him freedom may come to thought and teaching. We may, in time, be able to turn to the business of education and creating a university worthy of the name. It will not be soon. But hope has been born."

One of the faculty at the university at Oxford, Mississippi, is writing a book on thought control in education in the years since 1954. If the book finds a publisher, as is likely, it will explain a condition which made Mississippi, if not unique, at least somewhat "different" insofar as control of thought and restrictions on academic freedom are con-

Reprinted from *Saturday Review* 45 (17 November 1962), by permission of Mrs. Ralph McGill and *Saturday Review*. Copyright 1962, Saturday Review, Inc.

cerned. The White Citizens' Councils were organized in the state soon after the United States Supreme Court declared segregation on a basis of race to be unconstitutional. Within an incredibly brief time the Citizens' Councils were active in every county in the state. Their center of power moved inevitably from the Delta, where the idea was initiated, to Jackson, the state capital city. It became headquarters for the statewide Citizens' Councils Association because political power was centered there. A subsidiary of the association was the Citizens' Council Forum. State tax money soon was being paid to the association at the rate of five thousand dollars per month. The forum began to turn out films and taped programs for broadcasting on hundreds of radio and television stations. Since 1954 no governor and no legislature has been unaware of the association. Governor Ross Barnett is a member. It is estimated that about ninety-five percent of the legislature is affiliated.[268]

A block-by-block, house-to-house survey was held in Jackson, and in other towns, to determine segregationist "attitudes." That this was an indirect form of intimidation was obvious. When, in 1955, a petition for integrated schools was presented in Jackson by forty-three Negroes, all of them in private employ almost immediately lost their jobs.

By 1955, university professors and ministers had become used to the inevitable man with a tape recorder at public speakings or panel discussions. University and college students, reflecting what they had heard at home, or what they heard from radio or television or read in their newspapers, began to spy on professors and send in accusations, signed or anonymous, accusing them of being soft on communism or segregation. A great statewide silence fell save for the Citizens' Councils programs. In time there seemed to many Mississippians to be but one voice—that of the Citizens' Councils. As the power of the Citizens' Councils grew, it corrupted. Some of its investigators, in talking with teachers, ministers, editors, or any person who had voiced "moderate" opinions, subjected them to coarse, vulgar, and on occasion profane tongue-lashings and intimidations. In the span of about two years roughly one-fourth of

---

[268]See Neil R. McMillen, *The Citizens' Council* (Urbana: University of Illinois Press, 1971); Thomas P. Brady, *A Review of Black Monday* (Winona MS: Association of Citizens' Councils of Mississippi, 1954); James O. Eastland, *We've Reached Era of Judicial Tyranny* (Greenwood MS: Association of Citizens' Councils of Mississippi, 1955).

the faculty of Ole Miss left, on orders, on "advice," or in a great hurry to be out of the witch-hunting, thought-control climate.

But always there was a small, hard core of professors who, in a very real sense, went underground. Their contemporaries in states where there was academic freedom and a state government undominated by a semisecret society wondered why they remained. Some of this group had economic and family roots and responsibilities which made it impossible to quit. But all of them stayed on because of a sense of responsibility. They were suspect by those of the faculty who collaborated with the Citizens' Councils to maintain a Gestapo-like atmosphere. Some, indeed, were subjected to spying and denouncements by fellow professors. Nonetheless, they held on. There was in them that curious, stubborn streak which enables man to endure what he daily feels he cannot endure another day. There was, for these, a feeling of obligation to stay which they could not or would not put into public words.[269]

"In the days before, during, and after the riots and tensions at Oxford," said one, "it was inevitable that some of us thought of the but lately dead William Faulkner. His characters were fragmented, divided against themselves in objectives and the essence of themselves. So were we at Ole Miss and in Mississippi. We were in Yoknapatawpha County. It had been Faulkner's symbol of how the South, and more particularly the Mississippi South, became the victim of itself and its own institutions and those who made up its power structure. The riots seemed almost a post-mortem chapter."

Whatever their motivation, there were a relatively few good men who held on. It is they who now hope. It is they who will be the cornerstone of a free university if, as they hope, academic freedom one day does return to the state.

They believe, with reason, that the presence of James Meredith will force the university students, as few have, to think about the racial problem, the constitutional guarantees of citizenship, and their own relationship to the great social issue of their generation. The more sensitive faculty members have had long years in which to observe. They believe the students of the state university are, and long have been, isolated from

---

[269]See James W. Silver, *Mississippi: The Closed Society*, enl. ed. (New York: Harcourt, Brace, & World, 1966); Russell H. Barrett, *Integration at Ole Miss* (Chicago: Quadrangle Books, 1965).

the main stream of national and international thought and ideas. The student actions since the riots confirm what faculty members describe as a most unbelievable lack of interest in, and opinions about, events and ideas in the rest of the nation and the world. Some students still respond to the encouragement of the Citizens' Councils to harass Meredith and to continue disturbance.

There is no tradition of dissent or liberal thought on the Ole Miss campus. There are, to be sure, always the few individual rebels, the nonconformists. But they have no rallying point.

The College Characteristic Index found that Mississippi students place a high value on possessions, status, and the material benefits of education. They were at opposite ends of the pole from the values prevailing at liberal arts colleges and some state institutions.

Standards at the university have remained relatively low, despite efforts to raise them. One factor contributing to this is a state policy admitting any high school graduate who has completed the required secondary school courses—regardless of his grades. The curriculum is not regarded as sound, though some individual teachers are superior and obtain excellent results. The university supports no debating society, no student literary publication. It has never been able to obtain a Phi Beta Kappa chapter. Newspapers and magazines are not readily available on the campus or in Oxford. The student newspaper has been harassed by the state legislature and the Citizens' Councils.

The university, in a state with the lowest per capita income in the nation, has been starved by lack of adequate appropriations. Attendance costs are about $1,200 per year, at a minimum. This is beyond the means of most Mississippi youths. Some observers have described Ole Miss as more like a club than a university. When the riots came one observer said, "My God, this is the state's elite group."

It should be noted, in discussing standards, that Mississippi has the smallest national percentage of persons who vote. The adults also are isolated. Mississippi is one of the five remaining poll-tax states. The state was a part of the Dixiecrat rebellion against President Harry Truman's nomination in 1948. In 1960 it withheld its electoral votes from the national nominees and presented them to Virginia's Harry Byrd.[270]

---

[270]See Emile Bertrand Ader, *The Dixiecrat Movement: Its Role in Third Party Politics* (Washington DC: Public Affairs Press, 1955); V. O. Key, Jr., *Southern Politics in State and Nation* (New York: Vintage Books, 1949).

It is against this melancholy background that James Meredith has emerged as a symbol of change. Resistance remains strong, angry, and determined. But the state has reduced its payments to the Citizens' Councils Forum. The governor has had to call off a Chicago dinner at which he was to have addressed two hundred Midwest industrialists on the happy life and advantages in Mississippi. One hundred business leaders have called for a recognition of law. The faculty supporters of the Citizens' Councils no longer seem quite so arrogant and assured. They and the student informers have seen that the Citizen's Councils are not, after all, greater than the government of the United States. They have been forced to think on constitutional rights, common to all.

Hope, therefore, glimmers at Ole Miss. It is a tiny flame. But it burns.

Chattanooga—
Where the Mountains
Look at Each Other

T o me, moving to Chattanooga from a river farm about thirty miles north along the Tennessee, the towers of the city were top-less and glorious like those of Ilium. I was six years old then, and it was more than forty years ago. And ever since, whether by air, road, or rail, when the mountain passes have been cleared and the city appears there by her sinuously curving river, I have felt something of the old warmth of arrival.

I remember so many things. We came by rail from Soddy, to which we had driven from our distant farm. Our things were hauled in farm wagons to the new home in the then rising suburb of Highland Park. There I began to soak up history; attended school at the old, square, brick Fourth District building; rode a bicycle to the library for two books each day; went on to McCallie; knew the thrill of playing in foot-ball games at the old clay-baked University of Chattanooga field; ap-

Essay provided by Mrs. Ralph McGill from the McGill papers, now at Emory University, Atlanta. While the exact date of this piece is unknown, McGill's reference to Senator Estes Kefauver as "the current representative" of Tennessee indicates the es-say was written no later than 1963, for Kefauver died in that year. Also McGill men-tions Chattanooga's population as being almost 150,000; the census of 1960 placed that city's population at 130,009. The piece was probably written, then, between 1960 and 1963. *The Eighteenth Decennial Census of the United States, 1960*, vol. 1, part 44, Ten-nessee, 44-11.

peared in dramatic club plays in which the GPS [girls preparatory school] girls participated; fell in love with Sue Smart and with Rebecca Mathis; hunted minie balls and shell pieces on Missionary Ridge and bloody Chickamauga; went away to Vanderbilt University and have never been back to live, but always the returning to visit family and friends has had in it some of that first arrival when my child's eyes saw their first city.[271]

Chattanooga takes its name from the original name of Lookout Mountain, "Chado-na-ugsa," a Creek Indian phrase meaning "Rock that comes to a point," as old Lookout does, crowding closely to the city until her cliffs seem almost to rise from it. And about her, too, are Signal Mountain, Missionary and Walden's Ridges. The Indians said, "Here the mountains look at each other."

The most beautiful valley of the Tennessee lies here between the great ranges of the Cumberlands, which are in turn extensions of the ancient, folded Appalachians, which pushed up into their great, wide belt of peaks when the earth was young. It was the Appalachian barrier which held back the settlers for so long. Some of the tributaries of the Tennessee itself rise on the east side of the mountains, reaching the main stream by way of deep-cut, wild gorges, through which at last the restless pioneers made their way.

The Tennessee is a grand river, but there in the Appalachians, she was bothersome. She was one of the great highways of the early days, for Indian and settler, but few men loved her. Death came often on her waters, from storm or Indian foray. There were rough shoal waters, such as Muscle Shoals, the Frying Pan, the Tumbling Shoals, and, of course, the suck, or boiling pot. As a boy I looked often at the suck, located in the canyon of the Tennessee. It was fearful to a boy's eyes, as it must have been to those who came by flatboat and sail years ago. The TVA [Tennessee Valley Authority] dams ended it.

In my boyhood there were great steamers on the river, and I often went back to our old home place on the *Joe Wheeler*. I can see her yet,

---

[271]See *Ralph McGill: Editor and Publisher*, ed. Calvin McLeod Logue (Durham: Moore Publishing Co., 1969) 1:25-44. For an interview with Rebecca "Reb" Mathis Gershon see *Southern Encounters: Southerners of Note in Ralph McGill's South*, ed. Calvin M. Logue (Macon GA: Mercer University Press, 1983); also Ralph McGill, *The South and the Southerner* (Boston: Little, Brown and Company, 1964) 54-55.

and smell her cargo. I recall the roustabouts, the thick, heavy china, the many vegetables, the ham, fried round steak, and chicken on the table, and the mystery and skill of the landings at night—the powerful search-light with moths whirling in its beams, the shouts of the mate, the gang-plank pushed into the muddy bank—that was living.

Chattanooga was from the beginning a product of river and rail. She grew from the river. John Ross, son of a Scottish trader and a Cher-okee mother, had a ferry, and a town grew up about it. It was officially named in 1838. Albion, Lookout City, and Montevideo were suggested names, but Chattanooga won. The city was incorporated the next year.

Since that time the city has grown and prospered. The river and rails faithfully continue to nourish her. The river now and then would treat her badly. Floods came. As a boy at McCallie school, I worked in rescue work with a boat from off the school lake, and, along with an-other fifteen-year-old, Malcolm Williams, was armed with pistols and placed in the great refugee-packed armory building for one long night. During those days I rode down Main Street in a motorboat. The TVA changed all that.

She was a brawling, bustling, frontier-type city, straining the seams of her pants, and just taking on polish, when the Civil War came. Chat-tanooga lies in the foothills of the mountains which run on up into East Tennessee. She has to this day the mixed culture of a mountain and a flatland town. The East Tennesseans believed in Union. They owned few slaves. They had sent their sons to fight with Andrew Jackson and had helped elect him president. They remembered how he had threat-ened to hang John C. Calhoun for trying to break up the Union. Most of them were hard-working, small farmers, and they looked with sus-picion on the plantation, slave-owning class. But, as now, there was also pressure in Chattanooga from the lower South. It met and mixed "where the mountains look at each other."

In the super-heated election of 1860, Tennessee went for the Con-stitutionalist party—and not for the Southern-secession Democrats who had bolted at Charleston and Richmond and, at the latter place, nomi-nated Breckenridge. The Constitutionalist party was made up of old Whigs and dissatisfied Democrats. John Bell was its nominee, along with the great orator Edward Everett, of Massachusetts.

"The war," said the wise ones, "would never reach into the mountain valley and touch Tennessee." But the river and the rails, which were to make her, brought the war. Grant came, and after a harsh campaign, Braxton Bragg went. Chattanooga's roads lead through mountain passes into the South, and after a while, Sherman's troops moved through them toward Dalton, and the Confederate army camped there under a new commander, Joe Johnston. The roads ran on to Atlanta.

Once the wreckage and paralysis of war were overcome, Chattanooga began to come into her own. She had a great voice—Adolph Ochs, and his *Times*. Free enterprise men came to stain the skies with smoke from foundries, mills, and fabricating plants.

Education was always a burning light. The Reverend Thomas Hock McCallie, of a pioneer Presbyterian family, started a boys' school on Missionary Ridge, and Baylor School was established in downtown Chattanooga. It was later moved northward on the river. The University of Chattanooga has steadily presented a sound and accredited program. The city and county school systems are among the best in the state.

She is a city of churches and great preachers. I remember best Tom McCallie and Johnathan W. Bachman. The latter had been a Confederate veteran and he became, before he died, minister to the whole town, Jew, Catholic and Protestant alike.

I remember her politicians—of whom Senator Estes Kefauver is the current representative.

Textile and woolen mills came shortly after the turn of the century, and Chattanooga proceeded on its way to become one of the first industrial cities of the state and region. Her population is almost 150,000, and she is a city of beauty and intelligence.

The coming of the TVA was of great importance to the city and the entire Tennessee valley. It was first suggested in 1933 by the late Franklin D. Roosevelt. The region included portions of seven states, the watershed of the Tennessee. Kentucky, Virginia, North Carolina, Tennessee, Georgia, Alabama, and Mississippi are at least partially in "the valley," and it constitutes a region almost as large as the British Isles. Its hundreds of lakes have brought recreation and industry. It was the TVA which made possible Oak Ridge and the great secret project there, which later was to flame over Hiroshima and bring an end to the Japanese empire.

The city keeps growing. It has built on its mountains, its ridges, and beyond them. As a boy I used to hunt rabbits and birds in the woods beyond Missionary Ridge, where thousands now live, and walk the five miles of dirt road to Bird's Mill to fish. Now, it is a great highway, along which heavy traffic moves, and the modern airport is nearby.

Chattanooga keeps changing—growing, but retaining always something of beauty and of charm because her mountains, lakes, and her river are there as examples of both.

63

Where We Stand: Emancipation

S ome months after Abraham Lincoln signed the Emancipation Proclamation, an Iowa farmer was asked by a reporter how Lincoln stood in his state. "He stands high," the farmer said. "He stands seventeen feet higher than any other man in the United States."[272]

A century has passed, and today we can say that, in the United States, the free man stands high, higher than ever before.

There were volcanoes of hate, fear, and treasonous movements in 1863. They erupted in our time at Little Rock in 1957, in the street riots of New Orleans in late 1960, in Anniston, Birmingham, and Montgomery in the summer of 1961, and in bloody and murderous mob attacks on U.S. marshals and troops in Oxford, Mississippi, in the early autumn of 1962.[273]

There may be occasional spewings of hate and ignorance in 1963, but the eruptions will be fewer. The original volcanoes are already ex-

Reprinted from *Look* magazine (15 January 1963), by permission of Mrs. Ralph McGill and the editors of *Look* magazine. Copyright 1963 by Cowles Communications, Inc.

[272]For McGill's "Cooper Union Lincoln Day Address," 12 February 1960, see *Ralph McGill: Editor and Publisher,* ed. Calvin McLeod Logue (Durham: Moore Publishing Company, 1969) 2:153-67.

[273]See McGill's "Rebirth of Hope at Old Miss?" in volume 2.

tinct, or almost so. They are reduced to an occasional belch of abuse against the courts and the Constitution, a puff of preposterous demagoguery, largely lacking its old-time sulphuric content.

Nor is this all. Those areas in which such volcanoes erupted have discovered that an invisible but nonetheless real deposit of sociological and economic lava covered their cities and towns. It got into the wheels of business and slowed them. It caused new industries to turn away and teachers to leave for healthier climates. The dust of it stifled friendships and discouraged community life.

None of this was lost on the South and its people—especially the young ones. The young Southerner's leaders—political, religious, professional and business—are now on trial before him. He sees that, for generations, the basis of "Southern" politics has been a monumental, almost comic, irrelevancy. He is being freed from the myths of state sovereignty, from those that distorted the history of pre-Civil War days and sought to make of slavery merely an error in kindly paternalism.[274]

The young Southerner now knows, as do his elders, that while not all may like it, in the most pragmatic sense no governor, legislature, or secret organization can bring back the conditions of life that prevailed in the South up to the year 1954. The United States Supreme Court school decision of 1954 was, like Lincoln's Emancipation Proclamation, a great rock on which conscience could stand.

As we evaluate where we stand today, the story is one of progress almost everywhere. A number of states that had segregated systems in 1954 have entirely—or almost entirely—ended them. The three border states of Missouri, Oklahoma, and West Virginia are examples. In Georgia, the University [of Georgia] and the Georgia Institute of Technology last September began a second year of integration, without incident. The University [of Georgia] in 1962 presented its first diploma to a Negro, without objection. Emory University, a private institution, voluntarily admitted its first Negroes to graduate schools. The Atlanta public schools, in September 1962, admitted forty Negro children. No qualified pupil was barred. And there will be no turning back. These educators who have managed to rescue the administration of education from the politicians do not wish to turn back.

---

[274]For McGill's analysis of false Southern myths see the editor's introduction.

We have grown used to seeing Negroes at the head table in meetings of state Democratic committees in Southern border states. The desegregation of parks, public transportation, golf courses, libraries, and concert halls is the rule, rather than the exception. A half dozen Southern cities have desegregated hotels; more will follow this year. There has been no breakthrough—but a start has been made in breaking the barrier to job opportunity. Desegregated luncheons and dinners, save in the three or four states of defiance, are commonplace.

Race relations are much improved. There are those who mourn that relations between white and black have deteriorated in the South. It is not true. They are much better. They are not, to be sure, in the old paternalistic pattern. But respect and understanding are increasing, and the more meaningful relationships are sounder.

Court decisions in the field of voting rights are of vast importance. Paired with them is the dramatic reapportionment ruling, which very substantially reduced rural control of state legislatures and forced the grant of more equitable representation to cities and suburban areas. Reapportionment, with the Civil Rights Act of 1960, is unlocking many doors to rapid progress for the Negro in the South.

The belief has long been held that securing the vote for the Negro would give him the power to secure for himself the rights set out in the Constitution. Case histories prove that participation of federal government urgently is needed. A classic case is that of Macon County, Alabama, seat of the justly famous Tuskegee Institute. The brazen resistance to Negro voting there was in the courts almost four years before the right of registration without discrimination fully was established.

In Fulton County, Georgia—Atlanta—where voting discriminations long ago were removed, a Negro won a seat in the state senate in the first election after reapportionment. His election was unique in two ways: His opponent was also a Negro, and the battle between them— also a product of reapportionment—was one of the first two-party state legislative contests in the state's history.

Of course, there are parts of the South where the resistance to change still seems strong. In Mississippi, the monstrous evil of White Citizens' Council power has paralyzed churchmen, educators, and others who might support morality.[275] Alabama is almost equally handicapped, and there are problems also in South Carolina. But, however long delayed, change will come in those states too. Today, the national conscience is committed to what we have called the American dream.

There is much to be done. But it will be done.

---

[275]See Neil R. McMillen, *The Citizens' Council* (Urbana: University of Illinois Press, 1971).

64

Television Interview
about Africa

I *ntroduction:* Senegal, Guinea, Ghana, Togo, Dahomey, Nigeria, The Congo, all in Africa, all part of the changing face of the Dark Continent. WSB Television now presents *Atlanta Constitution* publisher, Ralph McGill, recently returned from a twenty-five-thousand-mile tour to these countries, and to report to President [John] Kennedy. Ray Moore, WSB Television News Director; George Paige, News Editor; John Palmer, News Editor; in a special report, "McGill on Africa."

Ray Moore: Mr. McGill, you were invited to the White House this week to report to President Kennedy and Secretary of State Dean Rusk. What do you consider the most important thing you were able to tell them about your African trip?

McGill: Well I think the conclusion [was] reached that, while racial violences and incidents hurt us and always will hurt us, . . . there is a great reservoir of good will toward this country and a belief in this country. I think our policies are bearing some fruits slowly but surely, under con-

Published by permission of Mrs. Ralph McGill and WSB Television, Atlanta, Georgia. McGill was interviewed by newsmen on 22 March 1963 concerning his tour in Africa that year of Senegal, Guinea, Ghana, Togo, and Dahomey for President John F. Kennedy.

siderable pressure from the Russians, because this [Africa] is a great rich continent and they're after it. But I was encouraged by the Americans I met there and by the slow realization of the people [Africans] that this country wants to help and that it is a country which believes in independence and believes in the rights of individuals; . . . this sort of thing is getting over to them.

Reporter: We hear a good deal, Mr. McGill, about neocolonialism. Tell us what it is and how we can help the Africans without being accused of it.

McGill: Well, neocolonialism is a favorite word or phrase used . . . by the Communists and by the . . . extreme socialist left. And by that they mean that while these countries have freed themselves of direct colonialism, . . . their economies are in such dire straits that big cartels are trying to come in and obtain possession of their mineral supplies or gold or diamonds. This is neocolonialism, a coming in, in another way, to re-establish economic control over their resources.

Reporter: How can we help them then; how can we put any capital into Africa without being accused of this very thing?

McGill: Well we can't, but [that brings up] . . . another thing that I wanted to report on. . . . I had a talk in Accra, Ghana, for example, with President Nkruma. Now Nkruma was educated in this country; he spent twelve years over here. He didn't have a very happy experience in this country, not altogether. And he was convinced that with the limited resources and capital of his country that he would have to have a socialist regime. Well now, while I was there President Nkruma made a talk in which he said that to obtain a capital base . . . [his country] would have to invite in other outside investments. And he let [be] set up a schedule of the profits which an investment—outside investor—would be able to have working under the laws of the country. Now this is a very considerable retreat for him, a change of mind.

Moore: Is there any evidence that he might change his mind once again after he has gotten the goals that he wants?

McGill: Yes, this is the great danger; this is why outside investment will be slow to come in, of course. You and I would think a long time, but . . . they're damming . . . [the Volta River] up, and the Kaiser Company of this country, our Kaiser aluminum and Kaiser engineering people, are building what is one of the world's great dams there.

Reporter: Are the Russians in on this dam project?

McGill: Not on this one. They're building a smaller one over in here on a smaller river. But this one is only about seventy-five miles out of Accra. And when it is completed by 1965, which is only two years away, it will supply an amount of cheap electricity which will put into operation a rather big aluminum plant which Kaiser also is building. Now, it will provide electricity for almost half of Ghana, this one dam, and the feeling is that once the aluminum plant gets going that there will be other corollary businesses spring[ing] up, appliance business and so forth.

Moore: Are these people trying to extract any promises for stability as much so as they could? What guarantees are they seeking that they won't be eventually nationalized?

McGill: Well, I think the reason to get nationalized [is that] these countries get desperate. . . . None of them has a real viable economy. Not one. They all have some unemployment. They're largely rural, that is, agricultural countries, and the agriculture isn't well developed. They desperately need jobs. So the temptation is to take over or seize, nationalize, an existing foreign-owned company. But if they should get a big aluminum plant going and plants near it which were using the output of aluminum to manufacture boats, cooking utensils, roofing, many other things for which aluminum is used—

Reporter: Mr. McGill, isn't this a very dangerous trend? I noted also in your columns and this disturbed me very much . . . that individual freedoms are being sacrificed to a great extent in order that they might get a momentary gain, a material gain; isn't this the basis of communism?

McGill: Yes it is; it's also the basis of fascism or something like Mussolini, or Franco in Spain; it's the basis of any totalitarianism. Ghana has gone pretty far along that path. But they will argue with you—I don't buy this—rather let me say I don't like it and it's anathema to me— but in a country where you have . . . relatively . . . few people who are contending for power, some of them will just tell you, well, the only way . . . if you get power, . . . to stay in power, is to exile the others or to put them down.

Reporter: Do they say that some day this will be changed?

McGill: Yes, they insist it will. But whether or not I don't know.

Reporter: How can you . . . expect democracy to work though in a land where your people are illiterate? They don't know what they're voting about when they vote on something. Can you really expect it to work?

McGill: No, not for the time being, you certainly can't. Now one other thing, Guinea, illiteracy is over . . . ninety-six percent in Guinea, maybe higher, [over] eighty . . . percent in Ghana, all very high in all of these countries, and as we were talking when we came on, . . . the impossibility of establishing a national unity right away for a generation or more [lies in] . . . the great variety of tribes with several million members each, all speaking different languages. The Congo was a Belgian colony, therefore its official language is French. There are 180 major tribes, all speaking different languages, none speaking French, 200 of the smaller tribes speaking different languages. So the terrific task of a government which doesn't yet have an army [is] trying [to] create unity in a country where the tradition of unity has been to tribal loyalties, to chiefs.

Reporter: Well, is there any other answer then to this authoritarian tendency of the leaders?

McGill: Well, in Congo, the UN has done the job, and the Congolese know it. If the UN were to pull out of there, you'd fall off into chaos right away. It may fall off into chaos anyhow; it's a touch-and-go business there, but for the time being the Communists lost out in the Congo; they bet on Lumumba; he was assassinated, and his party fell into disrepute. Then the Communists thought that the Kantangese secessionist movement would not be quieted or quashed, but it was. So for the time being, the UN has restored a sort of balance of government there. Now, if the UN can be supported, this great, rich territory may not fall into Communist hands or may not fall into divisive chaoses.

Moore: Is the United Nations the solution for other division elsewhere in Africa?

McGill: Well, I certainly think it is in the Congo. I would like to see . . . all the aid . . . channeled through the UN; . . . this would prevent the Russians from coming in and trying to set up big aid centers that would give them a foothold there, a political foothold as well as economic. It would prevent us from doing this, but then we say we don't want an economic foothold, and I don't guess we do, but at any rate, I think for the Congo at least channeling everything through the UN would be the best answer.

Reporter: So what you advocate is neo-United Nationsism (laughter).

McGill: That's right, for the Congo.

Reporter: How do we stack up now with the Russians? I noted in one of your columns that you mention that the Russians don't mix well with the people, and the Africans somewhat resent this. Do we do a better job in this area?

McGill: Yes, all the other embassies' representations hire local drivers, local cooks, local gardeners, local maids, and so on, . . . but not the Russians. They bring from . . . wherever they come, . . . all their drivers, their maids, even the fellows tending the flowers in the embassy yard— . . . [they are] Russian. They don't allow any other people to mix with them. They have one or two persons whom they assign to mix at the diplomatic functions. But other than that they don't—and the average African knows this, and he doesn't like this very much. Take the tiny little country of Togo, not much bigger than Vermont. The Russians have an embassy in there with a staff of roughly sixty-five. Now, they're using this as a sort of African school to train Communist African diplomats or agents. And they stay there six months or a year, and then they are assigned to other countries. The Russians are really pressing in; they won't let up, and this is something I think we must realize, and try to help these countries make a go of it.

Reporter: Are you saying we are losing the image of the ugly American if we ever had it in Africa?

McGill: Yeah, . . . I'm just pleased to say I didn't meet in any of this a single person I'd classify as an ugly American. In this country of Guinea, which is a very poor country, the wife of the American ambassador, a very beautiful, highly educated woman, speaks French fluently, as does her husband; she works in a local, little hospital two days a week from 10:00 till 2:30. She washes beds that they have taken sick people off of, she helps deliver babies, she took a course in midwifery, and every morning . . . sick people would come to the house, to the residence. She would treat boils, some of the most awful looking infections, and children and babies. Well now, she's certainly no ugly American. . . . I ran into, also in Togo, a fine young Georgia girl, Harriet Heery, whose brothers are architects here in Atlanta. She was teaching English at a village way up here in North Togo, which I'm telling you is a pretty primitive place.

Reporter: Is she a Peace Corps member?

McGill: Peace Corps teacher, English. She not only was doing her regular job, but she was so excited at the earnest desire of these people to learn, that she and two other girls had organized a class for adults. And they were meeting them three nights a week, teaching them English.

Reporter: What kind of questions did the young Africans ask you?

McGill: Well, I would say that two-thirds of the time they ask about incidents of racial violence in the United States. The other times they'd ask about American politics, American journalism; I even held a sort of journalism school for three afternoons, way up here in a city called Kaduna, in north Nigeria. They've heard of James Meredith, and they don't understand it.[276] They have a pretty good image of us. And they say, "why does your country, about which we've heard so much— . . . [and which] send[s] us Christian missionaries—why do you *do* this?" . . . One of them said, "It just hurts me in here for your country to do this to people." They want to know. They've heard of James Meredith, they've heard of Mississippi, and they've heard of Little Rock.[277] They've heard of the Atlanta Wall too, that was in all the newspapers in the big cities over there, was the Atlanta Wall.[278] I think we've got to realize that we live not in a glass house but in a glass world. When something happens anywhere it flashes around the world. One of the things

---

[276]Meredith was a black citizen who attempted to enroll at the University of Mississippi. See James Howard Meredith, *Three Years in Mississippi* (Bloomington: University of Indiana Press, 1966).

[277]President Dwight Eisenhower nationalized National Guard troops to uphold racial desegregation in the public schools of Little Rock, Arkansas.

[278]A street barrier between black and white neighborhoods.

that helped me in the many, many talks I made—I was able to say when the Bulgarians mistreated some Ghanaian students . . . here is an incident something like Mississippi [which] happened in Bulgaria. They could sort of understand that.

Reporter: Is the U.S. Information Agency doing anything to combat this? (McGill: "Oh yes") I assume they are doing something with the money, but if they have just heard of James Meredith and these things I wonder if they have not also . . . [had] the opportunity to hear about Clemson, about Atlanta's peaceful school desegregation?[279]

McGill: Well, they hear about Mississippi and Meredith, and so on, from their newspapers and radio. And don't forget that the Communists keep radio programs coming in there in six or eight languages every day. Not merely French and English but in the major tribal languages. Now we're broadcasting some of our information in some of the tribal languages, not as many as the Russians. . . . So . . . they hear about all these things—our people are combating it, explaining it, but of course you are vulnerable just as the Bulgarians were. How are you going to explain it? It happened. It [treatment of Meredith] was a very shameful, brutal thing.

Moore: What about when the president sent troops into Mississippi or when a judge in Atlanta orders the Atlanta Wall down? Does that get equal notoriety?

McGill: It did in the newspapers. This happens just the day I was leaving Africa, to go to Italy.

Reporter: You mean the wall being down?

McGill: The wall down. There was a two-column headline—I don't know whether it was on the radio—I assume it must have been. But I talked about the wall, and explained that this was really a small thing, and while it was a stupid thing, it was still a small incident. And I told them [that] . . . the same day the wall was being put up . . . we were seating the first Negro ever elected to our state legislature since Reconstruction times—that he and his wife attended the Governor's Ball without incident. And I was able to say this sort of thing is more meaningful

---

[279]There was relatively peaceful racial desegregation at Clemson University.

to civilization than this wall, which a real estate operator put up to try to protect, in his viewpoint, his property.

Reporter: Mr. McGill, does this go any further into a hatred for the white man? Can you talk of it that broadly?

McGill: No, I'm sure there are, or is, some hate for the white man, but not much of it through here [on map]. You get down in here, and you get back over here in Rhodesia, they tell me there is a lot of hate; I did not get into those areas. But not through here. I found disturbed people. They say, why do you do this? Why does your great country do such things? But I didn't encounter any real hatred.

Reporter: How about personal experiences? Were there, I'm sure there were many pleasant ones, were there some unpleasant experiences with the people that you met?

McGill: Most of them were pleasant. I would say that I had only three unpleasant evenings, when some Communist groups in the student questioning periods tried to harass me and tried to insult me and tried to make me lose my temper.

Moore: Did they succeed?

McGill: No, no (laughter). But otherwise it was very pleasant.

Moore: What about the experience that you had at the Nigerian television station?

McGill: Let me finish—you asked about the troops. The sending [of] troops into Mississippi was from the viewpoint of Africa the best thing that ever happened because this really impressed them. They said, "think of this, your country doing all that to protect the rights of one man." And of course, Meredith is a sort of symbol of American citizenship, and this is what we were doing. But this impressed them . . . "My, just think, really, how much did it cost?" they would say. "Just think of doing all that for one man."

Moore: Governor [Ross] Barnett was asking that question too (laughter).

McGill: But in Nigeria—Nigeria is the only country in West Africa or Central Africa that has television. Of course they have television in South Africa, and in another area, but of all these countries, Nigeria.

And I was in north Nigeria, a very pretty place up here called Kaduna. It is the capital of the north region. They had just had television about three weeks, and I was to go on with a show something like this, with three newspapermen questioning me, and we were waiting for a movie, the first . . . full-length movie to be shown. There was a little Nigerian girl about twenty-five or [twenty-]six sitting there who was doing the announcing in this precise British accent, you know, but she was following this movie just entranced, and it was coming down to the close where the villain was cornered and the hero reached out and slapped him, and she said, "Oh no!" (laughter) . . .

Reporter: Does the young African national have a sense of humor? From what we hear about him we think of him as a very intense individual that really doesn't have a sense of humor.

McGill: Well, when he's caught up in some crisis or when he feels that, you know, that his country is troubled or his beliefs are involved with something, he is an intense person. But they are wonderful, when they're not involved in some emotion, a wonderfully friendly people, good-humored people. I flew most of the time; I drove from Accra down the coast, and into this little country (on map), in Dahomey, and then over here to . . . about in here to Lagos. And the kids all the way— it was on a Sunday, driving in, and all along the way they would say "Welcome, welcome" to all the cars. And you go into a village and they say, "Welcome, stay with us, visit with us a while." . . .

Reporter: How did you file your column from the bush country or when you were out in a small town. How did it get back to Atlanta, and then syndicated?

McGill: Well, I got ahead before I left for Africa. And then I went right to work. From Dakar [Senegal] here, they have very good mail service, direct flights to New York. Then when I got down here to Guinea, there were only two flights a week out of Guinea. So I had to work like mad, and get about four or five columns written for each one of these mails. . . .

Reporter; In Allan Drury's novel, *A Shade of Difference,* one of the central characters is a young African leader, who is really a rank opportunist, . . . a power seeker, [seeking] power apparently for himself, rather than for his country.[280] He left this picture really undisturbed in his novel, I thought—apparently thinks that's what some of these leaders really are like.

McGill: Some of them are like that.

Reporter: What was your impression of the ones you met?

McGill: I must say that Nkruma, President Nkruma of Ghana is one of the most charming men I have ever met. Very beautiful manners, an excellent conversationalist, talked about American history; this was the most thrilling thing he knew was American history. He had in his office big bookcases, and he had a lot of American books in there; he had Sandburg's *Lincoln*, and he had other American history books.[281] But yet he is a man who has established pretty much of a police state for the time being. But he's also the man who has got the big dam going, built by the Kaiser Company. . . . Nigeria, the leadership there I thought was the best I met; they've held onto all of the processes of law. They don't arrest you without a warrant, they don't search your house without a warrant; if they do arrest you, they file a charge against you. In some of these others, they can just come and arrest you without a charge or warrant, and put you away. These [are] opportunist people struggling for power, a lot of them in the Congo. . . . A great many of [these tribal chiefs] . . . don't have much sense of national unity. They're still think-ing in terms of their big tribe. And they'll occupy an area, some of them . . . almost as big as Georgia. They hold great . . . land area.

Reporter: And they don't mind playing the East against the West?

McGill: No, this was the colonial powers that did this. To . . . keep a balance of power. To keep any one tribe from being too powerful. They would . . . play them off, one against the other.

Reporter: Mr. McGill, is the United States government doing enough

---

[280]Allan Drury, *A Shade of Difference* (New York: Doubleday, 1963).

[281]Carl Sandburg, *Abraham Lincoln: The Prairie Years*, 2 vols. (New York: Har-court Brace Jovanovich, 1926); Sandburg, *Abraham Lincoln: The War Years*, 4 vols. (New York: Harcourt Brace Jovanovich, 1939). See McGill's essay on Sandburg in *Southern Encounters: Southerners of Note in Ralph McGill's South*, ed. Calvin M. Logue (Macon GA: Mercer University Press, 1983).

now? What more should or could we do to try to win this important Africa, at least to make it a neutral so that it will not go into the Russian camp and be against us.

McGill: I don't know that we need to do a great deal more. I would think that we certainly ought to understand the importance of keeping the UN assisted in the Congo. Now these countries are doing a lot for themselves. They haven't much. Their economies are stagnant, largely so, but Nigeria for example, forty-two percent of its total budget is going into education. They're building universities and schools. I mentioned being up here in Kaduna, north Nigeria. In 1960 there were two secondary schools in that whole region. Today there are fifty-six. And they've built them all themselves. And there are more in other areas. There's a brand new university, two years old. And, so they're doing a lot for themselves; they aren't just depending on help. But I think that if we can help them with education, send them the technicians; they haven't got any technicians. Leopoldville [now Kinshasa, capital of the Congo] a city of seven hundred thousand people, there's one real electrician in that city. One!

Moore: Mr. McGill, at least one of your fans, and I put that in quotation marks, had occasion to wish that you might have attended a cannibal feast. You did not manage this did you? . . .

McGill: This is one of the old images . . . that the Russians like to have us . . . [use] and insult the Africans. . . . I'm sure that in some of the areas, back areas, you'd find some instances of cannibalism; this was a religious sort of thing, part of a pagan ritual; but this is really not a part of Africa today. . . .

Reporter: Are you optimistic about the hope for Africa?

McGill: I don't know if I'm optimistic; I'm hopeful. Let's put it this way (chuckle). I think if we can keep the Russian Cold War out of Africa, they can make a go of it. I don't know that we can keep it out; I hope we can. . . .[282]

---

[282]See McGill's essay on W. E. B. DuBois in *Southern Encounters*; and more on Africa in "Let's Lead Where We Lag," in volume 2.

65

A Sensitive Southerner's View of a Smoking City

A Southerner in New York attending a meeting discussing world tensions felt an occasional near-compulsive wish to break suddenly into loud, despairing laughter. Birmingham was smoking with hate where once the stacks of her mills stained the sky with their plumes. Hate ran through Birmingham's streets.

It was given a sort of ugly immortality by the cameras of television and newsmen. The tensions in Birmingham were as real as those in Berlin or Viet Nam.

Sitting there in his meeting, the Southerner could see in his mind's eye the streets of Birmingham, the Appalachian face of Bull Connor, who is not merely commissioner of safety, but of education, and the Anglo-Saxon hill countenances that fill up the city of Birmingham more than any other city in Dixie.

Now and then he would go to the phone and wait and ask, "In God's name, what is going on now?"

Birmingham is not a Southern city. It was born of coal, iron ore, and limestone. It never knew crinoline or lace. The chemical smoke and slag from its early furnaces made mock of magnolias and mocking birds.

Reprinted from the *New York Herald Tribune*, 14 May 1963, by permission of Mrs. Ralph McGill and the *New York Herald Tribune*.

It came into being just before the turn of the century, and it had a dramatic effect on the small farms of the state. Nowhere was the share-cropper and tenant evil so deeply and wretchedly fixed as in Alabama. The regular jobs at mine and smelter were like economic manna from heaven to men who had worked at heavy farm toil for a year and ended up deep in debt to the plantation owner.

The city drew them. They opened mines. They dug coal. They learned to make steel.

The Negro, also freed from sharecropper peonage, came, too. But he was, by and large, a plantation field Negro. He had as little learning as the whites, and he had even less sophistication.[283]

One of the wells from which hate and prejudice are drawn in the South, or anywhere else for that matter, is fear of economic competition. The poor white man, escaping from his tenant farm, or from the few worn-out acres where his father had worn out a life, had no more skills than the Negro.

The fingers of both were curved to fit the handles of plows and hoes. But, one had a white skin. And that was a symbol of being better and of deserving more.

So, the Negro, as he came to Southern cities from being a cropper or a tenant, was kept in his "place" there as rigidly as he had been on the cotton farm.

The new and magic city of Birmingham was made to grow and her night skies to glow with the pourings of steel by those persons, white and black, who hurried in from the poor, inadequate, segregated schools which, in the early days of the city's development, were open for only a few months each winter. Their stamp has been on it ever since.

The managerial class came and built on the slopes of Red Mountain and other hills that rim the city. Business came. The city began to read books, to go to college, to furnish audiences for concerts and art festi-vals. But the stamp of her beginnings is on her, and the prejudices, and the mores born with her continue.

---

[283]See Ray Marshall and Virgil L. Christian, Jr., eds., *Employment of Blacks in the South: A Perspective on the 1960s* (Austin: University of Texas Press, 1978); Brian Run-geling et al., *Employment, Income, and Welfare in the Rural South* (New York: Praeger, 1977); Edgar Streeter Dunn, *Recent Southern Economic Development as Revealed by the Changing Structure of Employment* (Gainesville: University of Florida Press, 1962).

There was something else, too, that helped condition the city and bring her to riots and bloodshed that shocked the world of our friends and delighted our enemies. Birmingham was a stronghold of anti-union strength.

The battle of the steel workers' CIO union, and more particularly, John L. Lewis' United Mine Workers, produced violence and men willing to commit it. Nowhere were the hard-won union victories more fiercely held. No Southern unions, in the beginning, more thoroughly saw to it that those Negro members whom the CIO said they must admit kept their place.

The Negroes, grateful for the union, were content then to sit on the back rows and listen. Dynamite blasts are nothing new to Birmingham. The union wars heard a lot of them.

There is yet another thing to say.

Commissioner Bull Connor is a symbol. He was a poor boy from the farm. He got to be a baseball announcer in the early days of radio. He got into politics.

Almost no Negroes voted then, and few, in that time, thought they ever would. Like others who came from the country, he brought with him a feeling that the Negro was inferior.

It is likely that Bull Connor was sincere in saying he didn't "hate niggers." He could say, and mean it, that some of his best friends were "niggers." But, in the saying, he revealed.

They were friends in another dimension. They were pleasant colored persons who took off their hats and said "Mr. Connor" and were very deferential as "niggers" ought to be to men like Mr. Connor.

One more thing—

Alabama is still a rural state. There is Montgomery, sleepy since Jefferson Davis took the oath there. (When U.S. Attorney General Robert F. Kennedy visited there a few weeks ago, one of those genuine Southern ladies hurriedly placed a wreath of flowers over the spot where Mr. Davis allegedly stood to become president of the Confederacy. The lady said she wanted to keep "the enemy" from stepping on the marker.)

Birmingham is the only really industrial city in the South. Here of late, hard times have been a-knocking at her door.

The governor of the state, George Wallace, was a Horatio Alger sort of boy. He worked his way through college and law school. But, like Mr. Connor, he had that inexplicable feeling that the Negro, somehow, didn't have the same rights as a white man and should be barred from all associations in schools.[284]

When Attorney General Kennedy visited him, in an effort to persuade him to accept court desegregation decisions, the governor refused cooperation. He would not, he said, accept such orders. The impression was that he wanted the federal troops to come—as at Oxford [Mississippi]—so he could say, "I did all I could. I was overcome by federal power."

Alabama has had a long, uninterrupted line of such guidance—from Jeff Davis's day of oath-taking to now. The newspapers, in the writer's opinion, largely abdicated their responsibility.

Birmingham—and Alabama—have many wonderful people who would have been willing to go with reform. But they had no forum. The churches had enough big givers with opinions and attitudes to match those of Mr. Connor and Governor Wallace, and so they did not join actively in the dialogue.

So, all roads led inevitably to the demonstrations and the prayer meetings led by Dr. Martin Luther King, Jr. There have been some who criticized his tactics, saying he should have waited. This is not, in the writer's opinion, valid. There has been enough waiting.

Dr. King's tactics had to be cut to fit the cloth. And the cloth was Bull Connor, and Governor Wallace. Dr. King didn't have much choice.

It is significant that the Black Muslims, an extremist group pledged to destroy the white man and to build a new, glittering ghetto for the Negro, also hate Dr. King. They, too, were critical of his tactics—presumably because they succeeded. It should not be overlooked that the Negroes have used neither guns nor dynamite. The hate has been lately one-sided. Dr. King's preachings and passive resistance ideas have won a great following. One of these days the South, even Birmingham, will be grateful to Dr. King.

---

[284]For McGill's essay on George Wallace see *Southern Encounters: Southerners of Note in Ralph McGill's South*, ed. Calvin M. Logue (Macon GA: Mercer University Press, 1983).

If a real hater—a Black Muslim—had come along with Dr. King's power of speech and personality, the South long ago would have been bloodstained. The South is lucky to have Dr. King.[285]

And the young, direct-action Negroes, too, are lucky to have been able to follow him and to have behind them the wisdom of the legal minds of the National Association for the Advancement of Colored People.

The real story of the South is progress. Most of the resistance, the furious, irrational defiance, the hate, the curses directed at the Negro, at Dr. King, at President Kennedy and the attorney general, are bent up, so to speak, in about two states and in a few rural areas of others. Alabama and Mississippi—where political communication pressures have prevented the other side of the story from being told, or known—are the most serious problems.

Elsewhere, the Southern leadership is moving ahead. The Negro will have what the Constitution guarantees. The ugly clamor and shrieking hate out of Birmingham should not blind us to the promise of our nation being fulfilled.

---

[285]For McGill's essay on Martin Luther King, Jr., see *Southern Encounters*.

66

Georgia Tech: Lighthouse to the Postwar South

I n October 1888, when the doors of the Georgia School of Technology were opened for the first class, Henry Grady, then editor of the *Atlanta Constitution*, pointed to the tower on the main building and said to friends with him: "There is a light that will cast its beams over the South. So lighted we can move into the industrial future." Grady, as his state, his city and region have demonstrated, was a better-than-average prophet. Grady's emphasis—and that of the men whose energy and vision created Georgia Tech—was on the new South—the South they could see changing all around them. Grady looked always ahead. Tomorrow meant more to him than yesterday.

Georgia Tech has been a lighthouse. Today, as the Georgia Institute of Technology, it is casting a beam that is brighter and broader than ever before. A nuclear reactor is a part of its increasing power. Looking ahead to tomorrow, one can predict even greater things.

Georgia Tech is, it is plain to see, the lengthening shadow of an idea, as well as of the character and purpose of the men who translated that idea into brick and stones, into classrooms, teachers, and students. Also there is, properly enough, something of General Robert E. Lee in the institution. The men who founded her had served the Confederacy. But

Reprinted from the *Atlanta Journal and Constitution Sunday Magazine*, 15 September 1963, by permission of Mrs. Ralph McGill and Atlanta Newspapers, Inc.

their lives had not been made narrow and bitter by that service. Defeat had not blinded them to reality. They had done what they considered to be their duty. They continued to do what duty indicated. Happily for Atlanta and Georgia, their vision, hopes and dreams were like those of their great commander-in-chief. In 1866, General Lee wrote, and most of his "Old Boys" read:

> I consider the proper education of the South's youth one of the most important objects now to be attained, and one from which the greatest benefits may be expected. Nothing will compensate us for the depression of the standard of our moral and intellectual culture, and each state should take the most energetic measures to revive its schools and colleges, and, if possible to increase the facilities of instruction, and to elevate the standard of living.

There were Georgians who read that—and pondered. Among them were the young Confederate soldiers who were to establish Georgia Tech.[286]

So profound had been the separation of the South from the pre-Civil War progress of the industrial revolution that few of its people had ever heard of a technical school. The fierce opposition to establishing Georgia Tech grew out of the South's old culture. In the prewar days schools taught the classics—Latin and Greek especially.

A technical school was viewed as a place to train blacksmiths, machinists, and so on. An engineer was a man who operated a railway locomotive. Very few Southerners knew that already Massachusetts and New York long had had such schools. The ex-Confederates in Georgia knew. They had learned, out of the bitterness of wartime defeats caused by lack of supply and transportation and by being confronted in battle by fresh troops, newly arrived by rail, that the future would require the South to move into the industrial revolution. The Civil War was, in a very real sense, a railroad war. The electric telegraph carried messages. There were observation balloons in use. Electric charges had detonated torpedoes.[287] Yet, nowhere in the South was there a school to teach young Georgians and their fellow Southerners how to participate in the new

---

[286]For more by McGill on Georgia, see "The Chattahoochee River," "Introduction to *The Old South*," "My Georgia," "Give me Georgia," and several articles on Atlanta, in volumes 1 and 2.

[287]See also "The Confederates' Torpedoes," in volume 1.

knowledge. If new industries were to come—and already in 1888 they were coming—it would be necessary to import trained personnel from the North to manage and direct them.

This "vagueness" about the meaning of a technical school persisted for years. Dr. Kenneth G. Matheson, the third president of Tech, recalled that a number of years after the first graduating class had gone out to waiting jobs, a wealthy banker from Atlanta irritated the students mightily in a chapel talk. "Young men," he said, "I am in favor of this school for I know we need more blacksmiths and plumbers." This ignorance of what an engineering school was revealed the lack of vision that was to make difficult Georgia Tech's early survival. The South was being kept poor because the raw materials were going northward to be made into finished products with added wealth.

The near nonexistence of a managerial, technically-trained class made it necessary for the new industries to bring their own managers. (It was not until about 1945 that the South began to be able to produce its own capital and managers.) There literally was no research done in the early South. That the legislature should have taken some years to agree to provide appropriations for Georgia Tech and that the public in general was very vague about the purpose of an engineering school, or a school devoted to technology, was a measure of the state's and region's need.

Today, when the twentieth century has but thirty-seven years to go, Georgia Tech is even more a lighthouse for Georgia and the South. Freshmen entering this year will (if they work hard), graduate in 1967. Its members will be middle-aged men when the twenty-first century begins. The imagination boggles at trying to picture what technology will be producing in the year 2000. As the century began in 1900 the kerosene lamp, the wood cook stove, the horse and buggy, the dirt roads, and the steam engine were ornaments of home and countryside. In war the weapons were the rifle, cannon, and Gatling gun. No century has come so precipitously into the industrial and scientific revolution of which all the wonders of space probes and earth-orbits are but the more spectacular window dressing.

Georgia Tech has been, and is, one of our most necessary assets. Certainly men of vision today see that whatever money is put into Tech, in teaching, research, and physical plant, will be multiplied in returns material and spiritual. Georgia Tech will light us into the next century, with its awesome portents, and it, and all it will require of us, is coming toward us swiftly.[288]

---

[288]See Ralph McGill, "Scandinavian Studies," in Ralph McGill and Thomas C. David, *Two Georgians Explore Scandinavia: A Comparison of Education for Democracy in Northern Europe and Georgia* (Atlanta: State Superintendent of Schools, 1938) 11-55.

67

An Interview
on Race and the Church
1963

A *lbert Hatch:* In the first place you've heard this many times before, but I'm one of the young clergy that's getting right punchy
because the *Atlanta Constitution* and other papers quite rightly
yesterday ganged up on the clergy saying they have not led and this is

On 19 September 1963, Reverend Bert H. Hatch interviewed McGill in his *Atlanta Constitution* office concerning the role of the church in society. Hatch wrote to
Logue on 22 January 1970: "The interview I did with Ralph for the Episcopal dioc-
esan paper so displeased the Bishop that he had the whole press run (7,500 copies) con-
fiscated and burned before we could distribute same." On 13 October 1963, the *Living
Church*, weekly record of the news of the Episcopal Church, stated that

> The Lovett School of Atlanta was declared outside "the orbit of the disci-
> pline of the Episcopal Church" by Bishop Claiborne of Atlanta, after the trust-
> ees of the school refused to admit Negro pupils. Celebrations of the Eucharist,
> however, continue at the school. . . . About 50 copies of *Diocese* were distrib-
> uted before the paper was recalled, according to the Rev. Canon Milton Wood,
> editor of the paper. . . . Canon Wood told the *Living Church* that he recalled
> the paper because he felt people might construe part of the interview as a blan-
> ket condemnation of the entire cathedral leadership . . . and because he feared
> that readers would confuse Mr. McGill's utterances with the thoughts of the
> diocese.

The interview printed here is from a tape recording provided by Bert H. Hatch, who
at the time was executive secretary of the Georgia Association of Broadcasters, Inc.

justifiable and when we do lead the congregation rises up in arms—[289]

Ralph McGill: Yes.

H:—and I am wondering that if you were in my position, for instance, at St. James in Marietta in this time and place what could you tell, what *would* you want to tell the people from the pulpit, say in the aftermath of Birmingham last Sunday? [Several black children were killed in a Sunday School bombing.]

M: I don't know what I would do. . . . I have an idea about [it] which I will get to but first let me say that I don't know if we really ganged up on you. I think the significant thing was that this young attorney [Charles Morgan] in Birmingham, finally unable to contain his long frustration, spoke out and said that Birmingham was the only city where it was necessary for the chief of police and the mayor to call the clergy together and ask them to act.[290] Now, I'm well aware that the clergy is a part of what is called the establishment or the power structure and I know this inescapably is true. The clergyman is trapped just as many editors are and many others who are in a position which requires them really to speak out or to have something to say. I have never thought a crusade was necessary. Well, occasionally you may have to crusade. But crusade usually becomes necessary because you've waited so long to speak out that a situation has become intolerable. It might not have become intolerable had there been some speaking out.

H: When the speaking out came earlier, say in 1963 in Savannah, I was involved in it, in the kneel-ins in Savannah. All hell broke loose then. When I did a simple token speaking out which I sort of thought you— I mean I'm touchy on the subject—I thought you took a dig at, rightly again, yesterday when you spoke of churches who had probably hypocritically agreed to go as far as letting a few Negroes attend services.[291]

---

[289]See McGill's "Let's Lead Where We Lag," in volume 2.

[290]See McGill's review of Charles Morgan, Jr., *A Time to Speak*, in this volume.

[291]In his *Atlanta Constitution* column on 18 September 1963, McGill criticized the condition that " 'moderate' now means to remain silent, to avoid controversy, to make no commitment, to avoid affirming belief in principle." Further, "moderates and the great body of Christianity" must "make up their minds whether by their silence they give consent to the Black Muslims, the White Citizens' Councils, or the dynamiters" of children in a Birmingham Sunday School.

M: I don't think it's hypocritical, nor did I say it was hypocritical. I think what I said [was] that there had been a great deal of . . . guilt pride taken in this sort of window dressing where a Negro or two shows up and you admit him to the sanctuary. . . . I think this is a revelation of our shame and our guilt when we . . . feel a great satisfaction and say, "Well, after all this Negro did come and nobody offended him." . . . For a Christian church to have to take great pride in so small a window-dressing thing as this I think is a measure of our problem. I don't think it's hypocritical, not at all hypocritical. And I'm sorry if I gave that impression.

H: You used—

M: I used the word *window dressing* or the phrase—

H: I believe you did. (Laughter) I went back to Savannah this past summer, first time in three years after I was almost run out of town and found that the congregation welcomed me with open arms and now I found that in the light of subsequent developments, the demonstrations they had down there, they were patting themselves on the back and saying, "Look what we did three years ago, but now let's don't do anything else. . . . We've done our bit."

M: "We've done our bit." This is what I mean. This is very revealing of the Christian church—any Christian church, just not that one. . . . But a couple of Sundays at this particular church, Episcopal church, there were a couple of Negroes or maybe three in the congregation. And it may have been just an oversight—I doubt if it was. But at neither time did the clergyman making the announcements remind the congregation that there would be a coffee hour afterwards and that everyone was welcome. Now, I'm not of a suspicious mind, but I rather think that he thought, "Well, we will avoid this if we can," and he just forgot conveniently to invite everybody to come to the coffee hour. But I—to get back to the original question. I wonder if it isn't possible for a clergyman who has a church in which the power structure is reflected to the point that he knows that . . . any change in the . . . social status quo will offend many of his parishioners. This is something he must think about. He would be a fool if he didn't think about that.

H: If they drive him out of the church on this issue he can't deal with them thereafter on any issue.

M: Well, it might come to that. I think he might get up and say, "Now, look. Let us talk here together. I'm not proposing that this church now take any action but I think that it is required of us as Christians and citizens that we discuss this problem, that we know what is being said, that we know what the problem is. We know that it is related to a world problem. We know that it has been coming a long time." The school thing for example. Any astonishing number of Americans who ordinarily are well informed took the 1954 school decision as a sudden thing. Well, actually, as early as 1948 federal courts had begun to rule in this field. Well before 1950 there were more than one hundred Negro students in the graduate schools of the University of Texas. Well before Mr. [Orval] Faubus came on the scene there were a great many Negroes in the University of Arkansas in its graduate schools. The Oklahoma and Missouri cases had been decided well ahead of the '54 decision. And yet we had a great many well-meaning people say, "This is an outrageous thing for the Court to act so suddenly without any warning. They should have brought this on gradually." The trouble was that it had been coming gradually; decisions had been made, about five major important decisions. And yet the minds were so restricted, or confined rather, to the comfortable confines of our life that they hadn't noticed this.[292]

H: They misinterpret here what comfortable—

M: Now, yeah, they say, "Well, why doesn't the Negro show some responsibility, and he must." They say, "Why doesn't he earn these rights?" Well, how could he? Let me ask *you.* Do you know when public education really began in Georgia for the Negro?

H: I read your book but I don't remember the—[293]

M: Well, about 1924. You go out and talk to the adult Negro leaders in this state, in our universities, in the professions—Georgia Negroes— they will tell you that when they got out of elementary school there was not a high school available to them. They had to leave the state to get a high school education. Now to be sure there were in some of the urban areas; there were some high schools. But in the great vast area of Geor-

---

[292]See editor's introduction.

[293]Ralph McGill, *South and Southerner* (Boston: Little, Brown and Company, 1964).

gia there were no high schools for Negroes. Now we have done this and yet we say, "Well, why aren't they—they aren't ready." And we blame them for not being ready. Well, what has society done to enable them to be ready? If there was not a school they couldn't go. Now, much of the building of Negro high schools began as late as about 1950. It was not until . . . that time that Georgia began to build them in the rural areas in any great number.

H: I remember incurring the wrath of my mother when she took me down and showed me the new Lucy Laney High School in Augusta—

M: Just built—

H: —just built. And I said, "That's the biggest pile of conscience balm—"

M: That's right.

H: "—I've ever seen constructed out of brick."

M: And the reason they started building them was [that] they were— they thought that if they could build a few decent schools that the Court might say, "Well, the schools are equal. They're separate but they're equal." And here was a great confession of guilt. Nothing had ever been equal. (Hatch: And still isn't.) And still isn't. And yet I—this is hypocrisy, for us to go around piously saying, "Well, the Negro isn't ready. Let him get ready." This is just, just an awful thing.

H: I buy this. This is what I've been preaching and teaching. Particularly the young people.

M: Now, is it possible to say this in a sermon?

H: It better be or I'm out of a job Monday morning.

M: Well I mean, it ought to be possible for a clergyman I would think to talk about this if he prefaces it, say [with] "now I'm aware that this congregation doesn't want any change and I'm not advancing it but I think that we as Christians must talk about these things."

H: Do you think perhaps that the clergy are gun-shy and don't give the laymen enough credit for being able to deal with this without getting apoplexy?

M: I think so. Also I know that you said earlier we might drive some people out of the church. Unhappily, it seems to be the big givers who are driven out. I don't know why too often money is associated with the status quo.

H: Doesn't the newspaper loose its big advertisers when things don't please?

M: Well, we have not lost—as far as I know we have not lost an advertiser. We have lost people who quit the paper, to be sure. A great many of them around have quit the paper. And we work very hard and we had a great many more to take it. But certainly it is very costly to speak out.

H: I have noticed that one of the best places I can work in this business is with the teenagers, which we have a great following there, a great number of them. And I've about come to the conclusion that I can't be heard because I don't have gray hair and am not—I'm thirty-two—I can't be heard by the Old Guard of the parish.

M: No, no, they won't listen to you.

H: And so I—

M: The young people will.

H: —have to write them off. Are these people outside salvation? Can't—

M: As a matter of fact we're at the point where we ought to let these people who don't want to hear this leave the church (Hatch: I said this once before—) and let them find one somewhere else. This is the—I think this the most unhealthy thing we can do because we're taking a negative attitude. We're saying, "Well, we don't want to lose these people because they will get angry if we tell them the truth."

H: But have we really got them in any way that will please the Lord.

M: So they're the tail wagging the dog. Now Eugene Patterson, our editor, went to the Cathedral a Sunday night ago to talk to the young adults. And he came back to me greatly disturbed. He said as I recall twelve or fourteen showed up. And I hesitate to mention this because . . . some people always get so upset about politics. But he came back tremendously disturbed saying that in the question and discussion that those who were articulate, and some kept quiet and said nothing—that those who were articulate denounced the Birmingham dynamiting of the Sunday School as wholly the responsibility of President Kennedy. That he had stirred up all this trouble and this was why they'd had the dynamiting. And here were young adults at the Cathedral who did not mention in any sense the moral issue. They did not seem to be concerned with the death of these children. They were just taking it as something that "Oh, well, the President has encouraged the Negro to the point where these things happen and this is just a very bad thing for Mr. Kennedy to have done." Now does this reflect what they have learned at the Cathedral? I think so. I think so.

H: This is what it reflects?

M: Now I don't know—Did you notice, getting back to the Birmingham thing, that after the murder of these children the churches initiated a policy of tolling the bells at noon and asking people to come in and pray. . . . The reports from there said that this received very little attention and very few people went, and in some places none went and there was nothing—it amounted to nothing. Well, I don't think we could expect it to amount to anything when these same churches had been silent before and when it was necessary for the mayor to call in the clergymen and say, "Please try to help us." I had a call from a good friend of mine over there who is an Episcopalian who said that the sermon on the morning in which these children were dynamited . . . was a very superficial little discourse on one of St. Paul's sayings. Now here was a city which even then was very tense. It had had the riots, trouble was brooding over it, violence was around. Everyone knew this. And yet this sermon had absolutely no relevance to the city.

H: This is inconceivable to me.

M: Well, . . . this was true. It interested me enough to pay for a sort of spot check. I checked about six of the leading churches over there and not a single one had a sermon that day that was relevant—that any way indicated that there was a moral problem or a problem of law in the city. Now, I don't know. . . . Have you read this book *Honest To God?*[294]

H: Yes sir.

M: Well, I know it's a controversial book, and I don't agree with all of

---

[294]John Arthur Thomas Robinson, *Honest to God* (Philadelphia: Westminster Press, 1963).

it either, but he starts off, you know, with the statement that . . . our culture has sort of accepted this image of a three-decker universe in which God is up yonder or out yonder and hell is down below earth and man is on earth. But God is not here in our image, he's up yonder, an old man upstairs. . . .

H: We find this same thing in the editorial in the back of the *US News and World Report.* Do you ever read Mr. Lawrence?[295]

M: Occasionally.

H: He spends two pages in the back of this week's issue . . . telling us that the church has no business taking part in freedom marches and so forth. He makes the uncanny statement that the church shouldn't be interested in politics, this sort of thing. He says, "Many preachers, moreover, have been inclined every now and then to give priority in their sermons to discussion of specific pieces of legislation currently before Congress though in recent years many laymen have begun to feel that the pastors are unwisely spending their time giving lectures on national issues instead of helping their parishioners to understand the difference between right and wrong in their daily lives." Well, how in the world can they understand right and wrong in their daily lives against the background of what's going on in the world they've got to try to be Christian in?

M: . . . Well, Mr. Lawrence is the great hero of the segregationists and the Ku Klux Klan. I actually know of one White Citizens' Council in Mississippi which has an enlarged picture of Mr. Lawrence on the wall. He is a sort of a hero to these ardent segregationists insofar as the segregationists are concerned. Well this is it. This Soviet spaceman came back and they too had this image. They said they didn't see anything of

---

[295]In the *U.S. News & World Report* on 23 September 1963, David Lawrence concluded that "a national organization of churches in any denomination should not become involved in politics." On 16 September 1963, in an article reprinted from 20 September 1957, *U.S. News & World Report,* Lawrence argued against the 1954 Supreme Court's desegregation ruling: "Never before had the nine Justices of the Supreme Court set themselves up as nine psychologists or sociologists to determine the mental reaction of students to their environment. . . . Will the federal courts be expected to issue injunctions with the threat of jail sentences, to all those persons who supposedly induce a feeling of 'inferiority' in others?"

God out in space. And this is where God is and we have a sort of—

H: Lord knows, you wonder if he's *here*.

M: Well, we don't want him here I don't think. We've got a sort of a Rotary Club ethic and it's pretty comfortable. Speak to the fellow with a badge, and he wears a badge so you'll know his name. They say fair dealings, let's don't cheat in business and let's—

H: We've domesticated God to the service of a tribal group, whatever group we happen to be in.

M: I think so.

H: Sir, not to take an abrupt tack, but in your opinion is the Lovett School as it now operates today Episcopally affiliated in the generally understood meaning of that phrase or "ain't it?"

M: It certainly is. Inescapably so. And I'm so sorry of this. This has been a great sorrow to me. . . . I don't see how in the beginning a board even if it were segregationist-minded . . . could ignore the priority of the church when children of Episcopal communicants apply. Now this, I'm unwilling to accept *any* excuse for barring them. I don't think there is any excuse. Here again it was said that they would lose some pledges.

H: They've got six hundred thousand dollars tied up—I've often wished that I had six hundred thousand dollars to give them right now and see what would happen tomorrow.

M: Well, they still wouldn't do it. As a matter of fact, this has not been published, but the board was given assurances that there would be some money available if they would, could make up any losses and they still wouldn't do it. Now if the dean of the Cathedral continues as chairman of the board certainly there is a moral affiliation of the Episcopal Church.

H: And the most sacred rite of the Episcopal Church is still being celebrated once a week.

M: Yes, celebrated by Episcopal priests and this is the sort of state religion, you might say, of the school and it is the priests of the church [who] are administering this rite. Most of the board are Episcopalians. Now this, I say, is complete hypocrisy. To say that this isn't a church-related school; this is utter hypocrisy in my opinion. And I'm ashamed of those—

H: It remains as it was, huh?

M: Well, not perhaps as much although the bishop has said it isn't a church school, but it remains one just the same. It wasn't before except that the dean was chairman, and they had the . . . sacraments adminis- tered by the clergy of the church, and most of the board members were Episcopalians. This is true. All that's happened is the bishop has said it is not a church school. But it remains one.

H: In a meeting of the clergy of the Atlanta area some weeks ago we had quite a discussion about whether we as individuals would feel honor bound to go or not to go if we were asked to conduct services in the church there at Lovett School. Some of us took the tack that no, we would witness by not going, we wouldn't go under any circumstances. Others took the attitude that this is a sick situation, and maybe we can minister to it.

M: I certainly wouldn't attempt to say what an individual should do. I have an opinion about it but I don't know . . . are you administering to a sick situation or are you perpetuating it?

H: Precisely, precisely.

M: You're perpetuating it, I think, but then I certainly would not con- demn any man who went. But I say it is a hypocritical situation. I think the Cathedral leadership has acted with hypocrisy, and I think that this is too bad.

H: One other area that I'd like to cover before we turn this off. How in your opinion can interested laymen help in a parish or mission, help their priests in the pressure that he has, feeling constrained to speak to this issue and yet getting so much opposition . . . usually from the Old Guard, so to speak.

M: Well, I don't know. I would like to see all the organizations in all of the churches which are utterly sterile, which go through the motions, like the men's organizations, the young adults, and the unmarrieds, and all of these. I think that they could schedule for themselves a study pe- riod on this, not just an acrimonious argument necessarily, but first they ought to be informed about it.

H: Perhaps having Negroes of their own social level meet with them. Most people don't know a Negro really, they keep quoting their maid—

M: They keep quoting their maid or their yard man. Interesting thing, if we would go ahead and move, nothing really would happen. Here in Atlanta where we've desegregated some of the restaurants including the most beautiful one in town, Stouffer's at the Top of the Mart, nothing really happens, because of economics. . . .

H: Is their business as good as it has been?

M: Yes, the business is fine. Not too many white people can pay prices of top restaurants—Herren's, Stouffer's. For that matter Rich's, Davison's—the other department stores which have desegregated their tea room—they have only an occasional Negro client, customer, because even here not many . . . people can afford to pay $1.50 or $1.35 to take the time . . . for lunch—so that the image we have of a restaurant suddenly filling up with yardmen or cooks or beggars . . . reveals, I guess, our own guilt or ignorance. The schools, we've seen here what's happening and going on very well; no schools are going to be overrun. The problem is in the poor areas, that's were the poorest schools are for Negro and white.

H: Doesn't it make your heart sick, though, to see the church schools being used as a refuge when they think the public schools are going to be integrated?

M: Yes, it does the church-related schools. . . . I think that Westminster and Lovett have, well, I think we can all be ashamed of what they have done. The Little Trinity School quietly and legitimately and honestly took three qualified Negro children who applied, and I'm told that this is going along very well. One of the things that you haven't asked about was the Charlayne Hunter Stovall marriage, and I think we ought to talk about that. This caused all of the extremists to say, "You see, this is what we've been telling you. This is what will happen."[296]

H: A local "chicken fryer" said this.[297]

---

[296]Charlayne Hunter was one of the first two blacks to attend the University of Georgia.

[297]Probably Lester Maddox.

M: And I'm sure that a great many people were shocked and said "Well, maybe this is what happens if they go to school." Well, my answer to that is this has been happening right along . . . very infrequently. Suddenly most people, knowledgeable people, Negro and white, know that the ordinary marriage is tough enough and involves enough problems. These marriages will never be many. I remember two instances in Georgia where the daughters of Georgia farmers ran off with sons of tenant, Negro tenants, on the place. These never got in the paper; you hear of all these things. But this one got in the paper.[298]

H: I am so delighted that it was the son of a well-to-do Douglas, Georgia man and not somebody from New Jersey, because they say, "See, just a misguided do-gooder."

M: Well now, let's come back to this. If a young woman, a graduate at the university and a young woman of good character and intelligence I'm told, if she'd had an illegitimate child this would have been the occasion of a great many giggles and laughter, and they would have said "Isn't that just like a nigger." But they got married and this shocks people more than an illegitimacy would have shocked them. Now let's think about that. And then a woman called me up and she said, "You have helped destroy these necessary laws that keep the races apart and this is why this marriage has happened." And I said, "Madam, these laws you're talking about that we've had that you say have now been destroyed—will you explain to me how Charlayne Hunter is almost white enough to pass as a white person? Will you explain to me why nineteen million of the roughly twenty million Negroes in America are mulattos?" . . . Are we proud of this? Does this shock us? Apparently not. But—

H: If the Negro is so undesirable and so dirty why out of all the girls available at the University of Georgia was this fine young son of the South attracted to her?

---

[298]Throughout his campaign for civil rights for blacks, McGill confronted the "fear" of racially mixed marriages; see the response of a member of the audience during McGill's "Editors View the South" speech at Emory University in 1957; see *Ralph McGill: Editor and Publisher,* ed. Calvin McLeod Logue (Durham: Moore Publishing Company, 1969) 1:159-60; also "America's Town Meeting of the Air," in this volume.

M: I don't know. After all, let's face this too. Here's a young man twenty-five years old, or, in his twenty-fifth or twenty-sixth year, I've seen both stated. He lived in Europe over a year. He's a fairly sophisticated man, twenty-six years old. Let's don't be childish enough to say that here is just a little innocent lad who was brainwashed by the wicked integrationists.

H: Or paid by the NAACP.

M: Oh that's of course—Actually, I've kept a little check. I don't know these people, but I'm interested. And actually he hasn't been able to get a job up to now. She's supporting him. They're having rather a hard time.

H: Society's not going to let them alone.

M: Society's not going to let them alone. They certainly weren't paid a nickel by the NAACP. . . . You hear this. At first they said—

H: Why didn't the *Constitution* deal with this editorially?

M: Well, Mr. [Eugene] Patterson had a very long discussion of it and I thought a very intelligent one. We thought that it was not necessary for both of us to do it. But we did deal with it in a fairly lengthy manner. (Laughter) I commend it to you.

H: I'm sorry I didn't see it. I was hoping they would; I was just hoping the paper was going to come out and say, "Before you start saying, 'We told you so'; this is their business, leave them alone."

M: Well it is their business. Society will make some rather cruel adjustments for them as it always does. I met a good friend in the war, during the war, the Second World War, who married a very fine Japanese girl, intelligent, wonderful young woman, an artist, fine university education. He was a Pennsylvanian, and he took her back home there. But they finally moved to San Francisco because the social pressures were such in their home town. Not that people were too cruel about it, but it just wasn't enough climate for them to be comfortable in. This is what I mean by saying that the intermarriage thing will never be much of a problem. There always has been some of it, there always will.

H: And in a polyglot sort of society like Hawaii where it just abounds it doesn't seen to hurt the intelligence of the society.

M: We're always running about fears, and we don't stop to think. I'm afraid [of] how much our life is negative—being afraid of something rather than being for something or interested in trying to understand something.

H: Could I ask you why the paper feels constrained to print the ads of Mr. [Lester] Maddox?

M: Yes sir, you certainly may.

H: I think just as you say that George Corley Wallace's rantings and ravings have created an atmosphere, I think printing his [Maddox's] ads will create an atmosphere.[299] A lot of people take them humorously and they think, "Well here's a little man, a wild man flailing his arms and isn't he funny." But there a lot of people who say "Go get 'em, Les."

M: I know this. He got a lot of votes when he ran for mayor. . . . I'm glad you asked. We submit each ad to a lawyer first, and most of them are changed because most every week there's a great deal of libelous material, not always, but many weeks. Secondly, we left an ad out a couple of years ago, maybe a year and a half ago, and promptly the neighborhood papers printed it and said this is what the daily papers wouldn't let you read. Then two radio stations read it every day for about a week. This was creating a worse sort of atmosphere so after some soul searching we decided, well, the lesser of the two evils is to submit it to a lawyer and print it. We certainly don't have any pride in it (Hatch: Oh, I'm sure of that) and we suffer the same thinking about it that you do.

H: Do you think Mr. Maddox is as rabid as he sounds, or is this a good way to sell fried chicken?

M: No, I think he believes it, and I'm a little confident that as time goes on, you match the murder of children at Sunday School against Mr. Maddox, he doesn't look so good. And maybe time and events will deal with him as they are with Mr. [George] Wallace.

H: Maybe. I sure thank you sir.

M: I've enjoyed it.

---

[299]See essays on Maddox and Wallace in *Southern Encounters: Southerners of Note in Ralph McGill's South*, ed. Calvin M. Logue (Macon GA: Mercer University Press, 1983).

68

The South Looks Ahead

" *E* bony magazine is to publish a centennial edition of the Emancipation Proclamation . . . will you contribute an article under the title, 'The South Looks Ahead.' . . ?"

Memory recalled the summer of 1959 and the journey to Russia and Warsaw with Vice-President Richard M. Nixon. The publisher of *Ebony*, John H. Johnson, and Mrs. Johnson were members of the press party. We had become friends and had had many talks. At Sverdlovsk (where Francis Gary Powers and the U-2 plane not long thereafter were to meet disaster) the Soviet journalists invited the visiting press corps to dinner—with dancing. The day had been long, hot, and exhausting, and we sat gratefully down to a good dinner. The courteous, competent young women whom Intourist had sent along as interpreters were present, neat and attractively clad for a dinner dance.

One of the Russian-speaking U.S. staff members sought me out and said, "I thought you might like to know that I have heard the Soviet newsmen talking. They are waiting to see if you, from that South about which they have heard so much and know so little, will ask Mrs. John-

Reprinted from *Ebony*, September 1963, by permission of Mrs. Ralph McGill and *Ebony*. Copyright 1963, by Johnson Publishing Company, Inc. Written for a special issue on the hundreth anniversary of the Emancipation Proclamation.

son to dance. If you do, they won't mention it in their dispatches. If you don't, it may well be a featured part of the news from here."

So, I sought out Mrs. Johnson. "Mrs. Johnson," I said, "I haven't danced in perhaps twenty years. I was never any good at it and, with general approval, gave it up. But I think we must dance for the honor of our country." I then told her the story. "I am exhausted," she said, "and my feet are, as the saying goes, killing me. But we mustn't disappoint them." So, later when the music began, I went to Mrs. Johnson and asked if she would dance. She would. Indeed, we were the first on the floor. There was no feature story from Sverdlovsk that night.

The harmful impact of America's racial injustices and the outbreaks of defiance, such as Little Rock had presented, were subjects of frequent discussion on that journey in Russia. But as I sat before the typewriter to do this article memory recalled that many conclusions of 1959 seem far, far back in time in the light of the swift-moving transition.[300] In 1963 some eighteen million Negroes have broken through the major barriers that for some two hundred years have separated them from equal participation in American life. Within the foreseeable future the system of segregation will be wiped out.

The acceleration of pace in pursuit of that objective will intrigue historians of the future. The ugly, murderous mob at Oxford, Mississippi, created by the folly of a Mississippi long withdrawn from the American dream and purpose, was a therapeutic event in that it shocked the national conscience.[301] After all, those who had before Oxford remained aloof from decision could not say, "I approve of Ross Barnett and the policies of the White Citizens' Councils." The fact that the government sent troops there to establish and maintain the constitutional rights of one man was reassuring. (In a trip to six West African countries and the Congo early this year I found that the prompt action of sending troops to enforce the decision of the U.S. courts had made a really profound

---

[300]See McGill's speech, "The South in Transition," 7 May 1965, Emory University, Atlanta, in *Ralph McGill: Editor and Publisher*, ed. Calvin McLeod Logue (Durham: Moore Publishing Co., 1969) 2:348-60; Raymond W. Mack, ed., *Changing South* (Chicago: Aldine Publishing Company, 1970).

[301]See McGill's "Rebirth of Hope at Ole Miss?" in this volume.

impression.[302]) It remained for Birmingham, Alabama, its police commissioner Bull Connor, the use of police dogs, the arrest of children, the brutal employment of high-pressure fire hoses, and statements callous and coarse, to provide the catalyst, the quickening of will, the resolution to act from the grass roots of the Delta's rich soil and the ghettos of cities and towns, large and small.

So it was that by midsummer, one could look ahead and see that New South—about which so many prophets have written and prophesied—coming down over the horizon. There have been, of course, many new Souths in the long history of that region. But this one of freedom from the expensive and spiritually distorting bonds of a segregated system will be one really new, and the first one of truly free and great expectations.

But one could also look ahead and see that there was, and is, a vast need of coordination of all agencies involved in the drive for full citizenship and a broadening of the base. This is not merely a movement of Negro citizens. It involves all those who are committed to the national principles, to all that is meant by the phrase *Western civilization*, to the meaning and strength of the Jewish and Christian ethics, and to all those sensitive to the human condition generally.

Such cooperation is of a first priority. There must be well-thought-out plans for what comes after the ending of segregated practices. (That these will hang on for a time in isolated rural pockets is a melancholy expectation, but not really important to the major need.) It is well understood today that lack of guidelines after emancipation and the end of slavery and the Civil War was disastrous. A hastily conceived reconstruction was concerned with immediacy, and not with the future. A new society might have been slowly and patiently constructed. But there were no plans to educate, to train, to communicate ideas or a philosophy of democratic development. Had there been, then and there, a blueprint, something along the lines of the Marshall plan that rehabilitated Europe politically and economically after the Second World War, the nation would have been spared much painful travail and an accompanying

---

[302]See "Television Interview about Africa," in volume 2.

human and economic loss. There was none. There were reaction and re-union in terms of the Rutherford B. Hayes sell-out.[303]

After Birmingham in the spring of 1963 had everywhere lighted a grass-roots fire in America, the organizations at work in the field of human rights began to feel more sharply than before the need for coordination. It all had seemed to happen so quickly (though, actually, it did not), that no overall plan of strategy or tactics existed. The Congress of Racial Equality (CORE), the Students Nonviolent Coordinating Committee, the Urban League, the NAACP, and individuals, led by Martin Luther King, had unity of objective. Yet, the more mature knew that even though civil rights were won after a long, hard fight, this, too, would be but a step. There would still be need for implementation.[304] There were others who knew that because of the long isolation of the Negro from American life, a cultural and educational lag existed which would make it difficult for many Negroes—especially those in the rural South and those who had gone from it, untaught and unskilled, to the industrial cities of the East and West—to take advantage of the rights attained.

There were knowledgeable persons who were aware that for many Negroes in the North, jobs were of more immediate emotional appeal than civil rights. A poor, unemployed Negro can see that discriminations lie more heavily on him than on a skilled Negro wage earner of the middle class or a successful professional man. In fact, the poorer Negro can look about himself and see a certain economic kinship, at least, with the long-jobless white man, who, also, more often than not, is a product of the segregated educational system that has cheated both. The organizations and those who spoke for them soon were commonly agreed on the need for coordination.

As one looks ahead, the NAACP comes strongly into focus. The direct-action groups were invaluable. They worked in fields where, often,

---

[303]See Monroe Lee Billington, *American South: A Brief History* (New York: Charles Scribner, 1971); Francis Butler Simkins and Charles Pierce Roland, *A History of the South*, 4th ed. (New York: Alfred A. Knopf, 1972); C. Vann Woodward, *Burden of Southern History* (Baton Rouge: Louisiana State University Press, 1960).

[304]See John Hope Franklin and Isidore Starr, eds., *The Negro in Twentieth-Century America: A Reader on the Struggle for Civil Rights* (New York: Vintage Books, 1967).

there was no "law." The student pickets and sit-ins, the freedom riders, and all those engaged in eyeball-to-eyeball confrontation with discrimination telescoped time. They achieved in a relatively brief time what lawsuits could not have won in years. But the NAACP always was, as the legal arm, the great rock in a weary land. It is the organization that must bear the major burden of the future. The attainment of civil rights is not really the major objective. Once these rights are secured, then will come the exacting and demanding task of somehow closing the gulf in education and training, jobs and housing. Talents, skills, and abilities unavailable to the nation because of segregation will be released for use in other fields of the nation's politically and economically complex life. The competitive erosion of that release will present many new problems, some as psychologically frustrating as those of a segregated society.

Ironically, as one peers toward the unfolding future, one sees that since only 18 million of the roughly 185 million Americans are Negro, it will be the white population—more especially that of the South, that will benefit most of all.

We know that the "Redeemer Democrats," after having sold out the Democratic candidate Tilden in 1877 for a promise by Republican President-to-be Hayes to remove troops and abandon the promise of civil rights for the newly freed Negro, established the one-party system. Commenting on the one-party system, the eminent historian, C. Vann Woodward said in *Origins of the New South:*

> Had the white man's party of conservatism been democratically organized, had the "party line" been determined and criticized democratically, the one-party system might not have been stultifying. But the organization and control of the party was anything but democratic. Issues, candidates, platforms—everything was the private business of a few politicians known by the discontented as the "ring" or the "courthouse clique." The extent of their domination and the nature of their machinery of control varied among the state rings, but the ring was always present.[305]

These "rings" or "courthouse cliques" still have considerable influence, but their grasp is being broken. The rings never voluntarily gave up any power. Candor compels one to say that only the federal courts have

---

[305]C. Vann Woodward, *Origins of the New South, 1877-1913* (Baton Rouge: Louisiana State University Press, 1951) 52.

initiated reform. Through the federal courts the white primary was barred. Court attacks on the sometimes brutal, always effective, restrictions on, and deterrents to, voting are having more and more success. Latest, and most important, were the federal courts orders to reapportion the legislatures so as to make them more representative. In Georgia the iniquitous county unit system, which long had made that state all but helpless against the most corrupt and vicious elements in its politics, also was sponged out by the courts.[306]

There are signs of a developing two-party system, and of Democrats who do not approve of the racist views of senators and congressmen whose long political life and power in congressional committees have depended on the one-party politics of the region. President Kennedy was continually harassed and denied by this sort of control of the rules committee in the House, and by other committees controlled by Southern Democrats who were subservient to the extremist groups in their constituencies.

Most of the pragmatic business of looking ahead in the South fell to the white Southerner.[307] As the Negro's image of himself changed, the image of the region inevitably took on a different aspect. This reached deep into the rural regions. Almost overnight the Negro farm tenant, cropper, or small land owner, seemed to be (and was) "different." He was not, as some said, a new Negro. But in the new climate of things he could publicly say and express thoughts and feelings long suppressed. One month, for example, the Mississippi planters and mayors of cities in that state could, and did, speak of contented Negroes who were being disturbed by outsiders. The next month many of these same Negroes were in the demonstration of discontent in Jackson, the state's capital. It is factual to say that in the rural South the white man was certainly astonished, bewildered, and usually resentful of this change. The trum-

---

[306]See V. O. Key, Jr., *Southern Politics in State and Nation* (New York: Vintage Books, 1949); Jack Bass and Walter DeVries, *Transformation of Southern Politics: Social Change and Political Consequence Since 1945* (New York: New American Library, 1977); Dewey W. Grantham, Jr., *Democratic South* (Athens: University of Georgia Press, 1963); Numan V. Bartley and Hugh D. Graham, *Southern Politics and the Second Reconstruction* (Baltimore: Johns Hopkins University Press, 1975).

[307]See Lewis M. Killian, *White Southerners* (New York: Random House, 1970).

pets of a new era had blown down the walls of the old Jericho.[308] It was less easy for the rural Southerner to look ahead. His whole economy and society was based on the old ways. But, change being relentless, this Southerner had to look forward, and even if he closed his eyes against what he saw, he nonetheless had to open them now and then.[309]

In the urban areas, and the South is largely urban, there was looking forward. It needs to be said that well before the pickets and the sit-ins there were some few industries and businesses which had looked ahead and begun to upgrade Negro employees and to hire more than before. By 1960 this number had increased, though comparatively it was small. By 1963, most of the large corporations and businesses had begun—or had plans ready to put into operation—to upgrade Negro employees who were ready for promotion, and to send others to training schools. Looking ahead, one could see a steady, accelerated improvement in job opportunities for Negroes.

In looking ahead, Negro and white began to understand they had to look back at the low quality of most of Southern education and admit that a segregated system, in a region lacking the income to pay for one good system, had penalized all children with an inadequate dual set-up. The penalty, to be sure, was heaviest on the Negro children, particularly those in the poorer rural areas. Many of those who came from the tenant cabins and the small farms were, therefore, neither prepared psychologically nor technically for an industrial society. But they were there— and more were coming. This made looking ahead by the white leadership even more imperative.

Looking ahead one may see that it is in the field of voting rights that the real revolution will come. Voting strength will quickly win better

---

[308]See Donald R. Matthews, *Negroes and the New Southern Politics* (New York: Harcourt, Brace, and World, 1966); Monroe Lee Billington, *Political South in the Twentieth Century* (New York: Charles Scribner, 1975); Thomas H. Naylor and James Clotfelter, *Strategies for Change in the South* (Chapel Hill: University of North Carolina Press, 1975).

[309]See Brian Rungeling et al., *Employment, Income and Welfare in the Rural South* (New York: Praeger, 1977); Ray Marshall and Virgil L. Christian, Jr., eds., *Employment of Blacks in the South: A Perspective on the 1960s* (Austin: University of Texas Press, 1978); Timothy Thomas Fortune, *Black and White: Land, Labor, and Politics in the South* (Chicago: Johnson Publishing Co., 1970).

schools, will end discriminations in relief benefits, jobs, housings, and other aspects of life. The South, free of its burdens or taxes wasted in supporting two systems and maintaining all the other financially and morally costly trappings of a segregated society, should become the great boom area. The South has sacrificed its children, colored and white, to inferior education, and has, across a hundred years, discriminated, in one degree or another, against all its people. A free South will be, in fact, a New South. The human condition always has had at least three yearnings . . . to be treated as a human being, to have an equal, fair chance to win respect and advancement as an individual in the economic environment, and freely to seek spiritual and cultural happiness.

All this means that attainment of civil rights is only a means to the more distant end—the long-term harvest of social, political, and economic reforms made possible by the possession and use of those rights.

Planning and foresight, which will enlist all Americans of whatever racial background to build a stronger nation of commitment and belief is the opportunity offered by the days and nights that move toward us. If we miss this second opportunity—one hundred years after the first—it is unlikely we will have another.

69

Radio
"Conversation Piece"

C ommentator *[Haywood Vincent]:* Our special guest, perhaps the foremost journalist in the United States, winner of the Pulitzer Prize, the author of *The South and the Southerner*, frequently called the conscience of the White South, Ralph McGill.[310] There has been a principal point of criticism in regard to Southern clergymen, Mr. McGill, and it's been called the silence from the pulpit. Might you comment on that, sir?

Ralph McGill: Yes sir. I have a compassion for a great many of these men. They undergo a real agony. They want to do what they feel Christian morality requires them to do; they want to speak out, but they may have a governing board that won't let them. They may fear that they will drive away some of their big givers or the big contributors. They probably owe a big building-fund debt. And so they feel trapped.[311] Now I

Radio talk show, WEEI Radio Station, Boston, Massachusetts, 1963, published by permission of the CBS Radio and Mrs. Ralph McGill.

[310]Ralph McGill, *The South and the Southerner* (Boston: Little, Brown and Company, 1964).

[311]For more by McGill on race and religion see "Southern Moderates Are Still There," "Let's Lead Where We Lag," "Church in a Social Revolution," and "An Interview on Race and the Church," in volumes 1 and 2.

know from talking with many of them and I know from those who have spoken out and lost their pulpits and been driven out. I know some twenty-five young ministers driven out of Mississippi, for example. Some out of Georgia and other states. This is real agony for some of them.

V: Well, the people who drive them from their pulpits, how can these people rectify in their own conscience the claim that they are "Christians" and their activities?

M: I don't know. I quite agree. I don't see how any person who professes Christianity can take this stand of driving a minister out or of denying the morality of this situation and the true Christian responsibility.

V: There's a fine moral point probably to be found in the current civil rights bill before Congress.[312] This involves itself with the right of a businessman who's got a public license to sell his services or his goods to those people that he chooses to sell them to. What about this?

M: This is a puzzler. And I can only express an opinion. What he really does is he chooses to sell them to anyone who comes along who is orderly and has the money to buy unless here of late it happens to be a person of color. Then he says that this is a private business and refuses to sell to this fellow. No matter he may have the money. He may be well dressed. He may be [a] perfectly quiet, decent person.

So I don't know. Are we in this time of history with great developments going on all around us with three-fourths of the world colored, with African nations emerging, with our own American Negro moving toward possession of full civil rights for the first time in centuries—can we really say that a man who has a public license to do business, can he then start saying, "Well this is mine, I will sell to only who I want to?" I don't know. I doubt it somehow myself. And of course this is what the public accommodation bill is about. I would like to see it done by a voluntary agreement.[313]

---

[312]Civil Rights Act of 1964, affecting voting, public accommodations, employment, and education.

[313]Until the late 1960s, when McGill reluctantly concluded that Southern states would not provide civil rights for blacks voluntarily, McGill argued that Southerners should treat all citizens equally in housing, law, education, employment, voting, and social services, without the federal government having to require it; see the editor's introduction.

V: This is taking place in some cities in the South, isn't it?

M: Yes. Some it is.

V: Is there too much waving of the Confederate flag these days? Is this a symbol?

M: This is one of the things that sickens a great many Southerners. The Confederate flag was certainly carried in honor; whether you agree with the Confederacy or not, it was carried in honor, and men died for it, the soldiers of that war. And now to see it displayed by young thugs with black jackets and hoodlum crowds, strung up near dynamited churches. This is a very sickening thing to see a flag be so degraded.

V: I think to the true Southerner this comes down to the very point of sacrilege.

M: Yes.

V: Let's find out what the audience has to say about all of this. You're on the air with "Conversation Piece" with Ralph McGill.

Woman 1: Mr. McGill. May I be the first one listening in to thank you for appearing on "Conversation Piece." I've been a great admirer of yours and your newspaper. Coincidentally, a thing happened this morning. My paper boy delivered the *Boston Globe*. This is not the paper I subscribe to. But there on the first page it mentioned that you were in town and that you wrote a column for the *Globe*. This I did not know. And I promptly called the newspaper and requested that I receive the *Globe* from now on.

V: The Taylor family will be extremely grateful, I have no doubt.

Woman 1: That, however, is not why I called. On September 16, the day after the Birmingham bombing, your fine editor Eugene Patterson wrote an editorial on the "CBS Evening Report" which touched me immensely.[314]

M: Yes. I think that Mr. [Walter] Cronkite read that.

Woman 1: No, he said that he would let Mr. Patterson read it himself. That is one of the things that I thought was much more effective. And

---

[314]Patterson was editor of the *Atlanta Constitution*.

The South and Human Rights

of course he said what we all felt—the shame and the wastefulness.

M: Mr. Patterson got several hundred letters in response to that.

Woman 1: Do you think that if I write to Mr. Patterson, do you suppose that he would send me several copies of that editorial?

M: Yes, if you wrote to him, and I am sure that he will. He has been getting a number of such requests, and I am reasonably sure that there are extra copies left. Just write to him at the *Atlanta Constitution*.

Woman 1: Thank you very much. Just one more thing. I don't want to take too much of your time. I'm a newspaper reader who reads all of the news. And it's unfortunate that the work that's been done towards desegregation takes such a small place in the newspapers or in magazines as a whole.

M: Well, television is helping out and doing a fine job. And radio also just such as we're doing here today.

V: Thank you very much for your call.

Woman 2: Mr. McGill, I too am a Southerner, that is if anyone from Atlanta would say that anybody from Maryland was a Southerner?

M: Well, I think that we'll just let you squeeze in there.

Woman 2: There's one thing that has impressed me with all of these affairs of the last two years. Especially the March on Washington. It certainly was a splendid demonstration.[315] Why is it that not one of these colored people has said any word of gratitude to the country that they're here. They're not in Africa. And not one—I have never heard one mention the fact that any Southerner had been kind to them.

M: Well, I think that maybe you've just had an unlucky experience. I've had a great many thank me and others who worked with me and in other states.

Woman 2: I have seen my father, he wasn't born until after the war (Civil War), and I've seen him take care of every one of his father's slaves, lower them in their graves, and weep. And we were taught the greatest

---

[315]During the "March on Washington," 28 August 1963, Dr. Martin Luther King, Jr., delivered his "I Have a Dream" speech.

respect. I have never seen anyone be unkind to Negroes. Every Negro should feel that there is some kindness and some friendship, probably not as a whole but as individuals. Did you ever hear anyone say in Washington any word that they were glad to be an American?

M: Well yes. I thought Martin Luther King . . . [did in his] speech in which he said that he had this great dream about the full meaning of America and the Negro being allowed and enabled to become fully an American.

Woman 2: And there's another thing too. Isn't it true that most—I live in New England now but I have lived in Virginia and I have a daughter there—Isn't is true that most Negroes would rather go to school with Negroes?

M: Well, that I don't know if I can answer. It may be true of some. I don't know that this has been at any time an effort of the Negro simply to go to school with white people. This is one of the points that I have been trying to make. What we're after is the right of the Negro to use the public facility which in the case we're discussing is a public school. Now it might have mostly white persons in it, or all white persons, but this is a very complex problem. But the Negro doesn't want to go there just because it's a white school but because he lives in the area; he is a citizen. I don't think that he's trying to go to school just to be with white people.

Woman 2: I don't either. But when you say that the facilities in the South are different; I know some years ago in Richmond, the Maggie Walcot colored school was so far ahead of Thomas Jefferson and John Marshall white schools that it was really ridiculous.

V: Throughout the overall Southern seven-states area this would be a spectacular and isolated exception.

M: This is true in some areas now, but what happened was that about 1950 or '52 a great many of the Southern states began to build as fast as they could some new Negro high schools and some elementary ones, hoping that thereby they would persuade the Supreme Court to retain the separate-but-equal provisions which had been in the Constitution or so interpreted. And it is true that a number of these new schools are better than some of the older white ones. But in general I think that you will have to admit that the Negro school has been far inferior.

V: Thank you for your phone call.

Woman 3: Do you agree with some critics who say that President [John] Kennedy always had and still is playing politics with the civil rights issue? What do you feel is the position that the president should take? Namely, moral leadership or real use of the executive power? Thank you.

M: Well, first I don't think that he's playing politics with it in any bad sense. Let's be honest. We're a political country. We elect everyone from our lowest official to our highest. If he's playing politics he isn't doing very well with it. He isn't able to move it through the Senate or the Congress. Now, we have to play politics in our state legislatures and in the Congress of the United States. We have a system of checks and balances: the courts, legislative, executive. And unless a man is playing corrupt politics, I don't object to him. He's got to do it from a political point of view. Or at least he's got to consider politics.

I believe that Mr. Kennedy is sincere in wanting to give the Negro full civil rights. I don't think that he is playing politics in any bad sense. Secondly, the president, I think, if you will check the facts on it, has gone about as far as he can go with executive orders. After all he can't move in public accommodations, for example. He can't move in other areas unless there is some legislation. So that I don't know what else the president could do. He's moved in the field of housing, in the field of employment. He can't touch private employment unless they have a federal contract, a defense contract, say. And I think that he has moved in all of these. I really don't know under our system of checks and balances exactly what a president could do that hasn't been done.

Woman 4: Every time the word *federal* is used in the South it seems to be a dirty word. Why in the world instead of saying that the federal troops have gone in can't the newspapermen say that the army has gone in? Now both the North and the South belong to the army. Everybody knows what the army is. Why do they have to be called federal troops?

M: I share your feeling that too much of the South uses the word *federal* as a dirty word, and this is all the more ironical because no region has benefited so much from federal programs as has the South in agriculture. They do use it as a dirty word. I think that probably the reason is that you have state National Guard troops, then all the states now have state highway troopers, and so because of these two state organizations we have just fallen into sort of an easy way of saying federal troops. But you do have a point.[316]

Woman 4: When that Little Rock mess was boiling up, I wrote Mr. Ashworth [Harry Ashmore?] that we had a forest fire and the army, not the federal troops, sent a detachment from Fort Devens to help put it out. Now if that had been in the South, it would have been said that the federal troops were sent in.

M: Yes. You do have a point.

Woman 5: I've just called to thank you for your marvelous work. I think that you are a great American and a humanitarian.

M: Well you're very kind to say that, and I appreciate it very much.

Woman 5: I've read all your editorials in the *Globe* and I think that they're just terrific.

M: Thank you so much for calling.

Man 1: I think that it's an acknowledged fact that in the South the Negro is discriminated against in his voting rights and certain other privileges. Does the *Atlanta Constitution* always print a full, fair, and unbiased account of most of the racial incidents?

M: Well, we try to, sir. We've staffed all of them. That is, sent our own personal reporters. We have not depended just on the wire services. Although we take all the wire services. We have spent a great deal of money in sending our own reporters and photographers to these places. I don't know how good a job we have done sir, but we've tried.

Man 1: Well, maybe this is the reason that many of the local newspapers, the *Boston Globe* for instance, has printed quite widespread news regarding the racial incidents in the South, but yet we have an instance here just in Melrose. There was a house that was set afire down here and several antiracial comments written on the side of the house. Yet we found that buried on page seven or ten. And if something of the same magnitude happens down South we see front page news quite often.

---

[316]See "Is the Federal Government Running Our Lives?," in volume 1.

V: Well, isn't there a certain natural tendency for us to each hide the family idiot, so to speak?

M: Well, I don't know if you just had somebody who set a house afire if that would have been on our page one. But certainly if the house was occupied—I'm not familiar with the story so I don't like to comment about it—we would have given it a good play. Sometimes a claim is made that these are racial incidents. We've had a number of cases in the last two or three years where people have claimed racial angles to something, and then we have found out that it wasn't true. They were just saying this to try to make a better story. But I don't know about the one that you're talking about, sir. . . .

Woman 6: Mr. McGill. Can you tell me how many of the Negroes in this country are pure African race and how many are blended with other races. What percent?

M: I don't have the exact figure, but I would say that since the American Negro has been here for quite a few centuries, that probably something over ninety percent are, as you say, blended. Or say less than certainly ten percent would be pure African strain, unless they have come recently. But this has been a process of several centuries.[317]

Man 2: Mr. McGill, when I was in the army I was down in Tuskegee [Alabama] and I had to fly planes in there. Some of the Negroes down there were the smartest and nicest looking, and they had the nicest wives that I have ever seen in this world. Why can't the rest of the Negroes in this country work a little harder instead of just having leaders that they are going to follow, like a bunch of sheep? When I was down in the South we also saw Negroes who worked ten days and then took two weeks off. After they had a couple of dollars in their pockets, boom, that was the end. You never saw them again.

M: Don't you also find white people doing the same thing?

---

[317]Throughout his campaign for civil rights for blacks, McGill confronted the fear of racially mixed marriages; see "Is the Federal Government Running Our Lives?," "An Interview on Race and the Church," in volumes 1 and 2, and audience member's response to McGill's "Editors View the South" speech in *Ralph McGill: Editor and Publisher,* ed. Calvin McLeod Logue (Durham: Moore Publishing Company, 1969), 1:159-60.

Man 2: Yes, you do, but there is more than ten percent white people in the country than are Negroes and they are not all crying about it.

M: I think, sir, that you have probably put your finger on it by saying that in Tuskegee you met a lot of educated, trained Negroes.[318] You saw some others who were a product of a segregated system. I often try to think, sir, just what my psychology would be if I'd been a Negro. If I had not been allowed to vote, and if I'd grown up as a child knowing that no matter how much education I got I couldn't get a job unless it was maybe as a school teacher or a laborer, or a Negro woman a job as a nurse—I—you knew that all opportunity was closed to you. You weren't going to be allowed to vote. If you weren't allowed to join the P.T.A., to participate in any community discussion. This does some things to anybody. I think that this is what I have been trying to argue and preach, sir. That we have created through several generations of segregation policy a lot of people who are deprived, who are at a disadvantage, white and colored.

Man 2: There's another thing that I'd like to say. Don't you think that with all this, I won't say propaganda, TV, radio programs, and everything else, that this is doing maybe the Negro more harm than it is doing him good? Because it is stirring him up so much that it is setting him back? I think that it's eventually going to come to race riots and everything else, faster than if we didn't have all the programs on the air and on TV.

M: I would hope, sir, that it will never come to any riots. I think that we as a thoughtful people have got to understand that this condition exists. Too many of these people, not all of them Negro, are not educated, not trained, not skilled to take jobs. And we can't leave them just jobless in slums without making some move to do something about it.

Man 2: Another thing, have you ever been down Massachusetts Avenue in Boston?

M: No, I don't believe so. I think that I had better say that I have done fairly extensive research into slums in four cities, but not Boston.

Man 2: Well, it's probably the same as anywhere else. A pane of glass

---

[318]Tuskegee Institute is located in Tuskegee AL.

costs you maybe fifteen or twenty cents, and anybody can put a pane of glass in a window. Yet you ride down that street and you'll see cardboard instead of glass in the windows. Now if it were my house I would go and buy a pane of glass. Now why can't they have even that much initiative?

M: Well, if you rent the house—

Man 2: I used to rent a house, and if the landlord didn't do it, I did it myself.

M: Is this a slum area that you're talking about?

Man 2: Well, it's on the fringe.

M: I don't know if you can buy a pane of glass for fifteen cents. The last one I bought was more like thirty-five cents.

Man 2: All right, say thirty-five cents.

M: Well, that makes the difference between a quart of milk, a couple of loaves of bread for your kids. I don't know just what the situation is in a house with cardboard stuffed in the windows.

Man 2: Then let me take up just one other thing. I heard on a program the other day that this Negro was telling his following in this certain city that if they came to that meeting that night that maybe they couldn't dress as well as the white people because they didn't have the money, but for goodness sake be clean. Now that is one thing that at least they could do. But he had to remind them to be clean.

M: I don't think, sir, that we can generalize on this. Look around you and you'll see many dirty people from all races. Thinking of somebody of a different race as being dirty or not smelling good, they might expect to say the same thing of some of us. I try to stay away from that.

Man 2: At a point like this in their history in the United States I don't think that they should have to be reminded of it. It should be uppermost in all their minds.

Woman 7: I received a letter from two friends of mine who recently moved to Atlanta and are teaching in a college there. They enclosed a letter which they sent to the *Atlanta Journal*, which was not printed. It was about a Reverend Jones who was arrested sometime last summer for taking Negroes to worship at a white Baptist church in Atlanta. His bond [was] set at twenty thousand dollars, and he was evidently charged with disturbing worship. My friends tell me that he—at this time he spent twenty-six days without food and water, this was voluntary, but he has evidently been treated quite badly in jail. They sent a letter to you or your paper asking that this be published so that the people in Atlanta could protest. I wonder if you could comment?

M: Yes. My paper is the *Atlanta Constitution.* And if they sent it to the *Journal* I didn't get it. We have published a number of letters on this case. It is a very sad one. This man is quite elderly. He has been arrested a number of times. I feel that the decision is very unjust. We have said so. An appeal effort is being made. There has been one effort at *habeas corpus*, but the judge in the case had been very adamant, and as yet it has not been possible to make it a federal constitutional issue.

This elderly man is as you say on a hunger strike, in an effort to dramatize this situation. It is a sad case, and I assure you that everything has been done which could have been done. A number of letters have been printed, and in the *Journal* too, I just don't know about that one.

Woman 8: We had occasion a couple of years ago to drive through your state, and we have sort of a local joke that we were going to go to Atlanta and say hello to our friend Mr. McGill, but unfortunately the kids won out with the Okefenokee Swamp. I had never been down South before, and it's beautiful country. I wanted to ask you because I feel an affinity with Atlanta because you lost a tremendous number of people down there in a terrible earthquake. How is your art museum doing?[319]

M: The art museum is doing fine. It might interest you to know that the sacrifice of these people, if you could call it that, more than a hundred of them, so aroused the people that we are now moving and are going to have a tremendous fine new art school; our museum is going to be enlarged and we are going to have a concert center.

Woman 8: I would like to make just one comment with regard to my feel-

---

[319]On 3 June 1962, 121 Americans, many from Atlanta, were killed in an airplane crash at Orly Airport, Paris, France. The Atlanta Art Association had sponsored the tour. The Atlantans the woman speaks of died in that crash, not in an earthquake. See McGill's essay, "The Caring People," in *Southern Encounters: Southerners of Note in Ralph McGill's South*, ed. Calvin M. Logue (Macon GA: Mercer University Press, 1983).

ings on the subject. As a Northern liberal I don't have to go through the whole business but personally I can't stand after having [reached] the ripe old age of forty-five this terrible feeling between the races. There is not the easygoing intercourse that there should be between people. So that you really can't discuss anything. You have to be wary of what you're saying, or you have to be afraid that you might be offending. And most of this is just due to the fact that we do not have this easy feeling between us.

So that this is the thing that bothers me mostly over and above all the inequities that go on. I was just curious to hear you comment as to what part industry will play. I noticed as we were traveling South that there were a number of new plants. Do you think that now that the South is finally becoming industrialized this will have a bearing?

M: Without any question. It already is having a bearing. A number of these plants and especially those with federal contracts—and a great percentage of industry today does have subcontracts or a direct one— . . . cannot practice discrimination. One of the big plants near Atlanta, about fourteen miles north of the city, employs about thirty thousand persons. They have some Negro engineers, technicians, et cetera. A great many companies which have no federal contracts are upgrading these people. Our paper began some time ago. Two of our top circulation people are Negroes. These are at the executive level. So this is beginning to come along now rather fast.

Woman 9: It is a privilege for me to talk to you. Your book was the high spot of the summer for me.[320] I have a daughter who is working in Albany, Georgia, with the Student Nonviolent Committee,[321] but in answer to the person who said that the Negro was in too much of a hurry, I feel that Martin Luther King is the best answer for that. He says that the Negro has not made a single gain in civil rights without determined legal and nonviolent pressure.

M: This is true. I'm glad you said that, because it literally is true that not a single—I'm sorry to say this and it embarrasses me to say this and

---

[320]Ralph McGill, *South and the Southerner* (Boston: Little, Brown and Company, 1964).

[321]Student Nonviolent Coordinating Committee (SNCC).

I say it only out of sorrow—but not a Southern state has made a conces-
sion. They have all come about by reason of federal court decisions or
legislation. We had to get rid of the white primary. We had to get rid of
other restrictions on voting through federal cases. The school decisions,
I don't know, I can understand some people saying that the Negro is in
too much of a hurry possibly because this thing has remained quiescent
for so long. If I were a Negro, however, I wouldn't think that they were
hurrying very much.

Man 3: Mr. McGill, is there any racial discrimination in the Negro Re-
publics of Haiti and the Dominican Republic?

M: Well, I have been to Haiti. It was some years ago. I was in Africa
this year. And certainly you will find, yet I think that anywhere you go,
you will find some degree of discrimination in race and religion. In Africa it takes tribal form. Where . . . [they've] had tribal rivalries existing for centuries, they will discriminate against one another. This is
a pretty universal problem of discrimination and prejudice.

Man 3: Well, they've had what—about eighty years in Haiti and the
Dominican Republic?

M: Yes, that's right. But you'll have to admit though, sir, that they've
not had governments which have tried to make any progress in this field.

Man 3: Didn't they have an all-Negro government?

M: Again, it was pretty much of an all-Negro government, but it was
very much of a class structure. And the [problem with the] government, as I think that we're all well aware of the problem of trying to give
aid in those countries, is that it never really gets down to the people. You
had a top sort of a Negro elite in Haiti, but it didn't reach right down
to the people. I never felt that you could call it a true government, and
I mean that. In neither of these places.

Man 3: I was wondering if they had equality there or what they were
doing about it.

V: It's been interesting that you have been called, Ralph McGill, "the
conscience of the South," and the spokesman for the sane white South.
What does this carry in the form of the onus or some degree of serious
responsibility to you, sir?

M: Well Mr. Vincent, first let me thank you for the privilege of being on the program and to say how much I always enjoy coming to Boston. The description of me as the "conscience of the South," I don't know whether I merit that or not. It was given to me some years ago because I have for about thirty years been writing on the problems of the South as they have developed. I think that there is an obligation on each of us in whatever field of information media we may work. That is, if we are commentators or editorial writers or editorial columnists, I think that we do have an obligation to have something to say and to have commitments. This I think is important today. That we believe and that we have commitments. And that we not kid the people, to put it in the vernacular.

The Southern people and many people in the East or North have not been well informed on the problem because it lay sleeping for so long. And so there is a great deal of misunderstanding, and people as always don't like to hear the truth. But I think that there is an obligation not to shilly-shally on this but to really come down to it. It is a very important thing. It affects our national security finally. If affects our unity as a nation. It affects the unity and the good will and the economic prosperity of a city. It certainly reaches into the church. It reaches into every aspect of our lives. And so I've tried to talk about it.

V: What is the truth concerning the South as you see it currently, Mr. McGill?

M: Well, first, Mr. Vincent, I try to shy away from saying the "South." The "South" differs. Today for example, the Supreme Court handed down a decision letting stand an order to admit the first Negro to the university at Clemson, South Carolina. Now South Carolina has chosen not to be a sick state politically or sociologically. They decided to go ahead and follow the Court orders.

So they have admitted the first Negroes to the university and to Clemson which is the technical school; a large private university, Furman University—incidentally, Furman was founded by a man who was an ardent advocate of slavery in the old days. But at any rate, South Carolina has chosen, so far at least, to go along with the processes of law. So has Atlanta, Georgia. So have a great many other Southern cities.

But just next door over in Birmingham, Alabama, we've had all of the riots. We've had the shocking uses of police dogs and fire hoses. In

Albany, Georgia, 175 miles south of Atlanta, we've had resistance. Oxford, Mississippi. All these things are a part of the South. I don't think
that you can generalize.

V: There is a great tendency, though, in our Northern press to completely generalize . . . all of the states that once composed the Confederacy in the same general category. And to depict the totality of the white
South as consisting of citizens who quite probably wear peaked caps and
make night rides terrorizing Negroes.[322] Would you comment on this,
sir?

M: I'm afraid that this is true. We sort of get into stereotypes and we
put quotation marks around the "South," the "North," and actually the
North is a great variety of states and cities. Boston certainly is different
from Philadelphia or New York. We all vary according to our past history and to the cultures that we've had. So it is with the South.

Of course the South has been and is largely agricultural. And one
of the rules of thumb is that the racial problem is more acute and resistance to change is more defiant in those areas which still retain a lot of
the old-plantation-type culture: in other words, where the Negro and the
white man are still largely rural and agricultural, where illiteracy is
rather high. . . . In a rural area or an agricultural region which always
has a lower income than an industrial one, we have for a good many
years, several generations, attempted to maintain two school systems.
And we really didn't have the money for even one good one.

The Negro got the worst of it. In the rural communities, many
white people also were discriminated against or deprived of an opportunity at a good elementary or secondary school education. So that there
has come out of the South for generations, persons who were rural people. Their hands are fitted to hoes or the handles of plows or tools. But
they didn't know any skills.

I drive around up here, and I see all of your astonishing electronic
industries, and you have these because you had a pool of skilled labor, a
sort of background of people who knew how to do these things or who
would learn quickly. This isn't true in a region which until relatively
recently has been growing just cotton and tobacco, where the only tools

---

[322]Ku Klux Klan.

were those on a farm. You don't develop an industrial know-how background.

V: In your celebrated book, *The South and the Southerner,* you refer to the fact that the Negro and the white man in the South and throughout the United States do not actually know each other, that they have a serious problem of simple communication. Would you expand on that, sir?

M: This is very true, Mr. Vincent. Here in the South we had laws which separated the Negro and the white communities. These were state and municipal, county laws. Here in the East or North you did not have such laws. But you had a more subtle form which rather effectively did separate them.

So that I think one of the tragedies is that the white America doesn't know the Negro America. And the other side of the coin is that the Negroes never really had a chance to know the white American. Now we each, all, have known a Negro or a few Negroes. Some of us have been to schools with a few. But we don't really know them. How many people in Boston know the Negro or the white slum resident? I've spent some time in Chicago slums and Philadelphia slums and in Harlem. Now the white community knows that these slums are there. But they don't know what the real situation is.

For example, in education, the last figures I had for the school year of 1959-1960—and I obtained these from school people in New York—in three Harlem schools the turnover of pupils in that one year was one hundred percent. In three of four other schools, the turnover ranged from sixty to eighty percent. Now I'm sure you have a great turnover in your Boston schools, though not so spectacular. At any rate, too many people have a stereotyped view of the Negro. And too often at least it's an unattractive one. A great many white Americans, the only Negro they've had a chance to learn about is someone who may have been poorly dressed or uncouth or illiterate, and so this is what they think of the Negro. And they think that when desegregation comes this is the only sort of Negro that you're going to see.

The average American because of the separation—and this has been more effective in the South, but it has also been true elsewhere— . . . [has] never really seen the middle-class Negro or the educated Negro. This is one of the things which deters us in this movement now to grant citizenship rights. The great problem that so many people have of the stereotype of an objectionable Negro.

V: Isn't this a two-edged sword to a certain extent, sir? Hasn't the Negro a stereotyped image of the white man as an oppressor, as a foe?

M: Surely. This is what he has gotten. Now it ought to be a fairly simple matter—I saw the last figures and we've now become a nation of 190 million people, of which only about 19, not quite 20 million, are Negroes—now this really shouldn't be much of a problem, Mr. Vincent, for 170 million people to deal with this. But it's concentrated. We've got all sorts of old stereotypes and myths. Irrational fears. And then we've allowed it by neglect to become really concentrated in some of the great industrial cities.

V: Has there been any sort of a calculated effort in your eyes, sir, to maintain this myth?

M: Yes. There is now. Some of the white citizens [continue] in the South. Particularly those in Mississippi where they have had state support, where they have carried on television and radio broadcasts and have distributed printed material. There are [people] right now trying to play on the fears of the average person in the North, that a very undesirable type of Negro is going to move next door to him. This isn't true, of course.

The statistics of Chicago show that less than one percent of the Negroes in all of Chicago could afford to buy one of the cheaper suburban homes, say in the fifteen-thousand-dollar- to twenty-five-thousand-dollar-class range. Less than one percent. I am sure that the percentage here in Boston would also be quite low. Probably one percent or less. It is in New York. It is in Philadelphia. It is in Atlanta. So that the Negro has been depressed [but] not alone. This segregated system has discriminated against white persons. But in the main it has been against the Negro. So we . . . have, I'm sorry to say, developed an uneducated, unskilled class in many of our cities.

V: There is a certain point that it's quite difficult for us to understand this far away, I believe, Mr. McGill. And that is the actual power of those White Citizens' Councils throughout the Southern states. . . . Would you explain some of this power to us? How they operate? What type of citizens are actually in their membership?[323]

M: Well, actually they have not made much progress except in Alabama and Mississippi. Now, to be sure, they are represented in other states, but they didn't really catch on. And I think that the reason is that they started first in Mississippi. The state gave them state appropriations, so it certainly must have been illegal though no one ever challenged it.

They set up literally at the grass-roots level in all the small towns. They carried on things which seem to me would have to be classified as coercive. For example in little towns and in . . . all of the larger ones— Jackson, the capital, is not really a large city; it's about 125,000 persons—they would have poll takers out who would come around to your house. They were taking a poll on racial attitudes and on what yours . . . [were]. Well, you work in the town. You have a little business in town.

This is just a nice little way of sort of reminding people. And then they carried on boycotts. Let's don't forget that at the University of Mississippi some years ago they would show up when a professor would make a talk.[324] They would show up on the front row with a tape recorder. They would show up in churches with tape recorders to tape a minister who might be making what they would call a liberal speech. They would show up at any visiting lecturer. They would show up at seminars and tape things that were being said. This took on some of the aspects of a real police state. This supervision of the teachers went down certainly to the high school level. And they had to stop, I know one or two years, holding religion-emphasis weeks at the university because they objected to some of the men who were coming in from the outside, ministers or theological teachers.

This thing was very thorough. Now, they provided radio taped programs, television programs for other states. Anybody who wanted them could get them free. They have attained power in Mississippi which is difficult for us to comprehend even though we live very close to it.

V: Do these councils represent considerable economic pressure? Can they

----

[323]See Neil R. McMillen, *Citizens' Council* (Urbana: University of Illinois Press, 1971).

[324]See McGill's "Rebirth of Hope at Ole Miss?" in this volume.

force radio stations into broadcasting these tapes? Can they force news-papers into publishing their side of the story entirely?

M: Well, let's say that they have done it. They have all published and carried these programs. And I think that it would have gone very hard on a radio or a television station or a newspaper which refused. Now the other side of that coin is that I don't know that any of them wanted to refuse. Hodding Carter's paper is an exception in Greenville, Missis-sippi.[325] He's been subjected to harassments, boycotts of circulation, and so forth. So have we, of course, in Atlanta. So that there are always these actions against you.

V: You have fought the fight in the Negroes' try for first-class citizen-ship for a long, long time. Yours has been a most eloquent and powerful of all fights in Atlanta. What type pressures were tried on you to silence you, Mr. McGill? They obviously failed.

M: There were a lot of boycotts. I've had a lot of help and associates in various fields who have worked on this problem. I haven't been alone by any means. This was in the book[326] so I'm not dragging it out here. Oh, for years very filthy and abusive telephone calls, my house was shot into, dumping garbage on the lawn. Just a lot of things like this.

V: Why have you continued this fight, Mr. McGill? It would have been easier for you. Your income and status would have remained the same had you chosen a simpler path.

M: I don't know. I've often wondered about this myself. Sometimes I ask myself, when things are going badly, "why are you doing this?"[327] I don't know. I don't see how you can live with something that you know is wrong. I'm not a poet. I'm not writing poetry. I'm supposed to be writing editorial comment. Well, how can you live with yourself if you

---

[325]Hodding Carter published the Greenville, Mississippi, *Delta Democrat-Times*; see Hodding Carter, *Southern Legacy* (Baton Rouge: Louisiana State University Press, 1950). When Carter's book was reissued in 1966, McGill wrote the foreword to that work, and that foreword is reprinted in volume 2.

[326]McGill, *South and the Southerner.*

[327]For more on McGill's motivation for campaigning for blacks' civil rights, see *Ralph McGill*, 2:21-23.

ignore what is the big moral and social problem that is all around you? And more than this. A business in a city which has not gone ahead or tried to meet this turns out to be very bad. Birmingham is a very sad city economically. Business is suffering terribly. I know other places where business falls way off. So this reaches into your city's whole aspect, its economic life, its spiritual life, its social life. You can become a sick city. You can't ignore this. I don't see how you can honestly ignore this. And so I try to talk about it and discuss it.[328]

V: Would you say, sir, that there is a sizable percentage of the white citizens in your own state and throughout the Southern states, who think as you think, who realize that they have been trying to live with something that is basically wrong?

M: I don't think that there's any question that there's a great many persons who so feel. Now I don't know that all of them have reached the point where they feel like acting about it. But I'm sure that they feel it. We were able in Georgia to elect a very good young governor who did not run on the race program. He defeated a racist.[329] We've been able to avoid the development of any real White Citizens' Council of any strength except in one or two areas of south Georgia. Georgia's a very big state geographically. It's the largest geographic state east of the Mississippi River, for example. I think that [we] have some people who believe this. Now they may not agree with the courts and they may wish that it hadn't happened. But they have not joined the violent. Now we have some violent ones who are really working at this all the time. We have them in Atlanta. They carry on very active propaganda. They are a threat.

V: Have the Muslims made any headway with the Southern Negro? They seem to be enjoying a certain degree of success here in the East.

M: No, not very much. I doubt if the Muslim group in Atlanta totals more than seventy-five or eighty. Very small really.

V: Is there coming out of the Southern states currently the type of en-

---

[328]See McGill's "Birmingham Rotary Club" speech about that city's involvement in social change, in *Ralph McGill*, 1:212-22.

[329]Carl E. Sanders was elected governor.

lightened political leader who will fight your fight, the Negroes' fight and the white man's fight, actually as an American?

M: I can't say that I can say yes, that they are coming out of the South. Here and there, one is developing. Here and there, governors are appearing or candidates for the legislature or candidates for the Congress who will say, "Well, we've got to obey the law. We've got to do what the courts say." This is helpful. This is what you must expect from a Southern politician as he develops now. If you can get one to say this it is a great help. Because if you're going to obey the law and do what the courts say, well, then you're going to come along. This is their way of making a step forward out of the old racist attitude.

V: Of course at the other end of this political pole we find George Wallace of Alabama. Would you comment on him, sir?

M: I have looked at Mr. Wallace with interest. I think he is a very sad man. There is a certain pathos to me in looking at Mr. Wallace. Here is a man who came up the hard way. A poor boy who worked his way through school. You would think that such a person would have a compassion, a feeling for other less fortunate persons. But Mr. Wallace seems to be one of these persons with a strong determination to maintain segregation in its old form. And he of course is fighting a losing battle. He moved very strongly with state troopers in Birmingham, and in one or two other cities, to prevent the school from being desegregated. But he didn't move in Huntsville, we assume, because this was a large government installation. It is a missile center.

He was not quite consistent in this. He was another one of those who tried to say "never." But the University of Alabama has been desegregated. Schools have in Birmingham, Huntsville, and so on. So I don't know. I wonder about a man like that. I certainly don't feel any malice toward him or anything like that. I wonder why he thinks that he can win such a fight. Rather, why he wants to win such a fight here in the last half of the twentieth century. I don't understand the man.[330]

V: Is it politically practical for him to take this stand here at this time?

---

[330]Wallace was elected governor of Alabama again in 1983. See McGill's essay on Wallace in *Southern Encounters*.

M: Well it is. But I think that it's rapidly ceasing to be politically practical.

V: On the other side of this racial aisle, do you find that you are satisfied with the Negro leadership in the Southern states? And nationally, as far as that's concerned?

M: Not all of it, of course. You couldn't be satisfied with all of any political leadership. Some of the Negro leadership has made mistakes. Some of the sit-ins of the more beatnik types have been sort of exhibitionist, rather than leadership in form. In general I think that the South in time will be thankful to Martin Luther King, for example.[331] Suppose he had been a Muslim type. Suppose that he had been preaching violence rather than nonviolence.

I think that the NAACP and not all of CORE [Congress of Racial Equality]. CORE has done a good job in trying to keep its membership and its leadership in the framework of responsibility and by and large they have succeeded. So have the others. But there is a great need for more responsible Negro leadership. On the other side of that coin is that they never had an opportunity to develop under a segregated system. And they've had to come awfully fast since about 1954, you might say.

V: Many of the racists try to maintain a certain degree of intellectual support for their thesis. Based on the study made by the somewhat celebrated anthropologist Dr. Carleton Coon, who maintains that he can prove quite successfully the thing that he calls the "actual inferiority of the Negro as a human being on all levels. As a thinking creature. As a social creature. As a cultural creature."[332]

M: I read this book. I don't know how celebrated he is—Mr. Coon. But

---

[331]See McGill's essay on Martin Luther King, Jr., in *Southern Encounters*.

[332]In their book, *Anthropology* (Englewood Cliffs NJ: Prentice-Hall, 1973) 189, Carol R. Ember and Melvin Ember conclude: "Carleton Coon's theory of racial classification has been interpreted, perhaps unfairly, as scientific support for racism. Coon suggests that the Negroid race evolved later than the Caucasoid race, a view which has been used to explain why the Negroid people are less 'advanced' culturally than white groups." See Coon, *The Story of Man From the First Human to Primitive Culture and Beyond* (New York: Alfred A. Knopf, 1954); Coon, *The Origin of Races* (New York: Alfred A. Knopf, 1962); Coon with Edward E. Hunt, Jr., *The Living Races of Man* (New York: Alfred A. Knopf, 1965).

certainly he is a very lonely anthropologist. I have notes—almost a non-existent support for his thesis, relatively nonexistent. I know that much more celebrated anthropologists have said that it's a preposterous claim and so forth. Certainly if we look about us, if we look at the United Nations, if we look at the Negro intellectuals who are appearing in literature and art, if we look at the people who are coming to the fore in the new African countries. It seems to be that this is a lot of bunk to say that they don't have the capacity for leadership or development. How does he know? They've never had the opportunity really. In Africa, I'm speaking about, where they did have it some of them have done very well.

Others are coming fast. I was in some of the African countries early this year. You'd be in a vast territory. And maybe they'd had only two small elementary schools. Most of the education was by mission schools, Protestant and Catholic. I would say that most of the top leaders in Africa today, men in their forties, fifties, and sixties almost without exception had their beginning in some mission school. There weren't many of these, so that the Africans had very little chance. It seems to me that you can't condemn a whole people on the basis of some anthropological study, which time is proving to be incorrect.

V: We have here in the East, Mr. McGill, a situation that is rather frantic. It would be funny if it weren't sort of tragic in a sense. In which various publishers, broadcasters, business leaders, even clergymen, will cry out that the South is doing a terrible thing. They will insist upon the instant integration of Houston and Atlanta and Birmingham. But then quickly if it suddenly comes anywhere near their own doorstep, they cry out "well, not next door to me." It has been said that the South isn't as concerned with integration as it is over interference from the North. Do you believe that this is a valid claim, sir?

M: Well, I think that I won't be able to answer it yes or no. Certainly we, and I mean by we, the South, have noticed that some of the people in other areas who have been supporting integration, when they suddenly are confronted with it, they want to back away. I suppose that this is human nature. They haven't really thought about it in practical terms. And this is something that we must do. This is a very practical thing. These people are in our cities, and there are great masses of them. They are white and colored, but mostly colored. But they are here, and they're in the main not trained to work. And they're not going to be able to get a job.[333]

I think that this is a human nature thing, to back away. But I don't think that the last half of your question would really apply. The South really is concerned about integration. And after all, I think that that word gets kicked around. What we're talking about really is not integrating a society. What we're after now is that the Negro shall be entitled to all public facilities that any other citizen uses. Later on comes the other things, jobs, housing, and so forth. But anyhow, let's not quibble about a word. The South is concerned about it as we've seen in many areas. I don't know that the North has interfered much. Now to be sure some probably well-meaning groups have come down and made asses of themselves. But in the main I don't think Northern groups have interfered. This is another thing with us. They say "outsiders" caused all this. "Our Negro citizens are really very happy if the outsiders just let them alone." Well, this is bunk. If the local Negro is very happy, he wouldn't be out there demonstrating or risking his life probably or that of his family and his job. This is the bunk. The Negro is not very happy.

V: Have some of the angrier, though, of these angry young men of the Negro race moved too far, too fast, do you feel? Have they lost some of the support of the white liberal in the South who was on his side to begin with but feels that some of his actions have been a shade too enthusiastic?

M: Yes, I guess this is true. I don't know how much they have lost. This is probably true on a national basis. But again I think that more is required of us, if we're going to be upset by something like that. And they say "oh, I'm going to turn my back on this whole problem." This is no good either because the problem is going to run over you. You can't turn

---

[333]Until late in the 1960s, McGill stressed obeying laws and acting responsibly to make available civil rights for blacks rather than "integrating" blacks and whites in society. He believed this strategy best for the dangerous times in which he lived. For example, even in his speech at Emory University, Atlanta, on 16 February 1959, on "Crisis in Schools," McGill stated: "Now I certainly, personally, do not have any policy of integration and have not had; I am sure you have no policy of integration."; *Ralph McGill*, 1:195-96. White persons' concern about racially mixed marriages was one reason McGill spoke so circuitously; see "Is the Federal Government Running Our Lives?" and "An Interview on Race and the Church," in volumes 1 and 2 and "Editors View the South" speech in *Ralph McGill*, 1:159-60.

your back on this. There's no place to hide. There's no place to run. And I don't [think] that a man, a really thoughtful man, even though he becomes very angry and has a reason to be, [is] justified. He's upset by being what he thinks may be shoved around. He's upset by some of the more violent actions of some of these groups. But I don't think you can condemn the whole movement. I think that he's got to rise above this. If you look back at our own history, in our early days of nationalism, there are some lessons to be learned.

70

Hate
Knows No Direction

Almost one hundred years to the day after Abraham Lincoln looked out on the great crop of death at Gettysburg and spoke with compassion and with faith in the national dream, our young president [John Kennedy] has been savagely done to death in the harvest of hate. We have learned from history that hate cannot merely destroy a president but bring the nation itself close to disaster. The harvest of the seeds of malice in Texas reminds us that whether it comes from the extreme right or left, hate that is blind, bitter, and relentless already is a poison in our national life.

The first suspect at Dallas was a typical product of the furnaces of madness. Although an American bred and born, and although he had worn his country's uniform, he had defected to the Soviet Union. Later disillusioned with communism, he returned to his native land and became involved, for hire, in one of the pro-Castro groups.

But he was not alone in his hate. His deed brought out the glee of the right-wing extremists. When news of the shooting and, later, the death of the president became known, some Southern newspapers received anonymous, jeering, telephone calls. "So they shot the nigger lover. Good for whoever did it." . . . "He asked for it and I'm damned

Reprinted from the *Saturday Evening Post,* 14 December 1963, by permission of Mrs. Ralph McGill and *Saturday Evening Post.*

glad he got it . . . trying to ram the damn niggers down our throats." These were samples. Some of this kind of joy was open and loud.

Hatred knows no direction. The American Communist-oriented and the right-wing extremist groups have dissociated themselves from their country. The danger comes from both. Some of the segregationist forces have for more than a year openly condemned their country, its government, and its leaders, and declared their hatred for it and their loyalty instead to a state or a leader. Extremists have for six years directly and indirectly encouraged violence and defiance of federal authority. The list of these includes politicians, evangelists, spokesmen for organizations dedicated to defying the United States Supreme Court ruling against racial discrimination, the more rabid anti-Semitic and outright anti-Negro groups, and those of the more outspoken Birch Society mentalities who called Dwight D. Eisenhower a Communist stooge and the late Secretary of State John Foster Dulles a traitor and a Communist.[334]

The more shrewd among the peddlers of hate against their country have been careful to avoid open and direct incitement of violence. But their words and other abuse directed at the president and the government have inspired many whose disturbed minds tend easily toward recklessness and criminal action.

Ever since Little Rock's school riots of more than six years ago, it has been obvious that psychopathically dangerous persons would not hesitate to use dynamite and gunfire against the established laws of their states and national government. Innocent children have been dynamited to death in Birmingham as they sat in Sunday school learning a lesson of Christian love.[335] In the long and dreadful night of rioting when James Meredith was enrolled at the University of Mississippi, two men were killed by sniper fire. U.S. marshals were subjected to a violent attack by stones, bricks, pieces of pipe, and other weapons.[336]

---

[334]McGill believed that "extremists in either direction almost inevitably provide dangerous and damaging leadership"; see editor's introduction.

[335]For an important speech by McGill delivered prior to the Sunday School bombing, see "Birmingham Rotary Club Speech," *Ralph McGill: Editor and Publisher*, ed. Calvin McLeod Logue (Durham: Moore Publishing Company, 1969) 1:212-22.

[336]See McGill's "Rebirth of Hope at Ole Miss?" in this volume; James W. Silver, *Mississippi: The Closed Society* (New York: Harcourt, Brace and World, 1964); Russell H. Barrett, *Integration at Ole Miss* (Chicago: Quadrangle Books, 1965).

After the dawn had come to that strife-torn city and order was re-stored, local residents told of seeing persons who came from "outside" areas, one of whom was heard to say, "I am glad to be able to fight against this damned Communist country." Days later in Mississippi a sniper, firing from the cover of darkness, shot and killed Medgar Ev-ers, an NAACP official.

We have grown used to seeing on television and in news and mag-azine pictures, the hate-twisted faces of young men and women and of their adult counterparts, crying out the most violent threats and express-ing venom against their country, its courts, and its authority. We have seen the frightening faces of screaming, cursing mothers during the de-segregation of schools in New Orleans. The lives of those persons who sought to stand for law have been disturbed by threats and abuse, by filth shouted over the phone, by prowlers and, now and then, by a shot fired into the house.[337]

The extreme right and left in this country have so well revealed their minds to us in their literature, public utterances, in floods of mail, mostly anonymous, filled with outrageous charges against, and lies about, the murdered president, that we have no excuse not to understand what they plan and how they operate. In some instances men of great wealth, all made in the nation they wish to change more nearly to their own dream of at least semitotalitarian power, reportedly help finance some of the more extreme organizations, left and right. There were businessmen who, in a time when profits were at an all-time high and the domestic economy booming, nonetheless could speak only in hatred of "the Kennedys." There were evangelists who declared the president to be an anti-Christ, an enemy of God and religion.

This hatred could focus on almost anything the president proposed. When he asked for legislation for medical aid for the aged, for example, there were doctors who succumbed to the fever of national unreason and began abusing the president. In locker rooms and at cocktail parties, luncheons and dinners, it became a sort of game to tell vulgar and shabby jokes about the president, his wife, and his family. Most of these

---

[337]See Numan V. Bartley, *Rise of Massive Resistance: Race and Politics in the South During the 1950's* (Baton Rouge: Louisiana State University Press, 1969).

were repeats of stories in vogue at the time Franklin D. and Eleanor Roosevelt were in the White House. Contributors to this pettiness and malignancy must bear a small share of the national guilt.

71

When a Man Stands Up to be Counted, He May Be Counted Out: Review of Charles Morgan's *A Time to Speak*

The title of Charles Morgan's book, *A Time to Speak*, is from Ecclesiastes 3:7: "A time to keep silence, a time to speak. . . ." A later verse in this chapter asks: "What gain has the worker from his toil?" Mr. Morgan here gives the answer.

The author was not long out of the University of Alabama Law School before there came for him a time to speak and act. His book is a quietly eloquent and moving human document. In it is faithfully recorded, with compassion and contempt, what came of speaking and acting honorably across a brief span of years in Alabama—chiefly in Birmingham, "The Magic City."

There arrived a day when the road taken separated him from his community. It is from a distance that he looks back and assesses the gain of his toil. It is considerable. And though the effect of it in the Magic City—and in the state that elected and acclaims Gov. George Wallace— is not yet apparent in any major change, it is there. The book is not,

Reprinted by permission of Mrs. Ralph McGill and the *New York Times*, 10 May 1964. Copyright 1964, by The New York Times Company. An earlier draft of this review is in the McGill papers, now at Emory University, Atlanta. Charles Morgan, Jr., *A Time To Speak* (New York: Harper and Row, 1964).

then, a success story in the sense of victory, but it is a trumpet call to conscience.

It will be widely discussed in the South, where there will be those to sneer at it, and curse it, as there were those to sneer at and curse Charles Morgan. Yet the indictment of this personal story is too plainly honest to be ignored. Its prose is lean and clean. So is its accusation. One can only hope that it will be scanned wherever an understanding of the evil that segregation has done and still does is lacking. If the honorable senators who deny the need of a civil rights bill have time, this would be a helpful book for them to read.[338]

Charles Morgan's parents came to Birmingham from Kentucky when he was fifteen. He remembers a wonderful mother, a kindly father who never seemed to have a prejudice but did have opinions and could make decisions. There is some of that in the son. In seven years at the University of Alabama he won two degrees, law school honors, and the campus leadership. He was there when Authurine Lucy "integrated" the university in 1956.

When she left, after a series of blunders and errors which allowed a small minority of students and off-campus toughs to thwart the court order, Morgan had learned his first lesson—one that other Southerners had learned, or would learn: "In this failure to speak and act at every stage of crisis, the moderates—the nice, good, safe, respectable people—bear the major share of responsibility for the acts of violent men in the street."[339]

On Authurine Lucy's departure she told the press her one moment of hope had come just before her entry to the campus—a student leader had called her and told her he would do his best to prepare her way onto the campus. Morgan was the caller.

---

[338]For more by McGill on Southern moderates see reviews of Brooks Hays, *A Southern Moderate Speaks*; Hodding Carter, *Southern Legacy*; Frank E. Smith, *A Congressman From Mississippi: An Autobiography*; "The Southern Moderates Are Still There" and "The Case for the Southern Progressive," in volumes 1 and 2.

[339]For McGill's explanation and criticism of the role of Southern moderates see the editor's introduction.

The following years brought practice in law, marriage, suburban life, football weekends, children, a career that prospered. In the state itself not a single political voice had been raised to prepare the people for compliance with law. There were fourteen candidates in the Democratic gubernatorial primary in 1958. From rostrum and TV screen the thesis was stated and restated, each seeming to try and outdo the others: "I will maintain segregation." "There will be no integration of the public schools of Alabama."

There was no dialogue (as there has not been in certain other Southern communities); there was only demogogic gibberish.[340] The responsible people had failed. The business interests, the civil leaders, educators, communications media, clergy, and public officials had "permitted the democratic processes of the state to disintegrate into raucous, dangerous demagoguery." The author records exhibits in support of this erosion.

A young Phi Beta Kappa preministerial student at Birmingham Southern College was arrested by Birmingham police, presumably for meeting for discussion with Negro students at Miles College. Henry King Stanford, president of his college, resisted alumni and political pressure to expel him. The Klan, of course, burned a cross. In the end the case was dismissed; he graduated with honors. Stanford left to become president of the University of Miami in Florida. Morgan, who had represented the student, learned that sometimes the place for an honest man is in jail.

The Reverend Robert E. Hughes of the Alabama Council on Human Relations lost his Methodist pulpit for refusing to present to a grand jury all records of donations and contributions made to the council—believing, as he did, that contributors would be subjected to harassment, and perhaps some would lose their jobs. Morgan stood off the grand jury and courts. Pastor Hughes lost his pulpit, then had it re-

---

[340]McGill often criticized citizens in communities who failed to discuss race relations constructively; he personally had helped continue a positive dialogue on race relations in Atlanta and in the South, as is evidenced by his daily columns in the *Atlanta Constitution*, essays in this volume, and speeches in *Ralph McGill: Editor and Publisher*, ed. Calvin McLeod Logue, 2 vols. (Durham: Moore Publishing Company, 1969).

stored so he could go (oh, the wonder of irony) as a missionary to Africa.[341]

A young Baptist minister, Norman C. Jimerson, a Pacific war veteran, was jailed for conspiracy, though he had tried to prevent a riot and demonstration. Attorney Morgan won him freedom from jail and a dismissal of the case.

On Sunday, 15 September 1963, a Negro church was ripped by dynamite. Four young girls were killed; others were maimed. Jewish temples had twenty-four-hour armed guards protecting them.

On Monday, 16 September, Charles Morgan delivered a speech—scheduled long before—to the Young Men's Business Club. It was his valedictory. He was graduating from Birmingham.

"Who is guilty?" he asked.

> A business community which shrugs its shoulders and looks to the police . . . for leadership? A newspaper which has tried so hard of late, yet finds it necessary to lecture Negroes every time a Negro home is bombed? A governor who offers a reward—but mentions not his own failure to preserve either segregation or law and order? And what of lawyers and politicians who counsel people to what the law is not when they know full well what the law is? . . . Birmingham is a city where four little Negro girls can be born into a second-class school system, live a segregated life, ghettoed into their own little neighborhoods, restricted to Negro churches, destined to ride in Negro ambulances to Negro wards of hospitals or to a Negro cemetery. Local papers, on their front and editorial pages, call for order and then exclude their name from obituary columns.

Charles Morgan knew fear, heartbreak and harassment because he did what he felt he was supposed to do—yet he can still remember, from a new start in another city, the pleasant things, the friends, the nice homes, springtime, and the happiness of their children, when they were young in Birmingham.

And in Birmingham? "Everything's been pretty quiet there lately."

---

[341]See Kenneth K. Bailey, *Southern White Protestantism in the Twentieth Century* (New York: Harper and Row, 1964); Samuel S. Hill, *Religion in the Solid South* (Nashville: Abingdon Press, 1972); C. Dwight Dorough, *Bible Belt Mystique* (Philadelphia: Westminster Press, 1974); also "Television Interview about Africa," "Let's Lead where We Lag," "The Agony of the Southern Minister," "Church in a Social Revolution," "Interview on Race and Church," and "Introduction to *God Wills Us Free*," in volumes 1 and 2.

72

A Decade
of Slow, Painful Progress
1964

F or a brief measure of time after the school decision by the Supreme Court of the United States in May of 1954, there was a
period of silence and hope. In the region then most affected,
outwardly it was just another spring. But much of the silence was sullen.
And hope was soon to be rebuffed by defiance and demagoguery at high-
decibel levels.

Later, recalling that period of relative quiet, a newsman was to say
that it was somehow remindful of Parsis Towers of Silence at Bombay.
Statutory and constitutional segregation of United States citizens by race
was dead and on view on the highest pinnacle of law. But the vultures
of prejudice, hate, and greed were soon to come and tear at it, vainly
seeking to destroy the evidence of that death.

The story of the decade now gone truthfully could be said to be one
of progress. Much has been accomplished, materially and morally.
Measured against the 1954 threats and promises of blood in the streets,
the dreadful violence and the several murders that did occur, largely in
Mississippi and Alabama, at least were not all the strident voices had
predicted. Nor did they have the effect that was in the hopeful minds of
those who promised it. The Oxford, Mississippi, riots and murders in

Reprinted from *Saturday Review,* 16 May 1964, by permission of Mrs. Ralph
McGill and *Saturday Review.* Copyright 1964, by Saturday Review, Inc.

that state; the dynamiting of Sunday school children, the police dogs, and the police brutalities in Birmingham; and excesses of prejudice and injustice in rural areas and towns in neighboring states served to shock the conscience of the nation and to confront even the more apathetic with the need to make a choice.[342]

The decision of May 1954 confined itself to the schools. But it served to open up the entire spectrum of discrimination—education, jobs, inequality before the law, housing and voting rights. It was as if a call-loan on which the South and the nation had been paying exorbitant interest rates, had suddenly been called. The cost of Jim Crow is great—and will be paid for at least a generation to come.[343]

Some idea of the expansion of the decision of May 1954 may be had from the summer program now planned by the Student Nonviolent Coordinating Committee. Mississippi and Alabama, in that order, are the largest reservoirs of resistance to civil rights, including the most fundamental one of voting.[344] The student committee, aided by volunteers from many universities and colleges, plans an educational program on a person-to-person basis to teach the younger Negroes of Mississippi something about themselves, their country, and the responsibilities of citizenship. This will be done in six-week courses at "Freedom Schools." They will be aimed at the eleventh- and twelfth-grade levels. They will include lectures in Negro history. Most of the history books being used in this country, and especially those in the cotton South, present only fragmentary bits of information about the Negro. Much of it is slanted and chiefly concerns itself with slavery and the Reconstruction period.

There will be, of course, seminars in constitutional law and in how to qualify as a voter. Mississippi seems to be agitated about this peaceful program and publicly is arming additional police and preparing for vi-

---

[342]For more by McGill on Mississippi see "Rebirth of Hope at Ole Miss?"; for more on Alabama see "A Sensitive Southerner's View of a Smoking City" and review of Charles Morgan's *A Time to Speak*, in volume 2.

[343]For McGill's public support of blacks' rights in law, education, employment, voting, housing, and social services, see the editor's introduction.

[344]For more by McGill on voting by blacks see "If the Southern Negro Got the Vote" and "The State of the South," volumes 1 and 2.

olence, which hardly will be started by the relative handful of students who will work at the Freedom Schools.

The irony of such a situation, and the danger of it, is further underscored by the fact that disfranchisement of the Negro voter and the abolishment of most of his citizenship opportunities began in Mississippi just before the turn of the century. Other Southern states picked up "The Mississippi Plan."

In 1901, an editorial in the *Atlantic Monthly* commented acidly on the cynicism of disfranchisement in the nation's new territorial acquisitions and in the Southern states. It was a time when Rudyard Kipling had chided Americans with his poem, "The White Man's Burden," imposed, as he saw things, by the acquisition of the Philippines. He bade them take up the burden of the new-caught sullen peoples, half-devil and half-child. The U.S. Congressional Hawaiian Commission, meanwhile, had recommended property and literacy tests as voting qualifications in this new territory.[345] Senator John Morgan of Alabama, chairman of the commission, had said the commission had acted for "one assortment of inferior races." To reject the tests, the senator said, "would be to turn the legislature over to the masses" and to "deprive the more conservative elements and property-owners of effective representation." Northern political sentiment, in the Congress and business areas, which favored the voting qualifications for the new possessions, was thus prevented from being critical of the ruthless rush of the Southern states totally to disfranchise the Negro. Indeed, Senator John L. McLaurin of South Carolina was so moved by a speech delivered by a Massachusetts statesman, Senator George F. Hoar, defending the American Imperialism and its methods, that he rose to thank his colleague from the Bay State for his "complete announcement of the divine right of the Caucasian to govern the inferior races."

The *Atlantic*, noting the application of the harsh and frankly disfranchising Mississippi plan to the Philippines, said:

---

[345]Early in his campaign for blacks' right to vote, McGill also placed some restrictions on who would vote: "The privilege of the ballot ought not to be given to the unqualified. Particularly do I think it should be withheld from those not literate enough to know the issues. I would oppose most vigorously permitting uneducated or otherwise unqualified Negroes to vote"; see the editor's introduction.

If the stronger and cleverer race is free to impose its will upon new-caught, sullen peoples on the other side of the globe, why not in South Carolina and Mississippi? The advocates of the "shotgun policy" are quite as sincere, and, we are inclined to think, quite as unselfish as the advocates of benevolent assimilation.[346]

The two phrases are, in fact, two names for the same thing. Southern reaction, especially on the part of those engaged in disfranchisement, was one of almost incredulous joy at their good fortune. The business of disfranchising the Asian and African Americans went forward simultaneously.

In the South there was some opposition from Populist groups. Many individuals spoke out against it. Of these, John Spencer Bassett, historian of North Carolina, said of his state's brazen disfranchisement law: "At best, it is an enameled lie . . . one more step in the education of our people that it is right to lie, to steal, and to defy all honesty in order to keep a certain party in power."[347]

Professor Bassett was prophetic. Having assumed the burden of a lie and of dishonesty clad as truth and virtue, the South and the nation moved from 1900 into a decade of savage violence. Race riots were many. Lynchings multiplied in numbers and brutality. Southern politicians, of whom Ben Tillman is perhaps the best example, lectured under the banner of Chatauqua, declaring the Negro to be subhuman and shouting "To hell with the Constitution if it says we cannot lynch to avenge the crimes against womanhood." Racist extremists reached a wide audience North and South. Edgar Gardner Murphy, then an Episcopal minister in Montgomery, Alabama, and one of the really remarkable men of his time and region, denounced this brutal and inhuman trend, saying that racist extremists had "proceeded from an undiscriminating attack upon the Negro's ballot to like attack upon his schools, his labor, his life—from the contention that no Negro shall learn, that

---

[346]*Atlantic Monthly* 88 (October 1901): 433-49.

[347]John Spencer Bassett, *Anti-Slavery Leaders of North Carolina* (Baltimore: Johns Hopkins Press, 1898); *Makers of a New Nation* (New Haven: Yale University Press, 1928).

no Negro shall labor, and (by implication) that no Negro shall live."[348] They ended by preaching, he said, "an all-absorbing autocracy of race," an "absolute identification of the stronger race with the very being of the state."

It is the fallout from the decisions of this period in American history that slowly has poisoned and sickened the nation, and, more particularly, the South. The burden of guilt and fear, the acceptance of a system immoral and expensive in human and economic terms, made inevitable a lack of first-rate educational opportunity for the average Southerner.[349] It doomed most of the people of the rural South to an existence so meager and unrewarding as to bring on, and yet be unable to sustain, the Populist revolution. The sharecropper tenant statistics of the 1930s revealed how great had been the cost in things temporal and spiritual.

That cost continues. In my opinion, it will be paid over and over for at least a generation to come, and it is perhaps fitting that it must be borne nationally. But, the South, inevitably, will pay the heavier share of it.

There is no quick adjustment of this debt. But it should be obvious that the sooner the Negro comes to the ballot, to education, and to jobs, the better. Then, and only then, can the bill be settled. As the Negro rises in the economy and the life of the community, the fears and myths will mainly disappear.

The ballot is the best tool. That is where the major pressure will be placed this summer and in the months ahead.

The decade since May 1954 has brought great progress. It is too bad that the folly of resistance should obscure what has been accomplished.

---

[348]Edgar Gardner Murphy, *Basis of Ascendancy: A Discussion of Certain Principles of Public Involved in the Development of the Southern States* (New York: Longmans, Green, and Co., 1909); *Problems of the Present South: A Discussion of Certain of the Educational Industrial and Political Issues in the Southern States* (New York: Macmillan Co., ca. 1904).

[349]See C. Vann Woodward, *Burden of Southern History* (Baton Rouge: Louisiana State University Press, 1960).

73

The Case for the Southern Progressive

One of the more melancholy commentaries on conservatism, Southern style, is the company it now keeps. A few examples will illustrate the dilemma. In Arkansas the more ardent [Barry] Goldwater Republicans prefer Democrat Orval Faubus for governor, rather than Republican Winthrop Rockefeller. Mr. Rockefeller has rendered the state yeoman service. His investments and payrolls are large. He has toiled hard, in all areas of the state, promoting interest in industrial development. His large, well-managed ranch has, by precept and example, stimulated beef production. It attracts thousands of visitors annually. No one denies the soundness, durability, and value of Mr. Rockefeller's contribution to the state. But, alas for him, he has a quietly decent record in race relations. This makes him unpalatable to many members of the state GOP, especially in the eastern section of Arkansas. Mr. Rockefeller is not, by their yardstick, a conservative.

In early May of this year, the last survivors of the conservative Republicans in Georgia, who in 1952 formed an organization that provided meaning and respect previously nonexistent to the state Republican organization, were ousted in a state convention controlled by Senator Goldwater's supporters flying a banner of "true conservatism."

Reprinted from *Saturday Review*, 13 June 1964, by permission of Mrs. Ralph McGill and *Saturday Review*. Copyright 1964, by Saturday Review, Inc.

Some leaders of 1964 were—not too surprisingly—those whose delegation to the Republican national convention in 1952 had been rejected by the convention. This was a seeming return to the old "Lily White" GOP policies of a generation ago.

In Tennessee, "conservatives" shouting for Senator Goldwater assumed control of the organization that twice carried the state for nominee [Dwight] Eisenhower and for [Richard] Nixon in 1960. For the first time in fifty years, the Tennessee Republican delegation will not include a Negro. In both Georgia and Tennessee, white and Negro leaders said that the Negro had been "read out" of the Republican party.

Further illustrations of this sort of conservatism, Southern style, exist in abundance. This is by no means to say that all conservatives in the South have a racial bias. But it is to say that those who are most vocal and politically dedicated and who have control of Southern state Republican organizations have such bias or permit it to reveal itself. The conservatives of 1952, who at great personal expense and effort began a true two-party movement in the Southern states, are, with few exceptions, appalled and angry by what seems to them a betrayal of the Eisenhower philosophy. They had won a majority of the Negro vote in 1952 and 1956. In Georgia, they lost it in 1960 after Senator Goldwater made three appearances in the state. These conservatives, ousted by the Goldwater conservatives, wryly and sadly note that at a time the Negro citizen rapidly is attaining the right to vote (registration already is considerable), the "conservatives," Southern style, are making him unwelcome in the Republican party. Georgia's new Republican chairman, from Savannah, admitted as much, saying, "We will make up for it by getting more white votes."

The Southern conservative, especially in business and the professions, who honors the word and who has been proud to wear it as a badge, increasingly finds himself disturbed and alienated by this mutilation of the conservative issue and philosophy.

Senator Goldwater flew from the Georgia convention to Bakersfield, California, where he addressed the United Republicans of California. This group is described in that state as an ultra-Republican faction that split off a year ago from the conservative California Republican Assembly because of the latter was considered too liberal.

Two features of the senator's appearance so well fit the pattern of the new and strident "conservatism" as to merit attention. On the platform at Bakersfield the Confederate flag was prominently displayed beside the national flag to welcome the senator from Arizona. Secondly, the senator, decrying the civil rights legislation before the Congress, was reported as saying, "You cannot pass a law that will make me like you or you like me. This is something that can happen only in our hearts."

The presence of the Confederate flag at a California ultra-conservative rally for the senator is not without meaning. One of the lamentable developments of the new Southern conservatism has been the prostitution of the Confederate flag. It has become the property of hoodlum Klan elements, the White Citizens' Councils, and dynamiters of churches and schools.[350] Leather-jacketed toughs fly it from the radio aerials on their hot-rod cars. The Bakersfield conservatives at least gave the flag of their country a place with the Confederate banner. The senator's fatuous comment about the inability of law to make him like others and others to like him is typical of much of the Southern conservative logic. It is at one with "You can't legislate morals," "You can't legislate equality," "Are you in favor of mongrelizing the races?" and "Civil rights agitation is a Communist plot to take over America."

Civil rights legislation is not, of course, aimed at legislating morality. Nor does any section or paragraph of it require that "you like me and I like you." The bill is designed to establish and protect equal citizenship rights, no more, no less. Nowhere in the legislation is there even a hint that the senator from Arizona at any time will be required to like someone or have them like him. There is no intent to legislate equality, but there is a determination to legislate equal citizenship. Southern conservative extremist groups, in and out of the Congress and in and out of state capitals, have persistently sought to distort the meaning and intent of equal citizenship rights by insisting that it invades the field of private social life and attempts to "legislate morality."[351]

---

[350]See Neil R. McMillen, *The Citizens' Council* (Urbana: University of Illinois Press, 1971); Francis M. Wilhot, *The Politics of Massive Resistance* (New York: George Braziller, 1973); Numan V. Bartley, *Rise of Massive Resistance: Race and Politics in the South During the 1950's* (Baton Rouge: Louisiana State University Press, 1969).

[351]For McGill's support of blacks' rights in law, education, employment, voting, housing, and social services, see the editor's introduction.

Even more dangerous and reckless is the segregationist program of declaring the civil rights campaign to be a Communist plot, conceived by Communists and executed by Communists or by their stooges. They were delighted by J. Edgar Hoover's statement that Communists were trying to infiltrate the Negro movements. This has never been a secret. It is the oldest Communist technique—to try to ride any horse of discontent that comes along. The Southerners have forgotten that the Communists also tried to infiltrate the sharecropper and tenant organization of the dreary years of the Great Depression. They made a major effort to exploit Negro suffering and discontent in those years. The story of Communist efforts in this decade is not the small success they have had, but Negro resistance to them.

It is one of the dismaying revelations of the minds of the rightist conservatives that they are willing to equate communism with the various movements seeking the right to vote, to have job opportunity, to attend school, and to eat in a restaurant or stop at a hotel. Communism couldn't manage that sort of propaganda with the aid of a dozen agents. The fact that the White Citizens' Councils, Klans, some editors, senators, congressmen, and commentators on TV and radio daily insist that a drive to join Americans as participating citizens is communistic must puzzle as well as delight the Communist party. But the practice remains and becomes more and more irresponsible.

Passage of civil rights legislation will not, of course, be a panacea. But it will provide a legal base from which to proceed against plain, undeniable injustice. The primary reason that much of the Negro crusade for acceptance as a citizen moved from the courtroom to the sidewalk was quite simple. There was no "law" applicable to the inequity at hand. The first such demonstrations began more than four years ago by students seeking service at lunch counters in variety and department stores. They were able to accomplish a constructive result in relatively short time, with surprisingly little disorder. They achieved a boycott of sorts. And, perhaps equally important, they revealed the preposterousness of the discrimination.[352]

---

[352]See John Hope Franklin and Isidore Starr, eds., *The Negro in Twentieth-Century America: A Reader on the Struggle for Civil Rights* (New York: Vintage Books, 1967).

In the variety stores Negro and white customers were used to standing side by side to make purchases. They could be shoulder to shoulder
buying underwear or toothpaste, but they could not walk to the next aisle
and shop for coffee or a grilled cheese sandwich at the same counter. This
made no sense. The same untenable, deadly parallel was drawn in the
department stores where each customer's dollar was invited at every sales
table except the one offering food.[353] It is fair to say that a substantial
number of operators of these businesses privately were pleased to have
the decision forced. They had—or believed it wise—to go through the
motions of resistance in order to placate the ancient prejudices before removing the discrimination. When they did, nothing untoward
happened.

So it is with the public accommodations section of the present [1964]
civil rights act. In most major Southern cities a majority of hotels and
the better restaurants and sandwich shops have been desegregated for
some time. Rare is one that has suffered any economic loss whatever. A
substantial number of those who have not voluntarily removed discriminations privately yearn for the law so that they may have "an excuse."

Here again is an area in which these "conservatives"—politicians,
editors, and Klans and White Citizens' Councils—who declare the
rights bill to be destructive of private-property rights are themselves
likely to be the more destructive. It cannot be for the health of the American enterprise system to equate property rights in the field of public services with injustice and personal affronts through discrimination. A
Playboy Club is a private restaurant and cocktail room catering largely
to the the expense-account trade. A private social club also offers food
and drink. But it seems likely that in the last half of the twentieth century, events and morality suggest that a public business is public, available to any orderly, properly clad person seeking, and able to pay for, the
services publicly offered.

Nor is this concept of public service "new law." There early was
brought into the laws of the several states the old English innkeepers'
statute that denied a general right to discriminate in turning away travelers. These laws were not widely tested in discriminations growing out

---

[353]See C. Vann Woodward, *The Strange Career of Jim Crow*, 3d rev. ed. (New
York: Oxford University Press, 1974).

of anti-Semitism and race because of their generality—or ignorance of their existence—but they provide a precedent, recognized in Elizabethan times, for the public accommodations legislation in this last half of the twentieth century. Those who insist that public-service operators are really private and have a right to discriminate run contrary to the opinion of a majority of restaurant and hotel keepers. They strongly feel that the American system will be heavily eroded if it insists that injustice and ugly discrimination is a "right" of a public entrepreneur.

There is constant mourning in the dovecotes of those who profess to believe in federalism but who resist the changes necessary to maintain it. They fret about what James Madison would think of today's amended Constitution. They are obviously regretful that the "general welfare" section of the Constitution has been so well used. Their text is the free citizen in a free society. But moves to make the Negro a free citizen in a free society are opposed because, they insist, the Constitution forbids it. Therefore, regretfully, say these Southern conservatives, we must wait. When those who have waited almost a century move to the sidewalk and, out of frustration and resentment, make unwise decisions, such as the World's Fair stall-in that failed, an excess of piety is added to the always constant flow of that commodity.

All attempts to make the American pledge of equality of citizenship an actuality are decried as "centralism." Some five million citizens in the long-isolated Southern Appalachians, their livelihood gone because their natural resources of timber, coal, and minerals have been ruthlessly exhausted or are now obtained largely by mechanization, may not be helped because it is "unconstitutional." And anyhow, Americans have become used to "the honeycomb life" and must somehow be made more rugged. This attitude, persistently defended, unquestionably adds to the frustration of Negroes—especially the younger ones. But more than that, it gives aid and comfort to the Black Muslims. It encourages the Communists to step up their efforts to infiltrate the movements so frustrated.

Those who profess to be willing to give the Negro citizens equal rights, to understand the needs provided by extreme poverty and the imperative demands for movement in area redevelopment, but who sadly declare it cannot be done because the Constitution doesn't permit, rarely mention Thomas Jefferson. He may have been the best authority of all.

Jefferson's message to the Congress in 1806 proposed a program of national development. A surplus was in prospect and he suggested using it to pump-prime a tremendous long-term plan of digging canals, draining and dredging rivers to make them navigable, and constructing roads and communications in general. In his dream, too, was the establishment of a great national university by the federal government.

The question was asked, "Could this be done under the Constitution?"

Jefferson replied he would move, three years in advance, to amend the Constitution if necessary. That he had also in mind use of the general-welfare clause is obvious. That he so acted when, lacking any constitutional authority, he made the Louisiana Purchase is undisputed.

In 1806 Jefferson, the strict constructionist, told the nation that he did not think the nation could, or should, be kept forever in the straitjacket of the original constitutional restraints. Jefferson said the Constitution was not a fetish to be worshiped and made sacrosanct against change, but an instrument of service to the nation, to be changed when changed conditions demanded change in the national interest or for progress.

That was 1806. Today, in 1964, there are petty, niggling constructionists who invoke technicalities and ghosts to sustain a strained and narrow conservatism. They attempt to make a fetish of the Constitution, declaring it to be sacrosanct and not subject to change. These persons are perhaps as dangerous to the validity of the Constitution as are the totalitarian groups who openly would destroy it. Those who would deny, in the name of the Constitution, an equal sharing of citizenship rights, who would stop a war on poverty and prevent urban and area redevelopment, who would oppose all programs designed to improve the general welfare of the country by a narrow interpretation of the Constitution, certainly would bring that noble and flexible document into jeopardy.

The political effect of racist conservatism is, at this writing, not yet jelled. Alabama and Mississippi are the major centers of the "independent elector" chimera. This is old stuff with those two states. It was Alabamians, led by Bull Connor, recently in the news of Birmingham's race riots, who created the Dixiecrat party in 1948.[354] In 1956, some electors went off the reservation. There is a chance that Mississippi, prisoner of the White Citizens' Councils, may not do so in 1964, but the odds are she will. Alabama belongs, for the present, to Governor George Wallace, who is working in a manner somewhat reminiscent of the late Huey Long to solidify his hold on the grass roots of his state.[355] Louisiana also has third-party or independent-elector pains, wholly because of the race issue.

Even if Senator Goldwater is nominated, it is doubtful that Alabama would give him her electoral vote. In 1960 Mississippi cast hers for Virginia's Senator [Harry] Byrd. Six of Alabama's electors bolted the nominees. Louisiana, for all her official commitment to segregation, should be kept in line by the influence of Senator Russell Long and others of that faction. As of this writing, Virginia and Florida are the two Dixie states where the Goldwater strength might give him a victory. But these are by no means sure. Senator Byrd has not made up his mind in Virginia. And Florida will be close.

Insistence by Goldwater Republicans on holding hands with the worst racist elements, and in frankly bouncing the Negro from the party in Georgia and Tennessee, will produce reaction. A surprising number of Southerners are uninformed about Negro registration. Behind the clamor of sit-ins, demonstrations, and protests, the Negro, where the opportunity is present, has been registering to vote.

A Voter Education Project, supported by local and national organizations interested in remedying the effect of disfranchisement in eleven Southern states, showed a net gain of 327,000 new Negro voters from 1 April 1962 to 31 December 1963. A later estimate, as of 31 March, added about 220,000 to that total. The drive ended 30 April. It is likely that well over 400,000 voters were obtained by the VEP proj-

---

[354]For more on Bull Connor and Birmingham, see "A Sensitive Southerner's View of a Smoking City" and review of Charles Morgan's *A Time to Speak*, in volume 2. See also Emile Bertrand Ader, *Dixiecrat Movement: Its Role in Third-Party Politics* (Washington DC: Public Affairs Press, 1955).

[355]For McGill's "George Wallace: Tradition of Demagoguery," see *Southern Encounters: Southerners of Note in Ralph McGill's South*, ed. Calvin McLeod Logue (Macon GA: Mercer University Press, 1983). George Wallace was elected governor of Alabama again in 1983.

490

ect. They, of course, must be placed with those who registered on their own.

Negro registration at year's end was estimated at 1,751,818. It now tops 2,000,000. This is about forty percent of the 1960 Census count of 5,016,100 Negroes of voting age. It is also about fifteen percent of an estimated total registration in the eleven Southern states of 14,295,420.[356]

In Alabama, where Department of Justice injunctions have eliminated some of the barriers to Negro qualification, registration has made good gains in Birmingham and in central Alabama. Resistance continues in the Black Belt areas. (The Black Belt is so called not because of Negro population but because of the black belt of soil.) In Louisiana and South Carolina significant gains have been made. Only in Mississippi are there determined tactics of preventing registration. Out of about 422,000 Negroes eligible to vote, only about 28,000 have managed to register.

Other Southern states also report substantial gains. This is especially true in North Carolina, Florida, Texas, and Georgia. This march to the ballot will not halt. Mississippi and those communities in Alabama that still seek to evade the law and the Constitution eventually will be required to obey. A steadily increasing Negro vote is in the future of the Southern demagogue and racist, the Senate filibusterers, and office seekers at the local level who oppose the legitimate aspirations of the Negro citizen and who delay the industrial and educational advancement of the region.

For years those who have helped disfranchise the Negro have evoked the specter of a bloc vote. There is ample evidence to prove that the Negro vote is not necessarily a bloc. In local elections in Atlanta, for example, the Negro vote has gone for some Negro candidates and against others. The fact is that the Negro votes like any other voter. When his interests are at stake he may vote in a bloc—but no more than labor or the farm bloc.

---

[356]For more by McGill on voting rights for blacks see "If the Southern Negro Got the Vote" and "The State of the South," in volumes 1 and 2, and the editor's introduction.

The Negro has been voting long enough in the South to demonstrate that he is a good friend of the more able and competent candidates. He becomes, therefore, an asset to improved government. This is not surprising. The Negro has been a victim of bad government for so long that he instinctively looks for improvement.

There will be more Negroes elected to local offices. Georgia has had its first modern state senator. His conduct in office has broken down much of the prejudice and fear that were a part of his election. In Tuskegee, Alabama, home of the famous Tuskegee Institute founded by Booker T. Washington, a federal court decision eliminated a vicious and cynical gerrymander and also enjoined slowdown evasions by registrars. There is a Negro majority. Negro candidates have been chosen to contend for office. Some will be elected. Faculty members at Tuskegee are included among the candidates. Great care was taken in selecting contestants. Each is superbly well educated and prepared. They will receive a fair share of white votes.

Passage of the civil rights legislation [1960 and 1964] and the surge of the Negro to the ballot will provide a very real emancipation for the South and the Southerner. The Southern politician of intelligence and ability will be able to serve his nation and state. He will not find it necessary to truckle to the worst elements of prejudice to hold his place. In the years since Reconstruction many Southerners have gone to the Senate who were first-rate men, worthy to be considered as presidential nominees. They could not be, because, to remain in office, they had to satisfy the worst in their states, not the best. A civil rights bill and the increasing Negro vote will free future candidates. Rights legislation will be resisted in some areas, but in time it will move the protests from the sidewalks to the courthouse. Business will be more willing to come to the South. Emancipation of the Southerner and his region is a sure development of the future.

Once that emancipation is had, the South, which has a truly large, varied, and positive contribution to make to the nation in the field of industry and the human condition, will be able to abandon its historic negative base and enter the mainstream of national life with strength and purpose.

74

First of All, Georgians are Americans

The people—the people of Georgia!
    They came first in 1733, led by James Oglethorpe. The British Crown wanted a buffer against Spain. But that is another story.
    Those first Georgians soon were to become part of a larger pattern. There were Dutch and Swedish colonies in the new land. Those in New England and Virginia already were beginning to exhibit a fact not then comprehended by the colonies and which would never be understood by a throne in London. This fact was that neither the law nor the customs of the Old World would fit the New. By 1658, seventy-five years before the first Georgians had come, the Burgesses of Virginia had considered the question: "Whether a regulation or total ejection of lawyers." The law was not to be accepted from London but to be improvised in response to practical present conditions.
    Harsh conditions prevailed in the new country. A high death rate was constant. Between 1606 and 1623, for example, about five thousand immigrants came to Virginia. Children were born. Yet in 1623 there were only a thousand persons left. It was so in New England. There was nature. And, here and there, hostile Indians. But the cradle, though

Reprinted from *Atlanta Journal-Constitution Sunday Magazine*, 26 July 1964, by permission of Mrs. Ralph McGill and Atlanta Newspapers, Inc.

emptied often, was kept rocking. By 1680 the native-born were dominant in the colonies.

But the immigrants kept coming. In the Old World the sources of immigration were increased. Presbyterians left Ulster in great numbers. Welshmen and Scots began to go. The fever of the New World spread to the continent. Germans, Swiss, and Frenchmen began to pack for travel. Religious refugees from England, Germany, and France sent special contingents. Quakers, French Huguenots, Spanish, Portuguese, and English Jews responded to the fever. There were some paupers and prisoners of debt among those gathered by Oglethorpe, but we must understand the semantics of the time. Many a man, yeoman or of noble family, fell into debt and, as the law allowed, was imprisoned.[357]

The original plan of the Georgia colony failed. It was semicommunal. It was to grow silk and indigo. The colony survived. The original Georgians were just another example of the new country. Men in a distant land made plans. But those who came learned they had to dream their own dreams and make their own plans.

The colonies from Maine to Georgia were English. In the eighteenth century the Dutch and Portuguese chiefly were interested in Africa and the Far East. France was the great antagonist. France was the great power of the Continent. Spain cast her lot with Paris. French armies challenged Britain in India, in Europe, on the seas and in the New World.

The Mississippi Valley was the key to the French plan. There were forts on the St. Lawrence. The plan was to build them to the Gulf of Mexico. The English came too fast. But British attacks on Canada failed.

Trade began. It grew. The slave trade grew. The plantations began to appear in modern form—mostly tobacco and rice. In the East, the small traders, shopkeepers, artisans, iron makers and builders began to grow in number. Provincial politics began to jar with those of the British crown. The colonists began to talk of "rights." New ideas came into being. Schools were set up.

---

[357]See Kenneth Coleman, *American Revolution in Georgia, 1763-1789* (Athens: University of Georgia Press, 1958).

The Georgians who came slowly became a part of all these forces. There was a greater one. The French and British became heavily involved. The name of George Washington began to be known. Once he led Virginia militia against the French. Twice he was on the staff of British forces. Each time they were defeated. The French and Indian allies were too strong. Most of the fighting was outside the New World. Actually, this war, which did not end until 1763, was the first world war. There was fighting on the coast of Senegal and in Asia where French and British interests clashed, as there was at Quebec and Ticonderoga. It reached, too, into Georgia. Spain, seeking to profit, and to aid France against Britain, harassed the young colony. In July 1742, the Spanish came by sea and landed a force near Frederica. On 7 July, battle was joined at a place later to be called Bloody Marsh. Scottish Highlander troops were the major strength of Oglethorpe's command. Spain's superior force of Indians and regulars was defeated. Men called the site where they died "Bloody Marsh."

The mainland was saved from Spain. There was no more war in Georgia. But it was not until 1763 that France lost Canada, and Spain lost Florida.

Note now how destiny works. History records many catalysts. In this case it was debt. Britain's population was eight million. The debt piled up by the years of war with France was a staggering 140,000,000 pounds. It seemed to the British Crown that the colonies, saved from France, should bear part of the burden. And so they would. But an ill-advised, arrogant government, unaware of what changes had been wrought in the colonies, did not plan well. They were not persuasive. They demanded. Edmund Burke warned the Crown that a "fierce spirit of liberty" was stronger in the colonies than anywhere on earth.

In 1776, after more than a year of open rebellion Tom Paine's insistence that faith in kings was dead and that the republic should be proclaimed was answered. The Declaration of Independence was written. The text was largely Jefferson's.

A month passed before the young colony on the bluffs of the Savannah River heard the news. A messenger rode a horse from Philadelphia to Georgia with a copy of the proclamation.

War smote Savannah and Georgia with a heavy hand. The city was occupied. A civil war between Tory and Revolutionists, operated guerrilla fashion, brought war to Augusta and Wilkes County. Indeed

Wilkes County became the refuge of the revolutionary government. There were hangings, murders, fire, and terror. But in 1780, Augusta was recaptured. The British held Savannah until after the defeat of Cornwallis. In July of 1782 the city was reoccupied. It was September 1783 before a peace treaty was signed. The new nation could then begin.

Georgia was one of the thirteen states of the Confederation. It fell soon into chaos because it had no central authority. In 1789 Georgia signed the new constitution that brought the United States into being and committed each state to the constitution. Georgia entered the Union with enthusiasm. The honor of the United States was her own honor.

The plantations were largely rice and tobacco until 1793 when Eli Whitney, a New Englander, visiting in Georgia, invented the cotton gin. Cotton plantations and farms multiplied—as did slavery. Economics began to shape the political thoughts of men. In the East there were new industries, canals, railroads. Georgia and the cotton states chose agriculture—rice, tobacco, cotton.

About 1820, economics, slavery and its extension, began to create sectionalism—a South and a North. Events began to move toward the senseless tragedy of 1861 when emotions supplanted reason.

All along, the story of the American people has been one of what sociologists call a pluralistic society finding a common nationality, accepting a common principle of equal opportunity and loyalty. There have been, and are, many differences. The story of the people of Georgia is not a separate one. Always they have—with others—been subject to events and forces that have impinged on all Americans—the French and Indian wars—the Revolution, the failure of the Confederation, the birth of the United States under a common Constitution in 1789—the Civil War, the coming of industrialization, the agricultural revolution, the growth of cities and population—we have shared—and now share—in all of these.

The past comes along with us. It is both blessing and curse. But the people of Georgia have their faces turned toward better schools, more opportunities for her children, and a peaceful settlement of differences rather than one of chaos and bitterness that comes out of strife. The space age is on us—and out in space are new worlds to find.[358]

---

[358]See Kenneth Coleman, ed., *A History of Georgia* (Athens: University of Georgia Press, 1977).

First of all we are Americans. We were, when the first Georgians came in 1733 and began to be shaped by the New World and contact with other colonies. Two great world wars, the mobility of population, the genius of our transportation system, the vast productivity of our farms and factories, and the need to sustain our principle of freedom against totalitarian communism or any other form of government that denies freedom—these commit us as a whole people.

The people of Georgia are Americans—they always have been—and will be—proud of the American heritage and loyal to its principles.[359]

---

[359]See McGill's "My Georgia," "Give Me Georgia," "Introduction to *The Old South*," and articles on Atlanta, in volumes 1 and 2.

75

From Atlanta:
The Political Assessment
1964

D uring the Southern tour of the Republican presidential nominee a comment frequently heard was that he seemed to be
running for Jeff Davis's old job. An example will illustrate.

On 16 September [1964] Senator Barry Goldwater spoke at the
Knoxville, Tennessee, airport. The port itself is in adjoining Blount
County. The eastern area of the state was heavily Union in the Civil War.
President Andrew Johnson, who succeeded the martyred Lincoln, was
born nearby. Maryville College, a small but excellent liberal arts
school, is not too far from the airport. During the Civil War the college
was one of the many centers of antislavery sentiment in East Tennessee.
East Tennessee almost certainly would have become the loyal Union state
of East Tennessee, following the West Virginia example, had the federal
government been able to move troops into Knoxville. Nearby, also, are
the birthplaces of Ben Hooper and Alf Taylor, two Republican governors
of Tennessee.

But on that warm and sunny September day when Senator Goldwater spoke in Blount County, Tennessee, he stood almost beneath the
folds of a massive Confederate flag. Well to his left was the state flag.

Reprinted from the *New York Herald Tribune*, 27 September 1964, by permission
of Mrs. Ralph McGill and the *New York Herald Tribune*. Manuscript provided by
Mrs. Ralph McGill from the McGill papers, now at Emory University, Atlanta.

But it was the stars and bars of the old Confederacy that flew over the nominee, the shadows of it repeatedly crossing his face as the breeze caught the folds of it and made then ripple slowly and sinuously in celebration.

Nothing better symbolizes Goldwater Republican leadership in the South. It has taken the Democratic party almost a century to cut down on waving the bloody shirt and exalting the issue of segregation as the most important domestic and political issue. Indeed, Democratic use of this demagoguery is now largely restricted to Mississippi, Alabama, and areas of Louisiana.

The Goldwater Republicans are somewhat more subtle. They employ the trappings of Confederate flags, the music of Dixie, and cast-off Democrats who help decorate the podiums with their presence. Senator Goldwater's speeches, however, were less subtle. He attacked the United States Supreme Court. He condemned reapportionment—which no states need so badly as the Southern states which are held more firmly in the bondage of rural control than their sister commonwealths. The nominee was for Southern states' rights and against big government.

It cannot be said that the candidate aroused his crowds to a pitch such as that attained by a [Theodore] Bilbo, a Cotton Ed Smith, or one of the several other demogogues of the past.[360] But his audience professed to understand. Reporters questioning members of Goldwater audiences had replies such as, "We know Barry can't talk straight about the need for segregation. But we understand that. You heard what he said about that damned Red-led court, didn't you? That's plain enough. We're satisfied. You didn't see any damned niggers around did you?"

There was a total lack of Negro presence in the Southern Goldwater crowds. This made them different. Even in the days when the worst of the Dixie demagogues were up there flailing away at "the nigger" there were always a hundred or so disenfranchised colored citizens on the fringes of the crowd, silently and patiently taking the abuse. They came, apparently, for the entertainment of the occasion. There is not always too much of that quality in the rural South. But they did not come to hear Barry Goldwater. Indeed, their absence led to a paraphrase of one of

---

[360]See Cal M. Logue and Howard Dorgan, eds., *Oratory of Southern Demagogues* (Baton Rouge: Louisiana State University Press, 1981).

Miss Joan Baez's songs. It began by asking "Where are all the Negroes gone?" and ended with the words, "Democrats picked them every one."

It cannot be said that the divorce of the Southern Goldwater Republican party from the party that ended slavery and wrote the Thirteenth and Fourteenth Amendments and its transformation to that of a lily-white party that frankly and openly has written off the Negro is the work of any central regional committee, or, indeed, of state leadership. The Goldwater Republican party in the South is not a mass movement led by a messiah. It is a collection of feudal baronies. Some are castles of Birch Society arrogance and wealth. Others are out of the redneck Klan klaverns. A few are anti-Semitic members of Gerald L. K. Smith's Christian National Crusade. Others are out of the split-level suburban country clubs. Others are "Democrats for Goldwater." A sample of these is that of Georgia, where Roy Harris, one-time national president of the White Citizens' Councils; and former governor of Georgia, ardent-segregationist Marvin Griffin, support Senator Goldwater. They presumably believe he may be able to impeach the Supreme Court of the United States and restore the rights of states to practice segregation and to restrict the registration of Negro voters.

The average Southern Goldwater voter fondly believes that under Senator Goldwater the able man who can make the money will be allowed to keep it because he made it and not have to pay it out in taxes to support the poor who are poor because they are lazy, or in aid to foreign peoples in the underdeveloped countries. The average Southern Goldwater supporter is, with few exceptions, proudly an isolationist who wishes to get out of the United Nations and all foreign entanglements and go it alone. He is better off than ever before; his company, or the one for which he works, is making higher profits. But there is something sinister, wicked, and wrong, and Barry, he thinks, is the man to set it right. As for the Negro, he is too violent and pampered and has come too fast. He needs to keep his place while the real Americans go forth to save the country from socialism and liberals. The baronies are separated in culture, income, and social status. Some of them are disappointed in their candidate's me-too tea parties with General [Dwight] Eisenhower at Gettysburg. They wish their man had more fire. But the rapport is there. As the red-necks say, they understand.

There are but few possible exceptions to the barony concept of Southern Goldwater Republicanism. William Miller, number-two man to Senator Goldwater, reportedly has described Alabama's John Grenier as the best political mind he has met. This would explain why Grenier was the floor leader of Southern Republican forces at the San Francisco convention and why he is in the national headquarters in Washington. That he is able none denies. He is credited with inspiring the whispering campaign around the South to be patient with Barry, even though the candidate can't say what all they'd like to hear. They can count on Barry doing what's right about the Court and states' rights.

Alabama has another of state stature, a former Democrat, Jim Martin, who in 1960 ran against Senator Lister Hill and gave him a scare. Mississippi has Wert Yerger, also possessed of political skills. The governors of Alabama [George Wallace] and Mississippi [Paul Johnson] also are helpful. But even so, the barony picture of the Dixie Republicans holds rather true in those states.

If Senator Goldwater is elected, the professionals may be able to bring the feudal barons under disciplined rule. But if Senator Goldwater is defeated the baronies will hold fast. It will require many years to move the Republican party of the South from its present reliance on segregation and racist prejudices. These make up the glue that holds it together today.

There was no real Republican party in the South until after 1952. The old "post-office" Republican organizations of pre-Eisenhower years were, with few exceptions, corrupt. They worked closely with, and often were members of, the legislatures of the Southern states and went right along with the one-party policies. The Eisenhower Republicans managed to get control of the state machinery in most of the Southern states after 1952. At the convention of that year old-line GOP delegations from Georgia and Texas were thrown out by convention action. The winners went on from there.

Whatever progress has been made in building a Southern two-party system belongs to the Eisenhower Republicans. They gave freely of their own money. The National Committee gave little financial aid. There was scant evidence of comeback by the old-line Republicans. The leadership, much of which was made up of busy professional and businessmen, grew careless. Some dispute this, saying they trusted Barry Goldwater and did not consider he would try to take over their state organizations. He was, they believed, one of them. Others frankly say they were fooled in their estimate of the senator from Arizona and even less comprehended the ruthless drive of those about him. At any rate, county meetings, which traditionally were sparsely attended, began to be well attended by men and women interested in Senator Goldwater. But even so, the callous ejection of the men and women who after 1952 had made the Southern party what it was came as a really great shock.

A few days ago Robert Snodgrass, of Atlanta, one of those who had given much of his energy and money to building a GOP organization in the state, talked to the local Rotary club. He spoke a day ahead of the appearance of the nominee.

"The Republican party of Georgia," he said, "cannot afford, and it must not be led by hatemongers like the Ku Kluxers, the John Birchites, the cast-offs and has-beens of the Democratic party."

Snodgrass, who had been national committeeman, and who was in charge of the radio and television operations at San Francisco, continued, "The GOP platform committee was completely dominated and controlled by the Goldwater forces. Normally in writing a party platform, there is a process of giving and taking. Never before in the history of the Republican party had there been such absolute discipline of delegates dedicated and pledged to a particular candidate. The Goldwater forces refused to give on any points."

Snodgrass further said, "All serious-thinking people agree that Georgia will be better served as and when there is a real two-party system. However, can the Republican party be built on a sound, firm foundation that is good for all the people of Georgia if this growth is built on hate?"

The Rotarians gave him sustained applause at the end of his speech and also interrupted him with applause after the "hatemongers" statement.

What happened in Georgia was, in its basic essentials, reproduced in other Southern states as the Goldwater forces culminated a quiet, dogged organizational drive that began in 1960 and gave them control of the Southern GOP machinery. Exclusion of the Negro was perhaps inevitable. Most of those who led the takeover were segregationist, states' rights minded, and were emotionally fired by opposition to the Court's rulings. Some were former Democrats who had joined the Dixiecrat movement that nominated Strom Thurmond after a walkout from their 1948 convention.[361]

In 1952 the Southern Negro vote went largely for General Eisenhower. In 1956 an even greater majority went along with Mr. Eisenhower. In Georgia and other states the party organizations were integrated. In 1960 Senator Goldwater made some speeches in the South. He recommended in Georgia, for example, that the party not try too hard to win the Negro vote since it was basically Democratic. (This was contrary to the results of 1952 and 1956.) The senator also spoke warmly of states' rights. An alarmed state GOP sought to counter this. They might have succeeded but for the 1960 incident of the arrest of the Reverend Martin Luther King and his imprisonment on a traffic charge. Nominee Richard Nixon was asked to protest. Republicans from Mississippi, Alabama, and other Southern states urged that there be no protest lest it cost them their states. While the national GOP headquarters debated and delayed, Nominee John F. Kennedy acted. In the 1960 election the majorities that had gone to Mr. Eisenhower turned to Mr. Kennedy.

This is the background. No matter whether Senator Goldwater wins or loses, it will be a long time before the racist prejudice and hates are rooted out of the Southern Goldwater Republican leadership. Indeed, there already is talk in some of the Southern baronies that if defeat is the senator's fate, the thing to do is to make the senator chairman of a national organization of all such baronies to work and plan for 1968. Only a really smashing defeat will prevent such a national organization under Senator Goldwater, or someone else should he refuse the post. The baronies of Kluxers, Birch types, suburban country-club freedom fighters, and those who would end-the-income-tax and get out of the United Nations and foreign-aid business will not simply go away. They have no commitment to Republican principles, even those in the platform. A tremendous victory by President Johnson will slow them down. But even so, "Real Republicans" will find it difficult to take away what the Goldwater Republicans have captured.[362]

---

[361]See Emile Bertrand Ader, *The Dixiecrat Movement: Its Role in Third Party Politics* (Washington DC: Public Affairs Press, 1955).

[362]See more on Goldwater in McGill's "Church in a Social Revolution," "Case for the Southern Progressive," and "Interview concerning John F. Kennedy," in volume 2.

76

From Boyhood Onward, the Course Was against the Tide: Review of Frank E. Smith's *A Congressman from Mississippi*

On a July day in 1926, in the Mississippi Delta county of Leflore, Frank Smith, Jr., an eight-year-old boy, was alone at home. His mother had been summoned to Greenwood where her deputy-sheriff husband was dying of gunshot wounds inflicted senselessly by an escaped Negro convict. A half hour later a carload of men pulled up before the home.

"Where are Frank's guns?" two of the men shouted as they came on the porch. "We're going out to help get the nigger that shot your daddy, and we haven't got a gun for everybody in the car." The small boy knew them vaguely as distant cousins. He showed them his father's guns, which they claimed, and departed.

There was no lynching. Before the father died he exacted a pledge against such action from the sheriff. "I've been a deputy trying to en-

Reprinted by permission of Mrs. Ralph McGill and the *New York Times*, 11 October 1964. Copyright 1964, by the New York Times Company. An earlier draft of this review is in the McGill papers, now at Emory University, Atlanta. Review of Frank E. Smith, *A Congressman From Mississippi: An Autobiography* (New York: Pantheon Books, 1964). See also, Smith, *Look Away From Dixie* (Baton Rouge: Louisiana State University Press, 1965).

force the law too long for us not to enforce it now," he said. The widow also urged against the very commonplace act of lynching. There was none.

Several years later Frank Smith was on the courthouse lawn on a Saturday morning. A large crowd was there discussing the capture of two Negro men accused of murder. There were then prisoners in the jail. Young Smith was attracted to a circle about his Sunday school teacher, a wealthy farmer and businessman. The old man doted on teaching, and the boys liked him because on Sundays he always gave out nickels to the boys who had best memorized the Scripture lesson for the day and who were keenest in their answers to the list of questions for the day in the Sunday school lesson book.

As the young boy worked his way into the crowd to hear what his Sunday school teacher was advising, he heard him say loudly and urgently: "They have no business locking those black sonsofbitches up and keeping 'em out of our hands. Stringing them up right now would be the cheapest and easiest way to handle this."

Frank E. Smith, whose autobiography discusses a Mississippi Delta boyhood, schooling, and twelve years in the Congress of the United States, demonstrates the truth of what psychologists tell us—that every man takes his childhood along with him. Smith had learned from his father and family that lynching was wrong. He knew other peace officers believed it right. He heard his Sunday school teacher urge a double lynching as being "cheaper" and "easier" than the processes of law.

Young Smith was subjected daily to contradictions. At no time did he ever hear in a Christian church a sermon or a discussion on race relations.[363] Out of a gradual accumulation of influences he wound up with an attitude different from that of those with whom he had grown up. These latter persons recognized the same influences but preferred not to respond to them in the face of deeply ingrained community pressures for conformity.[364]

---

[363]See Samuel S. Hill, *Religion and the Solid South* (Nashville: Abingdon Press, 1972); Kenneth K. Bailey, *Southern White Protestantism in the Twentieth Century* (New York: Harper and Row, 1964).

[364]See Thomas H. Naylor and James Clotfelter, *Strategies for Change in the South* (Chapel Hill: University of North Carolina Press, 1975); Lewis M. Killian, *White Southerners* (New York: Random House, 1970).

In a revealing, honest book, Smith shows how, using the technique of survival, he managed to spend twelve useful years in Congress. He believed he might be able to make some contribution to the ending of discrimination and to the acceptance of law and court decisions. He worked hard at it, at times shamed by his own appeasements and compromises; but, he was never a [Theodore] Bilbo or an [James] Eastland. He managed to attract a respectable and surprisingly large and loyal support.

After the United States Supreme Court decision of 1954, he knew he was finished. He tried hard. He brought the young Jack Kennedy to speak in Mississippi, and the occasion was a triumph. But in the end, nothing was saved. His enemies gerrymandered his district. In a campaign filled with typical slanders, lies, and demagoguery, vulgar and shabby, the White Citizens' Councils and the yellow-eyed haters defeated him.[365] Even so, he made a good race of it, and there is evidence that there are those in his district who remember him and what he tried to do. Change now is coming to monolithic Mississippi.

Smith discovered something long apparent to those Southerners who have not closed their minds:

> Because race is the beginning and end of every issue in the deep South, the net effect of race politics is that the people of the South have disfranchised themselves. They make decisions on national and international issues on no other basis. . . . Few Southerners seem to recognize the irony of their own position: that to keep the Negro from having any political power, they have given up their own political power.

Frank Smith's book effectively complements James Silver's book, *Mississippi: The Closed Society*. Silver wrote out of twenty-nine years as a professor at the University of Mississippi.[366] Now comes Smith to reveal, in an excellent, painfully honest book, what the cost is in political

---

[365]See Neil R. McMillen, *The Citizens' Council* (Urbana: University of Illinois Press, 1971); James O. Eastland, *We've Reached Era of Judicial Tyranny* (Greenwood MS: Association of Citizens' Councils of Mississippi, 1955).

[366]James W. Silver, *Mississippi: The Closed Society*, enl. ed. (New York: Harcourt, Brace and World, 1966); see also Russell H. Barrett, *Integration at Ole Miss* (Chicago: Quadrangle Books, 1965).

integrity in state and national life. Both are sad books with touches of glory, courage, and purpose.

77

Equality on the Firing Line: Review of Anthony Lewis's *Portrait of a Decade: The Second American Revolution*

A nthony Lewis has done a superb portrait profile of the decade 1954-1964, interspersing his narrative with particularly apt excerpts from articles and news stories in the *New York Times*. It is all here, the warts, scars, and unhealed wounds; the grandeur and nobility of men and women who have worked to fulfill the meaning of the revolution. And here are the failure of leadership and the ugliness and ruthlessness of those who shouted, "Kill the niggers," the viciousness of those who detonated the dynamite that killed and maimed; and the awful portent of those who, though wearing uniforms of law-enforcement officers, brutally battered those who sought their civil rights.

Now and then, reading the pages of this book, one could, out of the author's words and those of the *Times*'s reporters, hear the mobs at Little Rock; at Anniston, Birmingham and Montgomery; at Oxford, Missis-

Reprinted by permission of Mrs. Ralph McGill and the *New York Times*, 25 October 1964. Copyright 1964, by The New York Times Company. McGill noted that this text was "written from galley proofs from which were missing a chapter on Alabama and maps." Review of Anthony Lewis and *New York Times*, *Portrait of a Decade: The Second American Revolution* (New York: Random House, 1964). An earlier draft of this review is in the McGill papers, now at Emory University, Atlanta.

sippi; and the shrieking cursing mothers at New Orleans when a school there was desegregated. But also there moves through these admirable pages the forward momentum of social and moral progress.

Courage is a major subject of this book. When historians review the ten years portrayed here, they may well decide that no purer example of courage was shown us than that of the small Negro children who daily walked through the fiery furnaces of mob hate to their places in classrooms. They were too young to understand, of course.

But they knew they were the central figures, the ones about whom the courts had decided and whom the troops or police guarded. So they went, and they endured it. There was the courage, too, of the sit-ins and the freedom riders, who were beaten and slugged, cursed and reviled, for quietly asking for service at a variety-store lunch counter or the snack bar of a bus depot. Yet within two years they had won a majority victory for human dignity and for American values.[367]

We can now better understand what it has meant to be a Negro—to know daily humiliation, open scorn, and rejection not merely as a citizen but as a person. This book, too, reveals how utterly without truth was the comfortable view so widespread in the South that the Negro was happy and liked things just as they were.[368] We see Sheriff Z. T. Mathews, of Terrell County, Georgia, appearing with two deputies at the Mount Olive Baptist Church at Sasser, where thirty-eight Negroes and two white persons were holding a voter-registration rally.

"I tell you, cap'n," he said to a reporter, "we're a little fed up with this registration business. . . . We want our colored people to go on living like they have for the last hundred years. . . ."

There was something almost wistful in his voice, reporters said. His world was changing, and suddenly neither badges nor guns seemed adequate. The church at Sasser was later burned, as were three others which had also been holding voter-registration meetings. All were rebuilt. The *Atlanta Constitution* organized a campaign for contributions. Organizations outside the South helped. The Trappist Monks, near

---

[367]See John Hope Franklin and Isidore Starr, eds., *The Negro in Twentieth-Century America: A Reader on the Struggle for Civil Rights* (New York: Vintage Books, 1967).

[368]For McGill's analysis of false Southern myths see the editor's introduction.

Conyers, Georgia, made stained-glass windows for all four churches, and a firm of architects in Atlanta contributed plans.

Unlike many books on the South, Mr. Lewis's is complete, the first in which are gathered all the features of the second American revolution—the law of it, the court decisions, the effect of those, the acceleration of voting, and, of course, superb reportorial insights into the riots and the efforts of Southern Negroes to exercise their rights.

Mr. Lewis's conclusion that the exercise of the franchise was, and is, a top objective is accurate. A voter-education project, financed by private philanthropy, began in 1963 and is clearly a success in the face of bitter and violent resistance. There are about five million Negroes of voting age in the South; in 1940 the total registered was perhaps ten percent; and as late as 1961 only about twenty-five percent. But by late summer of 1964 the total was up to more than two million—about forty percent.[369]

In the states where registration was widespread, brutal sheriffs became gentle, and civil rights came along fairly rapidly. But in Mississippi there was, and is, savage resistance in most of the state. The three young men who were murdered near Philadelphia, Mississippi, in early summer were there to teach adults to read, write, and qualify as voters. As this is written there have been eighteen bombings since April in McComb, Mississippi, one of the towns where defiance of rights laws is terroristic.

In nearby Natchez the homes of the mayor and a Negro worker in voter registration have been bombed. Certain parts of Alabama, Louisiana, and Georgia are almost equally defiant.[370]

There is in this book clear evidence that in those states where there has been leadership from the governors, the mayors, the public sector, there has been a minimum of trouble. Schools have peacefully begun to desegregate; restaurants, hotels, motels, and all places of public service

---

[369]See Jack Bass and Walter DeVries, *Transformation of Southern Politics: Social Change and the Political Consequence Since 1945* (New York: New American Library, 1977); Steven F. Lawson, *Black Ballots: Voting Rights in the South, 1944-1969* (New York: Columbia University Press, 1976).

[370]See Numan V. Bartley, *The Rise of Massive Resistance: Race and Politics in the South During the 1950's* (Baton Rouge: Louisiana State University Press, 1969).

and entertainment have with but few exceptions, accepted the public accommodations feature of the civil rights legislation. These cities have
learned that the fears and myths had no validity—provided they were
countered with truth and action. In those states where governors and
lesser officials have preached defiance, mobs have been encouraged, and
the public has been deceived into believing that the law does not have to
be obeyed.

Perhaps the most somber and important portion of Mr. Lewis's
book deals with this corruption of law. Such situations are dangerous;
this one needs and requires the support of bar associations, of civic
groups, and of all persons interested in this nation continuing as one of
law.

Americans understandably were shocked by the lawlessness and loot-
ings in the slum riots of the past summer. But these are not the long-
range danger to law that comes when mobs (or individuals) and sheriffs
and law-enforcement officers violate constitutional rights ruthlessly,
brutally—and remain outside the law. The record is a frightening one.
Grand juries do not always indict, and juries rarely convict, no matter
what the evidence. The Federal Bureau of Investigation, called when local law enforcement fails, is attacked by newspapers, public officials,
and defense attorneys as an agent of "the enemy" in Washington.

It is one of the ironies of the bitter reaction to civil rights measures
in some areas that the breakdown of local law and government is complete, or almost so. And yet, the complaint from such locales against the
federal government is that it interferes with local government. The brazen, cynical disregard of federal law in a handful of defiant states is a
present danger that threatens every lawyer, court and, finally, our whole
concept of government by law.

Overall, however, despite defiance, violence, and brutality the decade has seen substantial progress. That some 160-odd million white
Americans have so difficult a time doing what is morally and legally
right about the human rights of 20 million other Americans indicts us
all. Facing such things requires some faith. That quality too, is in this
book. It is a balanced portrait of a magnificent revolutionary decade.
Fearful though much of it is, it is one in which civilization and decency
have taken a long step. The revolution will continue and the next decade
is not far off. Mr. Lewis's book asks of us what we will make of that.

78

The Church
in a Social Revolution

S ince the United States Supreme Court decision of May 1954 declaring segregated schools to be unconstitutional and discriminatory per se, no Christian church has held a meeting in which the morality and immediacy of this undenied century of ugly discrimination did not intrude itself.[371]

By now this problem is as bloody and earth-stained as was poor Banquo's ghost or the oft-stabbed body of King Duncan. Who would have imagined there was so much blood in what could—and should—have been a relatively simple problem of giving equal citizenship rights to some 20,000,000 Americans? That a heavy majority of about 162,000,000 Americans, who own most of the property and productive means of the nation, are unable and unwilling to do what is morally and legally right—and long delayed—causes the bloody problem to sit at the banquet table at every church and business meeting and to enter into every home.

Reprinted from *Church and Race*, December 1964, by permission of Mrs. Ralph McGill and *Church and Race*. Formerly published by the Executive Council Episcopal Church.

[371]For more by McGill on religion and race see "Let's Lead Where We Lag," "Southern Moderates are Still There," "Interview on Race and the Church," and "Introduction to *God Wills Us Free*," in volumes 1 and 2.

That the Christian church, with a few notable exceptions, has been paralyzed or semiparalyzed by this decision of racial justice is perhaps the single most melancholy aspect of what has been called the moral decline of our time. Indeed, most of the pulpits from which one hears so much about sin and moral backsliding are segregated or almost so, and while admitting a Negro Christian to worship, shudder at the idea of admitting said visitor to communion or membership. No Dixie demagogue has been more loud or pietistic in protesting that things are moving too fast or that "we are not understood" than the average Christian church.[372]

In the recent national election one of the candidates made a great play to cash in on a white "blacklash vote." The U.S. Supreme Court was condemned. The Civil Rights Act was criticized. The Confederate flag flew, and the American flag was missing in such speeches in the Deep South. To be sure, not all those who voted for this candidate were segregationists or urgent advocates of white supremacy. Yet, the undenied facts are that it was antagonism toward civil rights that provided the majority for this candidate in the Deep South states of Mississippi, Alabama, South Carolina, Georgia, and Louisiana, where racist appeals had been made, where racist violence has been at its worst, and where Christian churches have been largely timid with tokenism or outrightly hostile and defiant in defense of the status quo.[373] In a number of Southern churches prayers were offered for the repeal of the Civil Rights Act and against the "godless" Supreme Court.

The recent St. Louis sessions of the Episcopal Church did not make all bishops or laymen happy. Indeed, many came away sad and discouraged. A reporter for the *New York Herald Tribune* said that it seemed that the delegates and bishops spent most of their time trying to keep the

---

[372]See Charles Reagan Wilson, *Baptized in Blood: The Religion of the Lost Cause, 1865-1920* (Athens: University of Georgia Press, 1980); Samuel S. Hill, *Religion and the Solid South* (Nashville: Abingdon Press, 1972); C. Dwight Dorough, *Bible Belt Mystique* (Philadelphia: Westminster Press, 1974); Kenneth K. Bailey, *Southern White Protestantism in the Twentieth Century* (New York: Harper & Row, 1964).

[373]The candidate was Senator Barry Goldwater, campaigning for president of the United States; see McGill's "From Atlanta—The Political Assessment," "Case for the Southern Progressive," and "An Interview Concerning John F. Kennedy" in volume 2.

world from coming in through the doors—but that the world persisted in entering.

That the world will keep coming in is inevitable.

The average church failed, too, in giving members or communicants perspective on the slum riots during the past summer. There was, from most pulpits, merely condemnation or demands for more law enforcement. Rare was the discussion of the massive social problem of slums, the relative absence of churches, the growth of urban America into what is perhaps the nation's number one problem. Joblessness, illiteracy, frustrations of spirit and body, lack of opportunity, squalor, and a daily offering of the plate of humiliation and discrimination to the average American Negro will not be solved by police or courts.

There has been progress in race relations in America. In some areas it is considerable. But it has been more than ten years since the first school decision. Measured against years, the progress is small. And save for a comparative handful of bishops, ministers, and church bodies, the Christian church has been merely a bit player in the greatest social revolution of our time. A decade passes, but still most doors are closed, and the cry is not for action but, "Don't go so fast—Give us time—You don't understand our problem."[374]

---

[374]In 1968, McGill was still speaking out against segregation in churches. In a manuscript prepared for Joyce Leviton's *Time* magazine article, "On Being a Contemporary Christian," 12 April 1968, he wrote:

In my opinion, being a contemporary Christian requires a reliance on a personal faith which rejects the irrelevancies, the clamorous and contradictory dogmas and attitudes of too much of today's established religion. In the South, which I know best, the church is still almost entirely segregated. The Evangelical sects are, by and large, aggressive in their determination to remain segregated. With the usual few exceptions, the church is timorously trying to explore how it may do something in the slums without really getting its hands dirty or its vestments soiled. It is, I feel, a time for believing and for commitment to greater ethical principles, but rare is the church that is helping the individual attain this.

Manuscript provided by Mrs. Ralph McGill from the McGill papers, now at Emory University, Atlanta. It was not used in the final version of Leviton's story.

79

Review
of Hubert Humphrey's
The Cause is Mankind

N ow and then there comes along a man who takes genuine plea-
sure in being in the midst of competitive ideas, of clamorous
controversy, of debate, and of the great contest of political
skills. U.S. Senator Hubert Humphrey is such a man. To be alive and
to go forth and meet with what each day brings is a delight to him. Being
alive and eager is a wondrous gift.

All of this comes through in the pages of Senator Humphrey's book,
The Cause is Mankind. He took the title, he writes, out of memory of
the late President Kennedy's frequent quotation of Tom Paine's words of
1776: "the cause of America is in great measure the cause of all mankind."[375] The book offers a liberal program for modern America.

This ebullient and believing man brought with him from the Da-
kota prairies where he was born, and from Minnesota where he was educated and where he taught political science and made an entry into
politics, a faith in America that has moved past rebuffs and disappointments to achieve important legislative advances and reforms.

Hubert Horatio Humphrey, *The Cause is Mankind* (New York: Praeger Publishers, 1964). Manuscript provided by Mrs. Ralph McGill from the McGill papers,
now at Emory University, Atlanta. McGill was a strong supporter of the Democratic
party. (The editor noted that Humphrey attended McGill's funeral in Atlanta.)

[375]See McGill's "Interview Concerning John F. Kennedy," in volume 2.

There are Southerners, for example, who do not like him because they say that in 1948 Senator Humphrey, but recently elected to the Senate, defeated the Southern-nominated platform committee by bringing the civil rights issue to the floor and winning enough votes to put an intelligent rights plank in the platform. The fact is—and all but the closed minds know it—that had the South and the nation moved then to implement that plank the agony of today's changes would have been avoided. The young senator said, on that turbulent night of 14 July 1948, that his proposal for a rights plank was made with no single region, no single class, no single racial or religious group in mind. Every citizen, he said, has a stake in the emergence of the United States as the leader of the free world.

"For us to play our part," he stated—with prophetic truth,

we must be in a morally sound position. . . . Our demands for democratic processes in other lands will be no more effective than the guarantees of those practices in our own country. . . . There are those who say we are rushing this issue of civil rights. I say we are 172 years too late. There are those who say the issue of civil rights is an infringement on states' rights. The time has arrived for the Democratic party to get out of the shadow of states' rights and walk forthrightly into the bright sunshine of human rights. People—human beings—this is the issue of the twentieth century.

The plank went in the platform. But many minds remained closed. The moral position in the South and the nation was not sound. Our leadership has suffered. Our domestic life has been eroded by tardiness in accepting that challenge of 1948. The closed minds who have remained hostile since 1948 ignore the great growth and valuable contributions of Senator Humphrey since that time. He has given important assistance to the legislative creation of the Peace Corps, the Arms Control and Disarmament Agency, the National Defense Education Act, the Humphrey-Durham Drug Act, equitable farm legislation, and, of course, to passage of the 1964 civil rights act sixteen years after the Humphrey plank of 1948.

The book reflects the spirit, the idea, and the will of the man who serves his time and generation well. The program for use of our human resources is certainly not socialism, although the more reactionary will so charge. American capitalism continues to flourish because the profit dollar has been given a social duty. The Humphrey program for meeting the challenge of agricultural abundance is practical and fascinating.

American agricultural production increasingly will become a factor in foreign policy. The less-developed world, the Senator notes, is carrying a double burden—a population growth twice that of the West with a much smaller per capita availability of land and water and their natural resources. The "man-land" ratio is out of balance.

The four chapters on the quality of life and the upgrading of national values find the senator at his idealistic, practical best. His success in merging the ideals and realism is one of his more valuable assets.

The senator sees a need for congressional reforms, including as a starter the streamlining of procedures.

Back of all he writes is an abiding faith in the future and in the concept and duty of American liberalism that has given us more freedom and more prosperity than we have ever known. It is a challenging book from a challenging man.[376]

---

[376]See Michael Amrine, *This is Humphrey: The Story of the Senator* (Garden City: Doubleday, 1960); Winthrop Griffith, *Humphrey: A Candid Biography* (New York: Morrow, 1945); Allan H. Ryskind, *Hubert: An Unauthorized Biography of the Vice-President* (New Rochelle: Arlington House, 1968).

80

Race:
Results instead of Reasons
Review of Howard Zinn's
SNCC: The New Abolitionists
and *The Southern Mystique*

Howard Zinn is a passionate idealist and partisan. A part of his strength is what his friends have called an almost philosophic determination to express what is best about those whom he admires and those who are on his side. This is an admirable quality, but it also lends itself at times in these books to sentimentalizing and romanticizing.

SNCC: The New Abolitionists is an excellent book for our time. As the author says, it is not a history of the Student Nonviolent Coordinating Committee (SNCC—which quickly came to be called "Snick"); instead it offers a glimpse of its members in action. Some of these young people were his students, and, besides joining their picket lines, he worked at getting a number of them out of jails.

This reviewer shares Mr. Zinn's admiration for the SNCC groups. Now and then they acted unwisely and ill-advisedly. At times they acted impulsively, without adequate information or preparation. But in the

Reprinted from *Saturday Review* (9 January 1965), by permission of Mrs. Ralph McGill and *Saturday Review.* Copyright 1965, by Saturday Review, Inc. Review of Howard Zinn, *SNCC: The New Abolitionists* (Boston: Beacon Press, 1964), and Howard Zinn, *The Southern Mystique* (New York: Alfred A. Knopf, 1964).

main they were magnificent in their courage, dedication, and commitment. Let no one minimize the grit required to go into the Southern towns where there was (and is) so much hate and venomous resistance. The early sit-ins and the subsequent freedom riders were productive of the most, and the quickest, changes on the Southern scene.[377] Neither courts nor processes of law could so well have dramatized the immorality and irrationality of the segregated lunch counters and dining rooms in variety stores, bus depots, and department stores. The writer knows firsthand the inspiration these groups gave to fathers, mothers, aunts, uncles, and grandparents in the rural South. In a sense, they were bringing to life the meaning of the U.S. Supreme Court decision. They worked in a field where there was no "law." There was then no public accommodations section of a civil rights act. The smell of jails and injustice, of brutality and ignorance is in Mr. Zinn's chapters on Mississippi, Alabama, and southwest Georgia.

It is, however, a little difficult to accept the author's conclusion that the federal government has been deliberately negligent in not using all its legal weapons. He generalizes too much. Certainly the Justice Department made errors; the story of Albany, Georgia, is perhaps the best example of that. But the basic frustration of the federal government has been that local juries all too frequently ignore evidence and refuse to convict those brought to trial, no matter how good the case. Indeed, grand juries have often refused to bring in indictments because of prejudice against "the government." It was necessary for Washington at all times to try to bring about local settlements and to encourage any persons who were working for progress.

SNCC has continued its efforts in the months since Mr. Zinn's "glimpse" was written. Volunteers in Mississippi provided a good chapter. Three gave their lives in Philadelphia [Mississippi], in what will remain one of the more sadistic, brutal murders of our history. McComb, Mississippi, as of this writing, has had some eighteen bombings, including one at the home of the white mayor of Natchez. But, because of the work of SNCC and the superb support of Dr. Martin Luther King, the NAACP, and others, a beginning has been made in school

---

[377]See John Hope Franklin and Isidore Starr, eds., *The Negro in Twentieth-Century America: A Reader on the Struggle for Civil Rights* (New York: Vintage Books, 1967).

desegregation in Mississippi.[378] The monolith of defiance has been cracked.

The Southern Mystique is a collection of essays previously published as magazine articles. The first, "Is the Southern White Unfathomable?" is a psychological analysis of racial prejudice. Mr. Zinn is quite right in saying that the mystique with which the South has so long surrounded itself is beginning to vanish. Certainly the thoughtful person must agree with the author's premise that the wise and productive procedure is to ignore "cause" as a general philosophical problem and concentrate on "result." Mr. Zinn suggests—and is, I believe, on sound ground—that there is really no mystery involved in the Southern attitude. We are learning that, while the Southerner cares about segregation, sometimes fanatically, in his hierarchy of desires there are things he cares about more: "monetary profit, political power, staying out of jail, the approval of one's peers, etc."

The essay "The Mysterious Negro," proves, of course, there is no such thing. Like all of us, the Negro is a product of the complex factors that make up what we too glibly call "an environment." No other American, for example, has had so much daily humiliation in his environment as the Negro.

Since Mr. Zinn wrote these two books the slum riots have come and, for a time, ceased. The FBI has, by presidential order, examined them and found no basis to suspect organized inspiration or direction. But the inflammable materials of slum, crime, ignorance, frustration, hopelessness, and humiliation remain. Unless we act as a nation, cooperating on the local level, there will be more riots.

---

[378]See McGill's essay on King in *Southern Encounters: Southerners of Note in Ralph McGill's South*, ed. Calvin M. Logue (Macon GA: Mercer University Press).

81

The Clearest Truth
is in Fiction:
Review of Jesse Hill Ford's
The Liberation
of Lord Byron Jones

W hen I had finished reading Jesse Hill Ford's novel *The Liberation of Lord Byron Jones*, I sat thinking for a long time. The characters were strongly alive and jostling in my mind; the mood and motion of their life in the town had created a sadness and an excitement. Lord Byron Jones was liberated—true enough. And so, in a sense, were Somerton's police force, Willie Joe, and Mr. Stanley. Steve and Nella Mundine had escaped but were not free. There was no liberation for anyone else in Somerton. Certainly not for Oman Hedgepath, whose whole life had been one of captivity, a captivity as complete as that which had enmeshed Lord Byron Jones. Nor had there been any liberation of the people of Somerton. The town might be any one of a hundred or so county seats I've seen in a lifetime of being a Southerner, spending forty-four years trying to understand and know

Reprinted from *Atlantic Monthly* 216 (August 1965), by permission of Mrs. Ralph McGill and *Atlantic Monthly*. Copyright 1965, by The Atlantic Monthly Company. Review of Jesse Hill Ford, *The Liberation of Lord Byron Jones* (Boston: Little, Brown Co., 1965).

the region of my birth and why I loved it and yet wanted to be liberated from its hold. I recalled the voice of a long-dead novelist friend saying, "It is a region you love as a mother loves a crippled child—you want the child to be made well, to be healthy and strong." It is that, but that is not all.

I sat thinking that I must have seen and talked with at least a dozen or more small-town policemen and deputy sheriffs who looked and talked and thought exactly like those Jesse Hill Ford had pictured in fiction. In the months and years of electric cattle prods, police dogs, beatings, shootings, of bodies found in rivers and fields, Willie Joe and Mr. Stanley were principals in the cast of characters in most of the civil rights dramas. Oman Hedgepath was there, too, not really wanting murder to be done, or men to be mutilated and slugged or denied justice and dignity, but rationalizing it if it was done.

The book revived questions frequently asked by visitors (and, God knows, by myself and friends), posed in countless letters and raised in seminars: "What does the white South really think, especially the white South of the old-plantation areas?" "What does the Negro think, specifically the Negro in the country towns where he is at the mercy of the cold-eyed sheriffs and the power structure that becomes brutally violent when it loses its balance of tolerant paternalism?"

Out of Jesse Hill Ford's magnificent novel comes reply. The deeper answers, I believe, are to be found not in biography, autobiography, news stories, or personal narrative. They may be found, paradoxically perhaps, in fiction—not just any fiction, but in writing such as Mr. Ford has set down in what is a superb and moving book.

The lives of white men and women and Negro men and women are closely mixed, yet widely separated, in Ford's fictitious setting of a Tennessee town called Somerton. The town's name doesn't matter. What matters is that there were, and are, so many Somertons, so many Oman Hedgepaths, so many Willie Joes and Mr. Stanleys; so many places where barbarous, senselessly cruel things and mocking injustices have for so long survived year after year. As the years came and went the Somertons acquired country clubs, paved streets, subdivisions, and traffic problems. But never was there any drive toward removing the degradation, the daily affront to the dignity of man, and the many denials that flowered out of segregation. The Negro residents of their towns could not vote, could not make use of public accommodations in the same manner as did other residents, could not send their children to the same school that other children attended but rather were compelled to send their children to neglected, inferior schools. There was never any civilized thrust to change this pattern in the many Somertons, never any common sharing of courtesy and justice, but always the stifling paternalism, the gulf of separation that denied experience in the meaning of PTA, of town meetings to discuss taxes or bonds, and of other routine experiences. Injustice was older than the most ancient graves in the cemetery. The sheriff, the deputies, and the courthouse were not persons or a place to which a "nigger" could go in search of justice. They were—and too often are today—"men" and a "thing" to fear.

The form of Mr. Ford's novel is not traditional. There is a plot, but it is not one in which there is a single protagonist on whom the action centers. Nor can it be said that Lord Byron Jones, Negro undertaker and a bewildered, decent, Victorian moralist who wants to divorce his wife (who is sleeping with Willie Joe Worth, one of the town policemen), and Oman Hedgepath, lawyer, whose young nephew-partner persuaded him to represent the undertaker, are the dominant characters. This is a novel which reveals what people think and why, and what they do and why. They are all part of an enormously simple story in which the lives of its characters are complex because man himself, wherever he is, is essentially complex.

Somerton is black and white, mixed yet separated. So are the thoughts mixed and separated.

There is the black man Mosby, who had left Somerton at the age of thirteen and had come back to see Mama Lavorn, of Lavorn's Look and See Café and Tourist. It was a bar and whorehouse where on Saturday night, the white folks said, a nigger could get drunk and have nigger fun. Mosby remembers how Mr. Stanley had beaten him as a boy a long time ago. He never had been able to forget it. Willie Joe Worth had a good, hardworking daddy. But he died. And there was no one to advise Willie Joe, who had been a pretty baby, but who was "weak." Steve Mundine, whose mother was Oman Hedgepath's greatly beloved sister, had come from San Francisco to Somerton after the war at Uncle Oman's suggestion to be Oman's law partner. As for Steve's wife, Nella, whose grandparents still live in Norway, the South puzzles and disturbs her. Her Steve "hangs in the balance between liberality of thought and conservatism of mood. The Confederate dead . . . seem to hang sus-

pended over him sometimes like the very mist on the mountains. Another day the air will be perfectly clear. . . . He is thinking. I love him."

T. K. Morehouse, the federal marshal from Memphis, Lavorn,
Willie Joe, Mr. Stanley, Mosby—they appear and reappear in the pattern of Somerton. The White Citizens' Council speaker comes. There
is "thinking" at the country club on Saturday night. . . . Mr. Templeton, the druggist, moves out his soda fountain. "You can't blame him
. . . the niggers would be usin' it. . . . "

The day the president was shot in Dallas, the first word was that he
was shot, but not killed. At Johnnie Price Bulkhalter's hardware store
they had it on television. The store filled up. "God," says the mayor.
"Anybody that would come that close and then botch it. I just don't
know. I'll bet twenty-five dollars he don't die!" Druggist Templeton had
tears in his eyes: "God bless the South," said Templeton. "If he dies, if
some Southerner has killed him. . . ."

Oman Hedgepath thought, "After the first shock began to wear off
I had a moment of tears, afraid he would die and afraid he wouldn't,
because no matter how counter your feelings and beliefs run towards
those of another man, no matter *how* you hate him, still you don't wish
him death. You might want him dead; but you don't wish him death
. . . not this way."

The town "thinks" about the divorce. Oman thinks. So does Willie
Joe. And Mr. Stanley. There can't really be a divorce, of course, because
it would "come out" that Emma, Lord Byron Jones's wife, was with
child by Willie Joe. That would "hurt" everybody: Willie Joe's kids, the
town, and would unnecessarily upset a lot of people; so, there couldn't
be a divorce. But both Emma and Lord Byron Jones wanted one, and
like damn fools insisted on one. So it was necessary, finally, to liberate
Lord Byron. Before, during, and after the "liberation" we know what
the Negro South thinks and what the white South thinks, not as they
think in the universities or colleges, in CORE or the NAACP, or in
"liberal" circles, but as they think in the Somertons of the South. We
had evidence of this "thinking" in Philadelphia, Mississippi, in Birmingham and Selma, Alabama, in Oxford, Mississippi, and in other
towns and cities. But it is best comprehended—and more logically in

perspective—in fiction such as Jesse Hill Ford has written so powerfully in *The Liberation of Lord Byron Jones*.[379]

---

[379]For McGill's perspective of the world as poet, see the editor's "Ralph McGill: Man of Fire and Poetry," in *Southern Encounters: Southerners of Note in Ralph McGill's South* (Macon GA: Mercer University Press, 1983).

One Magazine Invisible:
Review of *One Hundred Years of the "Nation"*:
A Centennial Anthology

I n a good many years of reading books and articles about the post-Civil War and Reconstruction South, I learned that one came frequently upon quotes from the *Nation* and references to it. That the *Nation*, founded in 1865, was keenly aware of the plight of the ex-slaves and was quick to expose the corrupt practices of promotional combines was evident from the many times historians of later years turned to its pages for illustration and interpretation of the passage of the swiftly moving feet of history. The sometimes naive—but consistent—idealism of the *Nation*'s editorialists also is a part of the record.

After the deal that made Rutherford B. Hayes president and ended Reconstruction, the Southern states proceeded to repudiate many of the bonds floated in questionable companies that were to have built railroads, established factories, and dug canals—and hadn't. When some of the Negroes still in legislatures voted with the "Redeemer Democrats" to repudiate the bonds, the *Nation*'s editor, E. L. Godkin, had doubts about the Negro's fitting himself into our system of government. But succeeding editors didn't.

Reprinted from *Book Week, Sunday New York Herald Tribune*, 12 September 1965, by permission of Mrs. Ralph McGill, *Book Week*, and The Washington Post Company. Review of Henry M. Christman, ed., *One Hundred Years of the "Nation": A Centennial Anthology* (New York: Macmillan, 1965).

Now comes the *Nation*'s centennial anthology. It takes one pleasantly and insistently by the hand and leads one through a really impressive and magnificent selection of contributors taken from the pages that cover one hundred years of uninterrupted publication. Many of the outstanding names of the century are here. They were attracted chiefly by the *Nation*'s idealism. Contributors always were paid, though the magazine has been self-sustaining only during the period from 1938 to 1942, and the checks were not large. But one could say what one wished, and that was payment not always easy to come by. Idealists still support the *Nation*, and it has entered its second century with confidence and courage.

One of the objectives laid down in the founding of the *Nation* was a reform of the daily press. If it has not entirely succeeded in this worthy aim, the magazine has been a good watchdog, and by crying out in some of the more complex wildernesses, has helped to encourage greater accuracy and less emotionalism. It also offered a blueprint of news coverage that was neglected at great cost.

In the original prospectus of July 1865, for example, there was recognition, plainly stated, that the condition of the South's "laboring classes"—that is, the freed slaves—was a matter of "vital interest to the nation at large," and the editors also declared necessary to the nation the removal of the "artificial distinction between them and the rest of the population," and "the securing to them, as far as education and justice can do it, of an equal chance in the race of life."

There was vision, too, in declaring that public attention must be fixed upon the political importance of popular education and the dangers which a system like ours runs in the neglect of it in any portion of our territory.

The *Nation* sought to interpret the progress made, or lack of it, and to educate the nation to conditions in the postwar South. John Richard Dennett, a young Harvard graduate, was sent southward to write dispatches. These forgotten and unknown articles were for the first time published in book form a few months before this centennial anthology appeared. One of Dennett's reports, written from Vicksburg, appears in the latter volume. Dennett had a good eye and an unusually fine ear that caught all the nuances of the Southern semantics. The conversations he reported from Mississippi in 1865 are now being repeated, almost verbatim, in Mississippi and other Southern states in 1965.[380]

The *Nation*'s centennial anthology is, in a sense, an indictment of the media of newspapers, radio, and television in that the riots and troubles of our time reveal how inadequately the people of this country have been educated about the racial developments and their meaning. Only the merest handful of newspapers reported and, more important, interpreted the great shift of uneducated and unskilled persons out of the rural South. The migrations began with the industrial job opportunities of the First World War. The boll weevil of the early 1920s greatly accelerated the out-migration. The Second World War provided a tremendous movement out of the Southeast. Almost nowhere do we find public leadership, newspapers, magazines, or other media analyzing the meaning of the shift of millions of people, most of them Negroes, off farms to the industrial cities. Nor has there been adequate interpretation of the ultimate dangers in piling up, in the slums of cities, the illiterate and unskilled human material capable of violent, spontaneous combustion.

The *Nation* itself did not have the capacity or circulation to do this job. But in 1865 its editors did have the vision of what needed to be done, and through the years the magazine has done what it could.

As editor Carey McWilliams suggests in his fine introduction to the anthology, a key to the remarkable consistency of "tone and quality" across the century is found in the continuity of certain family influences. Wendell Phillips Garrison had a major editorial responsibility for the magazine from 1865 until his death in 1907, first as literary editor, and, after 1881, as editor. Henry Villard, railway tycoon, who purchased the magazine in 1881 (he also owned the *New York Post*), was a brother-in-law of Garrison and father of the energetic and imaginative Oswald Garrison Villard, who was the *Nation*'s editor from 1918 until 1932. The Garrison-Villard connection prevailed from 1865 to 1932.

The *Nation*'s founders were young men, all intense idealists with commitments and beliefs. Abolition of slavery had been their major interest before the Civil War. Frederick Law Olmsted, one of the found-

---

[380]See John Richard Dennett, *South As It Is, 1865-1866*, ed. Henry M. Christman (New York: Viking Press, 1965).

ers, who had written the antebellum classic *The Cotton Kingdom*,[381] was
the eldest at forty-four. E. L. Godkin, an Anglo-Irish journalist, the
first editor, was thirty-four. Dennett was twenty-six. All had been interested in saving the Union and abolishing slavery.

Selection of the anthology's contents seems to have been done wisely
with an eye to giving a well-rounded view of the contents of one hundred
years. Dennett's article, "The South as It Was—Vicksburg, Mississippi," is the "oldest" contribution. Francis Parkman's "The Tale of the
Ripe Scholar" appeared in 1869. Henry James looked at Newport in
1870 and wrote of its beauty and its peculiar society, so different from
the less refined crowd at Saratoga. Frederick Olmsted, in 1871, showed
how good a reporter he was by writing of "Chicago in Distress."

Bernhard Berenson wrote in 1894 of "Dante's Visual Images," and
in 1896 of Botticelli's illustrations to "The Divine Comedy." Ernest
Newman enlightened his readers of 1910 with a brilliant essay on
"Strauss and His 'Elektra.' " Sinclair Lewis and Theodore Dreiser in
1923 wrote pleasant back articles on their native states, Minnesota and
Indiana, respectively. H. L. Mencken is there with his mercurial article
on H. L. Mencken, the critic. Chaim Weizmann's 1924 article on
"Zionism—Alive and Triumphant," is recommended for reading today
in a time when Israel is established amid a hostile Arab world.

Upton Sinclair, Ezra Pound, Bertrand Russell, Norman Thomas
wrote of their idealism and of human rights. Leon Trotsky, as a con-
tributor in 1936, discussed what seemed to him a "Revolutionary In-
terlude" in France. A young Andre Malraux wrote beautifully, even
ecstatically, of the high pitch of life fighting for the Spanish Loyalists
against Franco's Fascists. He titled it "Forging Man's Fate in Spain."

Sherwood Anderson, Katherine Anne Porter, and Bertolt Brecht
contributed short stores to the *Nation*. Reinhold Niebuhr's "Halfway to
What" is certainly one of the more penetrating political articles of the
Nation's century. Edmund Wilson's article on Gogol is another of the
higher-level contributions. There are many other names that illumine
the books as they did the years in which they wrote.

---

[381]Frederick Law Olmsted, *The Cotton Kingdom: A Traveller's Observations on Cotton and Slavery in the American Slave States*, 1861, ed. Arthur M. Schlesinger (New
York: A. A. Knopf, 1953).

Poetry is represented by Edwin Arlington Robinson, Robert Frost, William Butler Yeats, W. H. Auden, Robinson Jeffers, Robert Lowell, and others of distinguished quality. First in the list is Robinson's "Mr. Flood's Party," published in 1920. The reviewer recalls memorizing this poem out of the *Nation* in 1920 while at college, and at this late date, is able to recite it. Mr. Flood was the first to assert the painful fact that most things break, including hearts.

83

Introduction to Robert McNeill's *God Wills Us Free*

Observers of the Southern scene across the past quarter century, more especially the past decade, increasingly have noted what came to be designated as the "Agony of the Church." There is almost unanimous agreement that the church and the synagogue have, with a few notable and magnificent exceptions, almost totally failed to come to grips with the most demanding revolutionary, social, and moral problem of our time—the complex one of race. That this was more true of the Southern church, though not exclusively so, was made inevitable by the fact of population and history. A shockingly high percentage of Southern churches was to be found utterly committed to the past and blind not merely to the future but to the present. Even more dismaying was the fact that so large a number of churches were forced to reveal themselves as putting material commitments first. Those who received the fatter pledges were inevitably the most strongly committed to the status quo.

The agony, therefore, was not so much that of the church itself but of those more sensitive ministers and rabbis who sought to present the

Reprinted by permission of Hill and Wang, now a division of Farrar, Straus, and Giroux, Inc., and Mrs. Ralph McGill. Introduction by Ralph McGill from *God Wills Us Free: The Ordeal of a Southern Minister* by Robert McNeill. Copyright 1965, by Robert McNeill.

moral questions and the ethical principles involved, Christian and Judaic, in the nation's race problem. In early 1965, the record revealed that more than twenty-three young ministers had been forced out of Mississippi alone, in the preceding two years. In the same period, pulpits had been emptied in other states in the Deep South. But those ministers who perhaps suffered most were those who early began to try to be literal shepherds of their flock. Some ministers began trying to prepare their congregations well before the 17 May 1954 school decision by the Supreme Court. Others, heartened by this long overdue decision, felt that surely their congregations would understand that there was no escape from commitment and that the old ways were done. Almost all these pastors endured shattering experiences.

One of these was Robert B. McNeill. In retrospect, it seems to me that this gentle and sensitive man of equally quiet courage and conviction is perhaps the most revealing symbol of Christian pastoral example that I have seen in a lifetime of looking at the Southern scene. He was, so to speak, born and bred in the briar patch. He was a typical white Southerner of tradition, descendant of the Scotch-Irish who spilled through the tortured Appalachian passes into what was to become the cotton South. Intelligent, well educated, stubbornly committed to the principles of his faith, he had attracted attention by his superior performance in small churches. He was called to a large church in the prosperous city of Columbus, Georgia, on the banks of the Chattahoochee River where the descending rapids have for many years turned wheels of commerce. There he spent seven increasingly useful years.

It is almost incredible, in the light of what change has wrought in the Southern scene since the years of 1959, that Robert McNeill was dismissed from his pulpit for the mildest of pleas—that the Southern problem of race be viewed in the light of Christian principles and Christian doctrine. Yet, it did happen. There was, indeed, a sort of crucifixion. There had been weeks of gossip, of abusive, even filthy, phone calls to his family; there had been the coolness of the members of his civic club, the hostility of some of the church members and the determined planning of some of the more influential ones to drive him from the pulpit. Even then it was an incredible action. Time has made it a preposterous one. Many members of that congregation insist that a sense of guilt remains in the church, haunting it as a faithful ghost.

McNeill's travail was just beginning. Shortly after his dismissal he was felled with a severe heart attack. Faithful members of his congregation maintained a vigil at his hospital door, greeting callers, taking messages, and giving word of his condition. The Bream Memorial Presbyterian Church in Charleston, West Virginia, had called him before his illness struck. When he recovered he went there. Slowly but surely Robert McNeill, with his gentle strength of character and commitment, and his fine wife and children have made a substantial place for themselves in that community.

Now he has written a book. It is, without question, a moving and revealing narrative of a man's life, defeats, victories, trials, and triumphs. It is autobiographical, but the reader will understand, as he reads it, that he is reading much more than the details of a dedicated minister's life in times of great disruptive social and political change in the Southern states and in the nation. There is something in this book of Everyman. There is much of Robert McNeill's soul and much about the mystique of the South's commitment to its past. The writing and the style are excellent.

Today, after little more than ten years have passed since the first of the court decisions, it is plain that if the Christian churches and the synagogues had moved into a position of quiet leadership, much of the violence, hate, fear, physical assaults, and murders that have strained so many areas in the South might well have been avoided. Robert McNeill is one of the several magnificent exceptions of men who tried to provide that leadership. Almost every one of these men suffered. What it has meant to live through these years in the role of a Christian minister is here told in eloquent simplicity, compassion, and commitment. This is a book which merits wide readership.[382]

---

[382]See Samuel S. Hill, *Religion and the Solid South* (Nashville: Abingdon Press, 1972); and McGill's "Let's Lead Where We Lag," "The Agony of the Southern Minister," "The Church in a Social Revolution," and "Interview on Race and Church," in volumes 1 and 2.

84

Statement
for Brotherhood Week

B rotherhood Week always has appealed to me as being one of those helpful products to conscience and to principle. Man's long search for the deeper meaning contained in the phrase *Brotherhood Week* has, of course, not met with success. Sometimes there is scoffing at the holding of an annual Brotherhood Week. The critics remind us that there are fifty-one other weeks in the year. They say that this week devoted to meetings, speeches, and resolutions is simply conjecture and that it has very little meaning. I do not agree.

Certainly we are not going to attain brotherhood this year or next. We perhaps never shall fully attain it. But I do submit that Brotherhood Week has very real value and that it has been, and is, one of the many mechanisms which have helped us make progress in the whole area of human relationships. We find those who deplore a decline in morality,

Statement prepared for National Conference of Christians and Jews, Ottumwa, Iowa. Reprinted by permission of Mrs. McGill and The National Conference of Christians and Jews, Inc. Manuscript provided by Mrs. McGill from the McGill papers, now at Emory University, Atlanta. The National Conference could find no record concerning the date of this statement.

an increase in violence, hatreds, et cetera. These are old complaints unchanged through the centuries.

Our tremendous population growth has skyrocketed all of our emotions and statistics. The sprawling suburbs, the decline of our central cities as living areas, the increasing dependence of man on an industrial society, which through automation and technology requires skills and educations heretofore unnecessary in the general labor market, have contributed to a widening of all of our stimulating statistics. (Something over thirty-one million Americans now work for a little more than seven thousand corporations.)

I strongly submit that despite evidence to the contrary, we are making progress. I do not think the civil rights legislation so long delayed would have been passed without the continuing activities of organizations such as that of the National Conference of Christians and Jews and the many others that have worked in this area. I do not think our national and local governments would be so concerned with human relations had it not been for all that is wrapped up in the meaning of Brotherhood Week.

So I hope that all concerned will not weary of the job of maintaining an interest in Brotherhood Week. It is one of the very important tools which we may use to do what is necessary in helping man with the problem of himself.

85

An Interview
concerning John F. Kennedy

C   *harles T. Morrissey:* Let me start by asking when you first met
John Kennedy.

McGill: I remember very well when I first met John Kennedy,
that is, to have a talk with him. I had been introduced to him before he
became a senator. In April, after he had become a member of the Senate
in January, Lawrence Winship, editor of the *Boston Globe*, was in Washington and had a small luncheon in a hotel suite to which he invited Senator Kennedy and Senator [Leverett] Saltonstall. This was at the time
when a great many of the Southern states were, as they still are doing,
unhappily, offering all sorts of exaggerated inducements to New England textile mills to move South. They were offering tax-free years;
they were building factory plants and offering them rent-free for the
first year, small rent the second year, and so on. These and other
inducements.

Senator Kennedy had spoken in the Senate against these because his
constituents were alarmed; they were losing jobs. Some of the cities and
towns were suffering. I remember that Lawrence Winship, editor of the
Globe, interjected to say that he thought this was good, and I remember

Oral History Interview with Ralph McGill, 6 January 1966, Atlanta, Georgia,
by Charles T. Morrissey, for the John F. Kennedy Library. Reprinted by permission
of Mrs. Ralph McGill and The John F. Kennedy Library.

him saying, "Ralph, you will never see an editorial in the *Globe* deploring the movement of a textile mill out of New England. For the most part," he said, "they're no damn good. They pay low wages. They try to bring everything in their cities down to the lowest common denominator. And the long net effect is that they are bad for the community—any community. You will rue the day you get them," he said. This, I remember, struck Senator Kennedy as a new idea, and we talked on at some length about that. I do know that he quieted down on his public utterances, and later on I talked with him about this—it must have been three or four years later—and he said that he did then begin to talk with other persons.

This was, I think, some of the motivation that led to New England letting the textile mills go without too much complaint and beginning a movement to being in industries which would take advantage of the great skills that were there in the labor force. So when he talked about that later, Senator Kennedy remembered that little point as having influenced him. We could already then begin to see that the South was suffering, and certainly it's true today. A great many of the smaller mills with old machinery which moved into our region in the South already have folded up, gone out of business, unable to compete. This is one little item of no real interest, but I find myself thinking of it as I look at our textile industry.

Then I remember a very personal thing. In December, a few days before Christmas, 1960, after Senator Kennedy had become President-elect Kennedy, my wife and son and I started for Key West, Florida. My wife was then quite ill, but able to ride in a car and walk a little bit. Actually, she had, as it turned out, just about a year to live.[383] I wanted to surprise her, and the evening before we would reach Palm Beach the next day, I telephoned a friend of mine, a reporter, [William H.] Bill Lawrence, then of the *New York Times*. And he set up for me a little surprise for my wife and son, but especially for my wife. The next day, at the appointed time, I told her that we would drive by and see where the Kennedys were living. Well, we stopped there and went in. He was out

---

[383]McGill married Mary Elizabeth Leonard on 4 September 1929; she died on 21 March 1962. Their son was Ralph, Jr. On 20 April 1967, McGill married Mary Lynn Morgan.

in the lawn, behind the wall which was around the garden of his home. We went in, and he was very kind and showed my wife about, and we talked there. Then he told me after a nice visit of some thirty or forty minutes that his brother Robert [Robert F. Kennedy] would like to see me. The president-elect and I talked for a few minutes about his ideas about the civil rights legislation and plans. He wanted to ask a few questions about some of the Southern states, some of the Southern leaders. We went from there over to see Robert Kennedy, then already named to the cabinet as attorney general, and had possibly an hour's talk with him. I will always remember with appreciation his great kindness to my sick wife.

I think the next thing I remember that might be of some interest is in January of 1963, I went for the State Department on a tour of some of the West African states. This included Senegal, Guinea, Ghana, Togo, Dahomey, Nigeria, and the Congo.[384] At all these places I made talks at the universities, a number of talks—three or four—because student groups had a number of various political organizations and political clubs and sometimes journalism classes. I also talked to some of the groups of teachers and journalists—always to journalists and to students.

So when I came back from this trip, which was one of a little more than two months, I was asked by the president to come by and sort of go over the trip with him. This I did, and I answered questions he had about Nkrumah, Kwame Nkrumah of Ghana. I had the good luck to have a long, forty-five-minute talk with President, or Premier, Kwame Nkrumah, and he is a puzzling man, as he is to this day, and certainly no friend of this country. I had tried to probe into that because Nkrumah had spent a number of years in the United States, had gone to Lincoln University, and had spent a total of almost twelve years, as I recall, in the United States. Much of this had been an embittering experience. He told me at one time of being desperate, broke, out of money, and sleeping on park benches. But he would not, curiously enough, be drawn into any discussion of his racial views. I thought then—and still think—that this was because at that time he had had a shock in that some of his students in Moscow had been physically attacked and had suffered beatings, including some head wounds that had to be bandaged. And, indeed,

---

[384]See "Television Interview about Africa" in volume 2.

some of these had arrived in Ghana while I was there. I've had the feeling that this led to a turn by Nkrumah toward the Chinese. Well, all of this and more I tried to relate to the president.

Then, what might be of some interest to the future is he was at that time troubled with civil rights legislation and with other domestic legislation. And the talk turned to Senator Richard B. Russell of Georgia, then, as now, one of the more influential members of the Senate, and a man who had, as the president noted, rendered very great service to the country in a number of hearings, handling them very well so that they did not get out of hand and embarrass the nation. Particularly, I recall, he mentioned, and we talked about, the hearings when General Douglas MacArthur had been removed from command by President [Harry S.] Truman. General MacArthur then made his historic, dramatic, "old soldiers never die; they just fade away" speech before the joint session of the Congress and so on. We talked at some length about the great assets and great contributions by Senator Russell.

Then I remember the president said, "I admire Dick Russell very much, and I wonder if you could explain to me a man like him. The Southerners, the really able Southerners that I've met in the Senate and in the Congress, have been extraordinarily gifted men in parliamentary matters. The good ones seem to have a grasp of government and how to carry out the political maneuvers quite beyond that of the able men of other regions." And he said, "I suppose that the South has always had a lot of politics and been interested in politics, although," and he grinned and smiled, "we could not exclude New England from that interest." [Laughter] "And perhaps the Eastern states. So, that can't be the answer. But," he said, "I don't know any person that puzzles me more than Senator Russell. Here's a man of great gifts and great capacity for friendships and loyalties. The whole world is changing, and the whole nation is changing. And yet this gifted man remains adamant and defiant in the matters of any measures which tend to enter the field of race—civil rights."

And he talked of how Senator Russell of course had great power and how for many reasons he did not want to have any open break with him. One, for the very practical reason that it would be bad politics and would make no sense and would divert the attention given the bill—civil rights bill—and one or two other pieces of legislation that Senator Russell was quietly holding back. "But," he said, "for the other reason, it just would make no sense to do this, and I wouldn't want to do it because I like Dick Russell." I remember he was sitting in a rocking chair and he kept rocking as he talked, rocking gently, and there was a look of puzzlement and concern on his face. Then he said, "I sometimes wonder if Dick ever looks to the future in this."

And he noted that Senator [Herman E.] Talmadge, also from Georgia, the junior senator, had taken a much more realistic view. He said he didn't know whether Senator Talmadge had changed any of his opinions, but Senator Talmadge knew realistically that it was no longer possible to deny the qualified Negro the vote, to have jobs, to participate equally in all of the gifts of our Constitution and citizenship in a pluralistic society. And Senator Russell, on the other hand, was quietly adamant.[385]

Also, it seemed to disturb President Kennedy as we sat chatting there—it was rather late; about 6:30 one evening—he wondered about Senator Russell because he had heard that Senator Russell was more and more withdrawing and that Senator Russell's friends were concerned that he was becoming lonely, that he was not well, that he tended to withdraw more and more from contact with fellow senators. It was obvious he had a real respect and affection for Senator Russell, but he felt kept at a distance. This is how I felt about it: Here was a president confronted with a very formidable adversary who was really holding up civil rights legislation, making it impossible to go along with it, and yet, it seemed to me that the president's concern for the moment was equally that for a human being whom he thought was a man of great gifts and potential who had yet found it in his mind to carry on what really seemed to be a petty, personal . . . oh, what shall we say? Not a vindictive feeling because I don't think the president felt there was any of that in it. But he wondered why a man of such gifts would have this sort of attitude when all the world was changing, when his own state was changing, when his fellow senator was changing. And it puzzled him to find this in a human being.

---

[385]See McGill on Russell, Talmadge, and civil rights, in *Ralph McGill: Editor and Publisher*, ed. Calvin McLeod Logue, 2 vols. (Durham: Moore Publishing Company, 1969) 1:193-204.

I remember thinking as I sat there, "This is an odd thing. Here is a troubled president, an overworked president, and he's sitting there rocking with this look of concern, or mingled concern and wonder on his face." And it became more or less a sort of philosophical discussion about man, man alone—sort of an existentialist thing about the absurdity of man at times. I will always remember this conversation which went on about twenty minutes. It began about, "If I knew why Senator Russell took such an adamant position . . ." And then he went on, and it quickly became the concern of a man for another.

This is, I think, my major personal memory—sitting there, the two of us, in his office. We had talked about the African trip, and he had asked a good many questions, chiefly about Nkrumah, as I said, because Nkrumah then, as now, has got his hand in all the subversions and intrigue that's going on in Africa, and was turning even more toward the Chinese. But we got away from that, and it came down to a talk of a senator who was in opposition and then a senator as a man and a human being. We went into this for some time—a sort of philosophical talk, discussion. At any rate, this I find one of my chief memories. I suppose that is about all that I have.

I have many other memories of brief talks on the campaign tour—moments of him. I remember one of the funniest ones we ever saw. We were all amused, and so was he, and pleased by the great fervor aroused. And we used to tease him a bit about how the ladies of all ages seemed to be so pleased. I remember we were in Ohio coming, as I recall, from Springfield, Ohio, back toward Dayton, and we were coming along an expressway or freeway. And as we approached an overpass bridge, it was thronged with people, and not only that, but they had climbed out, and they were seated on the grassy slopes all along the approaches to the bridge. And there was one middle-aged woman, I remember, seated there on the bank. She had rather ample hips which were revealed in pretty tight-fitting black slacks. And she had a gay blouse on and a black poodle. As the car went by, the president waving, in a sort of ecstasy she picked up this poodle and kissed it. And we teased the candidate that night—not then president—we teased him and asked him to explain the symbolism of this kiss. [Laughter] Well, a lot of things like that, but they don't belong in something like this. . . .

Morrissey: We would be interested in your other impressions of the campaign.

McGill: Impressions of the campaign. I do remember another time, after the campaign, and we talked about it. I'm sure that this is something that many persons have said who had this from him. Obviously, everyone will talk about the debates with Mr. [Richard M.] Nixon. And he talked about this, the debates. But he did say—and this maybe he didn't say—that he himself felt, after the debates, not any great surge of confidence that he was going to win necessarily, but he did feel a surge of confidence that he could cope with the whole campaign; that after these debates, nothing else would be any more difficult than they; that they were a sort of combined, contained encounter, as they literally were. They were in a private room with only one or two hidden technicians about, but millions of persons were looking on. But after the great tenseness, concentration necessary for these, he felt confident, he said, that out in the open then and seeing the audiences or the crowds face to face wouldn't be as difficult as that, and it would be easier because he felt that they had a sort of understanding of him and a rapport with him because of these debates. I'm sure that this is nothing new.

Then I had a talk with him once—that is of no great meaning—about the campaign. I said that I had all my life, since as a youngster I had gotten interested in Woodrow Wilson, been a real card-playing Democrat but that in the 1956 campaign, especially, while I was strongly for Adlai Stevenson, I had nonetheless developed a sort of liking for Richard Nixon, and I had tried very hard to understand him.[386] And I told him of an incident at that time. President [Dwight D.] Eisenhower early in that campaign, you will recall, was ill, not well. And for the first weeks of it, and indeed, for most of that campaign, Vice-President Nixon was carrying the major load.

I remembered and told the president about a talk I had had with Mr. Nixon. I'd had a private breakfast with him on his plane. The back part of the plane was curtained off, and we were making an early morning flight from El Paso into California—Sacramento, as I recall. And Mr. Nixon asked me to have breakfast with him in his curtained-off back quarter of the plane. He talked then very strongly about the Republican

---

[386]See McGill on Wilson in *Southern Encounters: Southerners of Note in Ralph McGill's South,* ed. Calvin M. Logue (Macon GA: Mercer University Press, 1983).

party: How he felt it had not gone after young people, young voters; how he felt that during the depression years, the leadership of the Republican party had been so unaware politically of the meaning of the depression that they had permitted the party to become what seemed to the nation simply a force which was opposing all of the reforms of the New Deal. And it was easy to translate this opposition, he thought, into the image of a party which didn't really care about people, which was a party only of wealth and of privilege and big business. He thought it was necessary to have a sort of rebirth in a great struggle to recreate the Republican party into a new image.

Well, I expanded a little bit on some more of these. And the president expressed also a respect for Mr. Nixon, but he agreed with me that he was a puzzling, complex man who was difficult to know and difficult to follow. I ventured the thought that perhaps Mr. Nixon, along with Mr. [Arthur] Larson and others, might have been responsible—that Mr. Nixon might have been one of those really responsible for the 1956 Modern Republicanism idea which was proclaimed at the Republican Convention that year. And the president thought this was certainly a possibility.

Looking back on it now from these days of the John Birch Society and of the really frightening, to me at least, frightening overtones of the Goldwater Convention and the people who had taken over Senator [Barry M.] Goldwater, of the split that has come in the party and the efforts of the party now to shake itself loose from all that is symbolized by the John Birch state of mind, I sometimes find myself even more puzzled about Mr. Nixon because I recall that at that time he had spoken of the Californian concentration of these as kooks and nuts and so forth.[387] But at any rate, I always had this feeling of wanting to know Mr. Nixon better and a feeling that there was something in this man that was very valuable—could be very valuable. But neither he nor the times could break it out of the shell of the man. I think the president shared this. I judge so from what he said. . . .

Morrissey: Theodore White emphasizes in his book on the 1960 cam-

---

[387]See McGill on Goldwater in "The Case for the Southern Progressive," "From Atlanta—The Political Assessment," and "Church in a Social Revolution," in volume 2.

paign that when Richard Nixon early in that campaign received a very affirmative response here in Atlanta, this response caused Nixon to think in terms of carrying some traditionally Democratic states in the South.[388] Did you ever doubt in 1960 that Georgia would stay Democratic?

McGill: I had fears, maybe doubts. I knew that the racial angers were rising. I was fearful for the whole of the old cotton South because we are still largely rural and most of our rural areas are depressed, and they're losing population. And there is a sort of permanent resentment in the depressed and sort of dying out rural areas. Their county seats are poor; their shops are closed; their movies—many of them—are closed; their hotels are closed down. So I was frightened, but Mr. Nixon quite missed the boat. I never thought his Atlanta performance had any meaning much beyond Atlanta.

What had happened here was that the old Republican organization, which had been known as the Post Office Republicans, who got active every four years and the rest of the time they were hand-in-glove with the worst of the Democrats in the legislature and around the capitol and all this. . . . There was no real Republican organization in the South, but beginning in 1952 in a few of the states—and more notably in Georgia than others—a great many fine people had gone over to call themselves Eisenhower Republicans. And they did get control of the party and oust the old corrupt—they were really corrupt, most of them—corrupt crowd that had been in there just as a shadow skeleton organization. This new crowd set up statewide organization at considerable cost. I would imagine that these Eisenhower Republicans in Georgia must have spent a quarter of a million of their own money because the national organization didn't have the money, didn't have any faith in it, and didn't put it in here in any amount.

Well, this again—I'm coming up to one of the inexplicable things about Mr. Nixon—local Republicans worked very hard and very intelligently in preparing a great welcome for him. They put out a lot of money. They organized Young Republicans; they had them dressed in blazer coats and straw hats, the old boater-type straw hats. They put on

[388]Theodore H. White, *The Making of the President, 1960* (New York: Atheneum, 1961).

a tremendous parade; they had a great crowd—a beautiful day, a great crowd in a beautiful little park we had. There must have been twelve, fifteen thousand people standing. Well, a great day. And they took Mr. Nixon out to the airport.

The next day I had lunch with one of the chief architects of the new Republican party in the state and one of those three that had put on the big welcome. I never saw a man. . . . He was proud of the great demonstration, but he said, "You know, Mr. Nixon never said, 'Thank you,' or 'It was a great job,' or 'I really appreciate this,' to any of us. I had a lot of men there who wanted to like Mr. Nixon." Incidentally, I told this story to the president as we talked about the campaign there. So at any rate, there was no great fervor for Mr. Nixon in Georgia. He did get a substantial vote, but, of course, Mr. Eisenhower had also received a substantial vote in two previous campaigns. But the only thing, chiefly, that worried us was the Roman Catholic issue. But the president's superb performance before a group of Baptist ministers in Texas had rather dispelled any real chance of the worst of the demagogues in that area doing anything.

But do you know, it may well be—and the president was aware of this, too—that the campaign turned right here in Atlanta, the 1960 campaign. Martin Luther King, the great Negro leader who had risen from Montgomery but who had moved to Atlanta where he had been born and where he had gone to school and where his father was pastor of a large church—Martin Luther King had been arrested and put in jail by a judge from an adjoining county to Fulton, where Atlanta is located.[389] It was so obviously an act of prejudice and really a distortion of legal processes and judicial power that a great many persons were outraged, but no one did anything.

At that time our mayor was Mayor William B. Hartsfield, a fine man, as indeed is the present mayor.[390] Mayor Hartsfield was indignant about this. At that time, you will remember, no one really knew what the Negro vote would do. It had not really jelled. Mr. Nixon had quite an appeal for many of the Negro leaders. Mayor Hartsfield tried very hard to get in touch with then candidate John Kennedy. He couldn't

[389]See McGill on King, in McGill, *Southern Encounters*.

[390]See McGill on Hartsfield, in McGill, *Southern Encounters*.

reach him. He was out West somewhere, as I recall, and moving by plane. He tried then to get Robert Kennedy and couldn't get him. But he did get some people high up and said, "The candidate ought to say something." And he said, "I'm going to say it, anyhow. And I'm going to move to do what I can to get him released." And he also told him that he knew that the local Republican Negro leadership was interested in this, too, and he felt sure they were trying to get in touch with Mr. Nixon or President Eisenhower to get him to say something about this.

Well, finally, the truth of it is that something had to be done, and Mayor Hartsfield, made absolutely confident, one, that John Kennedy would want to say something if he could be gotten in touch with and have the matter explained to him, and, two, that he should say something and that time was of the essence, Mayor Hartsfield really, in effect, did a very daring thing. He sort of quoted, if you would examine into it. He brought Jack Kennedy's name in by saying he was disturbed by this—he had never been able to get him—that he was disturbed by this and wanted everything possible to be done to try to alleviate it. Well, it's interesting that two Negro leaders were at that moment also in touch with people in the Republican headquarters in Washington.

You asked about Atlanta and Nixon. This had led me into this because I think the two are related. Of course, when later on Mr. Kennedy did get word, he did react exactly as Mayor Hartsfield had predicted. The Negro people were justly aroused about this affront to Martin Luther King. So was I, and so were a lot of us. We were editorially denouncing it here. It was a very outrageous act. Wholly aside from the political thing, it was just an outrageous action by a judge, a small judge. Well, that night, you will recall, John Kennedy—candidate John Kennedy—telephoned Mrs. Martin Luther King, expressed his concern, asked her if there was anything he could do, and expressed the hope and the wish that the authorities would correct this injustice.

Well, I really think, seriously think, that the whole national election may have been decided right here in Georgia because that was a catalyst which precipitated the Negro vote in the large cities of the East for candidate Kennedy. And I think it ought to be remembered that up to then they were not committed. They had taken no position. But this forthright act, really done by the mayor of Atlanta—also, as I said facetiously, a card-carrying Democrat all his life—this had precipitated it. Now, the fact is that the Negro requests from Atlanta had received a sort of bureaucracy treatment; that is to say, it had reached the proper authorities early, whereas Mayor Hartsfield was never able to reach them. He just issued the statement himself, without any authority, as it if were coming from candidate Kennedy and from the Democratic headquarters.

The Republican headquarters had it early. And they debated about it, and they called up Southern leaders. This I know. This isn't surmise or hearsay; I know they called up. And President Eisenhower thought something should be said, but he didn't want to do it. He bowed to the advice of the National Committee. At that time [William P.] Rodgers of North Carolina was the attorney general. He thought something should be done. I know this because he later told me so. So this isn't any hearsay either. He even prepared a statement. All the while the great minds were meeting on this, and they finally said, "No. We've got a chance to carry Georgia and South Carolina. We must defend the white segregationist vote because we've got to have the segregationist vote to carry those states if we do carry them." So they telephoned around, and of course, then these Southern states—South Carolina—said, "No. Don't have anything to say in behalf of Martin Luther King." And so the great moment passed.

Now if you go back and look at it—the majority of sixty-odd thousand votes—I feel very, very strongly that this one little episode here in Atlanta, Georgia, probably was the pivot on which the election turned and was won. I know that later on Mr. Kennedy felt this to be possibly quite true because it did turn. . . .

Remember, Mr. Nixon for some time had gone out of his way to support civil rights—never precisely or in any positive legislation, but the general concept of civil rights he had supported and, I am sure, sincerely so. So there was a great feeling on this. Some of the Negro leadership in Atlanta was pretty strong for Mr. Nixon until this one little Martin Luther King story broke, and the candidate John Kennedy telephoned. But this all grew out of a pretty unusual decision by Mayor Hartsfield, a great friend of mine and—he won't mind my saying—a somewhat eccentric man.

Morrissey: Do you recall during the 1960 campaign if candidate Kennedy ever commented on the importance of carrying the Southeastern states?

McGill: Do you mean publicly, privately?

Morrissey: Privately to you. I'm thinking of the two Carolinas and Georgia.

McGill: No, he didn't just to me, but I do remember him commenting about it. Let me see. It seems to me that it was at the time of his journey into Ohio. I remember he spoke in Dayton, Ohio, and that James M. Cox, who is the president of the company which publishes the papers in Dayton and in Atlanta and the son of James M. Cox, who was the Democratic nominee for the presidency in 1920 when he had a young man named Franklin D. Roosevelt as his second man on the ticket, presided. Mr. Cox presided over this speaking. Later there was a little luncheon. As we sat around talking at this luncheon, we began to talk about the whole campaign. Mr. Kennedy, John Kennedy. . . . I remember him saying then that it was going to be a hard race and he felt maybe that the religious issue was going to hurt him, but it was very important, he knew, to carry some of the Southeastern states. He didn't know if he could win without it or not because he had already been told there in Dayton that Ohio was pivotal and doubtful, that it would be very difficult. Yes, I recall—I can't pin them down except this one in Dayton after this small luncheon. But there I do remember that he spoke about it.

And certainly at other times he did talk about the importance of the Southeast. And he was so pleased with the fact that the Baptist Ministers Association in Texas had asked him to talk with them. This had been broadcast, and he felt that he had done very well in this question and answer period, as indeed he had.

Morrissey: Was that film shown widely in Georgia?

McGill: No, not widely, but it was shown. It did have the effect of quieting the doubts of some very influential Baptists here in the state. So there was no religious opposition to speak of in Georgia. Some of the small-town, you know, idiots got into it, but not really.

Morrissey: Before I went to work for the Kennedy Library, I was working for the Truman Library. Of course, Mr. Truman is a good Baptist and a good Mason, and he campaigned in 1960 for John Kennedy.

McGill: Oh, yes.

Morrissey: Do you think he was effective here in Georgia on the religious issue?

McGill: No, except very indirectly. Mr. Truman didn't come into Georgia.

Morrissey: Oh, he didn't?

McGill: But the fact that he was campaigning was well known. You know, you have a curious dichotomy now that's been here all our lives. The South has always been a great prohibitionist area. That is to say, it makes more moonshine liquor than any other region—and drinks more—but it's always had this split personality imposed by the Protestant tradition, I suppose. There's always a tremendous opposition to drinking. You get some of our Protestant ministers greatly agitated about the sale of liquor. These same men have never opened their mouths about the greatest social problem of our time—the one of race, civil rights—but you open a liquor store somewhere, and you can get a great crowd of these people out.

These same people didn't like Mr. Truman because Mr. Truman was a whiskey-drinking, poker-playing man. The description that John L. Lewis once applied to old [John Nance] Jack Garner, that he was an "evil, whiskey-drinking, poker-playing . . ." A lot of our more extreme Baptist ministers, especially in the rural areas, including some in our city, had great doubts about Mr. Truman, so I don't know whether he was any help in this particular, specific area. [Laughter]

Morrissey: You told me about John Kennedy's ruminations about Senator Russell. Did he ever ruminate about Mr. Carl Vinson?

McGill: No, not to any great extent, except I remember that he did have an admiration for the "Admiral," as all the Navy people used to call Mr. Carl Vinson. He was such a rugged old veteran that I think nearly everyone had an admiration for him. But I never had the opportunity to hear him talk to any great extent. "You can always count on Carl Vinson," I remember him saying. Carl, the great old fellow, he had done a lot for the Navy; he had done a lot for this. But I don't remember to any great extent. But he had a great admiration for him, appreciation for him. He could always count on him, he felt. That was true: he could count on him.

Morrissey: Going back to that first meeting you had with John Kennedy in 1953 about the textile industry. Do you recall his viewpoint at that time about the movement of the textiles from New England to the South?

McGill: Yes, I think I do remember. He thought this was deplorable, and he had made one of two strongly critical public speeches about this Southern attitude of these communities that would just buy a mill in. They said, "Come on in. We won't charge you any taxes. We'll give you a building free for three years." He thought this was wrong, and it was wrong—some of this is still going on, incidentally—and he had been strongly critical of this on the floor of the Senate. But after this little set-to with Larry Winship of the *Boston Globe,* as I recall it, he slowed off on this. And this might be sort of a key, because if he had kept on with this, he would have built up an image of himself as an anti-Southern fellow. This he never did. Of course, there were others doing it at the time. He was not alone. But I've often thought this might have been one of those little unimportant things of the moment which had importance, greater importance for a period later on.

Morrissey: One of the interesting aspects about his race for the vice-presidential nomination in 1956 was that he got extensive support from the Southerners, and his opponent, of course, was the Senator from Tennessee [Estes Kefauver]. And this has usually been described as anti-Kefauver sentiment being expressed as pro-Kennedy sentiment.

McGill: Well, that's true.

Morrissey: It is?

McGill: Absolutely true. I remember being on the floor. Mississippians gave John Kennedy great support in that. I remember, I think it was the chairman of the Mississippi delegation I was with, and we asked him about this. "How come you fellows from Mississippi are supporting this New Englander?" And he said, as I recall—maybe it wasn't the chairman; I think it was—at any rate, the spokesman said, "Well, we'd be for anybody against that damned, nigger-loving Kefauver of Tennessee. He's too damn liberal to suit us." This was a queer thing. It simply illustrates how very little national attention had then been given John Kennedy. It illustrates, also, how quickly he came to national prominence after that. Of course, it helped, the fact that he almost got the nomination there. I think back in politics many times when it is the little things that have meaning later on.

Morrissey: Going back to that Palm Beach visit in 1960, I was wondering if that picture was taken there.

McGill: Yes. That picture there by my desk was taken there. You can see the president standing there. When we came in, he already had his coat off. You can see in the picture that he has the coat on his arm. He had been talking with two or three visiting senators who had come in there to talk with him. They were just leaving as we arrived—my wife, son, and I and Bill Lawrence, then of the *New York Times*. In the picture made by some photographers there who were taking pictures of the senators, you see that the president had just really met us—my wife. I knew him. And he met my son.

Later, we chatted there in the sun, just under the edge of a tree there by the corner of the house. He later escorted my wife, who then was so ill that she walked with some difficulty, around back of the house to the sea wall, looked out at the sea, showed her the gardens, took her into the house and then came back out. And she and my son sat and rested while the president, the president-nominate, and I talked, and Bill Lawrence was with us. That was when he told me that his brother wanted to see me. Lawrence drove my son and wife and me to another house where Robert Kennedy and his wife were talking. And I remember we sat around the swimming pool there. I'll always be very grateful, too, for how gracious Mrs. Ethel Kennedy was to my wife.

Morrissey: Do you recall at that time what Robert Kennedy's attitude was to civil rights legislation?

McGill: Yes, I do. He had it very much on his mind, and this was what he wanted to talk about. He wanted to ask what I thought the reaction would be in Georgia and the other neighboring states. He asked for the names of some people whom he might call on and see. He asked for people who might be willing to serve in this area.

There's another little thing that isn't a memory so much about John Kennedy. I happened to be in New York at the time they had a little advanced showing of the Kennedy Library material with all the pictures and photographs and writings and documents and so on. I went and was talking with Mrs. Kennedy, Mrs. Jacqueline Kennedy, and with Robert Kennedy. And I was saying to Robert Kennedy that I regretted that I couldn't get back by commercial plane the next day to the morning ceremony at Carrollton, Georgia, which is a city about fifty-two miles southwest of Atlanta where is located a branch college of the University of Georgia, West Georgia College, where they were going to dedicate the next day a chapel named the John F. Kennedy Interfaith Chapel. Robert Kennedy said, "Well, look. We're flying. I can't leave till tomorrow either, and we're flying down in the morning. Join us and come on down."

So I did this because I had really wanted to attend and there simply wasn't a flight that I could get that would enable me to get to Atlanta and get a car to get over to Carrollton. So I flew down. Mrs. Ethel Kennedy and the attorney general and two members of his staff. . . .

I remember the students were ecstatic. They gave him a great welcome. The townspeople turned out very well. Then we had a luncheon at the president's house. Card tables had been set up; there was fried chicken—a very nice luncheon. There was a little fellow who was a member of the Board of Trustees. I remember this old fellow, who didn't like the Kennedys at all and especially didn't like Robert Kennedy, was at one of these card tables with Mrs. Ethel Kennedy. She's a charmer, of course. After the thing was over, and they were gone, I stayed over.

Anyway, I was saying, Mrs. Ethel Kennedy was at the little card table with this crusty, old fellow who disliked the Kennedys intensely, especially Robert Kennedy. I stayed over. I went out to the airport and was among those who saw them off, going back to Washington. And I stayed over in Carrollton, spent the rest of the afternoon and had dinner that evening with some people. I just sort of wanted to pick up reaction.

Incidentally, the little chapel, beautiful chapel, previously had served as an Episcopal mission chapel and then later as a Catholic mission chapel and then was given and moved to the campus. It had been located in the town. It was moved to the campus to serve as a center for the chapel named for John F. Kennedy.

At any rate, after they had gone, the president of the college told me an amusing story about this crusty old man who had disliked the Kennedys, especially Robert Kennedy. "Well, I'll tell you this," he said in a grudging, reluctant voice. "Any fellow that girl Ethel would marry can't be as bad as I thought he was." [Laughter] He had fallen hard for Ethel Kennedy. Everyone does, of course.

Morrissey: Before I came down to Atlanta, I went through the index of the White House appointment books and noticed you are listed on six occasions as coming in to visit the president. The first was on March 1, 1961, with the President's Advisory Committee on Labor and Management Policy, and likewise with the second and third. The second was on July 11, 1962, and the third on May 1. Do you have any recollections of those meetings?

McGill: Well, yes. The president came into these meetings and talked with us. I don't know that the committee ever had any great accomplishment, but it is, or was, the only labor-management committee that had met more than once. [Laughter] A number of them had been appointed in past years. But we kept meeting, and we turned out. . . . Well, members of the board: Henry Ford of Ford Motors, Walter Reuther, George Meany, [Richard S., Jr.] Reynolds of Reynolds Metals—some of the top leaders—and five public members, of which I was one. We turned out a number of reports that went to the president and to the Congress and which were, I think, of some value, minor value. But the president was eager to have this committee because he felt that it brought these leaders together and made it necessary for them to have a meeting of minds and discuss these problems when they weren't involved in an actual labor case. And it had a great value.

I can remember Mr. Reynolds saying one day to Walter Reuther, "Well, you know, Walter, I never really thought I'd like you very much, but I do. I enjoy being with you, and I want to tell you that a speech I heard you make the other day (it wasn't on a labor subject) was one of the best things I ever heard." Well, you get little touches like that. Mr. [Thomas J., Jr.] Tom Watson of IBM was on.

It was up to the public members to preside sometime in committee meetings. I remember once a furious debate—I would rather not name the two principals. Two notable economists got into a shouting, finger-waving argument; this was a committee meeting, not the whole board. I was trying to preside, and I can remember these two distinguished figures leaning across the table shouting. [Laughter] Yes. It was interesting to see the president. He thought this committee was of some value. President Johnson has continued the committee, although for the past year we've had no meeting. But at any rate, it was interesting to see the president and hear him talk. Sometimes he would come in and talk a half hour to these committees.

Morrissey: Do you recall him talking about the steel-price increase?

McGill: No, I do not.

Morrissey: In the White House appointment books you're down for October 2, 1962, off-the-record, with the president.

McGill: October 2, 1962, off-the-record. Oh, that was . . . I think, as I recall, that was something about the congressional races down here, some of the Southern political things. And the civil rights. . . . The usual things that it has been my fate to have to talk about. As I recall, that was it.

Morrissey: Do you recall specifically what was bothering him?

McGill: He was interested chiefly in, as I recall it . . . I could look that up, but I'm sure he wanted simply an evaluation of what these very hostile governors were likely to do and what could be done to help the situation with a fellow like Ross Barnett, then in Mississippi, and with Alabama and so on. And we were doing pretty well here in Atlanta and fairly well in all of Georgia. And he wanted to know what we had done and could it be applied to elsewhere.

It couldn't. Here you have newspapers, and you have a mayor; you have a business community that has wanted to go along even though they might not all have liked it. But in these other communities you had the opposite. You had a governor and mayor and newspapers and business community that was adamant, defiant. This was the real tragedy of the situation—the real tragedy of the terrible riots at Oxford at the time of James Meredith when they had an actual attack on the U.S. marshals and troops later. A great pity.

Morrissey: The last two meetings I have you listed for were March 22 and April 9, 1963, both off-the-record.

McGill: Well, I should have been sort of looking up. I don't keep a diary or anything. What were the two dates again?

Morrissey: March 22 and April 9, 1963.

McGill: Oh. March 22 was the meeting I discussed earlier, the talk about the African trip, and that's when we got off on Senator Russell. April . . .

Morrissey: I think that might have had something to do, the April meeting, with the U.S. Arms Control General Advisory Commission.

McGill: Oh, yes. Yes, it did.

Morrissey: Were you a member of that committee?

McGill: I'm a member of that committee, also. I'm sure that was it.

Morrissey: Do you recall what was discussed?

McGill: I do, but that's still very much off-the-record. I mean the whole committee. It's high-level security.

Morrissey: Did you have any discussion with President Kennedy or high officials in his administration about the integration at the University of Georgia?

McGill: Yes. I recall that one of these meetings. . . . I talked with the president on the phone a few times. I certainly talked with Attorney General Kennedy about that integration at the University of Georgia. And, also, I can't recall where, but I do remember the President laughing as I told him how the integration came about.

In the beginning it was rather humorous. Everything was very quiet. Nothing was going to happen in Georgia. The legislature was going to convene on Monday at 10 o'clock. There had been several days of meetings, and Governor [S. Ernest] Vandiver in the Sunday papers was quoted as saying, "Nothing is expected to come up in the area of segregation." The Georgia laws still covered it, and he didn't think any new legislation would be necessary. And everything was to be pretty quiet. So we got off to a nice quiet start.

Bang! Early Monday, the order had come in to submit these people's classes that morning. And so they were in classes at 8 o'clock, these two people, Charlayne Hunter and Mr. [Hamilton E.] Holmes. Well, by the time the legislature could meet, the University of Georgia was integrated. It was a *fait accompli*.

Then a curious thing happened. The Southern states—I suppose like any other state, but I have a feeling the Southern states, having had so difficult a struggle to attain public education. . . . Of course, the state legislature is quite an old one. We like to say we were the first state university chartered. And this is true. But we didn't get going until the University of North Carolina had actually already begun, but this is the second oldest. But I don't mean to . . . But public education in general at the secondary levels and branches of the university didn't begin to come until 1910, '12. So all over the state there is a great attachment to the university.

Well, a curious thing happened. The governor had either to close the university, the whole university. . . . And he could not close it just in Athens, where the integration happened, because all the other branches are literal branches under the same board of regents. He was urged at first to close it. Then some of the same people who were calling, when told that this meant closing a branch in their city. . . . And, of course, in any city, especially a small Southern city which has very little industry, a branch of the university is the biggest industry and the largest payroll in the town. So there began to be second thoughts.

As the day wore on, and the governor did nothing . . . By the next day, the legislature and the governor were beginning to get telephone calls and telegrams saying, "Well, don't close it. I'm angry. I'm mad. I don't like it a damn bit. But," some of them would say, "my boy is over there, and he's going to graduate this year. My daughter's over there, and I don't want her education interrupted." They would damn the Kennedys and damn the government, but, "Don't close the university."

So they had a little riot over there one night which was largely, if not entirely, actively created by the White Citizens' Council element, and the Klan joined in it. I know—not by hearsay—I know the White Citizens' Council people in this state, the leaders of it, one leader, at least, sent money to some of the students to help organize and create this student riot. Only a few students joined in. Some of the people from neighboring small towns, a few from Athens, a Klan group from Atlanta and other areas went over. Six of those were arrested, put in jail. So the integration went off really rather well.

They were lucky in having Miss Hunter and Mr. Holmes. Charlayne Hunter is a very nice, intelligent, outgoing person. And Holmes, a serious, quiet, introvert student. I was pleased that when his grades made him eligible for Phi Beta Kappa, the Phi Beta Kappa chapter at the University of Georgia elected him. And then he went from there to Emory University Medical School and is doing very well there. So the university was lucky in having Miss Hunter and Mr. Holmes. Both of them did a very good job there.

Morrissey: President Kennedy developed the custom of meeting occasionally with editors from a state or a region of the country. Did you ever attend one of these sessions?

McGill: No. If you will look at the lists, he did a pretty smart thing. He did it on the advice of other people in the newspaper business. If you look at it, he invited, for the most part, editors from smaller towns who would rarely get an opportunity to be in Washington and to see the president. You won't see on those lists many persons who had an opportunity to see the president other times. This was after discussion and by design and planning. And I think it was an intelligent way to handle it. . . .

Morrissey: Thank you very much.

McGill: Thank you.

86

Review
of C. Vann Woodward's
Strange Career of Jim Crow

C. Vann Woodward's second revised edition of *The Strange Career of Jim Crow* nudges us once again with the reminder that this American historian is the most knowledgeable and articulate voice in any discussion of portrayal of things Southern.

No people of the several American regions, reflecting as they do the events and history of their regional environment, are so lamentably lacking in understanding of their own history and their share of the evolutionary processes of their country as are the Southerners. Other peoples may reflect local chauvinisms and a euphoria of regional nationalisms with symbols such as cowboys and Indians, Puritans and abolitionists, First Families and pioneers, "Massa and ole Miss," old "Black Joe," "Mammy," and banjos twanging happily in "de quarters." But the Southerner was, and is, condemned to schizophrenia of mood and emotions. His lack of knowledge of himself and his history and his sense of isolation and of being alien and outside the movement and destiny of his

Reprinted by permission of Mrs. Ralph McGill. Manuscript provided by Mrs. Ralph McGill from the McGill papers, now at Emory University, Atlanta. Apparently this piece was prepared on 18 January 1966, for *Life* magazine, but not published by that journal. Review of C. Vann Woodward, *Strange Career of Jim Crow*, 2d rev. ed. (New York: Oxford University Press, 1966).

country are an indictment of the crippling economic and social effects of a century of a segregated system still hotly defended.

The average Southerner's long obsession with race and his blind, irrational commitment to a system of injustice and discrimination that distorted and weakened all his institutions, public and private, are a tragedy not experienced by the people of any other American region. So closed was the Southern mind in the 1880s and 1890s that discovery of the prevalence of pellagra and hookworm actually brought protests from editors, legislators, and lay leaders against impugning the perfection of Southern life.

A conversation from a writing tour of the collapse of the Southern agricultural one-crop system in the autumn of 1936, comes to mind. A lanky, past-middle-age farmer, his face, neck, and hands burned a brick-clay red, sat on his small, dusty, weather-stained plank porch and talked. After a while he paused and said, despair in his voice: "There just ain't no damn lights to guide a man any more."

He was not a reader of books or history. But had he been, there still would have been "no damn lights to guide." It was the dilemma of the Southerner that the slave-culture oligarchy looked to Europe for linen, education, books, wines. There developed a mystique about Southern culture, but save for that built on the leisure afforded by slavery, there was no real "Southern culture."[391] The Southerner had no books to guide him about his own region or the antiserfdom and antislavery forces already strong in Europe and Russia. In 1860 the distinguished J. L. Petigru,[392] of Charleston, could say of his native state as it compulsively moved toward beginning the Civil War, "South Carolina is too small for a republic and too large for a lunatic asylum." In 1897, near the turn of the century, J. Gordon Coogler,[393] a sort of early Ogden Nash, wrote:

---

[391]See C. Vann Woodward, *Burden of Southern History* (Baton Rouge: Louisiana State University Press, 1960).

[392] See James Petigru Carson, *Life, Letters and Speeches of James Louis Petigru: The Union Man of South Carolina* (Washington DC: W. H. Lowdermilk & Co., 1920).

[393]J. Gordon Coogler, *Purely Original Verse*, 1897 (Columbia SC: Vogue Press, 1974), with original reviews and biographical sketch by Claude Henry Neuffer and Rene La Borde.

Alas for the South; her books have grown fewer
She never was much given to literature.

It was the tragedy of the South that it did not know its own history, nor did it know the meaning of what went on outside its borders. This was true before and after the Civil War. To be sure, George Washington Cable[394] of Louisiana, and Lewis Harvie Blair[395] of Virginia, both Confederate veterans, published important books in the 1880s, exposing the folly and ruin that a segregated system of discrimination would produce. But few read and those who did condemned the authors as "enemies of the South." The paternalistic, sentimental, tender Uncle Remus stories merely served to enhance the memory of "Mammy," "Uncle Tom," "the Big House," and the soft side of slavery. They were not intended to do so, but they reinforced old stereotypes and attitudes. Thomas Nelson Page's novels incited and glorified the violence of the Klan.[396]

Young Southerners in 1936 were inspired by Howard Odum's brilliant *Southern Regions*. This book gave them identity and understanding of their "place" in history and economics and of their sociological dilemma.[397]

---

[394]George Washington Cable, *Creoles and Cajuns: Stories of Old Louisiana*, ed. Arlin Turner (Gloucester MA: Peter Smith, 1965); *The Grandissimes: A Story of Creole Life* (New York: C. Scribner's Sons, 1880); *John March, Southerner* (New York: Grossett & Dunlap, 1894); *The Negro Question: A Selection of Writings on Civil Rights in the South*, ed. Arlin Turner (Garden City NY: Doubleday, 1958); *The Silent South, Together With the Freedman's Case in Equity and the Convict Lease System* (New York: Charles Scribner's Sons, 1885).

[395]Lewis Harvie Blair, *A Southern Prophecy: The Prosperity of the South Dependent Upon the Elevation of the Negro,* 1889, ed. C. Vann Woodward (Boston: Little, Brown Publishers, 1964).

[396]Thomas Nelson Page, *Among the Camps: Young People's Stories of the War* (New York: Scribner, 1898); *Bred in the Bone* (New York: C. Scribner's Sons, 1904); *Burial of the Guns* (New York: C. Scribner's Sons, 1894); *General Lee: Man and Soldier* (London: T. W. Laurie, 1909); *Marse Chan: A Tale of Old Virginia* (New York: C. Scribner's Sons, 1892); *The Negro: The Southerner's Problem* (New York: C. Scribner's Sons, 1904); *Old South: Essays Social and Political* (New York: Charles Scribner's Sons, 1966; New York: Haskell House Publishers, 1968); *Red Rock: A Chronicle of Reconstruction* (New York: C. Scribner, 1900).

[397]Howard W. Odum, *Southern Regions of the United States* (Chapel Hill: University of North Carolina Press, 1936).

C. Vann Woodward's *Tom Watson: Agrarian Rebel* was published in 1938.[398] It was the first book that gave the Southerner an insight into his region during conditioning years of the Populist movement—and the surrender of both Populism and "The Redeemers" to racism. Wilbur J. Cash's magnificent and comprehensive *The Mind of the South* appeared in 1941.[399] But the South had to wait until after 1945 to begin to learn its own history and thereby to have more lights for guidance.

Since 1945 there has been a vast surge of books about "The South," some good, many bad. If we admit, as we must, that the problem of race and its many ramifications is the most important of our domestic issues, then *The Strange Career of Jim Crow* is perhaps the one really indispensable book. First published in 1955, it now has been revised to include events of the last decade and make them relevant to the past so that we better understand the present.[400]

It is not merely the Southerner who needs to read this book. It would be enormously helpful if every American interested in understanding what Gunnar Myrdal called "the American dilemma" would become familiar with it.[401] Vann Woodward traces "Jim Crow" from his northern origin and the fixing of the Jim Crow system in the South where "the peculiar institution" and its post-Civil War complexities were concentrated.

Thousands of Negroes voted before the turn of the century. A number held municipal and state jobs. Time was when there were no separations in transportation, at theaters, or in eating places. Populism took the Negro in as a political partner and taught him that the "establishment" separated him and the poor white in order more readily to exploit both. But disfranchisement policies came. Their coming and the ugly, cancer-like growth of the closed white society make up a dramatic, im-

---

[398]C. Vann Woodward, *Tom Watson: Agrarian Rebel* (New York: Oxford University Press, 1963).

[399]W. J. Cash, *Mind of the South* (New York: A. A. Knopf, 1941).

[400]C. Vann Woodward, *Strange Career of Jim Crow*, 3d rev. ed. (New York: Oxford University Press, 1974).

[401]Gunner Myrdal, *An American Dilemma: The Negro Problem and Modern Democracy* (New York: Harper & Row, 1969).

portant, and fascinating section of American history.[402] The story of it touches every American life today. It has handicapped the South so that in all statistical totals of education, income, and literacy the South still trails other regions. The out-migration from the South and the big city ghetto slum problems are an outgrowth of it. Jim Crow and all that is wrapped in the words is responsible.

There are today but two large hyphenated minorities. They are the Negro-Americans and the Southern-Americans. They have lived together for three and a half centuries. They have, in a very real sense, shaped each other's destiny. Each has helped shape the character, accent, experience, and culture of the other. The romance, tragedy, and despair of the more than three hundred years are understandable only as one knows about *The Strange Career of Jim Crow.*[403]

---

[402]See James W. Silver, *Mississippi: The Closed Society*, enl. ed. (New York: Harcourt, Brace, and World, 1966).

[403]See "Radio Program concerning the South" with Woodward and McGill, in volume 2.

87

Radio Program concerning the South 1966

*A*nnouncer: Good evening, ladies and gentlemen, and welcome to the 397th edition of "Yale Reports." There are many people who say that the climate of the South can never be changed until the media of communication are fundamentally altered. There is one man who almost single-handedly, for over twenty-five years, has proven this to be true. Ralph McGill, today's guest, has been a columnist, an editor, and is currently publisher of the *Atlanta Constitution*. He has brought to a time of crisis a sense of true responsibility which modified extremist hysteria and maintained a sense of balanced inquiry, never losing the confidence of his readers nor the certainty of his purpose.

Participating in tonight's discussion are Mr. C. Vann Woodward, Sterling Professor of History at Yale University, one of the foremost

---

A "Yale Reports" radio program, Yale University, held on 1 May 1966. This was the 397th edition of "Yale Reports." Mrs. E. T. Stickney wrote to Logue on 29 April 1970:

> Our program is one that is prepared on current and interesting topics and people who visit the university. It is heard over 103 stations and reaches over a million people. It is on educational and commercial stations, and so reaches all walks of people, not necessarily college people, who write and ask for transcripts. We send out 70,000 requests a year.

Interview is reprinted by permission of Mrs. Ralph McGill and "Yale Reports."

Southern historians of our generation and a longtime close friend of Mr. McGill, and Mr. John H. Rothchild, managing editor of the *Yale Daily News*. Mr. Vann Woodward will begin the discussion.

Woodward: Mr. McGill, I have often wondered, as an old resident of Atlanta, Georgia, how it came about that the *Atlanta Constitution*, between the 1920s when I first encountered it and the last decade, came to the leadership in the South of enlightened opinion on public affairs and particularly the race problem.[404]

McGill: Well, sir, you're very generous to think that we have. I don't really know. I came to Atlanta in sports. I'd sort of fallen out of a political reporter's job in Nashville, Tennessee, because the sports editor got fired, and I'd played a little football at Vanderbilt so they said sit here for a while till we can find a sports editor. So I sat in for about nine years.

Woodward: When did you come?

McGill: Well, I stopped writing sports in 1938. I kept writing outside things and in 1937 a young faculty man at Emory University, where you were, came and asked if I would like to apply for a Rosenwald Fellowship. I'd been trying to write some things about the collapse of the cotton economy during the thirties and the unemployment, and the sharecropper tenant-tenure problem.

At any rate, I was then still writing sports, but I was doing all these articles on the side, chiefly with the Sunday paper. So the paper gave me leave at half-pay and I stretched this fifteen-hundred dollar fellowship out for almost a year in Europe, and I earned a little doing other things and was on half-pay. So, while I was there I was writing a great deal about the Scandinavian countries, particularly for the first three months in Denmark. And I went there because their population was about the same as Georgia's, a little over three million. They had a lot of small farms, as did Georgia, but they were making a great success of farming even on small plots, and they were doing it largely, though not entirely, because of cooperatives. So I began to write about all these things in Denmark.

---

[404]For more by McGill on Atlanta and the *Atlanta Constitution*, see "She Sifted the Ashes and Built a City," in volume 1.

Woodward: But Denmark doesn't have a race problem.

McGill: No, but then they wrote me and said, when you come back we want you to go on the editorial side. Then, about two months before I came back, the editor died. He was a man whom you might associate, his name was Francis Clark. He had a brother named Eli Clark, who was connected with the Klan.

Woodward: Well, that wasn't a source of liberal leadership that I was trying to find out.

McGill: At any rate, I came back, and no one told me anything. I was made editor of the paper, and I started just writing the way I felt about things, and no one told me to stop, although they got very worried at times. I know I'd been working only about a month, when to my astonishment, I didn't know I'd said anything really, the Klan staged a big Saturday night parade up and down in front of our building with their hoods and sheets on, with placards denouncing me.

Woodward: What did this do to circulation?

McGill: Well, it hurt the circulation some. It's been a very expensive thing since about 1954. James Cox, who is the owner, and the staff have a meeting and the circulation managers cry about lost circulation. Boycotts here and there knock off a few hundred papers today, a few hundred tomorrow, but we have been lucky.[405]

Woodward: Well it's evident that the people of Georgia responded to this, or you wouldn't be in business.

McGill: Well, our circulation now is higher than it ever has been.

Rothchild: How has the liberal stand of your paper changed the image of the *Constitution* in Georgia, would you say?

McGill: Well, after all, I have been working on the editorial side since late 1938. I don't know, I guess it has changed the image with the older person, not so much in Atlanta. Atlanta gets a continual enrichment of people from outside Georgia, and I don't know that they would notice any real difference in it.

Woodward: I held a theory about these editorial changes—they have a

---

[405]See also "An Interview on Race and the Church," in volume 2.

good deal to do with personality and the people who are in charge, and it seems to me that your paper and Hodding Carter's paper are reflections of individuals, in a considerable measure, and their impact on the society they live in and the response to it.[406]

McGill: Well, I have not thought of it in those terms, but I think that is probably correct. I have been lucky, and I appreciate the luck of just being left alone.[407] I have been wrong lots of times, I have made mistakes. I know the first owner in the thirties and forties at one time was very uncomfortable. But even though he was supporting somebody else, he let me go ahead and support another man for governor or for president. I know when we supported Adlai Stevenson in 1952, I don't think anyone else on the paper was for him but me almost, but I was the editor, so they let me go ahead.[408]

Rothchild: Isn't it unusual for a person to be named publisher of a paper without actually owning the paper's controls?

McGill: It is a little unusual, yes sir. Although there are a few other examples of it, and I own a very modest amount of stock in the paper, and I assure you it is modest. But it's just one of those situations.

Rothchild: Do you think the failure of a conservative paper in Atlanta last year, the *Atlanta Times*, which was supposed to represent the White Citizens' Council and some of the other conservative groups, reflects a dying point of view in the South and in Georgia?[409]

---

[406]Hodding Carter, editor, Greenville (MS) *Delta Democrat-Times.*

[407]In the editor's interview with McGill on 29 December 1965, McGill stated: "I think that I must say, and I *regret* to say, but now will say, namely that—I would not like to mention anybody's name—but there was a period here [at the *Atlanta Constitution*] when I had a rather difficult time with some of the management which was opposed to me writing what I wanted to write. This took about three years . . . in the forties," and later McGill added in "the early 1950s"; See McGill, *Ralph McGill: Editor and Publisher,* ed. Calvin McLeod Logue (Durham: Moore Publishing Company, 1969) 1:22-23.

[408]For more by McGill on working relationships at the *Atlanta Constitution* see "An Interview on Race and the Church" and "A Conversation with Ralph McGill," in volume 2.

[409]See Neil R. McMillen, *Citizens' Council* (Urbana: University of Illinois Press, 1971).

McGill: No, I do not think it represents a dying point of view. I think that point of view is greatly fragmented; I mean the various groups who have this point of view are fragmented, and they have no common philosophy unless it is the philosophy of racism. This paper was started for the wrong reasons, for a vindictive reason, and it didn't please anybody. It was not a White Citizens' Council paper as those people thought it ought to be. It didn't suit the John Birch extreme view, so they ended up not pleasing anyone.

Woodward: Well, the history of the *Atlanta Constitution* embraces a great deal of the history of the South, starting in the 1860s. It had some famous editors; I suppose your most famous predecessor was Henry Grady, a man of great attractiveness but a man of very sharply contrasting views to your own. I think of him, though his reputation is somewhat different, as a pretty conservative man, especially on social and racial questions.

McGill: I think I would certainly agree with that. He was a great orator in the style of that time, but he was very conservative and he was one of the great leaders of the so-called New Departure Democrats. I remember first reading this in your book, *Tom Watson: Agrarian Rebel*.[410] Watson used to say that Grady would help get a new cotton mill and he would see the smokestack with the smoke staining the sky, and this was perfection. He never noticed, said Watson, the pale, thin, wan children who were working in the mills ten to twelve hours a day, nor did he notice the filth about their shacks. Grady had no social viewpoint. I think this was probably true. I talked to a great many persons who knew him. When I came to the *Constitution* his secretary, James Holliday, was still there, and I had many talks with him.

Woodward: Grady died in 1889.

McGill: Grady had just passed his thirty-eighth birthday when he died of pneumonia. His wife wouldn't have anything but homeopathic physicians. I don't know if they could have done anything with pneumonia in those days anyhow, but he never had a real doctor. But Grady had the

---

[410]C. Vann Woodward, *Tom Watson: Agrarian Rebel* (New York: Oxford University Press, 1963).

paternalist view so prevalent then, and up into our time.[411]

Woodward: Well, his time was succeeded by an era typified by the man you just mentioned, Watson, and the outburst of Populism, which is, I suppose, a mixed blessing, if it was a blessing. Do you find that heritage still prevalent in Georgia?

McGill: You find it in some places, but it seems to me, sir, that it is being diffused, maybe, by the New Deal, the Great Society, and so on. I remember when Senator Richard B. Russell was running for the Senate, and former governor Eugene Talmadge was active and thought at the time that he might be a candidate. He later was a candidate against Walter George.[412] But I remember we had a big meeting in Thompson, Georgia, where Watson lived and had his big home, and reference was made to Gene by an old "pop," as they called him, and he said, "Why, the mantle of Tom Watson, if put about Gene Talmadge, would fit him like a mother hubbard on a June bug!" Very apt. You don't hear much of that any more. The old "pops" have sort of died out.

Rothchild: Do you think that your Southern heritage and the fact that you are a Southerner has been able to help change the views of some men? I remember that in 1959 you reported Bill Hendricks of the Florida Ku Klux Klan was changing his views. Do you think you've been able to help these people change?

McGill: I don't know that I've changed a single viewpoint. I have no evidence of it. Old Bill Hendricks—Bill just was a pretty decent sort of fellow, and he got just fed up with some of the more violent people in his outfit, and just decided he couldn't go on with it, and that was all. I used to have a great sympathy for the Klan. I think the Klan in the twenties, for all of its evil and wickedness, of which we certainly were aware, and which we tried to combat, still there were some pretty good people who got mixed up with it.

Woodward: Well, you mean you sympathized with the people, but not

---

[411]Paternalist view of many whites toward blacks.

[412]See McGill's essay on Walter George in *Southern Encounters: Southerners of Note in Ralph McGill's South*, ed. Calvin McLeod Logue (Macon GA: Mercer University Press, 1983).

with the Klan?

McGill: Not with the Klan, yes. But I sympathize with the people who get pulled into it. Now the Klan of our time has never been very large, and it has become chiefly a refuge for terrorists. They develop a secret little group, the identity of which is not known to the members. Now, they try to get as many members as they can, and they charge them ten, fifteen dollars, and then they get ten or fifteen dollars more out of them for regalia, and then they usually sell them a ring or a pin, some of them even have insurance that they sell. But the real danger of the Klan and the Klan's mentality has been the terrorists, I think, such as the bombing of the church in Birmingham, killing a Negro army officer on the road in Georgia, and killing three civil rights young men in Philadelphia [Mississippi]. The Klan is related to all of these. I don't know of one in which the Klan isn't implicated.

Rothchild: How much trouble have you had on the *Constitution* lately, or yourself, with threats from the Klan. Any at all?

McGill: Well, not too many. Well, yes, for a time; you don't know where they come from. You get harassments on the phone and sometimes all night. My house has been shot into once, but we didn't know about it till the next morning. It was shot through the window and a .22 bullet was in the back of a chair that sat just by the window. And after a big Klan meeting one night, they came out and shot up my mailbox, which is just at the road, and put six shots through it, a six-shooter. Two or three times they have dropped big paper cartons, large ones, on the lawn, full of garbage. That's a curious mentality to me. After all, I could get it cleaned up. Here's a fellow who had hoarded garbage and got it loaded up, and trucked it out to my place, and dumped it on the lawn.

Woodward: Well this is an old strain of violence that we know, and it keeps cropping up. I must say, in my more pessimistic moments, I don't see it diminishing much.

McGill: No, I don't either.

Woodward: It flares up again and again. Criminal law, even with federal backing and enforcement, doesn't seem to be enough. What's the hope when this guard of justice against violence is not effective?

McGill: Well, sir, I don't want to embarrass you, but I would like to tell this audience that most of what we Southerners know, we've learned from Mr. C. Vann Woodward. You brought it out in *The Origins of the New South* the way violence had a really unaccountable surge upward after the disfranchisement proceedings of the late 1800s and then the early 1900s.[413] After they had legally excluded the Negro from all participation, then violence against him took a great surge upward.

Woodward: Well, yes, and now we have a wave of violence with the reenfranchisement of the Negro, and I don't see that I've found any pattern here.

McGill: I can't see any pattern. I remember in 1929, when I came to Georgia, there was in existence then an Anti-Lynching Association in Georgia. It was devoting itself to trying to create public opinion to reduce lynchings.

Woodward: That was a woman's organization.

McGill: Essentially a woman's organization, although it had some men who worked with it. They were trying to influence judges and trying to get a federal law. It seems to me almost incredible how much opposition there was then to a federal law against lynching. It used to be mentioned and introduced every now and then. And they would say, "Leave it to the States."[414]

Woodward: Well, that aspect of violence has, of course, greatly diminished, but it breaks out in many other ways, and they are quite as nasty.

McGill: Much—in a way, more nasty—because it's more concealed. The horror of the lynchings was they were pretty much in the open.

Rothchild: You talk in your book, *The South and the Southerner,* which I

---

[413]C. Vann Woodward, *Origins of the New South, 1877-1913* (Baton Rouge: Louisiana State University Press, 1951). See also McGill's reviews of Woodward, *Burden of Southern History,* and Woodward, *Strange Career of Jim Crow,* in this volume.

[414]Although McGill consistently opposed discrimination against blacks in the South from the 1940s until his death in 1969, for many years he argued that one more federal law was not the answer, both in response to a federal antilynching law and the Federal Fair Employment Practices Commission (FEPC); see the editor's introduction.

think is a tremendous book, about people as being twigs, sort of bent back perhaps. Do you think that some of this violence might come from a lashing forward, perhaps, a compensation, or a backlash from ideas that have [been] held for so long that are now being broken through?

McGill: I don't know if I would describe it as a backlash; I wish I had time to think a little more about that. But I think it is some sort of evil compensation, wouldn't you say, psychological compensation. You wonder about a mind that would put dynamite under a Negro church in Birmingham, and put it under the Sunday School area, and time it to go off when you knew they would be there.

Woodward: This is a disease of a grave sort. And do you get at that by criminal law, by the trial system?

McGill: The trial system of course has been debased and distorted and prostituted in many areas. It's an interesting thing, and a dismaying thing. I seriously doubt if there are really many places, maybe none, in the South, where you could really get a completely fair-minded jury, if the element of racist prejudice were present.

Woodward: It's said that Hugo Black has two goals in his career. One is justice for the Negro, and the other is the protection of the jury system. Are these compatible, do you think?

McGill: Well, ideally they are, but they are not yet compatible in fact. That's very sad, and frightening.

Woodward: Is the answer in the direction of federal courts?

McGill: I reluctantly believe it is. And I think this may be the next step: some federal legislation. I don't know what it'll be, or how you will make it effective, and this worries me. Even if you had federal legislation, how would you get into the minds of men? And these men can protect themselves pretty well, by lying or violating their oaths, which they do not hesitate to do.[415]

Woodward: These recent decisions, of course, were about a statute that was passed a hundred years ago.

Rothchild: If I may change the subject for a minute, you were at Van-

---

[415]See "Is the Federal Government Running Our Lives?" in volume 1.

derbilt at a time of an exciting literary revolt, and I think from a student point of view, we would wonder what you think about the new student revolt, let's say the "God is Dead" movement in Atlanta. Do you think this is representative of a new feeling? Are there differences between your generation and ours that you could describe, perhaps?

McGill: I doubt if there's any essential *human* difference. I think this generation is much better informed than mine was. I think it is probably more determined, and those who express themselves are more determined to commit themselves to some form of social service. I don't know that that's true. But it seems to me it's true. We weren't so troubled in my generation with sociological problems. When I went to Vanderbilt, we didn't seem to get around to it very much; it wasn't reflected in the faculty, it wasn't reflected by discussions on the campus.

Woodward: That was the preoccupation of the next decades.

McGill: It was in the thirties, yes, but not in the twenties. In the twenties, the Fugitive poets at Vanderbilt were not so much in rebellion against society as they were against the English department, the man who was then head of the English department, and the refusal there to really have modern poetry as any part of instruction or discussion. He was a wonderful old man, the head of the English department, who never got much beyond Browning, Tennyson, and Keats, very good poets, let me say, but Eliot was the beginning, and Eliot was not in any of the classes. So they began, not in any manifesto or rebellion, but just by meeting together, writing poetry, and discussing it. Finally, they began to publish it, and they published first under assumed names, or pen names. They attracted a great deal of attention and someone, I forget who it was, said that the Fugitive poets represented the total literature of Tennessee. It was Mencken, Henry Mencken.

Woodward: Well, you have followed this literary renaissance and have found some notable examples of it in Georgia. I'm thinking of Carson McCullers and Flannery O'Connor.[416] Do you see this literary upsurge as a continuing thing?

McGill: Yes, I do. James Dickey, of Atlanta, already has become one of

---

[416]See McGill's essay on McCullers in McGill, *Southern Encounters.*

the two or three best-known American poets, young poets. His recent volume was selected for one of the National Book Awards. In Tennessee, where I still have associations, I know some writing that's beginning to come out. I think it's going to continue. I don't know if it'll reach the peak of Carson McCullers or Flannery O'Connor, but maybe it will.

Rothchild: Well, from a journalistic point of view, how do you see a changing expression, perhaps in journalism? Do you see a changing mode of expression in newspapers, or will it continue to change, if there has been a change?

McGill: I think it must change. I know the impact of television is such that papers everywhere are affected by it, and what they will do, what we will do. We give a lot of thought to this. For instance, you don't see the newspaper extra any more, you haven't seen it for years. Radio really just about knocked out the extra. Television can do a great many things that newspapers can never do. The picture of the actual event, the whole sequence of it, the quick news flashes. They can do superb documentaries—not all of them are superb—but they do have some very intelligent men in television. Newspapers have not yet been hurt as much as the national magazines, but they are hurt in that this takes away circulation, the eyes and ears of people.

We think that the best kind of thing you can do is have more news articles, or rather more reporting in depth, to use the phrase that's now current, or more interpretative articles, combined with the news. We find this is helpful. Then you must get busy and dig up your own local news; what's wrong with your state mental hospital, what's wrong with your prisons. We had a young reporter who, for example, took a number of beers, till you could smell it on his breath, and then pretended to be drunk. He got himself arrested, and sentenced to the city prison, where he stayed for a week. The articles he wrote about his experiences in there brought about an overhaul of the city prison system, and attracted a lot of attention. We've done other things like that. A few years ago because of a reporter's lucky break and doing a real fine job of investigation, we were able to change the whole mental hospital, which has been a great block on us. It's one of the largest mental hospitals in the world, and badly run, even now, but we got great reforms. So I think newspapers are going to be forced to do things like this, otherwise, they become something like just a big shopping guide, with advertisements and type in between them.

Woodward: Has the wave of consolidation swept over your part of the country?

McGill: Yes, sir. We have a city that has a combined morning and afternoon publication. I don't know if you can really call it a monopoly any more.

Rothchild: How about a monopoly of editorial viewpoint. Do you think a city of the size of Atlanta should have a liberal and a conservative viewpoint expressed intelligently?

McGill: I think that would be ideal. Happily, in Atlanta, the *Atlanta Journal* is much more moderate in its viewpoint. We often differ editorially. We never have an editorial meeting together, we rarely see the people on the afternoon paper. We have separate elevators—old Governor Cox insisted on this—separate elevators, separate staff, separate city rooms, and we're on different floors in the building, and so we differ almost always on something editorially. This isn't planned, but it just happens that way.[417]

Announcer: You have been listening, ladies and gentleman, to "Yale Reports."

_____

[417]As of 1982 Jim Minter was editor of both the *Atlanta Constitution* and the *Atlanta Journal.*

88

Foreword
to Hodding Carter's
Southern Legacy

I n 1950, when the South's ever-present materials of spontaneous combustion were smoking but not yet in flames, the Louisiana State University Press published Hodding Carter's *Southern Legacy*. This was in a time, too, when federal court decisions based on suits filed by Negro students in Oklahoma and Texas had opened doors to graduate schools in those states, because, the court said, the states had discriminated against them by denying them entrance and at the same time providing no schools they could attend. An uneasiness had begun to come over the South because all but the most intransigent could sense the coming of the decision which finally would arrive on 17 May 1954. The South was confronted with the necessity to understand something about itself. *Southern Legacy* was one of the very best mechanisms for such understanding. The time for bitterness, acrimony, sit-ins, protest demonstrations, the ugly facts of big slum life, and the equally unattractive features of rural slum life had not come to occupy pages of our newspapers and screens for our televisions and our consciences.

Hodding Carter is an urbane, intelligent, courageous, and civilized man. His book *Southern Legacy* had wide readership. It is a personal

Foreword to Hodding Carter, *Southern Legacy* (Baton Rouge: Louisiana State University Press, 1966). Reprinted by permission of Mrs. Ralph McGill and Louisiana State University Press.

book. In it an able writer uses a great wealth of personal experience to illustrate and clarify the major issues of his state and his region. Many Southerners read it and were helped by it. Many persons in other areas were enabled better to understand what we call the Southern problem. But the greater challenge was to the Southerner. He was asked to comprehend the legacy of his regionalism.[418]

Now, in 1966, the Louisiana State University Press is reissuing the book. This is what may be called a genuine public service. Much progress has been made in removing many of the harsh and unworthy discriminations which Hodding Carter discussed in the first edition. Many Southern white men and many Southern Negroes have accepted the responsibility necessary to cope with change and with opportunity. There still are those who betray their legacy by interpreting change as something which enabled them to have and to hold a special privileged status. There still are those who persist in thinking that their Southernism enables them to be outside the laws and obligations of their national citizenship. This paperback edition of *Southern Legacy* will be helpful reading to all those who have yet to honor the legacy of their Southern heritage.[419]

---

[418]Carter was the publisher of the Greenville, Mississippi, *Delta Democrat-Times*. He also wrote *Angry Scar: The Story of Reconstruction* (Garden City NY: Doubleday, 1959); *South Strikes Back* (Garden City NY: Doubleday, 1959); and *First Person Rural* (Garden City NY: Doubleday, 1963).

[419]See McGill's review of Carter, *Southern Legacy*, 1950 edition, in volume 1.

89

Foreword
to Margaret Anderson's
The Children of the South

W hen I had read the manuscript of Margaret Anderson's book *The Children of the South*, the fragment of a Proverb intruded into my mind. I looked it up. It was Proverbs 4:23: "Keep thy heart with all diligence; for out of it are the issues of life."

Margaret Anderson kept her heart with all diligence. This chiefly is why this excellently written book will be remembered and kept when many other books coming out of the fever and ferment of the South will be forgotten. It is a book that will be picked up for rereading of well-remembered pages and for the dignity and bravery of children in moments and hours of terror when adults had lost their reason and were mad with the poison of hates. She does well to say, on the dedicatory page, that the book is for "the Negro children of the South." They earned it—at Clinton, at Little Rock, at New Orleans, and other cities and towns of the South.

Margaret Anderson was teaching in Clinton High in 1956. (She still is there. Lucky Clinton.) The U.S. Supreme Court decision had been handed down in May 1954. Clinton's school was ordered deseg-

Reprinted by permission of Mrs. Ralph McGill and Farrar, Straus & Giroux, Inc. Foreword to Margaret Anderson, *Children of the South* (New York: Farrar, Straus & Giroux, Inc., 1966).

regated. All was quiet. There were some who did not like it. And then came a man named John Kasper. He had the gift of demagoguery. He soon became a racist Pied Piper, followed by all those who before had lacked someone to articulate their prejudices, fears, and hates.

Margaret Anderson introduces him and goes on with her narrative, telling of the lives of the people of Clinton—the children, their parents, the townspeople. It is perhaps fitting to say here that there came a day when a federal judge, one of the Taylors of Happy Valley, a family who long before had produced governors and a United States senator, sat patiently on the bench while Kasper's defense brought out all the ugliness of prejudice that was admissible. It was so bad and there was so much of it that the jury and the townspeople were sickened. Kasper went to jail. Tennessee's Governor Frank Clement sent state troops in to keep Clinton's school open. (He was a year ahead in setting this precedent. A year later, at Little Rock, Governor Faubus sent Arkansas troops to prevent the schools from opening.) Clinton's school later was literally destroyed with an estimated hundred sticks of dynamite. It cost over half a million dollars to replace it. Children in many cities each bought a brick. Voluntary donations helped. The county board of education found extra money.

This is some of the background. But this book is about children and their parents, especially their mothers and grandmothers. It is the story, too, of children who came to school in those early, grim days between rows of cursing, hot-eyed men and vicious, shrewish women whose language was filthy beyond that of men. It tells of the Negro children in the classes and corridors in that first year when children from the homes of the hate-filled men and shrilling shrews brought the same tactics to school. It probes skillfully and deeply into the powerful and melancholy influence of many years of segregation in the South and its impact on the white and Negro population both.[420]

The book goes deeper than that—much deeper. It is good that a teacher should reveal so vividly, weaving her story out of the lives of children, what the costs of generations of segregation were, and are, to

---

[420]See C. Vann Woodward, *The Strange Career of Jim Crow*, 3d rev. ed. (New York: Oxford University Press, 1974); C. Vann Woodward, *Burden of Southern History* (Baton Rouge: Louisiana State University Press, 1960).

some twenty million Americans. Mrs. Anderson places the necessary emphasis on the installments paid on a debt that will take many years to be cancelled out.

Out of her years of experience Margaret Anderson writes:

> The Negro child *is* different from other children, even other children of deprived backgrounds, because he has problems that are the product of a social order not of his making, or his forebears'. . . . The Negro child comes to us [teachers] an overburdened child, taxed in a hundred ways that make him old beyond his years. The road for him is three times as hard as for the average white child, even the poorest white child. Although the poor white child has much in common with the Negro child in that both have experienced deprivation, the Negro has handicaps which do not shackle a poor white child so noticeably. At every turn there is an obstacle, and forever and ever, the Negro child must ask himself, "Why?"

I can testify to the accuracy of Margaret Anderson's words. The Negro child, caught from birth in segregation, shut off from the nation's political, cultural, and values system, grew up almost inevitably with a low estimate of his own possibilities. It was hard not to have a poor self-image when the child's mind could not conceive of being much more than what his parents were. Segregation deadened initiative, suppressed personal confidence. Many of these children—too many—came from homes where neither parent could read or write. These and other factors in the long years of segregation created a handicap that even today is not quite fully understood.

Margaret Anderson's conclusions are supported by my own years of work and experience. The Supreme Court was never more right than when it found that a segregated system was and is, per se, discriminatory. It was, terribly so. The agrarian South, with a per capita income considerably below the national level, attempted to carry two school systems, though money was lacking for even one good one. The Negro schools were far inferior. The Negro teachers were, as a rule, less trained, because of the segregated teaching schools. The South has been sacrificing generations of its children. But segregation was more than that. It was, especially in the rural regions, almost total alienation from the community. In some towns and communities the Negro occupied almost exactly the place of the untouchables in India. We are just learning that while segregation was a "system" designed to separate the Negro from the rest of the community, the effect was like that of the "system" of slavery. All who lived in it were affected by it. The Negro, being a minority, was the more penalized. But the white majority could not escape. The results are visible in educational and economic lags as well as in the area of moral convictions and in religious health. The costs will be paid for a long time. The umbilical cord that stretches from the generations of segregation to the slum riots in large Eastern and Western cities is unmistakable.

Margaret Anderson illustrates her findings of the overall damage done by segregation with the stories of children in her class. They tear at the heart. Let us take, for example, the story of Roberta. Margaret Anderson met her first when Roberta was twelve. A school census was being taken.

Roberta came to the door. She had a tiny baby in her arms. She invited the teacher in. Roberta's mother had left word about her coming. The house was a low-ceiling hut with three rooms: living room, bedroom, kitchen. There were no closets or bathroom. The floors were of unfinished planks. One could see through the cracks. The walls were papered with newspapers. In the center of the main room was a pot-bellied stove. There was one bed in the house, an old iron bed with a thin, sagging mattress, lacking a sheet. Pallets on the floor served the children.

There were eleven children. The mother had left a notation of the names and ages of each. There had been different fathers, and none was living with the family. Roberta was in charge. She talked of her keen desire for books and reading. She "couldn't wait" to get to high school. Roberta did go to high school, to the school that was once all white. She, "a child hungry for books," wore a dress made of feed sacks and a dingy white blouse. Her glasses, provided by public assistance for eyes too long neglected, kept slipping down on her nose. But for Roberta the material things did not then matter. She was happy, enthusiastic. She scored high on her mental tests. She had determination and will. She would rush home when school was out, always with books, to do a full day's work before sunset, and when this was done she turned to her books. In the Negro elementary school she had led. In high school, for which she was ill-prepared, she had trouble making average grades. By the second year, the toil with eleven children to care for and the house and the hard schoolwork "to keep up" had begun to do something inside her. But she never asked for help. She went to summer school, working to help pay her way. A new baby was on the way at home. And then Roberta dropped out of school.

Margaret Anderson went to her and asked why.

"I woke up one morning and looked about me," said Roberta, "and I just decided it was too much to overcome."

Margaret Anderson properly asks what is going to happen to all the bright, good minds such as Roberta's. What symbols will these young people look for? To what in their environment will they respond?

"The Negro students in today's schools are in the process of becoming what they will be tomorrow. . . . So often have I thought how carefully we would teach them if we were wise. . . ."

This is a book that everyone interested in the tremendous processes of desegregation and integration, and the problems of life and education, should read. Margaret Anderson devotes several chapters, based on case histories, to what Southern education needs. Parents of white children who still oppose desegregation of schools would profit enormously from this book. So would congressmen, senators, and all those confronted with educational problems. Much of the white South, victimized and psychologically distorted by generations of segregation, might obtain understanding by reading *The Children of the South*.

It is a book written with much compassion and understanding—out of life and out of the heart of a great teacher.

Review
of William Stringfellow's
and Anthony Towne's
The Bishop Pike Affair

D uring the reading of *The Bishop Pike Affair* I found myself, somewhat to my astonishment, thinking of Truman Capote's *In Cold Blood*.[421] There was only one bit of relevancy. Capote had used the record of a brutal crime and multiple murder to tell his story. He was neither partisan nor judge. It was up to the reader to evoke from the pages his own emotions, his judgment of right and wrong and of the forces at play, outside the principals and within them.

William Stringfellow and Anthony Towne have done this in *The Bishop Pike Affair.* They have put together the record of it (the affair), of what led to it, and what is following after. It is, I believe, for this reason, a book of meaning for every Christian and for those outside the church who retain interest in it, secular though that interest may be.

For the Christian, it seems to me, this book is one which may not be dismissed. The reader may think, as many do, that Bishop Pike is a

Review of William Stringfellow and Anthony Towne, *The Bishop Pike Affair: Scandals of Conscience and Heresy, Relevance and Solemnity in the Contemporary Church* (New York: Harper & Row, 1967), from *Presbyterian Survey* (September 1967), by permission of Mrs. Ralph McGill and *Presbyterian Survey*. Copyright September 1967 by *Presbyterian Survey*.

[421]Truman Capote, *In Cold Blood: A True Account of a Multiple Murder and Its Consequences* (New York: Random House, 1966).

naive man who employs shock treatment to attract attention—or that he is a jaunty egotist. The important thing here, in the reviewer's opinion, is that such conclusions are wholly irrelevant. It does not, after all, matter so much whether Bishop Pike is naive or enjoys shocking the more orthodox. What does matter is whether the "Pike affair" reflects the Christian church in general and the Episcopal church in particular. If it does, as the reviewer believes, it may explain why the Christian church today is, almost certainly, in a cul-de-sac.

Ohio Northern University's commencement baccalaureate sermon this past June was delivered by Bishop Odd Hagan, president of the World Methodist Council. Bishop Hagan's theme was that the Christian church had as its basic mission witnessing for Christ—not "going from victory to victory. . . . If Christ is to come at the end of history, then we are in history. . . . We cannot be outside it," he said. "It is this witnessing, testifying—that is the objective of Christian life."

He then shocked at least most of his listeners with a statistic. "If present trends continue," he said, "only nine percent of the world's population will by the year 2000 call itself Christian." The year 2000 is only a little more than thirty years away.

This statistic is evoked by *The Bishop Pike Affair* and by other records of the Christian church's failure to "be in history." The statistic is made understandable by the fondness of much of the Christian establishment for the extreme political right in America as well as by the church's position of withdrawal from, or careful neutrality in, the heated social revolution of our time. (Individual churches provide modest but noble exceptions.)[422]

The statistic is reflected, I think, in too many mortgages ranging from two hundred thousand dollars to more than one million dollars in the continuing building of more stately mansions—the edifice race. The statistic also is present in the defections from the priesthood of both Protestant and Roman churches and in the firing of young ministers by Protestant churches for their activity in racial or other social issues.

---

[422]See McGill's "Let's Lead Where We Lag," "Agony of the Southern Minister," "Church in a Social Revolution," "Introduction to *God Wills Us Free*," in volumes 1 and 2; and Samuel S. Hill, *Religion and the Solid South* (Nashville: Abingdon Press, 1972).

So it may be said again that *The Bishop Pike Affair*—and the record of what happened to the bishop—is of major importance because of what the reader evokes from it. It is, for example, incredible to see—though perhaps not too surprising—as the personalities have their brief hour upon the stage at the Wheeling heresy and censure proceedings, that the Episcopal church, like all other professions including that of journalism, has its share of clowns, straw men, and the petty and malicious.

What happened to Bishop Pike, therefore, is of relatively little importance. He will survive. He will continue to make men think. He will stir controversy and shock the orthodox. What is of dominant importance is what this record, so thoroughly, nonpartisanly, and honestly set down, starts in motion in the minds of Christians or those who still find the Christian church and its theology subjects of interest and concern.

The story of the "Louisiana Purchase" in the record of the Episcopal church, which also is a part of the record in *The Bishop Pike Affair,* is far more damaging to Episcopal—and all Christian—integrity than Dr. Pike's skepticism about the classical doctrine on the Trinity and the Virgin Birth. (The "Louisiana Purchase" is Stringfellow's label for an attempt to bring peace and harmony between right- and left-wing factions in the Diocese of Louisiana.) In a time when sex education properly is taught in high school and presented to many church youth groups, when a great many persons no longer think it necessary to "free" Saint Mary from the "sin" of conception, to censure a bishop for disenchantment with the orthodox doctrine on this subject is not likely to seem other than preposterous to a majority of today's questioning, intelligent young men and women who seek a "place" in Christianity. The "Louisiana Purchase" is much more a heresy of morality and spirit than anything Bishop Pike has said. (This reviewer happens to find the explanation and purpose of the Holy Spirit, or Ghost, as unimaginative translators put it, enormously satisfying and clear in meaning. But the orthodox Trinity is tough going for many committed Christians—not merely Bishop Pike.)

The Bishop Pike affair began with creedal trouble in 1959. In that year the *Christian Century,* Protestant and ecumenical, began publishing a series of articles by well-known churchmen under the general heading, "How My Mind has Changed." Contributors included Reinhold Niebuhr, Billy Graham, Martin Luther King, Karl Barth, Will

Herberg, John C. Bennett, and James A. Pike.[423] These men were asked to describe how their general views had changed and how they had changed theologically—or not. Bishop Pike's theological position in 1959 was:

(1) I am more broad church, that is, I know less than I used to think I knew; I have become in a measure a "liberal" in theology.

(2) I am more low church in that I cannot view divided and particular denominations as paramount in terms of the end-view of Christ's church, and I do not regard the gospel as the all-important and as the only final thing.

And (3) I am more high church in that I more value the forms of the continuous life of the Holy Catholic Church as best meeting the needs of people and best expressing the unity of Christ's church. These forms include liturgical expression and the episcopate.[424]

The article revealed his disenchantment with doctrine on the Trinity, the Virgin Birth, and salvation through Christ alone. It also contained what later came to be called "typical Pike smart-aleckness" in the form of irreverent insouciance that angers the most fastidious, especially those whose manner of speech is pedestrian and lacking in any lightness.

"The church," he wrote, "was centered around the truth of the gospel, but the Bible came along as a sort of *Reader's Digest* anthology."

Before the magazine article was published, Bishop Pike attended a special meeting of the House of Bishops in Dallas, Texas. The bishops were to prepare, and did, a pastoral letter on the reaffirmation of the creeds, especially the Nicene Creed. The letter was intended to deny any susceptibility of the creeds to cultural, social, or scientific mutations or changes. The letter, rather ponderously seeking to avoid the irritant of science, said: "When the creeds speak of the 'descent' of the eternal Son

---

[423]Niebuhr, "The Test of the Christian Faith Today," *Christian Century* 76 (28 October 1959): 1239-42; Graham, "What Ten Years Have Taught Me," *Christian Century* 77 (17 February 1960): 186-89; King, Jr., "The Church and the Race Crisis," *Christian Century* 75 (8 October 1959): 1140-41; Barth, "Karl Barth's Own Words," translated by RoseMarie Oswald Barth, *Christian Century* 76 (25 March 1959): 352-55; Herberg, "Historicism as Touchstone," *Christian Century* 77 (16 March 1960): 311-13; Bennett, "How My Mind Has Changed," *Christian Century* 76 (23 December 1959): 1500-1502.

[424]James A. Pike, "Three-pronged Synthesis," *Christian Century* 77 (21 December 1960): 1496-1500.

to take our manhood into union with Himself, or of the 'Ascension' of the risen Incarnate Son, we know that 'descent' and 'ascent' are movements between God and Man and not in interstellar space."

There were other portions equally obfuscating and Bishop Pike opposed them with vigor. In the end, however, the letter was adopted about as written.

About a year later, a number of Episcopal clerics in South Georgia importuned the bishop of that diocese to bring charges against Bishop Pike because of the *Christian Century* article. They did not charge heresy, but said there was "grave doubt about Bishop Pike's suitability for exercising jurisdiction as a Bishop of this church."

It has been Bishop Pike's good luck always to be attacked by relatively handicapped men insofar as contending with him is concerned. His reply to the Georgia clerics provides an example of this luck.

Reminding them that his remarks were quite within the bounds of doctrinal orthodoxy, he said:

> Our Lord has reminded us that those who do the will of the Father will know the doctrine. It would be interesting for the *New York Times* to inquire of this Georgia clericus as to how many of their churches are racially integrated following the clear and official teaching of this church and the Anglican communion. The Bible also reminds us that doing the truth is as important as saying the truth.

William Stringfellow and Anthony Towne bring the record on to the heresy meeting at Wheeling, West Virginia, which convened on Sunday, 23 October 1966.

Along the way the record introduces the many new developments in theological discussion, controversies, and so on. The many new books (among which *Honest to God* was but one),[425] the "God is Dead" theory, and the many variations on the critical role of the church in the last half of an exciting, traumatic century, were a part of this period. The near abdication of the church in the social revolution, particularly that of race; the openly stated plans of right-wing conservative organizations to

---

[425]John Arthur Thomas Robinson, *Honest to God* (Philadelphia: Westminster Press, 1963).

control local congregations, purge local pulpits, and censor and control the schools and textbooks were a part of the trauma.[426]

Also traumatic to the spirit and the status quo were the various "marches," particularly that of Selma where Unitarian minister James Reeb and other persons were killed. In Selma, the Episcopal church, as the march began, refused to allow even visiting white Episcopalians to enter for Sunday worship.[427]

The Wheeling heresy meeting was a sad melancholy affair. It reflected no credit on Christianity or the church. The House of Bishops was sorely divided. Some members of it were anguished and distressed. Others, known to be openly hostile to Bishop Pike, proceeded ruthlessly.

In the end a censure verdict was voted. The vote was 103 to 36. There followed an incredible event. A resolution to create a council to help the bishops "re-think, restructure and renew the church for the life of the world today" was unanimously adopted. The irony of this action was that the essence of the resolution was almost precisely what Bishop Pike has been urging for four years.

There also followed a predictable event. Bishop Pike's luck had held. He stood and demanded, under the guarantees of canon law, a full and thorough hearing on "reports, rumors, and allegations affecting my personal character and official character." As the authors of *The Bishop Pike Affair* concluded, "The censure motion had prevailed, but Bishop Pike had seized the ball, and where he would run with it only time would tell."

Since the Wheeling meeting of the bishops, Episcopal churches in his old diocese have been denied the privilege of inviting him to speak or preach in them.

This reviewer wishes again to remind prospective readers that the book is written from the records—not from the pro or con conclusions of the authors. Any Christian interested in, or concerned about, the pos-

---

[426]See McGill's "An Interview on Race and the Church," in volume 2.

[427]For more about voting and civil rights activities in Selma, Alabama, see Jack Bass and Walter DeVries, *The Transformation of Southern Politics: Social Change and Political Consequence Since 1945* (New York: New American Library, 1976) 11, 63, 83; Steven F. Lawson, *Black Ballots: Voting Rights in the South, 1944-1969* (New York: Columbia University Press, 1976) 278, 282, 308-11, 329, 348.

ture of Christianity and the church can hardly afford not to read it. As an afterthought, it is quite possible that the poems dealing with Bishop Pike, written by an Episcopal priest, are worth the price of the book. They are much more clearly revealing than the *Book of Revelation* itself.

91

The American South

My subject is the South—the American South. It is a region in which I was born, reared, educated, and one in which I have worked as a journalist for almost half a century. It also is a region in which, by reason of a number of influences, I early was made to see the inequities and injustices of a system of racial segregation. When I was made editor of the *Atlanta Constitution* in 1938 I was able to begin writing on this subject. But it is about today—now in the last months of the year 1967—that I wish to write.

As I write, the news comes in of demonstrations being made in a Southern city by black pickets against the racial imbalance still persisting in desegregated schools. But it is interesting that of those persons meeting to resolve the situation, four are black men who are members of the Georgia State Legislature. There are nine black men in the legislature (or parliamentary body) of Georgia, and all had large support from white voters as well as black ones. Georgia was one of the old Con-

Reprinted by permission of Mrs. Ralph McGill and the United States Information Agency. Manuscript provided by Mrs. Ralph McGill from the McGill papers, now at Emory University, Atlanta. Also, Eugene Rosenfeld, assistant director for Public Information of United States Information Agency provided a version that the USIA's "Press and Publications service used on its Wireless File in 9 October 1967." He wrote: "I enclose a copy of this as it was sent, plus a tearsheet from a Johannesburg, South Africa paper which used it"; letter to Logue, 19 September 1969.

federate states in the Civil War, which was fought to save the Union and to enable that Union then to abolish slavery. These nine legislators are a larger number than any other states have elected with two exceptions—the states of Illinois and Michigan.

As I write there is understandable unrest in the poverty ghettos of American cities. But, also as I write a black man has been nominated by the Democratic party, with the support of many white voters as well as black ones, as its candidate for mayor of Cleveland, Ohio.[428] Cleveland is one of America's largest cities—a major industrial center. It is located on Lake Erie, one of the properly named Great Lakes. There are five of these lakes. Their northern shores are in Canada. Canals have made them into a vast inland sea, insofar as transport and shipping go. Chicago is another city on these lakes. The St. Lawrence River flows into them, and the shipping of the world now may come to the lake city docks. The importance of these cities will increase. Twenty-five percent of the employees of the city of Cleveland are black men—and they are in all levels of employment. It is quite likely the next mayor will be a black man.

As I write there are protests in some of the Southern states of America about the discriminations shown black men by the sheriffs and courts of some of the counties (provinces, arrondissements, parishes).

But, also, as I write, Thurgood Marshall, whose grandfather was a slave, has just taken the oath as one of the nine justices of the United States Supreme Court. In stature and prestige a justice of this court ranks very close to the office of the president of the United States.

I admit that these examples, selected to illustrate progress and the need for more of it, do not get down to details. Before getting to a summing up, I would like to make this point: what is happening racially in the United States is, in general, necessary and productive of progress. The violence is not a good thing. Those who commit the really violent acts of shooting and burning are few in number. (There is actually one small group of black men, for example, who wish to set up all-black communities in the apartheid manner.) It is essential to keep in mind that revolutions or social protests do not come except in a time of ad-

---

[428]Mayor Carl B. Stokes.

vancement and rising expectations. They do not come from a truly depressed people, unable to make protest.

What happened in America is what is happening in all the world. It occurred first in this century. Beginning in about 1922 there was massive out-migration from agricultural regions to the industrial cities. This movement to the cities was accelerated in the 1950s and 1960s. Perhaps six million or more persons moved out of rural areas. They had no skills and little education.

Progress is everywhere. There are black men in jobs at all levels. There are not enough prepared and skilled men to fill all jobs open. There are black men in all our colleges and technical schools. But, there is left the big job of the very poor, the unskilled and untaught, on which the full attention and planning of the national government is centered. "We will overcome."

92

Comment on Pat Watters's and Reese Cleghorn's *Climbing Jacob's Ladder*

Pat Watters and Reese Cleghorn have done a book which is, without question, one of the solid books done on the Negro and his impact as a voter and as a citizen on the South and the nation. Perhaps the phrase *here is a book that must be read for understanding* has been overly used in a time when the greatest story of the last half of the twentieth century is inspiring publication of many books; nonetheless, I must say it for this one.

Since it is the story of the arrival of Negroes in Southern politics it is equally the story of the reaction of "white politics" to the Negro. What happened to some of the Southern senators and congressmen and so-called leaders in this entirely factual, intelligently organized book is almost cruel. Cruelty is not of intent. It is, instead, a pitiless way in which the surgical knife of facts, including the statistics of voting records and of publicly expressed attitudes and opinions, eviscerates some of those Southerners who have had the longest records in the Congress and who have been most influential there.

A comment by McGill of 19 October 1967, perhaps upon the request of the publisher, on Pat Watters and Reese Cleghorn, *Climbing Jacob's Ladder: The Arrival of Negroes in Southern Politics* (New York: Harcourt, Brace & World, 1967). Manuscript provided by Mrs. Ralph McGill from the McGill papers, now at Emory University, Atlanta.

Climbing Jacob's Ladder is a compassionate book. It also has an in-dictment. The story is here told in very human terms of how this country withheld many things from some twenty million of its people, including, incredibly, the fundamental right to the ballot. This is not a book of statistics and dry facts, although they are there in adequate number to provide a very firm foundation for the stage on which the human characters play their parts.

93

The South's
Glowing Horizon—If . . .
1968

Only a large, questioning "if" stands on the glowing horizon toward which the South's future economic development is moving. A growth rate greater than that of any other region is an attainable goal. For once, the always ebullient chamber of commerce prophets are supported by statistical conclusions reached in studies made by competent economists and business analysts.[429]

Not since that autumn of 1792 when young Eli Whitney came to Georgia from New England to shake the region—and the world—with the invention of a cotton gin, a machine that later was said to have been born into original sin, have so many forces sifted and sorted out the South.

Soybeans, turnip greens, okra, and vast forests of pulpwood pines grow where once only cotton bloomed and blew. Grain elevators rise surprisingly out of Mississippi's Delta, where once men said that God had

---

Reprinted from *Saturday Review* 51 (9 March 1968), by permission of Mrs. Ralph McGill and *Saturday Review*. Copyright 1968 by Saturday Review, Inc.

[429]See Brian Rungeling et al., *Employment, Income, and Welfare in the Rural South* (New York: Praeger, 1977); Thomas Dionysius Clark, *Three Paths to the Modern South: Education, Agriculture, and Conservation* (Athens: University of Georgia Press, 1965); Francis Butler Simkins and Charles Pierce Roland, *A History of the South*, 4th ed. (New York: A. A. Knopf, 1972).

put land just to grow cotton. They were the same men who said no machine would ever equal two black hands at picking cotton. Interstate highways are magnets attracting towns and trade to their whirring strips.[430]

Negro voting registration is now fifty percent of the voting-age Negro population in every Southern state—and it is increasing. The biggest gain is in Mississippi, where Negro voter registration has escalated from seven percent to sixty percent of Negro citizens of voting age. The number of Negro office holders in the eleven states of Dixie now is more than twice what it was when the voting act was passed by the Congress in 1965. Eleven Negroes are now members of the Georgia state legislature. Tennessee has elected six, Texas three. Some two hundred or more Negroes have been elected to local offices, including two sheriffs. In Georgia it is estimated that Negro registration now has passed the three hundred thousand mark.[431]

There is excitement in the South, mixed with days of despair growing out of the setbacks caused by those who mobilize the worst of the past to hold back the future. Decades ago plowmen in slavery sang:

Day, oh Day,
Yonder comes day. . . .
Day done broke into my soul. . . .
Yonder comes day. . . .

---

[430]See Vivian W. Henderson, *Economic Status of Negroes: In the Nation and in the South* (Atlanta: Southern Regional Councils, 1963); Timothy Thomas Fortune, *Black and White: Land, Labor, and Politics in the South* (Chicago: Johnson Publishing Company, 1970); Ray Marshall and Virgil L. Christian, Jr., eds., *Employment of Blacks in the South: A Perspective on the 1960s* (Austin: University of Texas Press, 1978); and McGill's review of James G. Maddox's *The Advancing South* and F. Ray Marshall's *Labor in the South*, in this volume.

[431]See Margaret Price, *Negro Voter in the South* (Atlanta: Southern Regional Council, 1957); Donald R. Matthews, *Negroes and the New Southern Politics* (New York: Harcourt, Brace and World, 1966); Steven F. Lawson, *Black Ballots: Voting Rights in the South, 1944-1969* (New York: Columbia University Press, 1976); Chandler Davidson, *Biracial Politics: Conflict and Coalition in the Metropolitan South* (Baton Rouge: Louisiana State University Press, 1972); and McGill's "If the Southern Negro Got the Vote," "State of the South," "Case for the Southern Progressive," and "Letter to *Center* Magazine," in this volume.

The day is breaking after many long years, but there are still those who try to darken the sun. Still, the winds keep blowing—so many things already are gone with the wind—with more that must soon be gone.

In the continuing collapse of the old agricultural and social system, the South's industrial mix is making adjustment from low- to high-wage industries. These producers attract others who supply, buy or distribute. More and more of these enterprises find available managerial skills in the South, though the import of this asset is still large. The quality of the region's work force slowly improves. If near full employment holds, the South's percentage of jobholders is expected to increase at a more accelerated pace between 1960 and 1975 than in the 1950s.

There is a sound base for saying the South has the essential resources to become the next "boom" center. The region's chief handicaps in competition with other, more developed geographic areas of the country for rapid-growth, high-wage industries are familiar ones. They are the shortage of trained and educated workers and stubborn attachment to the remnants of "values" and "traditions" that for so long have retarded the South in its efforts to attain full development of its resources—human and material. Until these slowdown liabilities are removed, the industrial-technical advances will progress at a slower pace than necessary—"day" cannot fully break into the South's soul.

The change from rural-agrarian to urban-industrial has been rapid but spotty. It is not yet complete. There are many minds among the region's policymakers at the county and state levels that do not have any clear understanding of development goals or the resources at hand. There are large declining rural areas as empty of industrial development as the Sahara is of wells. A large, unskilled, and inadequately educated agricultural work force, no longer needed on mechanized farms or on the millions of acres owned or leased by pulp and paper mills or cattle and dairying, is not ready for skilled work.

A big percentage of these displaced and deprived persons historically has been moving northward. They went in large numbers in the boll weevil decade of the 1920s. Their out-migration slowed in the depression years of the 1930s. In the decades of 1940-1950 and 1950-1960, more than three million Negroes and several hundred thousand white persons equally deprived of skills and education left the South. This export of the many and varied evils and paradoxes contained in the phrase *the segregated system* now is a critical national problem wrapped in another phrase—*the ghettos*.[432]

Change has not been confined to the agricultural South. The entire economic and social structure of the isolated and "different" South that developed after the Civil War is changing in the trauma of birth of the first really new South.[433]

The mythical South of the magnolias, mansions, and general munificence of manners and life never was. The post-Civil War South, whose corrosive poverty of life and spirit was such that it produced the Populist revolution and violent political and racial repressions, was followed by what might be called the cotton-mill South. The once-upon-a-time "lint-head towns"—gray always with poverty, dusty in summer with lint and the red or tan soil from the largely unpaved streets and roads, and harshly gothic in the rains and mud of winters—are about gone.

Some of the old towns, indeed, are dead. Others are dying. With the coming of crowded roads and interstate highways, many have moved from the traditional square with its statue of the Confederate soldier—eternally facing northward—to build their shops, filling stations, "bar-b-q" and fried-chicken "shacks," and drugstores and discount houses along the new highways. The old town about the square, half deserted, seems—and is—half asleep. Some of its stores are boarded up. Occasionally one will have become a gospel house of some obscure evangelical sect. The old squares are listless with apathy and neglect. Business is out

----

[432]See C. Vann Woodward, *Strange Career of Jim Crow*, 3d rev. ed. (New York: Oxford University Press, 1974); Woodward, *Burden of Southern History* (Baton Rouge: Louisiana State University Press, 1960); Robert Haws, *Age of Segregation: Race Relations in the South, 1890-1945* (Jackson: University Press of Mississippi, 1978).

[433]See Charles Pearce Rowland, *Improbable Era: South Since World War II* (Lexington: University Press of Kentucky, 1975); Paul E. Mertz, *New Deal Policy and Southern Rural Poverty* (Baton Rouge: Louisiana State University Press, 1978); Raymond W. Mack, ed., *Changing South* (Chicago: Aldine Publishing Company, 1970); John C. McKinney and Edgar T. Thompson, eds., *South in Continuity and Change* (Durham: Duke University Press, 1965); Thomas H. Naylor and James Clotfelter, *Strategies for Change in the South* (Chapel Hill: University of North Carolina Press, 1975).

there on the highways where automobiles move ceaselessly and shopping is a convenient drive-in stop.

Now and then near an old and decaying town one will see the ruins of a cotton gin. Even middle-aged men will remember when the cotton wagons were lined up for half a mile waiting their turn at the gin. Those were the flourishing days of trade when the little towns were alive.[434]

It is necessary, in thinking of that mythical South, to recall that it was only about seventy years from the invention of the cotton gin to the Civil War. There was not time for the creation of a civilization built on leisure and slavery that rivaled, as the myths have it, that of the slave-supported civilization of the ancient Greeks. A few—but only a few—cities attained wealth and great mansions.[435]

A South that was backward in education, dwarfed in technology, and imprisoned in a so-called one-party political system that fostered the status quo and extolled provincialism and described the customs and traditions as virtues, now is developing a Republican party of real potential. It is merely a part of the inevitable evolutionary growing pains that many of these new Republicans are former Democrats who defected out of resentments over civil rights decisions by Democratic administrations, rather than principle. Now, however, there are state and local Republican organizations—and young voters less and less inclined to follow their fathers or to vote merely out of prejudice, are active in them.

It was the cement of race that created the old "solid South." Actually, it was never solid unless the issues of race and white supremacy were raised. There were always many Souths.

A two-party system was not possible in the South until the federal courts began, about 1940, to hear cases on Constitutional rights, many of which had been untested since the Tilden-Hayes steal in 1876-1877, in which Southerners enabled Hayes to be president in exchange for an

---

[434]See Harriet Laura Herring, *Passing of the Mill Village: Revolution in a Southern Institution* (Chapel Hill: University of North Carolina Press, 1949).

[435]See T. Harry Williams, *Romance and Realism in Southern Politics* (Athens: University of Georgia Press, 1961); Carl N. Degler, *Place Over Time: Continuity of Southern Distinctiveness* (Baton Rouge: Louisiana State University Press, 1977); Paul M. Gaston, *New South Creed: A Study in Southern Mythmaking* (New York: Vintage Books, 1970).

end to Reconstruction. States' rights were restored with this agreement. It included the state determination of Negro rights—the United States Constitution notwithstanding.

Disfranchisement of the Negro and his exclusion from jobs by the newly rising labor unions, especially the railroads and larger craft unions, came on quickly. A combination of laws, amendments of state constitutions, and party regulations bypassed the Fourteenth and Fifteenth Amendments. These included such devices as the poll tax (also deliberately designed to restrict the franchise of poor whites), property ownership as a suffrage qualification, the white primary (which limited voters in the Democratic primary to white persons), and various "rules." These "rules" required a voter to "read, understand, and explain" to "the satisfaction of the registrar" a section of the Constitution. Rare was the Negro applicant—and rarer still was one who could "satisfy" the registrar.

Therefore, there could have been no two-party development in the South until the white primary was ended by the United States Supreme Court in 1944, a mere twenty-four years ago. Nor was a "New South" possible until the U.S. Supreme Court school decision in 1954. It was the first of several necessary constitutional decisions. There was, and is, much resentment and resistance by the states that were politically and economically freed by those decisions.

The unanimous school decree of 1954 was followed, in 1964, by congressional enactment of a broad civil rights act. This act created a legal, constitutional base that removed discrimination in public accommodations, in federally assisted programs, in job opportunity, and in voting. This latter constitutional right was more firmly established by an important complementary act to the one of 1964—a voting rights measure.

There followed one of the typical paradoxes of the South (some of them have been almost unbearable in their violence and stupidity, as various members of many generations have learned). The Court's rulings actually freed the Southern white man more than the black man. By accepting the legal direction to obey the Constitution and do what was morally right, the Southern white man was freed to advance his economy, to remove his political system from bondage, and to begin improving the quality of his education so that it would give Southern children equal opportunity—on the average—with children in the rest of the nation.

The Court's rulings should have produced a real year of jubilee. Nothing of the kind happened. Southern governors, congressmen, mayors, legislators, ministers, and laymen fiercely demanded that they be allowed to remain in political bondage, to keep their children in inferior schools, and to be politically chained—all for the sake of a long-discredited, immoral, unconstitutional racial status quo.[436]

Nevertheless, despite infamous and disgraceful delays, evasions, and dishonorable actions, progress was made. It was said that the schoolhouse doors would run red with blood before a single Negro child was admitted. It was cried from the rooftops of state capitols, from klan klaverns, White Citizens' Councils, pulpits and civic-club podiums, from newspapers, television, and radio that the South's answer was "Never!"[437] But there were Southerners aplenty who said otherwise. There were a handful of churchmen who opposed emotional idiocy. There were newspaper, television, and radio editors and executives who did not join the mobs."[438]

Sad to say, it was the dollar that really was most effective in allowing progress to be made. It was expensive to go into court and defend discrimination. Too, restaurants, hotels, and motels found that opening their doors to the total public enriched them instead of destroying business. Retail customers did not mind being waited on by Negro clerks. The myths of the old segregated order proved to be as unsubstantial and untrue as did the myths of the old magnolia South.

---

[436]See Numan Bartley, *Rise of Massive Resistance: Race and Politics in the South During the 1950's* (Baton Rouge: Louisiana State University Press, 1969); Bartley and Hugh D. Graham, *Southern Politics and the Second Reconstruction* (Baltimore: Johns Hopkins University Press, 1975).

[437]John Bartlow Martin, *The Deep South Says "Never"* (New York: Ballantine Books, 1957); Neil R. McMillen, *The Citizens' Council* (Urbana: University of Illinois Press, 1971); Francis M. Wilhoit, *Politics of Massive Resistance* (New York: George Braziller, 1973).

[438]For more by McGill on Southern moderates see "Southern Moderates Are Still There," "Case for the Southern Progressive," and reviews of *A Southern Moderate Speaks, Southern Legacy, A Congressman From Mississippi,* and *A Time to Speak* in volumes 1 and 2.

Hence, in 1968 it may be said that there is, on the whole, as much, and maybe more, of an overall acceptance of the civil rights laws in the South as in other regions. As would be expected, there are some paradoxes. Even some of the schools in rural county seats have desegregated and opened up the high school football and basketball teams to Negro youths. Some of them are the stars of their teams. It is nothing to see the crowds cheering themselves hoarse for these players. But once the game is done, the Negro boy is again separate and goes home to his section of town.

Let this not be too depressing. The Southerner is a great status-quo man, but once he has accepted—and cheered—a Negro boy, he will move on to a better attitude. The number of Southern school districts that refuse federal aid so as to hold on to segregation and low-quality education as long as possible is few. The winds blow—"things" go with them.

There is today a Negro member of the United States Supreme Court. Only the more rabid opposed confirmation of the able and experienced Thurgood Marshall. There are other Negroes in the federal judiciary. The list is too long to belabor. It can no longer be argued, however, that the present participation of the Negro in the American government and in its elective processes is mere tokenism.

The big problem nevertheless remains. The civil rights laws did not, and do not, really touch the life of the slum poor, most of them exports from the South during the past several decades. This problem of human beings, deprived by the customs and rules of the past, is not really one of "civil" rights. It is one of justice, morality, conscience, and practical, economic common sense.

The South, with its huge share of rural poor as well as its slum-city demands, is confronted with another of its paradoxes. The region can lead the nation in economic progress. It has the potential for prosperity never before experienced. The big "if" blurs the South's horizon of hope and expectation. The economic, political, and social future depends on the South's ridding itself of racism and second-rate education and declaring itself in behalf of a progressive program for all its children and adults.

Meanwhile, on the region's political seas, three men—two governors and an "assistant governor"—have put to sea in a leaky tub named *States' Rights*. They cannot destroy the South's future. They can, however, retard and distort it. They can, and do, encourage the worst of the segregationist elements in their states. This is not done directly. But if the state's chief executive proclaims himself a segregationist and damns Washington's "interference," those who are willing to defy the government in the area of civil rights legislation feel the governor privately is on their side. All statements about law enforcement are cynically received in light of the many gross examples of discrimination in law enforcement concerning the Negro citizen, often a victim of the law itself.

In January 1968, John Bell Williams was inaugurated as the fifty-fifth governor of Mississippi. On the platform with him sat, among others, Governor Lester Maddox of Georgia. Present in spirit was "Assistant Governor" George Wallace, inventor and sole owner of the American Independent Party of Alabama. It is "American" as Mr. Wallace defines Americanism. It is "independent" as he directs. He then was far away in California, driving toward the number of petition signatures necessary to get his name on the state's ballot for the June 4 primary.[439]

The new governor's speech was—like the weather—warm, but reporters said a slight chill could be felt in both. There was no mention of racism in Governor Williams's twenty-nine-minute address. Speeches by the cotton South's states'-righters today are purified by a new, political Magnolia mouthwash. It is guaranteed to clear the vocabulary of all sounds of "Nigger! Nigger!" and to prevent the belch and bellow of racism, which until recently was so integral a part of Dixie campaign oratory.

Another new product of the speech writer's factories is the camellia-jasmine deodorant, also a new Southern political product. It has given to the one-time citadels of demagoguery an air that, in the opinion of the veteran reporters of the Southern scene who remember the old days, seems almost dainty. It is dainty and cleansed of what we once heard from the Barnetts, the Bilbos, the old Talmadges, the Cotton Ed

---

[439]For more by McGill on Maddox and Wallace, see *Southern Encounters: Southerners of Note in Ralph McGill's South,* ed. Calvin M. Logue (Macon GA: Mercer University Press, 1983).

Smiths, and those who went before them, such as Ben Tillman and James Vardaman.[440]

The technique is verbally germicidal unless, of course, one knows the nuances of the new political idiom. When Wallace, for example, shouts against crime in the streets and says, "If you don't know what I mean, ask your taxi driver or the policeman!" the crowd roars. And if one doesn't know the new language and does ask, one is told, "He means them niggers rioting in the streets." "Liberals," "intellectuals," and college professors also feel the Wallace lash in a manner reminiscent of the old days of Joe McCarthy.

Mr. Maddox, nominated in Georgia's Democratic party runoff, became the nominee by virtue of an estimated seventy-five thousand Republican voters who entered that primary and voted for him because they thought he would be easier for their nominee to defeat. Thus nominated, Maddox could not get a majority in the election. A reluctant, somewhat embarrassed legislature had to cast its votes to select a governor.

All three of these men had found GOP nominee Barry Goldwater more "satisfactory" on the race issue in 1964 than President [Lyndon] Johnson. They publicly supported the senator from Arizona.[441] Williams was disciplined by his party peers in the House after the 1964 defection. He was deprived of seniority and committee appointments. In his inaugural address he said that Mississippi would, if necessary in 1968, again set aside partisan (political) consideration.

Maddox has said he would not support President Johnson, but is still "a Democrat." He is, emotionally, closer to Wallace. There still is a possibility that Maddox will not go for a third party, but doubt grows. In mid-February, Wallace came to Atlanta and publicly associated himself and his party with Georgia's former governor, Marvin Griffin, who attained national notoriety as an uncompromising segregationist. He pledged to close all public education facilities, including the university,

---

[440]See Cal M. Logue and Howard Dorgan, eds., *Oratory of Southern Demagogues* (Baton Rouge: Louisiana State University Press, 1981).

[441]For more by McGill on the Barry Goldwater campaign in the South, see "From Atlanta—The Political Assessment," "Case for the Southern Progressive," "Church in a Social Revolution," and "Interview Concerning John F. Kennedy," in this volume.

rather than admit even one Negro. His acceptance of a place as a Wallace man was in character. "I'll stay there till we tree the coon," he said, beaming. He added that he had always been for Wallace, but still hoped he could remain in the Democratic party.

Furthermore, Maddox's fundamentalist religious position pleases the rural evangelical sects. Taking a drink is a sin; dancing and mini-skirts are suspect.[442] He opens each day's work with a prayer service. "Isn't it wonderful that Governor Maddox has brought God back to Georgia," wrote a lady chairman of a rural church's mission program. Like many others, she sees no paradox in sending money to help Africans become Christians and barring American Negroes from church. The consensus on Governor Maddox is: "Not as bad as we feared—not yet, anyhow."

The influence of these three men will likely give two or three Southern states to George Wallace. But this is not assured. The "dump Johnson" hate vote, which blames President Johnson for civil rights, "interfering with state's rights," "and trying to ram" various "things" down Southern throats, normally would go to the Republican nominee. They loved Goldwater, who was "satisfactory." They do not, however, like either former Vice-President Richard Nixon or Governor Nelson Rockefeller. This is a compliment to these men, but it does not assist them politically in the South. A heavy vote for Wallace, such as that which went for Goldwater in 1964, might enable the Democrats to hold a doubtful state.

Thus, the three men sail on in their tub of *States' Rights*. And invisible thousands who follow these men symbolically sail aimlessly with them. These men know that the image they create of their region and their country is harmful and ugly. But their attitude is, "Who gives a damn what the rest of the world thinks!"

Progress, since 1945, and since the Court decision of 1954, is considerable when measured against the past. But the gains made and the regional boom that is possible highlight what must be done to attain a

---

[442]See Samuel S. Hill, *Religion and the Solid South* (Nashville: Abingdon Press, 1972); Kenneth K. Bailey, *Southern White Protestantism in the Twentieth Century* (New York: Harper & Row, 1964); and McGill's "Let's Lead Where We Lag," "Church in a Social Revolution," "Southern Moderates are Still There," and "Introduction to *God Wills Us Free*," in volumes 1 and 2.

growth rate higher than that of any region in the nation. The pace of regional advance depends on how readily and with what acceleration the South brings quality education and skills to her people and abandons the discriminatory practices of the past.

The future of the South then, is bright, if the Southern people will to have it so. But there remain the three men in the tub—and big "if" on the horizon.

94

The New Confederacy: Review of Robert Sherrill's *Gothic Politics in the Deep South*

I n *Gothic Politics in the Deep South,* Robert Sherrill offers us a verbal
Madam Tussaud's Museum. Mr. Sherrill writes very well indeed,
and the word portraits of the characters in his exhibition reveal
them much better than the best artists in wax could have done.

Among the main characters in this gothic tale there is Leander Perez
from an oil-and-sulphur-rich swampy parish in Louisiana: "Proud, arrogant, boastful, a crafty publicist of his often-imagined deeds of anarchy, Judge Perez looks the part of the backwater tyrant that he is. He
has a blockish body, a boomish voice, a sweeping pompadour, a cast-iron
mouth, a ready but humorless laugh, a limitless capacity to harangue, a
bottomless fund of spite and grudge." Of ex-Governor Orval Faubus,
Mr. Sherrill writes that "There is in Faubus's makeup a weakness that,
in moments of pressure, makes him act seldom from logic, often from

Reprinted from the *New York Times,* 22 March 1968, by permission of Mrs.
Ralph McGill and the *New York Times.* Copyright 1968, by The New York Times
Company. An earlier draft of this review is in the McGill papers, now at Emory University, Atlanta. Review of Robert Sherrill, *Gothic Politics in the Deep South: Stars of
the New Confederacy* (New York: Grossman Publishers, 1968).

fear, and even more often from whatever the last stress happens to be before action is demanded of him."

In George Smathers, soon-to-retire U.S. Senator from Florida, Mr. Sherill finds "the perfect case of the southern politician who, having treated his constituents to the public orgy of a witch-burning, is thereafter left alone to the private orgies of serving special interests and himself." And there is ex-Governor George Wallace, "the little Judge, the Barbour Bantam, the greatest disturber of the political peace in this generation, a neurotic, raving egotist, a skilled imitator of political gimmickry that others had shown to be useful, but at the same time possessing more imagination and drive and artistry of debate than all the other contemporary Deep South politicians put together."[443]

Mr. Sherrill, who also is the author of *The Accidental President*, a study of President Johnson viewed by some critics as the most merciless hatchet job since Lizzie Borden's, is a man of chrome-plated opinions.[444] He manages to take a few slashes at Mr. Johnson in this present book, but they are few and are largely decorative. Mr. Sherrill writes so well his opinions glitter, but they are quite rigid and firm. His style might itself be said to be gothic in an architectural sense in that it is "characterized by the converging of weights and strains at isolated points upon slender vertical piers and counterbalancing buttresses." His book is immensely entertaining and informative. And if some of his chrome conclusions and opinions are inaccurate, there are not too many of those and they are, one may be sure, made in good faith on the basis of talks with sources considered sound.

Mr. Sherrill's theme as I understand it, particularly from his final chapter titled "The Future: Still Black—and White," is that the Deep South is content, even though it has been "dragged into disrepute once again by its leaders." These leaders will, he argues, "keep the same old masters riding the bandwagon and the same old philosophies wheezing out of its calliope. Look therefore for no great changes."

---

[443]For more by McGill on George Smathers and George Wallace, see *Southern Encounters: Southerners of Note in Ralph McGill's South*, ed. Calvin M. Logue (Macon GA: Mercer University Press, 1983).

[444]Robert Sherrill, *The Accidental President* (New York: Grossman Publishers, 1967).

Mr. Sherrill seems to have done much of his research on the politicans and the late fundamentalist college president, Bob Jones, in the late 1940s and 1950s. He sees these men as symbolic of what he calls an unbroken mold and concludes, therefore, that the South is largely unchanged and that the region will alter its gothic ways slowly and reluctantly.

In his look at the future, Mr. Sherrill asks what will prevent a new and perhaps more subtle and therefore more successful wave of segregationists from coming to power. This reviewer agrees that the future assuredly is not clear. This is a time in which a white backlash, sustained largely by various ethnic groups in Northern cities, is confusing and endangering the progress of racial amity in its fullest meaning. The Southerner, looking at his region, hopefully finds reason to believe that the Negro in the South may be brought into a position of full citizenship at a pace more rapid than that in the larger cities of the North and West, to which millions of the victims of the old Southern system of segregation and educational lacks have been exported.

The men he has chosen to sustain his theme are certainly representative of the variety of influences, personalities and events that have given Southern politics some of its more macabre and contradictory gothic qualities. Leander Perez and George Wallace are the only two in his museum likely to give readers nightmares. The reader will find them all interesting and instructive in understanding at least some of the traumas and changes in the South.

At this point, however, it seems necessary to speak of an inconsistency in Mr. Sherrill's theme and to document it. He describes the men in his exhibit as "Stars in the New Confederacy." Yet, by his own reckoning the hourglass soon must run out for Leander Perez. Bob Jones already has gone to his fundamentalist heaven. Senator Strom Thurmond, who bolted the Democrats in 1948 to be the nominee of the shabby and abortive Dixiecrat party, is now a Republican Senator. If he ever had any star qualities, which is a doubtful claim, they have burned out. He talks; few listen. Senator Eastland is a mere boy of sixty-four. Faubus is pushing sixty. Of the younger personalities, Senator Smathers is retiring from the Senate this year because of poor health. George Wallace and Senator Talmadge are young enough to win actuarial votes for being around for some years.

608 No Place to Hide

But as Mr. Sherrill notes, Senator Talmadge is "adapting." (And better had.) George Wallace is a fiery star. In Alabama the faithful say that only three men can walk on water: George Wallace; Bear Bryant, Alabama's football coach; and Jesus Christ. (They always put the Nazarene last.) But George Wallace doesn't fit into the present well enough to walk on water for many more years. He is more comet than star.[445]

This reviewer cannot agree that the mold is unbroken and that changes will be as slow as molasses in January, to use a Deep South saying. Until 1964 the politics of the Deep South were indeed almost hopelessly gothic, offering horrors, vulgarities, a murky atmosphere of despair and decay, and incidents involving violence of unrelieved brutality. There also are cadenzas of humor and preposterous contradictions.

But it was simply not possible for the South really to change until the 1966 voting laws were enacted. Since midsummer 1967, Negro voting registration in Mississippi climbed from 199,000 to 264,000. This is 58.8 percent of the black voting-age population. Registration continues. A substantial percentage of the gains have been made since Mr. Sherrill did his research and editing. In the other Deep South states the registration percentages now are: Georgia, 334,000, 54.5 percent; Alabama, 255,000, 53.1 percent; South Carolina, 189,000, 50.8 percent; Florida, 304,000, 64.6 percent.

Negroes have now been elected to legislatures in six Southern states. Georgia, of the Confederate South, leads with eleven. The old apathy of the rural Negro, which Mr. Sherrill properly notes, is fast disappearing. In the cities, where most of the population is, the Negro voter is aggressive, organized, and active. It has been recognized that black power, flowing out of a ballot box, not a gun barrel, may after all be good for health of local government.[446]

Georgia's political predicament was unique. Neither a two-party system nor representative government could become a reality until the

---

[445]George Wallace was once again elected governor of Alabama in 1983.

[446]See Margaret Price, *Negro Voter in the South* (Atlanta: Southern Regional Council, 1957); Donald R. Matthews, *Negroes and the New Southern Politics* (New York: Harcourt, Brace and World, 1966).

county-unit system was declared unconstitutional in 1962.[447] In 1917 Georgia's Democratic-controlled legislature had given statutory authority to a county-unit system for selecting candidates in the Democratic primary. This included the nomination for all state offices and for Congress, both Senate and House. Eight counties had 6 unit votes each, 30 counties had 4 votes each, and 121 counties had 2 votes each. These units were arbitrarily assigned, and there was never any change in them, despite the great shift of population to urban centers that began after World War I. Thus, for a politician, editor, or citizen who attempted to participate in progressive politics in Georgia, the choice almost invariably was one of less attractive alternatives.

The late Eugene Talmadge used to say he would never campaign in a county that had a streetcar in it—he didn't need to. The unit votes of rural counties would elect him. The more populous urban areas were in bondage. Elimination of the unit system in 1962 and enactment of voter laws in 1964 enabled Atlanta and the state to be free. Lester Maddox was elected by the legislature, not the people.

Mr. Sherrill, who seems mildly hung up on "Atlanta's money kings," "Atlanta's slickers," and "the Top People of Atlanta," writes, by way of illustration, of the late Senator Walter George's withdrawal in 1956.[448] This left the way open for Herman Talmadge to be unopposed. Mr. Sherrill describes it, from information given him, as a betrayal by the Atlanta power structure. It was not. Those whom Mr. Sherrill describes as in power tried every possible way to save Senator George from having opposition. The polls and the county leaders showed the aging senator could not get the unit vote. Mr. Talmadge knew this. There was no betrayal. In those years the unit system was the real power structure.

Mr. Sherrill reports that the late Eugene Talmadge, never once supported by me, at one time asked me to write the Talmadge biography.

---

[447] See V. O. Key, Jr., *Southern Politics in State and Nation* (New York: Vintage Books, 1949); Jack Bass and Walter DeVries, *Transformation of Southern Politics: Social Change and Political Consequence Since 1945* (New York: New American Library, 1976); Dewey W. Grantham, Jr., *Democratic South* (Athens: University of Georgia, 1963); Monroe Lee Billington, *Political South in the Twentieth Century* (New York: Scribner, 1975).

[448] For more by McGill on George, see *Southern Encounters*.

He did, and I appreciate having the offer recalled. The suggestion was dismissed. "I wish you would," said the former governor, "I've already thought of the title."

"What's that, Governor?"

"The Life of Eugene Talmadge, by his Enemy, Ralph McGill."

"I am not your enemy, Governor. I just never have agreed with your ideas."

"I know," he said, "but it would sell a hell of a lot of books."[449]

The pre-1962 and 1964 molds are already broken. There is a lot of gothic left. And there really are some new stars in the political skies.

---

[449]In *Gothic Politics in the Deep South*, Sherrill chides McGill for staying merely "one step" ahead of citizens on human rights (pp. 49-52).

95

Review
of James G. Maddox's
The Advancing South
and F. Ray Marshall's
Labor in the South

T he sometimes melancholy but always challenging story that marches through the pages of two recent books on the South is an enthralling, enlightening one. The books complement one another in a most happy, extraordinary manner.

It has been one of the common attitudes of the Southerner to be defensive and unreasonably sensitive, not merely to criticism, but to factual recitals of his history—military, social, and economic. He likes to believe that he and his region are somehow different; that neither is appreciated or understood. But this stain of bitter myrrh in his mind has created a psychological attitude somewhat akin to that of the parents of a crippled child who are, understandably, the more fiercely protective of that child and extremely sensitive about any comment or discussion, however well meant, on the child's welfare.

Reprinted from *Monthly Labor Review* (March 1968), by permission of Mrs. Ralph McGill, Bureau of Labor Statistics, and *Monthly Labor Review*. Review of James G. Maddox, E. E. Liebhafsky, Vivian W. Henderson, and Herbert M. Hamlin, *The Advancing South: Manpower Prospects and Problems* (New York: Twentieth Century Fund, Inc., 1967); and F. Ray Marshall, *Labor in the South* (Cambridge: Harvard University Press, 1967).

Even now, as the twentieth century draws on toward its end, veteran Southern senators and congressmen, many with the records of distinguished service to their country, are angrily opposing federal legislation designed to improve the quality of education because the bills at issue are "not fair to the South" and do not recognize its "peculiar problems." That the South's long delay in development is in the main due to lack of education for all its children, more especially the Negro child, does not matter. What matters is that none tread on the toes of the South's "customs." For largely the same reasons, the same Congress will show a heavy majority of Southern senators and congressmen in various anti-labor stances.

Professor Maddox and his staff—all Southerners but one—have produced a book which is earnestly recommended to boards of corporations who may be considering plant investment in the region.

The South (the eleven states of the Old Confederacy plus Kentucky and Oklahoma) is increasing its real per capita income at a rate faster than the rest of the nation. (It had, and has, a larger gap to close.) Its share of the nation's investment in plant and equipment is also growing.

The collaborating economist-authors carefully, but nonetheless courageously, offer a projection of the South's likely growth rate at least through 1975. They are, with a few reservations, optimistic.

Much depends on what the South does with its inferior schools and its racial problem. Great progress has been made. Much of it has been reluctantly permitted. There still is considerable resistance. And, candor demands, some states and counties have made token, or fingers-crossed, pledges to carry out congressional civil rights legislation. They drag feet and hide evasions by various means.

Professor Maddox and his associates urgently advise that the symbolic chains that remain on the legs of the South's economy be eliminated with nondeliberate speed. Until the chains are removed the economy will limp.

It is precisely here that the more thoughtful boards of corporations investigating investment in the South can protect and enhance their own opportunities. They can—and in this reviewer's opinion, have a national responsibility to do so—select for investment location those areas which honestly have eliminated, or are sincerely eliminating, all the old ugliness and violence of discrimination from their communities.

To assist with capital investment a community that still retains a Klan-type mentality and that does not honestly and earnestly offer equal educational advantages to all children and to its young men and women cannot be a profitable long-run policy.

The Southerner reading this book will be impressed with the clarity and coherence in the presentation of the historical developments—the reason why the South became and remained agricultural and why, after the Civil War, it endured so much trauma of violence and corrosive poverty in all things of the spirit.

It is a scholarly summation. (If there is one omission it is that of a few paragraphs on the effect of the Hayes-Tilden election machinations and the effect of the reestablishment of states' rights over the race problem. But the omission is not really important.)

The central theme of the book is the South's progress, especially since 1940, and what must be done if the pace is to continue. (The writer recalls talking with the president of a large retail company in Atlanta who said, in 1945, that his new expansion, covering about a city block, was the first large construction ever built in the state without going outside Atlanta sources for financing.)

In 1938, President Roosevelt's committee on the economic condition of the South reported it to be the nation's number one economic problem. Many conditions have been corrected. But in 1967, the findings are that the greatest problem is "a large, unskilled, poorly educated agricultural work force that is no longer needed to till the land and is insufficiently trained to meet the requirements of the expanding manufacturing and service-producing industries."

In 1938, the region was not really competing with other geographic divisions. Today it is. The authors assert that the South's "greatest handicaps in competition with other regions for rapid-growth, high-wage industries are the shortage of a trained work force and the remnants of values and traditions that attach too little importance to developing the full potentials of the region's human resources." The truth of this conclusion is every day made abundantly clear.

The South must increase its per capita productivity, these economists say, in order to accelerate its economic growth.

Giving maximum priority to the development of the region's human resources, they believe, will provide the means; that is, to make quality education available to all with "greatly expanded public expenditures for education by State and local governments, and Federal aid and Federal action on a much more massive scale than at present."

The study stresses that intense effort must be devoted to the disadvantaged and underprivileged, both Negro and white; the federal government should establish and run a regionwide system of racially integrated training and child-care centers for preschool children available to all without cost; at the adult level, local, state, and federal agencies must find new and better ways to expand opportunities for the many rural and urban citizens the region failed to educate and train in the past.

Some of the South's cities have had and will have more protest violence. The slums, with their quota of untrained and uneducated men and women, were once mute indictments. Today they are militant and vocal.

It will be a great pity if this book is not widely read by all Southern business, professional, and educational people in particular. In its inclusion of projections to 1975, it is, I believe, the best book on the Southern region since Howard Odum's historic *Southern Regions*, published in 1936.[450]

It will be even more sad if Southern politicians, newspaper publishers, and editors do not read it. Too many of these people, along with a distressing number of the clergy, have helped perpetuate the more fatuous and false myths of the South and the nonexistent virtues of segregation, disfranchisement, and injustices that have kept the South's social and economic progress and its mind, as well, in repression.[451]

Professor Marshall's history of labor in the South follows naturally as a second reading insofar as a historical perspective of the South is concerned. His views on attitudes toward labor, the use of the "church" as a barrier to labor's efforts to attain the right to bargain collectively, the often solid front of the church, the press, and the "respectable" community against labor are best understood after reading the Maddox book.

---

[450]Howard Odum, *Southern Regions of the United States* (Chapel Hill: University of North Carolina Press, 1936).

[451]For McGill's evaluation of false Southern myths see the editor's introduction.

But one must hasten to say that *Labor in the South* also stands alone. It is a history, but the first of its kind. Strangely enough, no comprehensive chronicle of the Southern labor movement had been written until Professor Marshall did this.

This reviewer knew the able Bill Mitch, who in the 1930s worked at organizing Alabama coal miners and, later, steelworkers throughout the South; Steve Nance, highly esteemed and respected, who worked at textile organization in the turbulent 1930s; Miss Lucy Randolph Mason, the legendary Virginia aristocrat of historic lineage, who was my good friend and who was, incredibly, a successful CIO organizer and troubleshooter; and many others who came and went in those days of depression and hope. As a boy I recall seeing the National Guard called out to the Tennessee coal fields and hearing the talk of farmers who, in winters when crops were laid by, would work in the mines.

They and many others who pioneered before them and those who came after are in this remarkably interesting book, which manages to be a story of human beings while recording a labor movement in a unique region.

Professor Marshall quotes economist John T. Dunlop as having demonstrated that "features that are ordinarily regarded as distinctive to a national system do not enter equally into each industrial relations system within its borders."[452] He then demonstrates that the American South is sufficiently unique to provide a significant comparison with the rest of the country. There is no questioning his success in so doing.

The South's individual characteristics are being dissolved by industrialization. Its pattern moves closer to that of the nation. But it is not yet there, and from a historical viewpoint, the region remains unique.

Introduction of manufacturing came to the South more abruptly than elsewhere. Industrialization came on the heels of the humiliation of the Reconstruction. Broadus Mitchell, an economic historian, in 1921 wrote the *Rise of Cotton Mills in the South*.[453] He said of these industrialists that

---

[452]Quoting John T. Dunlop, *Industrial Relations Systems* (New York: Henry Holt and Co., 1958) 24-25, in Marshall, *Labor in the South*, 3.

[453]Broadus Mitchell, *The Rise of Cotton Mills in the South*, Johns Hopkins University Studies in Historical and Political Science, 39 (Baltimore: Johns Hopkins University Press, 1921) 107-281.

their tools were only such as were offered by determination in the midst of poverty. These things gave to the whole movement a social sanction, I might almost say social sanctification, which was largely lacking elsewhere. An added element to this end was the fact that the industry, particularly the cotton factories, furnished bread and meat to the hordes of poor whites who waited to be reclaimed after the destitution which slavery had entailed upon them.

This, I believe, is a paragraph most necessary to one's reading of the Marshall book. There was a "sanctification" quality to the mills. In fact, a feature of religion in the South was that the various sect religions, by a sort of osmosis, took the South's mores of prejudice, custom, traditions, and attitudes into the body of religion. It became, therefore, "religious" to support segregation in the years before the Civil War and to give God's endorsement to segregation and white supremacy after the end of slavery.[454]

Hence, it was not at all unusual for evangelical preachers to go off into the most extravagant, hypnotic denunciations of labor organizers. This reviewer recalls hearing CIO organizers denounced as representing the anti-Christ—John L. Lewis.

Some manufacturers provided a church and a "mill-paid" preacher. Foremen seemed always to be deacons or elders. Others, whenever an organizer was reported near, would summon one of the fiery-mouthed, pulpit-pounding tent evangelists. He would set up for business and nightly flay the evil men who would lure good Christian men and women into the sinful snares set by the devil's serving. Many of the stately churches in cities also were sounding boards of opposition.

County sheriffs and, indeed, the official power structure usually could be counted on to help ride the organizer out of town on a rail or, more politely, put him in a car, give him a good beating or scare, and deposit him beyond the county line.

There were other factors in the uniqueness of the South. Presence of a huge number of unskilled and uneducated Negroes—"the last hired and the first fired"—tended to hold down wages and to make the job-

---

[454]See Charles Reagan, *Baptized in Blood: Religion of the Lost Cause, 1865-1920* (Athens: University of Georgia Press, 1980); Samuel S. Hill, *Religion and the Solid South* (Nashville: Abingdon Press, 1972); Kenneth K. Bailey, *Southern White Protestantism in the Twentieth Century* (New York: Harper & Row, 1964); C. Dwight Dorough, *Bible Belt Mystique* (Philadelphia: Westminster Press, 1974).

holder fearful of replacement. Those were years when much of the labor was unskilled or semiskilled. Automation was not a problem. The race question and white supremacy put economic or bread-and-butter issues in second place.

Despite the coming of cotton mills, saw mills, turpentining, and other plants to the South, the region historically has been underindustrialized. Today, although much progress has been made and a real industrial boom is indicated if the South responds to the need for improved education and an end to its racial tensions, the region is still below the national average in industrial capacity.

Professor Marshall organized his book well. The labor history of each industry is given adequate treatment. We also get a look at development and problems of unions before 1928. These were primitive years. One finds in them the stories of strikes against plants for hiring Negroes and the development of patterns of discrimination. Low costs had begun early to bring New England textile mills to the cotton South. Strikes against Negro workers soon made the new mills "lily white," save in the positions of janitors, sweepers, and cleaners.[455]

There was considerable violence in the long years of efforts by textile workers to unionize. From Louisiana up to North Carolina, where the Gastonia story, involving charges of Communist activity, made national headlines, violence made news across a decade or more. The names of some of the mill towns where violence occurred in the 1920s and earlier have reappeared in the news of racial violence during the past four years.

The 1930s, with the passage of the Wagner Act and other labor legislation, and the coming of the CIO, are thoroughly and accurately discussed and analyzed. The excitement of those days comes through. Those were the years when some mills had barricades of cotton bales before them, and on their roofs they had riflemen and, in some instances, machinegunners who had learned those weapons in the First World War.

In the concluding chapter, "Future of the Unions," Professor Marshall says that trends are favorable for continued growth of unions in the

---

[455]See Ray Marshall and Virgil L. Christian, Jr., eds., *Employment of Blacks in the South: A Perspective on the 1960s* (Austin: University of Texas Press, 1978); Timothy Thomas Fortune, *Black and White: Land, Labor, and Politics in the South* (Chicago; Johnson Publishing Company, 1970).

South, particularly the Southwest. He believes that increase in Negro voter registration in the South will provide a favorable influence.[456]

Growth, however, may not be easy. The South, he says, will have to increase its union memberships by 1,455,000 between 1962 and 1972, just to hold its proportion of fourteen percent of the nonagricultural work force. Meanwile, the blue-collar worker force decreases. In the South the white-collar service employees are even less drawn to union affiliation than in other regions. Nonetheless, concludes Mr. Marshall, the base for growth exists and is good.

---

[456]See Edgar Streeter Dunn, *Recent Southern Economic Development As Revealed by the Changing Structure of Employment* (Gainesville: University of Florida Press, 1962); Brian Rungeling et al., *Employment, Income, and Welfare in the Rural South* (New York: Praeger, 1977).

96

Letter
to *Center* Magazine

T o the editors: Harry S. Ashmore was at his superb rational best
in his article "Black Power and White Inertia" (January).[457]
An astonishing number of things have happened since Mr.
Ashmore manned the journalistic ramparts at Little Rock in 1957. His
nostalgic reference to his old friends who survive down where the soybeans bloom and grow in old cotton fields, was especially appreciated.
After all, Little Rock was the first assault on the United States Supreme
Court decision of 1954. Many, nay, a horde, of newspaper, magazine,
and TV reporters visited the city to see the long run of that dreadful and
shabby show inspired by the actions of then Governor Orval Faubus.
The only drinking oasis in the town was at the Little Rock Club, a private one. Member Ashmore and his publisher at the *Arkansas Gazette*,
Hugh Patterson, bought so many drinks for the visitors that they legitimately became known as "the battle and bottle scarred" heroes of Little

Reprinted from *Center* magazine, March 1968, with the permission of Mrs.
Ralph McGill and *Center* magazine.

[457]*Center* magazine. In a draft of the letter in the McGill papers, McGill had writ-
ten "discussion of the books, *Black Power: the Politics of Liberation, The New Romans:
An American Experience*, and the Southern region," rather than "in his article 'Black
Power and White Inertia.' " Manuscript provided by Mrs. Ralph McGill from
McGill papers, now at Emory University, Atlanta.

Rock. The *Gazette* was then suffering financially because of the boycott brought on by the clamor of the idiot "never, never" segregationists. I often have wondered how much the bar bill added to the debt. Happily, the *Gazette* prospers and the Ashmore-Patterson war debt was paid long ago.[458]

It was pleasant in the Little Rock Club. The Negro waiters, quiet and scholarly in manner, cast covert looks of love and admiration in Mr. Ashmore's direction. This offset the glares and the not always muted phrases of the power-structure members. There was a great loss of weight among the fat cats of Little Rock in those long weeks of red-neck anarchy and of law by federal troops. When the big men came to lunch and saw Ashmore and his publisher standing at the bar with visiting journalists, their appetites went with the wind. They dribbled soup on their chins and merely nibbled at the chef's salad or peas and croquettes. Mostly, they fingered their martinis and muttered. A man can get thin on that diet.

Ever since 1957 it has been my belief that one of the most revealing, and perhaps significant, sentences in the history of the move to admit the Negro to the First and Fourteenth Amendment clubs was the wailing shriek of a segregationist lady. She was a part of the crowd watching when the troops brought the courageous young Negro children to school. There were hopes of barring them. But they were moved in through a side door. When this news spread this woman let out a wailing cry, "Oh, Lordy, the niggers is already *in* the school!"

And they were.

Events between 1957 and the appearance of the book by Stokely Carmichael and Charles Hamilton that Ashmore writes about are many. In a sense, all America has been in a classroom since that time. The inevitable number of illiterates and dropouts failed the tests. But America has learned a lot and is pained by how much more it has to learn.

Perhaps the best comment on the Carmichael book is a story out of Atlanta. SNCC's national headquarters are here.[459] The building has

---

[458]See text of McGill's "*Arkansas Gazette* Pulitzer Winners Speech," in *Ralph McGill: Editor and Publisher*, ed. Calvin McLeod Logue (Durham: Moore Publishing Company, 1969) 2:103-11.

[459]Student Nonviolent Coordinating Committee. See McGill's review of Howard Zinn's *SNCC: The New Abolitionists*, in this volume.

been closed for some time and the telephones cut off for lack of payment of bills. SNCC is reduced in numbers to perhaps 150. It long ago lost its credit cards. A reporter recently gained admission to the building. There were, he said, several boxes containing copies of Carmichael's book. They were growing musty. No one had been interested enough to do anything with them.

SNCC, like Carmichael and his book, is a melancholy story. From its beginning in North Carolina through the freedom rides, the freedom schools, and the long contests with segregation before the public accommodation law, SNCC was an inspiring organization. I do not think I have ever seen any more courageous, any sweeter or more dedicated lot of young people. They endured jails, abuses, brutalities. Some were killed.

When Carmichael opted for an antiwhite Black Power group he cut them off. I quite understand how three or four years of life in small rural Mississippi, Alabama, and south Georgia towns would torture and distort perspectives. But Carmichael's book, as Ashmore properly says, reveals more about Carmichael's lack of organized thought than it does about Black Power or the "politics of liberation." In essence Carmichael reduces Black Power to what high-school civic books have been saying about ethnic groups and their struggle to attain political power. The whole book is an immature product. One gets the feeling it surely must have been written at least two or three years ago. Its contents, save for the abusive and defiant rhetoric, are not really about Black Power.

Mr. Ashmore accurately argues that the presence of a brilliant lawyer, Thurgood Marshall, on the U.S. Supreme Court and the election of Negro mayors, legislators and judges, plus the grass-roots election of some two hundred local officials in the Southern states, including two sheriffs, are not "tokenism." Nor is the job opportunity for educated and trained men and women tokenism.

The dilemma is that the civil rights laws do not touch, save in the voter area, the lives of the really poor, unskilled, and uneducated. Several million of these, along with a few hundred thousand white persons, have migrated out of the South. The great exodus began in the 1920s with the arrival of the boll weevil. It slowed in the 1930s and was much accelerated in the 1940-1950 and the 1950-1960 decades. These have filled up the ghetto slums. Many are middle-aged and older. Their future is a new, acute economic and social problem.

Power in this country flows out of the ballot box—and the Negro registration figures are meaningful and will be more so.[460] Black Power means an end to discrimination in philanthropy in its gifts to higher education as well as an end to discrimination in overall job opportunity.

Black Power also means the attainment of pride in being a Negro, an identity with one's historical past and culture. Neither "black" nor "white" is a color in the technical sense. But certainly it is true that black is as beautiful as any color, technical or literal. There are other elements of which the ballot remains the best tool.[461]

---

[460]See Margaret Price, *Negro Voter in the South* (Atlanta: Southern Regional Council, 1957); Donald R. Matthews, *Negroes and the New Southern Politics* (New York: Harcourt, Brace and World, 1966); Steven F. Lawson, *Black Ballots: Voting Rights in the South, 1944-1969* (New York: Columbia University Press, 1976); Chandler Davidson, *Biracial Politics: Conflict and Coalition in the Metropolitan South* (Baton Rouge: Louisiana State University Press, 1972); and McGill's "If the Southern Negro Got the Vote," "State of the South," and "Case for the Southern Progressive," in volumes 1 and 2.

[461]In an earlier draft of this piece in the McGill papers, McGill ended the letter as follows:

Carmichael, who seemingly tries to be the opposite number of the Southern racist Fascist, is the big and helpful symbol to the Southern red-neck and the Southern "power structure" figure of like beliefs. He has added thousands of votes to the Wallaces, Maddoxes, and Williamses. His book is so poorly organized and immature one expects him any day to apologize for it. He was not even true to the Carmichael he has shown us by deed and spoken word. Black Power is not to be attained by hating whitey. Nor can true Black Power emerge from separatism. As for Mr. Keats' book, alas, I have not read it. I apologize. I have, however, obtained it and will soon have done so.

97

Foreword
to David M. Abshire's
The South Rejects a Prophet

I n my early boyhood, on a farm some twenty miles north of Chattanooga, and later, as I grew into my teens in Chattanooga itself, I heard stories of David M. Key, of William G. (Parson) Brownlow, and of the bitter and violent division between Unionists and those who sided with Jefferson Davis and the Confederacy.

Mr. Abshire's book is much more than an able biography of David M. Key. His book makes a valuable contribution to understanding the complex machinations of both South and North that were involved in the "steal" of the 1876 presidential election, in which conservative Southern leaders, including a number of newspaper editors and former Confederate generals, joined to make Rutherford B. Hayes president of the United States. This was one of the great pivotal points in American history. The conservative Southerners wanted railroads and new industries to be developed in the South. They also wanted an end to Reconstruction. In going with Hayes, they obtained both.

The costs of this decision to the nation were evident early and are now coming due in full measure. In ending Reconstruction with the

Foreword reprinted by permission of Mrs. Ralph McGill and Frederick A. Praeger from David M. Abshire, *The South Rejects a Prophet* (New York: Frederick A. Praeger, 1968).

Hayes election, the Republican party and the victorious North abandoned the newly freed Negro and returned him wholly to the control of the states under states' rights. There were then no segregation laws. The ballot was open to the Negro. But both parties had been guilty of manipulating and corrupting the Negro vote. Once states' rights were again in the saddle, the various black codes, segregation, and the several devices that would effectively bar the Negro from a voice in choosing his representatives and that would separate him from the processes of democratic citizenship began to multiply.[462] The consequences of this folly and injustice are being felt now, because millions of persons have migrated to the nation's industrial and urban centers, coming from a South where a segregated system debased education for both white and Negro citizens and denied millions of them the opportunity to acquire literacy and vocational and professional skills.

David M. Key, an emotional and yet a thinking man, saw far beyond his time. Originally deeply committed to the Confederacy, he lost patience in the postwar years with those who sought to return to the past. Many of these Southern leaders preached a new attempt at secession and war. It was a turbulent time, and none participated in it more fully than Key.

Mr. Abshire's book is an excellent portrayal of this important period in history and of the efforts of one man to contend with the violent forces then loose in the land.

---

[462]See C. Vann Woodward, *The Strange Career of Jim Crow*, 3d rev. ed. (New York: Oxford University Press, 1974); Woodward, *Burden of Southern History* (Baton Rouge: Louisiana State University Press, 1960).

98

We Must Go Along Together for Better or Worse

I am into my thirty-ninth year with the *Atlanta Constitution*, having come here 2 April 1929. When I look back to the Atlanta of that year and contrast it with that of 1968, I am almost awed by the changes that have come and by the progress made. However, I am well aware that the progress has been largely in a few areas and that advances have not been general. Nevertheless, I have always had hope. And I now believe that much of the old inertia is dissipated and that there is a general forward movement. I am sure this forward advance will be one of increased tempo.

You ask for observations. I feel that one of our great failures has been the neglect of Negro history and the many important contributions of the black American to our common country. This contribution began, of course, with the revolution that brought independence and it has continued. I am of the opinion that the white American needs this particular phase of education equally as much—if not more—than does the black American.[463]

Reprinted from the *Atlanta Inquirer,* 3 August 1969, by permission of Mrs. Ralph McGill and the *Atlanta Inquirer.* The piece was written on 23 July 1968, for the eighth anniversary of the *Atlanta Inquirer* and for that paper's "salute to black progress and history."

[463]John Hope Franklin, *From Slavery to Freedom: A History of Negro Americans,* 5th ed. (New York: A. A. Knopf, 1980).

As I look back to my early years in Atlanta, I believe that a part of our local education could be an appreciation of the important role played by much of Atlanta's Negro leadership in the bygone years. I do not believe it is either fair or productive of accurate evaluation to judge persons outside the context of their time. I know that today many persons tend to brush aside the contribution made by the late A. T. Walden. He had to cope with his environment and that environment was not that of today.

The same would apply to the late Dr. Rufus E. Clement, and to others I could name. They dealt with situations and an environment which was rigid beyond belief. They showed courage and ingenuity. Dr. Benjamin Mays, who, fortunately for all of us, has lived into our present, is an example of a man who wrought well in an old environment and is effective in the new.[464] I believe a part of the educational process for Atlanta's younger black and white students should be instruction in this aspect of an older Atlanta and an older South.

In looking ahead I can see that the constructive effect of black power in its political and public-opinion aspects will continue. Certainly we know that those black Atlantans who have been elected to public office have strengthened our political system. I am sure this process will expand and continue.

I can well understand the more militant demands for separatism, but I cannot see how separatism in any country is a workable concept or policy. We have only to look at certain European and African countries where large ethnic groups have tried separatism to see how impossible of success it is. I think our situation is somewhat like that expressed in a wedding ceremony. We must go along together, for better or worse.[465]

I salute the *Inquirer* and congratulate it on the role it has played in helping make Atlanta a better city.

---

[464]Benjamin Elijah Mays, *Born To Rebel: An Autobiography* (New York: C. Scribner, 1971).

[465]In his speech to students at Booker T. Washington High School in Atlanta, 3 February 1969, the day he died, McGill, in response to a question from a person in the audience concerning the black separatism movement, stated: "I don't think this will work. I would be sorry to see it tried on any great scale. . . . You can't separate yourself from the world. You can't separate yourself from your fellow man. Finally, you've got to be a part of life"; see McGill's speech in *Ralph McGill: Editor and Publisher,* ed. Calvin McLeod Logue (Durham: Moore Publishing Company, 1969) 2:495-513.

99

Preface to Carl Sandburg's
Chicago Race Riots

How much do cities, a people, a nation learn in fifty years? Not much. Half a century ago, on a hot and steaming July day, a Negro boy swam past an invisible line of segregation at one of Chicago's public beaches. He was stoned, knocked unconscious, and drowned. Police shrugged off requests from Negroes that the rock-throwing white men be arrested. After the body was pulled from the water fighting was renewed. This and other forms of violence did not stop for three days. Thirty-four men had then been killed, twenty Negroes, fourteen whites. An uncounted number, more than a hundred, had been wounded. Several houses in the "black belt" had been burned and damaged.

A young reporter and writer, Carl Sandburg, was assigned to write a series of newspaper articles on the riots. They were published in book form in 1919 by a newly established publishing firm, Harcourt, Brace and Howe.

It is from these reports that we learn that a city, a nation, a people, don't learn very much, if anything, about themselves in half a century.

Reprinted from Carl Sandburg, *The Chicago Race Riots* (New York: Harcourt, Brace & World, 1969), by permission of Mrs. Ralph McGill and Harcourt, Brace & World, Inc. Copyright 1969, by Harcourt, Brace & World, Inc.

There were commissions in 1919. They discovered there was much poverty. They found that the hearses haul more babies out of poverty areas than from those where the wages and hours are better.

There were other facts revealed by investigation.

Chicago's black-belt population of 50,000 had more than doubled to at least 125,000 by 1919. (The black population was 812,637 in the 1960 census. An early estimate for 1969 was near 1,000,000.)

In 1919 no new tenements or housing had been built in Chicago to absorb the pressure of doubled population.

The black doughboys had come home from France and war cantonments. They had a new voice—or wanted to have one.

Thousands of Negroes had migrated from the South where "neither a world war for democracy, nor the Croix de Guerre, nor three gold chevrons, nor any number of wound stripes, assures them of the right to vote or to have their votes counted or to participate responsibly in the elective determinations of the American republic."

Housing, war psychology, politics, and organization of labor and jobs fueled the Chicago riot in 1919.

That and several other riots of half a century ago were a good school of experience. But we were all dropouts. Few Americans learned anything.

The decade of the 1920s was about to begin—the era of wonderful nonsense.

During that span of stock-market frenzy, few north of the Mason-Dixon Line were to pay any attention to the cotton South—where the boll weevil had arrived. He had made a long journey of many years from South America into Mexico, across the Rio Grande and the waters of the Mississippi, into the region where for so long a time cotton had been king. The boll weevil makes tiny noises. It lays an egg in a cotton ball. The hatched-out weevil chews away—just enough to kill the boll. The clicking of the stock-market ticker tapes drowned out the weevil chorus.

By 1922 and 1923 cotton plantations and farms that had been producing thousands of bales of cotton were turning out 150 or 220 bales. By the late 1920s many of the two-storied houses were empty and deserted. So were thousands of cabins and shacks where the tenants and sharecroppers had lived. The hearthstones about which families had warmed themselves in grief and hope were cold. Doors swung drunkenly in the wind. Many a man owing "the man" and the county-seat store with its marked-up prices had vanished silently in the night.[466] Numerous cabins were burned. Careless hunters, huddling inside in a sudden slash of November rain, would start fires that sometimes got out of hand. There were hundreds of lonely chimneys in the 1920s. (They were even lonelier in the 1930s.) Nearly 200,000 men, black and white, left the South in the 1920s—the boll-weevil decade. Most of them went to Dee-troit, to Akron, to Pittsburgh, to South Chicago . . . anywhere there were jobs that unskilled hands could do.

The very corrosiveness of the depression years of fear, unemployment, and grief brought a temporary halt to most of the migration from the South. Those years also delayed the development of resistance to racism that was plainly visible in the riots of 1919.

A. Mitchell Palmer, U.S. attorney general of that period, was far ahead of a later Joe McCarthy in creating a "red" hysteria. Woodrow Wilson sought to calm Palmer.[467] He could not. The Palmer raids and charges yielded no results save that he was for a while a hero. The costly effect of A. Mitchell Palmer's becoming a hero was that he gave free rein to all the ugliness and violence in America.

Anti-Semites had their inning. They printed and distributed *The Protocols of the Elders of Zion*, long before proved to be one of the more hoary fakes. The anti-Semites aroused the more simpleminded with tales of Jewish conspiracy. The anti-Catholics were also in full bloom. They blamed the war on the Catholics and the Negro. They printed smears and lies about Catholics and the plot for the pope to come to America and take over. The Ku Klux Klan staged a revival out of Atlanta. America was so spiritually bankrupt that the nightshirt and mask

---

[466]See A. E. Parkins, *The South: Its Economic-Geographic Development* (1938; reprint, Westport CT: Greenwood Press, 1970); Paul E. Mertz, *New Deal Policy and Southern Rural Poverty* (Baton Rouge: Louisiana State University Press, 1978); Brian Rungeling et al., *Employment, Income, and Welfare in the Rural South* (New York: Praeger, 1977); Edgar Streeter Dunn, *Recent Southern Economic Development as Revealed by the Changing Structure of Employment* (Gainesville: University of Florida Press, 1962).

[467]For more by McGill on Wilson, see *Southern Encounters: Southerners of Note in Ralph McGill's South*, ed. Calvin M. Logue (Macon GA: Mercer University Press, 1983).

business flourished nationally. The Klan stronghold was in Dixie. But it also established strong centers in Indiana, Oklahoma, and Oregon. Never have all the peddlers of hate and lies had so great a harvest. The Negro suffered most.

Lynchings reached a crescendo in the South. Mob violence had been a part of Reconstruction. In exchange for Southern support to make Rutherford B. Hayes president in 1876, the North's political and economic power structures had abandoned the Negro. He was literally "turned back to states' rights." Black codes, disfranchisement, and segregation by law were quick developments. That horror—the mob at a frenzy of bloody killing—was accompanied by laws and states' rights decisions that declared the Negro inferior and defined his "place." These mob activities also sent Negroes northward in search for jobs that were less and less to be found in the South, where fear and the boll weevil were at work.[468]

But it was not merely the Negro who left. He was the more numerous in out-migration. But the poor white went too—and all the Negro's liabilities also were his. He had but one advantage—he had a white skin and he had been reared to believe this gave him supremacy and status.

So, when Negro migrants came asking for jobs at factories and mills, the white jobholders, especially the immigrants from Dixie, reacted with fury. In east St. Louis in 1917, forty-seven persons, mostly Negroes, were killed and hundreds more wounded in vicious race riots growing out of resentment against Negro employment.

In July of 1919, in Washington, the nation's capital, several thousand troops were called out to halt the white-black rioting. That same summer there were riots in New York and Omaha—all in addition to those in Chicago. In the South that summer there were seven riots. Most of them grew out of the "impudence" of returned Negro veterans demanding their rights as citizens.

Reporter Carl Sandburg's accounts were not easy to get. They are not always, as he himself said, in exact sequence. But it was a fine, down-to-earth job.

---

[468]See C. Vann Woodward, *Strange Career of Jim Crow*, 3d rev. ed. (New York: Oxford University Press, 1974); Woodward, *Burden of Southern History* (Baton Rouge: Louisiana State University Press, 1960).

Among the many revealing sentences from his reports, one will illustrate:

"During 1918 there had been 30,000 applications for jobs and 10,000 placed. . . . There is a steady influx of colored population from the Southern states. . . ."

Let us go back also to some lynching headlines out of the year 1919.

> April 5, 1919—Blakely, Georgia: When Private William Little, a Negro soldier returning from the war, arrived at the railroad station here a few weeks ago, he was met by a band of whites who ordered him to remove his uniform and walk home in his underwear. Bystanders persuaded the men to release him. Little continued to wear the uniform as he had no other clothes. . . . Anonymous notes reached him warning him to quit wearing it. Yesterday Private Little was found dead, his body badly beaten, on the outskirts of town. He was wearing his uniform.

> May 1, 1919—Shreveport, Louisiana: A Vicksburg, Shreveport and Pacific train was held up by an armed mob here today, about five miles from Monroe, and George Holden, accused of writing a note to a white woman, was taken from the train and shot. . . . The note was in plain handwriting. According to friends, Holden was not able to read or write.

> May 15, 1919—Vicksburg, Mississippi: Lloyd Clay, Negro laborer, was roasted to death here last night. He had been accused of entering a white woman's room. . . . A mob of between 800 and 1,000 men and women removed the prisoner from the jail. He was taken to the corner of Clay and Farmer Streets, covered with oil, set afire and hoisted to an elm tree. Bullets were fired into the body. . . .

These are samples.

During the first six months of 1919, lynchings declined as against the first half of 1918. The total was a mere twenty-eight in comparison with thirty-five in 1918. Of those lynched in the first half of 1919, one was a Negro woman.

The exodus from South to North continued. The depression decade slowed it. But by 1940 it was at a greater peak than ever. It was speeded again by World War II, when lend-lease factories working overtime were a tremendous magnet for labor. The disaster at Pearl Harbor turned much of this tide of labor westward to build planes, ships, and weapons for retaking the Pacific.

The out-movement of people has never stopped. Indeed, the largest migrant movement was in 1950-1960. Since 1940 almost four million

Negroes have left the South. When the war plants closed they stayed on, for they had nowhere else to go. They filled up the central cities. They are the ghetto, the slum people—they and enclaves of poor "hillbilly" whites. The latter, also cheated and degraded by the system, no longer have a meaningful skin value.

Their bitterness and alienation increases.

In 1940 about seventy percent of all the Negroes in America were in the South. And now? Maybe fifty percent. We shall need to wait for the 1970 census. . . .

Carl Sandburg's reports of half a century ago are a serious indictment of us as a people. We are again confronted with our incredible neglect of social facts and our lack of awareness of their meaning.

One of his chapters reproduces the demands of the National Association for the Advancement of Colored People following the Chicago riots. They are mild compared with those of 1968. One wonders what might have happened to the social, political, and economic health of America had those modest demands been met half a century ago.[469]

There cannot be a repetition of the past. There will be renewed attempts to thwart, delay or ignore the laws and the gains. They can hardly succeed.

In 1919 there were few Negroes registered to vote—and almost none in the South. In 1944 there were about a quarter of a million Negroes registered in the South. The voter registration laws were not enacted by the Congress until 1964 and were not implemented until 1965. In 1964 there were over two million black voters registered in the states of the old Confederacy. In 1969 the total is certainly three and a quarter million. There now are 385 Negroes elected to public office in the South— the heaviest concentration of such officials in the nation.[470]

---

[469]See John Hope Franklin and Isidore Starr, eds., *The Negro in Twentieth-Century America: A Reader on the Struggle for Civil Rights* (New York: Vintage Books, 1967).

[470]See Steven F. Lawson, *Black Ballots: Voting Rights in the South, 1944-1969* (New York: Columbia University Press, 1976); Chandler Davidson, *Biracial Politics: Conflict and Coalition in the Metropolitan South* (Baton Rouge: Louisiana State University Press, 1972); Jack Bass and Walter DeVries, *Transformation of Southern Politics: Social Change and Political Consequence Since 1945* (New York: New American Library, 1976); and "If the Southern Negro Got the Vote," "State of the South," and "Case for the Southern Progressive," in this volume.

The melancholy aspect of this progress is that the South and most of its congressmen, senators, public leaders, editors and clergymen opposed the advances. But they came on. (Open-housing legislation, for example, was stalled until the assassination of Dr. Martin Luther King, Jr.)

The lesson of 1919 and of later years has not been fully learned. There still is resistance to creating an unsegregated society in which the Negro is free to be his own self—not an imitation white man, but a Negro or black citizen of his country.

This reissue of Chicago's riot reports of fifty years ago is a bitter-tasting medicine. It indicts us as a people addicted to folly and violent resistance to healthful social and political change.

If the gentle reader is in need of a chill tonic, then let him open up the bottle of Carl Sandburg's report of fifty years ago and take a dose.[471]

---

[471]See McGill's essay on Sandburg in *Southern Encounters*.

100

Introduction
to John Osborne's
The Old South

I t is an evocative phrase—*The Old South*. Four of the five states that make up this old cotton South were the heart of the old Confederacy, which also reached westward from Virginia to include Arkansas and far southward to bring in Florida, a teenage state of sixteen years when the Civil War began. Mr. Osborne eloquently and with fine clarity discusses the culture and economics of that Old South. It was a region compulsively preoccupied with agriculture in general and cotton in particular. While the East and New England were developing a skilled working force and an increasingly significant class of merchants and exporters, most of the South clung stubbornly to growing cotton. Slaves were its labor force. Moreover, planters, out of an expressed fear and concern about security, usually forbade any education to this labor force. With the same preoccupation with the "system," they rented out

Reprinted from John Osborne, *The Old South: Alabama, Florida, Georgia, Mississippi, South Carolina* (New York: Time-Life Books, 1969), by permission of Mrs. Ralph McGill and Time-Life Books. An interesting draft of this introduction is in the McGill papers, provided by Mrs. Ralph McGill, now in the Emory University Library, Atlanta. For example, this paragraph is found only in the early draft of the essay: "Even the ante-bellum Old South was a region of yeomen. On the whole, they were isolated, without books and newspapers. The rivers were their thoroughfares. They had the stubborn independence and the fixed attitudes of yeomen. And, unhappily for them and the Union, there was no possibility of dialogue to ameliorate those attitudes."

their slaves to work in the few factories that existed or to do carpentry or building. There was, therefore, no opportunity for a skilled artisan class to develop. The South was "different," as it felt itself to be.

But what the Old South was not is almost as important as what it was—and is. It never really was "a land of cavaliers and cotton." The thousands who poured into Alabama and Mississippi in the 1830s and early 1840s never became a class of goateed gentlemen in broad-brimmed black hats, sitting on the verandas of big pillared mansions, drinking juleps stirred with a silver spoon and served by adoring black servants. When the Civil War came, about seventy-five percent of the Southern white people owned no slaves at all. A small planter class, by reason of its wealth and influence, managed to impress its politics and its legends on the cotton South. The facts just now are catching up with the romantic myths of a luxurious civilization that was, the makers of myths said, like that of Greece, built on slave labor.

Mr. Osborne is at his forthright best in his analysis of the course of Southern political leadership after Appomattox. The leaders did bring down upon themselves a radical Reconstruction. This was the first post-war tragedy. The second was the abandonment of the Negro by the North. This immoral decision was part and parcel of the Hayes-Tilden election steal in 1876. The Confederate Democrats privately agreed to halt any serious opposition to Rutherford B. Hayes's receiving the disputed electoral votes that had been sent in from three Southern states— South Carolina, Florida, and Louisiana. In return the Hayes government then removed remaining occupation troops and returned states' rights and the Negro problem to the several states.

"The New South" of the 1880s was the invention of an eloquent young editor, Henry Grady of the *Atlanta Constitution*. The antebellum South of slavery and secession was dead, he remarked. The South of union and freedom, however, was "living, breathing, growing every hour."[472] Grady was an optimist with his eyes on the stars. He wanted industry and jobs for the South. In many ways he was ahead of his times. But on the critical issue of Negro voting rights, disregarded in spirit

---

[472]Henry W. Grady, "New England Club Speech," in Joel Chandler Harris, ed., *Life of Henry W. Grady, Including His Writings and Speeches* (New York: Cassell Publishing Co., 1890) 83.

after 1876, and viciously denied after 1890, Grady was part of the consensus. He would not agree to such rights. Nor did he mention—nor did his audience ask about—the unconscionable violence in lynchings and other acts of physical repression that then disgraced the South and were to continue to do so until well into the twentieth century.

In the years since, many prophets from many and varied watchtowers have proclaimed a "New South." Still, the old past, the old convictions, and the old attitudes remain. The agricultural revolution and the exodus of millions of uneducated and unskilled Southerners to the cities of northern America have helped provide the inflammatory material for urban riots, set off the flight to the homogenized suburbs, and created a massive race problem throughout the country. But all this has paradoxically obscured the progress made in many areas of American life— and especially in the Old South. For despite the continued existence of old attitudes and prejudices, tremendous strides have been made in this region.

It is this presence of progress, I believe, that stimulates and continues my affection for the South. There is a mystique about the region, a feeling of attachment and warmth not easily translated into explanatory sentences. Even when one is frustrated by the many contradictions of the Old South, one feels this sense of moving on, of being a part of what is now, and what is ahead.

I remember some years ago, on a plane to Chicago, being seated beside a young Negro woman. She was, it developed, a teacher in a town near Atlanta. She was on her way to visit her parents in Chicago. They had migrated there years before, in the outflow of agricultural people that for so long has been a continuing chapter in the story of the South and the nation. She had come back to Georgia to teach. I asked her why.

"Well," she said, "I can tell you. Today I'm going back to Chicago. I'll see the girls who were in my class. They all have fairly good jobs. But, you know, their lives seem sterile to me. They go to the movies. They bowl. But, you know how it is in the South. That's where the big change is taking place. You can be a part of it. You feel you are making a contribution. The South is alive—in motion. That's where I want to be." (She still is here. That conversation took place a decade ago. Her town has changed for the better. And she has been a part of the process of change.)

It is not the old myths, the legends or the roll of drums and the squeal of fifes as the bands strike up "Dixie" that hold one in the South.[473] The Southerner in the Old South often muses about himself and his region. It is a pleasant place. There are flowers that grow the year around. In February the yellow jonquils bloom and in March clumps of yellow forsythia show richly golden in the hedges and along paths. The nights are deep-starred. In the piney woods of Georgia, Alabama, South Carolina, Mississippi, and north Florida one rides for miles in a corridor between endless pines. They are best seen on a bright day with the myriad sun shafts shining through them. But even on rainy or foggy days they have a dark, ghostly beauty. The magnolias are like some antique, unbelievable beauty of ivory and carved jade leaves. In the Deep South summers one may turn off any of the interstate highways at dusk and quickly find side roads that smell heavily of honeysuckle. There are white-pillared mansions and poor farm cabins. There are manners, and there is arrogance.

But this is not "the South." The Southernism of the South is an arcane thing. It is not an agrarian civilization, as Vanderbilt University's "Fugitive" poets once dreamed and wrote.[474] Nor is it the reek and rumble of an on-the-make bulldozer society.

The South is many Souths—many things. It is a region of white and black people, long separated and unknowing, groping painfully and arduously toward each other so that in good time they may clasp hands and together walk the glory road of the old hymn toward a time of jubilee.[475]

"The South" is standing at night atop one of Atlanta's new towering buildings—with trees and fountain below—and looking out toward the

---

[473]See Paul M. Gaston, *New South Creed: A Study in Southern Mythmaking* (New York: Vintage Books, 1970), and McGill's explanation of false Southern myths in the editor's introduction.

[474]As a college student McGill studied with members of the "Fugitives" while at Vanderbilt University; see *Ralph McGill: Editor and Publisher*, ed. Calvin McLeod Logue (Durham: Moore Publishing Company, 1969) 1:34-41.

[475]See Francis Butler Simkins and Charles Pierce Roland, *A History of the South*, 4th ed. (New York: A. A. Knopf, 1972); Monroe Lee Billington, *American South: A Brief History* (New York: Scribner, 1971); Idus A. Newby, *The South: A History* (New York: Holt, Rinehart and Winston, 1978).

distant, dark horizon. Yonder, the mind says, are the Big and Little Kennesaw Mountains around which red-bearded William Tecumseh Sherman fought his way into Atlanta. There ended the last meaningful resistance of the Old South. Once in the city, Sherman regrouped his forces, burned Atlanta and moved on, marching to the sea and up through the Carolinas to receive a surrender from Joe Johnston and to end the anguish of war in this region.

"The South" is driving through and seeing the miracle of Florida's growth and development, its beaches and citrus groves, and its industry. "The South" is coming up through Mississippi and remembering it twenty-five years ago—forty years ago—and seeing it now, moving away from cotton and isolation into the national future.

There is a New South, not yet here—but coming. One sees it in the faces of young Negro children in school singing lustily and confidently: "This land is your land/This land is my land. . . ." The New South is in the faces of students, white and black, and in the faces of the young executives, Southern trained and oriented. All these are a part of the new breed making a new South.

There is an excitement in the South. It is an excitement of the spirit and of reality. A recent Twentieth Century Fund study concludes that the South has a tremendous potential for growth and is undergoing "a slow-moving social revolution of significant proportions." The study emphasizes the need for improved education and upgrading the training of the work force.

That will be done—it is being done.

101

The New South
and a New America

The sociologist Howard Odum was an early hero to a number of Southerners who in the 1920s and 1930s were trying to understand themselves and their region. He was on the University of North Carolina faculty, but, happily, he was frequently on the move in the states south of Chapel Hill. He was a kindly, generous man, and he enjoyed having us meet with him and talk, seeking interpretation and faith.[476]

Odum was the one who early taught us that there were many "Souths"—but always *The South* and its amalgam of myths and realities. He was the one who made us see that the maddening paradoxes and incredible contrasts were often quite logical and credible because of our historical environment. There was no "new South" in those years. It was, as he said, a South that was going along about as it always had, getting better and getting worse at one and the same time.[477]

From the 1969 *Compton Yearbook* published by Encyclopaedia Britannica, Inc., by permission. A draft of this essay entitled "The Cumulative Push," is in the McGill papers, now at Emory University, Atlanta.

[476]See Howard W. Odum, *Southern Regions of the United States* (Chapel Hill: University of North Carolina Press, 1936).

[477]For McGill's analysis of false Southern myths see the editor's introduction.

He and Will W. Alexander, another of the pioneer white men to give themselves wholly to trying to awaken conscience and law in the area of race relations, kept asking Southerners to look at themselves and their region and ask a simple question: had the violence done by lynchings and the many tyrannies practiced in the name of white supremacy to keep the Negro "in his place" benefited the average white Southerner?[478] If so, where were those benefits in terms of good schools, educated citizens, per capita income, jobs, libraries, art galleries, symphony orchestras, concerts, or any of the many aids to the spirit and the so-called inner man?[479]

If the Southerner looked about him he saw only the poverty and the lacks of a civilized life. The 1920s were the last decade of the system of sharecropping and tenancy that was all too often peonage, or something near it, for the white man and the black. It was in this period that some Southerners became understandingly aware of just how much psychological satisfaction the Southerner, even the poorest and most illiterate Southerner, obtained from being white and, therefore, "better" than the poor black man. Even the poorest and meanest white man did not seem to care that the segregated system had deprived him and his children. He was "better."

We learned, too, to study the relationship of religion and the organized churches to the South and to see how they had lent their strength and prestige to keeping the Negro in his traditionally designated place. The church, most especially the evangelical churches, although none were guiltless, sustained slavery and, later, the segregated system. Rare was the churchman who protested the brazen evidences of the injustices of segregated practices, some of them hideous and repelling, all of them destructive of human dignity. Now and then a minister in a city church would inveigh against lynchings, burnings, or other savage retaliations against those who "didn't know their place." But these were rare. In rural areas there was emotional support of white supremacy and Negro inferiority as established of God himself. "God was the first segre-

---

[478]See Wilma Dykeman and James Stokely, *Seeds of Southern Change: The Life of Will Alexander* (Chicago: University of Chicago Press, 1962).

[479]For more by McGill on civil rights for blacks, 1946 to 1969, see the editor's introduction, and other essays in this volume.

gationist" was a familiar pulpit utterance. "Our task is to save souls—not to preach social reform," the church insisted, with but few dissenting voices.

Even when the light of the new South began to signal its dawning on 17 May 1954, with the rising sun of the U.S. Supreme Court decision that declared segregated schools unconstitutional, there was to be but little help from the church. Almost a decade and a half have passed since that May date of 1954, and there is a consensus that, with the usual notable exceptions, "the church" has been perhaps the single greatest failure as a creative force in the social revolution of those years.[480]

So little has the Southerner obtained from his "traditions" and the segregated system that, even as the decade of the 1960s moved toward an end, the public schools of the South were below the national average in all the major indices of teacher pay, money spent per pupil, the quality of teacher preparation, and so on. In the autumn of 1968, for example, a study was released revealing that Georgia was fiftieth (or had the highest rate) in the ranking of states in school dropout rate. Kentucky was forty-ninth. Alabama and Mississippi were tied for forty-seventh; North Carolina was forty-sixth; Arkansas was forty-fourth; Tennessee, forty-third. Not a single state in Dixie was higher than thirty-fifth in the dropout ranking. Yet Georgia's schools were attracting teachers from its neighbors because of better pay. Always the paradox.

It is against this background that one must attempt to assay the present and future. None may say what might have happened had the political leadership of the East and North not sold out to the South in the Hayes-Tilden contest of 1876-1877. In so doing, the leadership handed back the race problem to the states' rights dogmatists. The new Fourteenth and Fifteenth Amendments to the Constitution were abandoned. Again, one cannot know what might have ensued had the political leaders of the South accepted the Court ruling of 1954. For a few weeks it looked as if there were a chance. The more blatant and racially demagogic of the Southern governors, senators, congressmen, and local of-

---

[480]See McGill's "Let's Lead Where We Lag," "Church in a Social Revolution," "Interview on Race and the Church," and "The Agony of the Southern Minister," in volumes 1 and 2; also Samuel S. Hill, *Religion and the Solid South* (Nashville: Abingdon Press, 1962).

ficials were, for the moment, silent. It remained for the Virginians, with an early history of dedication to human rights, to proclaim "massive resistance." They thereby lent respectability to the more virulent resisters.

The major riots that followed amounted at times to brief civil wars. This was especially true of those at Little Rock in 1957 and at Oxford, Mississippi, in 1962. Violence of lesser scope, though intense enough, occurred in school integration moves in New Orleans; Birmingham and Tuscaloosa, Alabama; and other cities and towns.

Two magnificent stories of the South in its search for its soul were those of the SCLC of the Reverend Martin Luther King, Jr., and the SNCC.[481] The latter functioned in the rural South. It drew students from across the country, black and white. They taught reading and writing classes, helped register voters, and held classes in history and on constitutional rights. They picketed tearooms and lunch counters of department stores, variety stores, and bus depots. They tested, too, the segregated waiting rooms. They were working—in the period before Congressional enactment of the public accommodations act—in an area where there was no law. They were, I believe, by and large, the sweetest, gentlest, most courageous youngsters to emerge in the period beginning in April 1960. They were the freedom riders whose buses were burned and stoned. They endured the coarsest and most brutal treatment from the worst stereotypes of the rural Dixie sheriff and his deputies. Some of these young persons were murdered. The ugly chapter of the three who were killed and their bodies buried near Philadelphia, Mississippi (James E. Chaney, Andrew Goodman, and Michael Schwerner), is the most notorious of the several killings of civil rights workers.

The chapter written by the early biracial SNCC was a fine, inspiring one. The organization began to wither away when some of its leaders became more and more militant and split into power factions, some antiwhite. SNCC was the first biracial organization to prick the national conscience—and to capture the conscience of black and white students. In those early years Stokely Carmichael and H. Rap Brown, whose

---

[481]Southern Christian Leadership Conference, and Student Nonviolent Coordinating Committee.

names later were to be associated with antiwhite extreme militancy and violence, were friendly co-workers and organizers.[482]

In June 1966 Mississippians along the route of the James Meredith Freedom March heard Carmichael's cry of "black power."[483] It was grist in the mill of the "segs," an all-inclusive word that identifies members of the Ku Klux Klan or a White Citizens' Council and all others opposed to any breakdown of the old supremacy concept. Martin Luther King pointed out that all U.S. ethnic groups had reached for and attained power and that the Negro was belated with his effort.[484] Few listened.

The SNCC and CORE groups had more or less gone along together.[485] By 1966 the leaders of both had become more and more disillusioned by the old concept of working with white people. Disillusionment set in after the passage of the Civil Rights Act of 1964 and the Voting Rights Act of 1965. For SNCC, the failure of the Democratic party convention of 1964 to seat delegates of its newly formed Freedom Democratic party had increased militancy and a distrust of the white man. (In 1968, a black and white coalition of Mississippi Democrats, led by Aaron Henry and Hodding Carter III, brought about a unity of forces in the Magnolia State in a convention at Jackson, Mississippi, a week before the Democratic National Convention. This delegation was seated instead of the one offered by the regular Democratic party.)

By late 1966 both SNCC and CORE had abandoned any pretense of nonviolence and were, instead, urging armed self-defense and retaliatory violence. A pivot point in the civil rights movement was reached in that year. There was a split, and stress became a way of life for all civil rights institutions. The NAACP and even King's SCLC were in some

---

[482]See Stokely Carmichael, *Stokely Speaks: Black Power Back to Pan-Africanism* (New York: Random House, 1971); Stokely Carmichael and Charles V. Hamilton, *Black Power: The Politics of Liberation in America* (New York: Random House, 1967); McGill's review of *SNCC: The New Abolitionists*, in this volume.

[483]See James Howard Meredith, *Three Years in Mississippi* (Bloomington: University of Indiana Press, 1966); McGill discusses the Meredith case in "Television Interview about Africa," in this volume.

[484]See David L. Lewis, *King: A Critical Biography* (New York: Praeger Publishers, 1970).

[485]"CORE" is the Congress of Racial Equality.

No Place to Hide

instances denounced as "Uncle Tom" in character. King's prestige was too high for any direct or open attack. Yet it is true that, in the year before his tragic assassination, the young militants were increasingly critical of the middle-aged leadership and membership of the SCLC. King and his staff were aware of this and were moving to correct it. The shift to more direct contact and work with the poor—the Poor People's March and the Resurrection City in Washington, DC—grew out of this planning and concern.

The decline of SNCC began with the decision of its more militant members to take over. Stokely Carmichael was elected to replace John Lewis as chairman in the spring of 1966. Lewis resigned not because of Carmichael or of the black power concept, in which he believes, but because of Carmichael's interpretation of the phrase in terms of guns and violence. Some stalwarts of the old SNCC left; others remained.

In 1967 Carmichael was replaced as chairman by Rap Brown, then twenty-three years old but a veteran of Black Belt service in Alabama.[486] The writer recalls both Brown and Carmichael in the early days of the nonviolent coordination. Their embitterment and personality changes are easily understandable. They stayed too long in Mississippi and Alabama, enduring the intolerable conditions of that time.

King, martyred by assassination at Memphis, Tennessee, was the one tremendous force of the pre-1966 pivot. From the time he, as a young and unknown preacher in Montgomery, Alabama, took over the bus boycott there in 1955 until the enactment of the civil rights and voting rights legislation, he was the essence of moral power in the movement.[487] It is fair to say that such legislation would not have come in the decade it did had it not been for his superb courage and moral force. It was his nonviolent confrontation with the volatile violence of police and the public in Birmingham that stirred the Congress to action on the rights bills. He was everywhere that black rights were at issue. The man's fearlessness was unbelievable. Hatred for him was so deep that police and state troopers were seen to grow pale with anger and to grit

---

[486]See H. Rap Brown, *Die, nigger die!* (New York: Dial Press, 1960).

[487]See Martin Luther King, *Stride Toward Freedom: The Montgomery Story* (New York: Harper Publishers, 1958).

their teeth in ill-concealed rage when he appeared with his marchers and his pickets. The wonder is that an assassin's gun did not reach him before it did. In death he remains a goad for the nation's conscience.

It was inevitable that the SCLC, without King, would have difficulty with its program and its direction. The power and personality vacuum left by King's passing was tremendous. Filling it was not easy. The poverty of the rural and urban Negro is the obvious objective, and the SCLC will turn more and more in this direction.

Militants speak of today's civil rights movement as being divided into pre-Watts and post-Watts. They despise the old-timers who envisioned a United States shared commonly by all citizens and see it as impossible and undesirable. They see everything before the riots of 1965 in the Watts district of Los Angeles, California, as a middle-class movement aimed at a sharing of white values. They insist there must be two Americas—a black one and a white one.

The fiery young militant will tell you that the fires of Watts (and the later fires in Newark, New Jersey, and Washington, D.C.) ended the old days of King, of nonviolence, and of cooperating with whites.

Eldridge Cleaver, the Black Panthers' minister of information, articulates this, and related philosophy, in a manner persuasive to many young Americans. For example, he scornfully dismissed SNCC members as merely "black hippies"—not true revolutionists.[488]

The times are, for a fact, post-Watts. But they also are post-Montgomery bus boycott. They are post-Oxford riots, in which mobs attacking U.S. marshals and, later, troops, sought to prevent the registration of one lone black man—James H. Meredith. There are laws on the books, and despite the rather widespread hostility to those laws in areas North, South, East, and West, they will not be ignored.

The young militant scorns the progress made—and that is understandable. He has pride—and he got that not merely from Watts and all the other acts of resistance, but also from the cumulative push of the Court decisions, the laws enacted, the violence and the nonviolent campaigns, the murders of civil rights workers in Mississippi and Ala-

---

[488]See Eldridge Cleaver, *Soul On Ice* (New York: Dell, ca. 1968); Robert Scheer, ed., *Eldridge Cleaver: Post-Prison Writings and Speeches* (New York: Random House, 1969).

bama, the days and weeks spent in Southern jails, the beatings, the brutalizing by sheriffs and jailers. All these, plus successes, have given the old and young black people pride and determination, a pride the white people are sharing.

The Black Panther type of revolutionist and the two-Americas propagandist have rhetoric, much of it on a par with that of the great orators of past revolutions, both abortive and successful. But they are, even with their commitment to violence, mostly rhetorical, not revolutionary.

The Afro-American pride will grow—as it should. Those who somehow are dismayed by African hair styles, African fashions and decorations, must understand them to be comparable with a Scotch-American in kilts dancing to bagpipes.

The next year or so likely will be rough in transition; it will be something to live through. What we must "live through" may be extended if there is not a realization that the really poor of urban and rural areas number in the millions. They are a product of a past that neglected education and training, a past blind to the meaning of technological development and urban crowding by those made obsolete by technology.

The tremendous migration, or export, of Southerners, black and white, but mostly black, is a direct example of what neglect and the sickness of separation, alienation, and apartheid policies can do to a region and a country.

The future of the U.S. race problem is tied inseparably to poverty in the cities and in rural areas. Civil rights per se cannot do much for the desperately poor. The rhetoric of revolution cannot feed or clothe them. If the "second separate nation" were instantly created, it would include most of the poor and would be helpless to cope with their condition. The old slogans, like "Burn, baby, burn," now seem to belong to the past. A reactionary, "conservative" Congress in 1969 and a national will weakened and made afraid by the racist elements of the 1968 political campaign can make hideous the experiences we may have.

There is, however, enough evidence of what we can do in the story of what we have done to make one hold fast to faith in a United States commonly shared by all its people. It is not mere rhetoric to say that any form of apartheid will be destructive of all things. It has been a relatively brief but tremendous and exciting sweep of years since that 17 May 1954. We have come a long, long way. The political processes, so long denied, do work. There is already a common sharing of the country undreamed of in 1954. The critical national problems of our neglect and segregation practices are our poor and our unprepared.

Apartheid obviously is not an answer.

We have tried that already.

102

A Conversation
with Ralph McGill
1969

W hen Ralph McGill was named executive editor of the *Atlanta Constitution* in 1938 there was a parade in his honor. A mob of robed Ku Klux Klansmen marched on Forsyth Street displaying placards denouncing McGill and his newspaper. Today, thirty years later, his published views on discrimination and bigotry have not changed, but the KKK is almost out of existence.[489]

A friend of presidents, longtime champion of the Negro, winner of the Pulitzer, holder of many honorary degrees including one from Harvard, the celebrated publisher of the *Constitution* has written a daily column for forty years. It is syndicated in more than a hundred newspapers and attracts millions of readers.

He has been threatened, attacked, and abused; he is loved by many for his compassion and hated by many for his unrelenting stand on civil rights.

Ralph McGill is almost certainly Atlanta's best-known citizen and is certainly among its most distinguished.

Reprinted from *Atlanta* magazine, February 1969, by permission of Mrs. Ralph McGill and *Atlanta* magazine; from interviews held 27 November 1968 and January 1969.

[489]As of 1983 the Ku Klux Klan continued to be quite active.

Questioner: Mr. McGill, there is very little middle ground on the subject of McGill. You're admired by a lot of people, but you're hated and distrusted by many. Has it always been this way?

McGill: I suppose so. If you're in the daily press for as long as I've been around, and you're regularly expressing your opinion on great issues—issues that affect a great many people—you either change your opinion or stay silent or pick up a few enemies. I get hate mail and used to get some pretty rough phone calls at home, but I've tried to take it impersonally. These are people—these haters—whose lives are cheerless and empty. I feel very sorry for them.

Questioner: For example, the *Great Speckled Bird* is very often extremely critical of you.[490]

McGill: Well, that's another category of people. These young people are not haters. I read that paper, and I'm sometimes a little puzzled as to why they say some of the things they do, because on a truly factual basis they've been absolutely wrong in their charges, but that doesn't worry me. I think the *Speckled Bird* has a place as I think all of the so-called underground press has a place. I think they're making a protest; they see what they think is wrong, and by all means I think they should be able to say so.

Questioner: One of the subjects on which they were critical was a column you wrote about Hubert Humphrey's loyalty to LBJ. Do your views remain the same?

McGill: Sure. As I recall, what I said in that column was that Mr. Humphrey had to either be loyal to President Johnson or resign. I still feel that way. Hubert Humphrey wanted to be a candidate for the vice-presidency. When elected, he accepted it, and so doing he accepted the obligation of being what a vice-president is. And that is, in a sense, an assistant to the president who selected him. I think it would have been highly immoral of him to have made any public statement condemning the administration or to have engaged in any public opposition to the president.

I have very strong feelings that if you enter a political contest you must abide by the results. The only time this country failed to do that

---

[490]An underground newspaper in Atlanta.

we had the Civil War as a result of it. The South refused to accept the results of the election of Abraham Lincoln. No, no, I haven't changed my views at all. Humphrey was honor bound to the president.

Questioner: Mr. McGill, a recent issue of the *Nation* carried an article by Arlie Schardt which was extremely critical of Atlanta Newspapers, Inc., and of the *Constitution*. Can we discuss that for a minute?[491]

McGill: Of course, and I must say it was a very harsh article.

Questioner: For one thing, the article intimates that the editor of your newspaper—Gene Patterson—was either forced out or fired in a dispute over a column written by B. J. Phillips which was critical of Georgia Power Company.

McGill: Well, that's ridiculous. And it's absolutely untrue. Gene Patterson was neither forced out nor fired. He's an outstanding editor and the *Constitution* hated to lose him. In the last hours—almost literally—before he left, Jack Tarver, Jim Cox, and I made it clear that we would be pleased if he stayed on as editor, but that we wished him well in his new job [Managing editor of the *Washington Post*].

Questioner: B. J. Phillips, who worked directly for Patterson, also quit, did she not? Was that because of criticism of her column criticizing Georgia Power's rate increase?

McGill: That's possible. B. J. is a very nice young girl, and she and I are good friends. She did quit, yes, and she quit on the heels of that column. It may be said that she quit out of reaction to criticism of that column. But let's consider the nature of the criticism. As I understand it, Jack Tarver [president of Atlanta Newspapers, Inc.] read the column in

------

[491]In his article, "Atlanta in Suspense: Crisis of the *Constitution*," *Nation* (23 December 1968), Arlie Schardt wrote that Atlanta "needs a conscience. In the past, it was provided one . . . by the newspapers. But today that nettle is gone. . . . The budget continues to rule the press at profitable" Atlanta Newspapers, Inc. "Although he carries the title of publisher, McGill's authority is essentially limited to his column. . . ." When McGill died, the *Nation* concluded that the Georgian lived during "a time of opportunity for Southern journalists, and Ralph McGill was one of the best. . . . While Ralph McGill had responded to the new times the Atlanta *Constitution* had not. . . . McGill never in fact controlled the paper." 17 February 1969.

the first edition and called Gene to suggest that the rate increase was a rather difficult and complex subject for a columnist to be dealing with at that time.[492] Remember, this was the first edition, with a number of editions of the paper not yet printed. The column could have been killed. It wasn't, and there was never any thought of killing it.

Questioner: Still, Patterson did quit rather suddenly.

McGill: He did, yes, and I don't think it would be bad manners for me to discuss some of the background which led to that. Gene, who is forty-five, wanted to find his best opportunity in life. That's natural; it's much easier at forty-five than at, say, fifty. Well, two days after this incident we're discussing, my friend Ben Bradlee, who had just been named editor of the *Washington Post*, called me. He said he wanted to hire Gene Patterson as managing editor of the *Post*. Bradlee had been managing editor of the *Post* before being named editor. He had thought, he said, that he could handle both jobs but now felt the need for a strong managing editor. And he said, "I want him now. We need him today."

Gene was out of town. He was in Louisville. I called him, chased him around, and finally reached him at the airport. He called Bradlee, got an excellent offer, and they got together. The *Post* needed him immediately, so, with our consent and blessings, he left suddenly. I won't say there was never any acrimony—there always is on a newspaper—but those are the facts.[493]

Questioner: Schardt's article also commented at length on the number of good newsmen the *Constitution* and *Journal* have lost in the last few years, men like Jack Nelson, who won a Pulitzer. Is there any reason for this?

McGill: Yes. They did what all of us do—they looked for what they considered to be a better opportunity. Some of them found it; some of them

---

[492]See McGill's essay on Jack Tarver in *Southern Encounters: Southerners of Note in Ralph McGill's South*, ed. Calvin M. Logue (Macon GA: Mercer University Press, 1983).

[493]On 14 February 1969, after McGill's death, *Time* magazine concluded that McGill served as the South's conscience, but "as the *Constitution's* editor, and particularly as its publisher since 1960, McGill proved too kindly to crack the editorial whip." See "Reb" Gershon's judgment on McGill as editor and publisher, in McGill, *Southern Encounters*.

found they had made a mistake. Any newspaper like the *Constitution* will attract a certain number of good young journalists. Then—and this applies to the *New York Times*, the *Washington Post*, and a lot of other good newspapers—something else comes along and your good young journalist leaves. Why? Why not? They leave for more money, a location which suits them better, for more prestige. We've been lucky. We have some good men now who one day may leave us. Specifically, in the case of Jack Nelson—who is a good man—I understand he was made an extremely good offer by the *Los Angeles Times*. So he took it. There is really much less intrigue than one imagines.

Questioner: With a new editor—or rather, editor of the editorial page—do you feel that the paper will undergo a change? Will Reg Murphy effect serious changes on the *Constitution?*

McGill: Well, the editorial page has already changed somewhat. That's completely natural. An editor effects his own changes, and newspapers often grow with the changes. Reg is a very dedicated man, and he'll be dedicating himself to making ours the best editorial pages in the country. As for the newspaper as a whole, the *Constitution* will continue on the course it's been pursuing for so many years.

Questioner: A few weeks ago the *Constitution* ran an editorial on the Worth County situation which seemed to strike at the heart of the question. It was a strongly worded editorial of the type you have often published. Later, a few days later, a second editorial appeared which was, in the eyes of many, almost an apology. Why was that?

McGill: In the first place, it was certainly not an apology, nor was it intended to be. Some of our facts in the first editorial were incorrect, and, in what I consider to be the proper tradition of newspapers, we ran a second editorial with the factual corrections. We simply corrected, as quickly as we could, an honest error. We certainly didn't ease our position on the problem.

Questioner: I think it's reasonable to assume that you—that is, the newspaper—considered the matter of libel. All of us—every publication—is acutely aware of the libel laws. Why are your newspapers so concerned with libel suits, and incidentally, whatever happened to the libel suit by General [Edwin] Walker because of your column on his actions in Mississippi?

McGill: Why do we consider the matter of libel? First, we don't want to libel anybody. The truth is almost always more interesting than fiction, and the truth is all we are interested in. Second, there is a matter of thirty million dollars in libel suits which have been filed against us. That's both papers and it's over a good number of years. But most of them have been dropped. You know, the person filing suit decided, after all the publicity, not to pursue the point in a court of law. But a newspaper must be aware, very alert to the possibility of libel and a libel suit. The *Constitution* is not alone in that awareness. As to General Walker, he sued for libel and dropped the suit. He withdrew.

Questioner: What do you think the South's posture on the subject of nondiscrimination and equal rights will be in the immediate years to come?

McGill: I don't expect any miracles. There has been a lot of progress, but, remember, we had a very great way to go. The Negro won't—and shouldn't—give up this struggle. There's so much more to do, here and everywhere in this country. My hope is that we can do it peacefully.

Questioner: Can we?

McGill: I don't know. A lot depends on Mr. [Richard] Nixon. His relationship with Strom Thurmond at the Republican National Convention leaves a lot to be desired. I personally think that, while Mr. Nixon obviously went along with it, the deal with Senator Thurmond was probably a brainchild of Mr. Bliss, the Republican party chairman.[494] Will he—President Nixon—really go along with Strom Thurmond? There's been talk of turning the schools back to local authorities and about abolishing some major federal programs such as Headstart, Job Corps, equal opportunity things. You can't turn school systems over to the worst kinds of demagogues and segregationists in these small towns. I just can't believe President Nixon will do this.

If he did, we would be in trouble, terrible trouble, and he would be in trouble. Yes, of course, if something like that happened they would take to the streets. You would see monumental disobedience.

Questioner: President Nixon has talked—during the campaign, that is— of "Black Capitalism." What are your thoughts on that?

---

[494]Ray C. Bliss.

McGill: I think the idea, if it is properly implemented, is a good one. The idea originated, I might add, with Roy McKissick of CORE.[495] There is a great move on for business, through tax incentives and so forth, to help black people set up their own businesses in the poor areas. But this isn't the total answer by any means. This is a good idea, but what are you going to do about the really poor people? They won't be able to participate in what's called "Black Capitalism."

Questioner: If that happened—if, for example, there was a serious abandonment of some of these federal programs—do you feel the country would be in for dangerous civil strife?

McGill: I don't know what you mean by "dangerous civil strife," but there would certainly be serious trouble. We've had serious trouble already. They would certainly take to the streets, but I would hope they wouldn't take to final violence and utter violence because this would be met with responsive violence and repression and would play into the hands of those who want just this sort of thing. But we've got to realize that some of these moves, if they occur, by the federal government won't be taken quietly or by sitting down.

Questioner: What was your reaction to the rioting at the Chicago convention?

McGill: Well, of course, it was extremely unfortunate. I was there. And I'll tell you that a heavy percentage of them were the so-called kids. My wife and I walked among them one afternoon and talked to a lot of them. I thought they were just fine. Let's come back to the central fact that this hard-core group was led by a couple of men who were twenty-eight to thirty years old and weren't kids by any definition. They were using these kids, the real kids, and they were doing so very skillfully.

And I don't think this was a Communist thing. That's a comfortable story to believe, but I think it was the work of the real revolutionists. I thought the youngsters were just fine; the twenty-eight and thirty-year-old "kids" were not so fine.

Questioner: Some of these same youngsters are saying nowadays that you ran a man out of town, a teacher named Don West.

---

[495]Congress of Racial Equality.

McGill: How ridiculous. I haven't thought about this in a long time, so please forgive me if my dates aren't correct, but it seems to me that this occurred in the late thirties. Mr. West was a teacher at the time, and there was a big uproar then among parents of his students. A lot of charges were being made, principally that West was teaching Communist ideology. We heard a lot about it, of course, so I tried to get in touch with Mr. West, but couldn't do so.

Now, remember, there were at the time avowed Communist organizers in most of the major cities of the South. Atlanta had one; his name was Homer Chase. Well, Chase and West were involved in a number of things together.

Anyway, I wrote Don West a registered letter to outline the situation as I knew it and to question him about it. I don't know how to be fairer than that. He wrote me back and said it was none of my damned business. So I did write some columns on the subject, but they were honest and straight. If they were tough, well, I had my facts straight.

As to my running him out of town, I don't know that he ever left the city. Far as I know, he could still be here.

Questioner: The Viet Nam war does seem to be somewhat dominant in our past conversations. Why is that?

McGill: I think this war—well, first it came on slowly. It reached its first escalation under President Kennedy and then higher escalation under President Johnson. It began under President Eisenhower in Laos and then began to spread over to Viet Nam before he left office. You remember we—I think it was in 1954—were almost ready to lend our air support to the French–Viet Nam under Eisenhower. So, the thing had been going on a long time, and there was an undeclared war and also the draft and selective service laws are not equitable. They're really not fair, so I can see where a lot of the young people who are subject to the draft see it as unfair.

Questioner: Do you think that we may, at social functions, for example, and in our conversational involvement with the war, be overreacting?

McGill: Well, really, a war which was, in one sense, as unpopular as the war in Viet Nam was our war with Mexico.

Now, it didn't attract a lot of youth organizations, but if you'll read history, you will find that there was a great deal more public opinion against that war. There were a great many more outspoken senators and congressmen against that war than the war in Viet Nam. And there was very heavy editorial public condemnation of the war with Mexico. It was a very unpopular war. Too, we were pretty neutral in the First World War, even, until the Germans began to sink ships, the *Lusitania* and others. And I ask you to remember that even in the Second World War, the Selective Service Act failed to pass renewal—failed to pass in Congress. It was a tie vote in the House and the vice-president had to cast the deciding vote to give us a renewal of the Selective Service before we got into the Second World War. And there was tremendous opposition to anything except neutrality. Had not the Japanese attacked Pearl Harbor in the manner they did, we might well have stayed out of that war and managed to help by a continuation or stepping up of "Lend Lease." So, I never go along with all this talk of our having all of this—having always a military, a militarist nation. This just isn't true. History doesn't sustain that.

Questioner: Thank you, sir. I'd like to come back now to the question of whether the *Constitution* may be changing. Some people feel that a lot of "Lester" has left the editorial page.[496]

McGill: Well, that's a relative point. I wasn't aware we had that much "Lester" on the page, and I'm not sure that it has changed that much. I think that Gene Patterson had been here as editor about ten years. Certainly, when he went away—he was a brilliant young man, one of the very finest writers that's come along—it was a loss. I would say to you that Reg Murphy, a young Georgia man, is just about the same age now as Gene Patterson was when he became editor, and I would say to you that Gene Patterson in his first couple of years was not so well known. He rather quickly made himself known. I don't think I've seen a young man come along as fast as he did. But still, I would be glad for any committee, whether a very partisan one or an anti[partisan] one, to take what Reg Murphy has written and see if it any way weakens or deviates from the position which Patterson and I have both tried to maintain. Reg is a man of honor and integrity—and naturally you must assume that all of this was talked about before he came to work. He would not

---

[496]"Lester Maddox" and the issue of civil rights.

have taken the job if he had in any sense wished to change the direction of the paper. His mail—his critical mail—is running about as heavy as Gene's, and that's rather quick. This paper isn't going to change its policies or position or the thrust of its beliefs. I wish someone would examine all of Reg's columns—one of last week, for example—in which he was saying it was time for the civic clubs of this city and the white urbanizations to begin to take in and use Negro membership. This was something that hadn't been said before, and you will be seeing other things like this because he believes this. I don't think there's any need to worry about what direction we're going. If our direction does change it won't be because of any higher authority or it would simply be because Reg and I both don't measure up in it.

Questioner: Well, the *Constitution,* and you in particular, has helped to usher in this new era Atlanta is enjoying.

McGill: Well, you're kind to say it. I am aware of how many things have happened, but certainly if I were a black person today, especially a younger one, I would be very impatient with anyone who talks about how far we've come. But I do remember when I was made executive in 1938, on the very first day I came in the office I sent down instructions that the word *Negro* should be spelled with a capital *N* because this was proper according to the rules of English usage. I didn't go into anything else. We had two printers who sent word up that if it ever came to them they'd be damned if they would set it. But that's all that happened. We had a few letters of complaint, but not many people noticed it. At that time, as I recall, there was not a paper south of Philadelphia that was spelling the word *Negro* with a capital *N.* You'd see it in national magazines and books thirty years ago spelled with a lowercase *n.* I mention this very small thing to show that from that small sort of beginning, other changes have come. I'm not a pessimist, nor am I a Pollyanna, but I do believe we are going ahead, and I can't urge too strongly that we all support the real teaching—the real part the Negro has played in American history, the debt owed him for his part and his contribution. The white man has underemphasized this and has in fact almost omitted it entirely. This is an interesting thing. Nobody ever sat down and said, "Look, all you textbook writers, keep the Negro out of history books," nobody ever did that. It was a sort of acceptance that this is the way things are. This was one of the many evils of this system.

Questioner: Mr. McGill, we were talking a moment ago about Atlanta's new era, which is to say the boom Atlanta has enjoyed in the past ten years. Ivan Allen, Jr., has played a significant role in that boom, and now he has withdrawn as a candidate for the next term.

McGill: He is a great mayor. I think he would agree that he—the right man—came along at the right time for Atlanta. I also think that he would agree that his leaving the post will not stop this city. If he thought that, he would never have pulled out. But this city, like all of urban America, is going to be faced with some hard problems in the next few years. Atlanta is going to need a strong mayor, a man in the tradition of Bill Hartsfield and Ivan Allen, to keep things on the track. [497]

The election ought to be a very interesting thing. A lot of good men want the job, and the Negro vote is going to be a serious factor in deciding who will succeed Ivan. I don't think our mayor will be a Negro, but I hope the black people and whites can get sufficiently together so that the right man is elected. I would hope that we could at last see a black man have the opportunity to be elected vice-mayor. I see that as a distinct possibility. [498]

Questioner: On the subject of politics, how do you rate the job Governor [Lester] Maddox is doing?

McGill: Well, as you know, Lester Maddox is the subject of conversation all around. He can be amusing; he's had the support of a lot of people. But running the state of Georgia is certainly a major business enterprise, and I don't feel he has the competence for the job. And I'll tell you another thing; I think he is an evil—a political evil. Despite all of his religious talk, I think he's an evil. [499]

Questioner: One final question. You're seventy years old, and that's a few years past the normal retirement age. Have you any plans? Do you ex-

---

[497]For more by McGill on William Berry Hartsfield, Robert F. Maddox, Frank Neely, Martin Luther King, Jr., Jack Tarver, and Robert Winship Woodruff see *Southern Encounters*.

[498]Maynard Jackson and Andrew Young, blacks, served as mayor of Atlanta in the late 1970s and 1980s.

[499]See McGill on Maddox in *Southern Encounters*.

pect to retire soon?

McGill: No, no. Somebody may come into my office one of these days and tell me that my working time is up, but I don't expect that. No, I'll probably not retire. I'm feeling good and working hard; I'm married to a fine, beautiful woman; I like what I'm doing for a living; and I'm not nearly finished with what I hope to get done.[500]

---

[500]McGill married Mary Elizabeth Leonard on 4 September 1929; she died on 21 March 1962. On 20 April 1967, McGill married Mary Lynn Morgan. McGill died on 3 February 1969.

Index

A Congressman from Mississippi, 503
"A Few Figs from Thistles," 348
A Shade of Difference, 410
A Time to Speak, 473
Abshire, David M., 623
Accidental President, 606
Adams, Henry, 335
Advancing South, 611
Africa, 384, 402-412, 437, 447, 466, 476, 480, 537, 540
Afro-American, 646
Agar, Herbert, 23
Agrarians, 336, 364, 637
agriculture, xl, 6, 16, 27, 61, 149, 158, 189, 220, 232-33, 369, 404, 458, 515-16, 558, 593, 595-96, 613, 628, 636
Alabama, xxviii, 33, 97-98, 121, 148, 187, 192, 236, 250, 270, 277, 306, 324, 328, 330, 342, 355, 357-58, 378-79, 382, 396, 400, 413-17, 438, 461, 463-66, 477-79, 488, 491, 500, 507, 509, 512, 518, 553, 586, 606, 608, 615, 635, 637, 644-45
Alabama Council on Human Relations, 475
Alexander, Will W., 640
Allen, Ivan, 658
Almond, J. Lindsay, 248
American Federation of Labor, 91
American Independent Party of Alabama, 601

American Revolution, 495
Americans, confident, 351
Anderson, Margaret, 576-80
Anderson, Sherwood, 528
Anti-Lynching Association, 569
anti-Semitic, 327, 487, 629
Appalachia, 355
Appomattox, 20, 326, 635
Arkansas, 1, 12, 192, 223, 244, 261, 292, 298, 345, 407, 437, 450, 470, 482, 507, 576, 619, 634, 642
Arkansas Gazette, 619
Arms Control and Disarmament Agency, 515
Arnall, Ellis, 92, 94, 128, 141, 187
Arp, Bill, 299
artisans, 635
Ashmore, Harry, xxx, 450, 619
Asia, 478
Atlanta, 156, 168, 269, 293, 298
Atlanta Constitution, 86, 418, 450, 454, 508, 562, 566, 588, 625-26, 648, 652
Atlanta Journal, 453-54, 573
Atlanta Times, 565
Atlanta University, 316, 384
Atlanta wall, 407
Atlanta Water Works, 361
Atlantic Monthly, 479
atomic bomb, 220
Auden, W. H., 529
audiences, xx, xxi, xxiii, xxv, xxxi, xl

Augusta GA, 186
Augusta Constitutionalist, 21
authors, 128
automobiles, 597

Bachman, J., 396
Baez, Joan, 499
Baker, Newton D., 172
Baldwin, William H. Jr., 35
banks, 40
Bar-b-q, 159, 596
Barnett, Ross, xxxiv, xxxvi, 593, 601
Barth, Karl, 583
Basset, J. S., 480
Bell, Burton, 359
Bell, John, 11, 395
Bellamy, Ralph, 312
Benét, Stephen Vincent, 64, 329
Benjamin, Judah P., 20
Bennett, J. C., 584
Benson, Ezra, 232-33
Berenson, B., 528
Bible, 584
Bilbo, Theodore, 73, 121, 125, 352, 498, 505, 601
Bill of Rights, 349
Birmingham AL, 413-17
Birmingham Southern College, 475
Birmingham Sunday School bombing, 423
Bishop Pike Affair, 581
Black, Hugo, 570
Black Belt, 28, 325, 331, 490

Black Codes, xl, 630
Black Muslims, 416, 487, 496
Black Panthers, 645
Black Power, 621, 626, 643
blacks, "apathy," 331; attitudes of, 226, 467; attitudes of North toward, 624, 635; ballot, xxviii, 34, 104, 138, 190, 193, 220, 248-49, 274-81, 323, 327, 330, 442-43, 479-81, 483, 489-90, 499, 502, 508, 539, 592, 594, 608, 618, 622, 632, 642, 658; capitalism, 653; children, 375; churches, 280; citizenship, 145; College Fund, 316; colleges, 137; contributions of, 625; denied jobs, 598; denied rights, 88, 119, 242; discriminated against, 325-27, 579, 595; disfranchisement, 329-30, 480, 489; economic status, 44-45, 277; education, 36, 78, 190, 376, 425, 481, 483, 590; elected to office, 378, 400, 588, 608, 626; employment, 138, 190, 439, 442, 481, 617, 630; equal citizenship, xxxix, 195, 265, 379, 445, 459, 462, 511, 607; exclusion of, 501; exploitation of, 82; facilities, 467; false myths about, xxxviii (see myths); farmers, 40, 124, 309; free to travel, 383; harmed, 457, 478; history, 478, 625; housing, 113; humiliation, 508; image, 380, 441; in North, 439; in unions, 415; income, 124; "inferiority," xxxix, 640; influence, 3; integration, 70, 209, 291; intimidation of, 80, 323, 329; jobs, 42; judicial treatment, 275; leaders, 103; migration, 27, 124, 191, 318; open housing, 633; paternalistic attitude toward, 567; patience, 194; policemen, 132, 269; politics, 591; population, xxxviii, 5, 270, 525; Populist, 32; religion, 383; rights, 598; soldiers, 374; spirituals, 283; students, 330, 574; teachers, 375; unemployment, 513; voting, 90-91, 120, 135; waiters, 620; working with whites, 100

Blair, Frances P., 19
Blair, L. H., 559
Bliss, Ray C., 653
Blossom, Virgil, 262
boll weevil, 45, 58, 122, 147, 219, 527, 621
Bolton, William H., 52
Boney, F. N., 8
Booker T. Washington High School, xliii
Booth, Edwin, 301
Booth, John Wilkes, 301
Boston Globe, 446, 450, 535, 549
Boyce, William W., 19
Bradlee, Ben, 651
Bragg, Braxton, 283
Brecht, Bertolt, 528
Breckenridge, John, 11
Brooklyn, 342
Brotherhood Week, 533-34
Brown, John, 329
Brown, Joseph E., 19
Brown, Paul, 187
Brownell, Herbert, 262
Brownlow, W. C., 623
Bryan, William Jennings, 172, 198
Bryant, J. B., 165
Bryant, Paul "Bear," 608
Bull, William, 55
Bull Moose Party, 38
Burke, Edmund, 494
Burke, Emory, 80
Burleson, Albert S., 38
business leadership, 321
businesses, 327, 379, 392, 399, 486, 596, 612, 614
Butler, Fanny Kemble, 130
Butler, Paul M., 214
Butler, Pierce, 6
Butler, Richard C., 247
Byrd, Harry F., 248, 489

Cable, George Washington, 559
Caldwell, Erskine, 128
Caldwell, Harmon, 71
Calhoun, John C., 10, 60, 118, 336, 395
California, 483, 541, 564, 601, 645
capitalism, 338, 515
Capote, Truman, 581
Carmichael, Stokely, 620, 642-44
carpenters, 635

Carter, Hodding, 144, 462, 565, 574, 643
Cash, W. J., 144
Catholics, 292, 352, 544, 629
Cause Is Mankind, 514-16
Center Magazine, 619
Chaney, James, E., 642
Chase, Homer, 655
Chattahoochee River, 146, 305, 354-61, 531
Chattanooga TN, 393-97
Cheney, Brainard, 257
Chestnut, Mrs. James, 21
Chicago Race Riots, 627-33
Chicago Round-Table, xx
children, 365
Children of the South, 576-80
Christ, Jesus, 294, 584
Christian, J. J., 28
Christian Century, 585
church, segregated, 385-87
Churchill, Winston S., 238-40, 254
CIO, 91, 102, 415, 615, 617
civic clubs, 599
civil rights, xii, xv, xix, xxiii, xlii, 101, 118, 122, 134-40, 261, 439, 509, 603, 646
civil rights bills, xxviii, 233, 323-26, 329, 374, 400, 484, 486, 491, 510, 512, 538, 598, 600, 621, 643
Civil Rights Commission, 280
civil rights movement, 643
Civil War, xxxiv, xlii, 15, 78, 127, 182, 193, 248, 255, 282, 316, 335, 337, 338, 339, 341, 447, 497, 525, 527, 559, 589, 616, 634, 650
Clark, Eli, 564
Clark, Thomas D., 369
Clay, Henry, 13
Cleaver, Eldridge, 645
Cleghorn, Reese, 591
Clement, Frank G., 251, 577
Clement, Rufus, 278, 626
Clemson University, 457
Cleveland, Grover, 38, 172, 182, 198, 221, 286
climate, Southern, xl, 60
Climbing Jacob's Ladder, 591
close the schools, 602
coal miners, 615
Cocking, Walter D., 69

Collins, LeRoy, 318, 327, 346
Columbia Broadcasting Company, 173
Columbia University, 175
Columbia Valley Authority, 181
Columbians, 80
communications, 304
Communist, xlii, 101, 111, 176, 194, 205, 212, 374, 389, 405, 470, 471, 485, 654
Confederacy, 13-14, 21, 48, 171, 300, 335, 339, 357, 396, 446, 484, 495, 497, 588-89, 608, 612, 634
Congress of Racial Equality, 439, 465, 643, 654
Connor, Eugene "Bull," 413, 438, 488
conservatism, 484, 565, 585, 623
Constitution, xliv, 202, 210, 327, 350, 373, 389, 399, 417, 478, 487, 539, 641
Coogler, J. Gordon, 558
Coolidge, Calvin, 176
Coon, Carleton, 465
Copperhead Movement, 18
Cornwallis, General, 495
cotton, xl, 13, 20, 27, 39, 57, 92, 189, 303, 337, 352, 363, 369, 458, 478, 495, 594, 617, 628, 635
cotton gin, 495
cotton mills, 596, 617
Coulter, E. Merton, 21
county government, 332
county-unit system, 441, 609
courts, 323, 350, 399, 437
Cox, James M., 547, 564
craftsmen, 8
credit, 7
Crommelin, John G., 328
Cronkite, Walter, 446
Crump, Edward H., 141
Cuba, 165
Culpepper, Caughey, 359

Dabbs, James M., 241
Dabney, Virginius, xii
Dalton, Theodore R., 248
Daniels, Josephus, 38
Davidson, Donald, 336
Davidson, Jim, 148
Davis, Henry W., 20

Davis, Jefferson, 12, 103, 254, 283, 415, 497
Davison, Francis W., 30
Declaration of Independence, 494
defiance of courts, 328
Delaware, 320
demagogues, xxxviii, 17, 102, 154, 230, 304, 326, 490, 498, 512, 544, 577, 601-602, 653
democracy, 338
Democrats, xvi, 4, 25, 97, 101, 119, 135, 143, 170, 172-73, 187, 193, 214, 236, 285, 332, 400, 440-41, 498, 525, 543, 546, 602-603
demonstrations, 441, 489
Denmark, 563
Dennett, J. R., 526
depression, the, 45, 219, 485
desegregation, xxi, xxvii, xxxv, xl, xlii, 45, 69, 209, 223, 226, 241, 266, 269, 349-51, 379, 400, 457, 459, 464, 486, 508-509, 519, 576-77, 588.
Dewey, Tom, 177
dialogue, xxxvii
Dickey, James, 571
Dirksen, Everett, 178, 180
discrimination, xxiv, 456, 511, 558, 578
Disraeli, Benjamin, 109
District of Columbia, 320
Dixiecrat movement, 121, 142, 151, 235, 391
Dixon, Frank, 100
Dixon, Harry St. John, 49
Dodd, Lamar, 129
Dominican Republic, 456
Douglas, Stephen H., 11
Drew, John, 312
Drury, Allan, 410
DuBois, W. E. B., 36
Duke, Dan, 87
Duke University, 272
Dunlop, John T., 615
Durr, Virginia, xii

Eastland, James, 505, 607
Ebony, 436
economy, xxi, 17, 29, 124, 153, 250, 328, 371, 414, 442-44, 486, 598, 603, 611, 617
education, xxiv, 157, 418-21, 448, 481, 612

Eisenhower, Dwight D., xxviii, 46, 79, 99, 180, 182, 196, 216, 232, 248, 261, 364, 378, 483, 499, 502, 541, 655
electors, 328
electric telegraph, 419
emancipation, 398, 436
Embree, Edwin, 70
Emerging South, 369
Emerson, Ralph Waldo, xvi
Emory University, xxx, 159, 399, 563
Emory University Medical School, 555
employment, xxii, xxiv, xxviii, 287
England, 492
English, Mildred E., 308
Etheridge, Mark, xxiv
Everett, Edward, 395
Evers, Medgar, 471
extremists, xviii, xxx, 326, 328, 350, 372, 432, 470, 480, 531

factories, 635
Fair Employment Practices Commission (FEPC), xxv, 42, 102, 123, 136, 180
family, 3
Farley, James A., 172
farm support, 207
farmers, xli, 31, 41, 43, 198, 203, 284, 331, 360, 459, 615, 628 (see agriculture)
Farragut, Loyall, 340
Fascists, 528
Faubus, Orval, 236, 244, 260-62, 271, 319, 482, 577, 605, 607
Faulkner, William, 258, 390
federal aid to education, 614
Federal Bureau of Investigation (FBI), 510
federal government, xxiv, 7, 196, 449
Federal Housing Administration, 116
federal programs, 598
Fifteenth Amendment, 598, 641
filibuster, 326
fire hoses, 457
First Amendment, 620
Fisk University, 316
Fleming, B., 128
Flinn, Richard O., Jr., 308

Florida, 184, 196, 306, 318, 324, 327, 330, 346, 490, 567, 606, 608, 634, 637-38
Flynn, Ed, 97
folkways, 365
Folsom, Jim, 98
Ford, Henry, 552
Ford, Jesse Hill, 520-24
Ford Foundation, 212
forests, 593
Forrest, Nathan Bedford, 282
Fort Benning GA, 358
Fort Sumter, 12
Fortune, 111
Foster, L. H., 188
Fourteenth Amendment, 23, 620, 641
Fowler, Thomas N., 52
free society, 487
free speech, xix
Freedom Riders, 379
Freedom Schools, 479
fried chicken, 596
Frost, Robert, 529
Fugitive poets, 571, 637
Fulbright Student Exchange, 212
Fulbright, William, 236
Fulton, Robert, 341

Garner, John N., 172
geography, 284
George, Walter, 187, 567, 609
Georgia, xiii, xxviii, xxiv, xliii, 1, 48, 54, 59, 63, 68, 89, 106, 126-27, 129, 148, 156, 170, 186, 192, 236, 250, 270, 289, 306, 324, 328, 330, 334, 354, 362, 367, 378, 396, 466, 483, 490, 492, 494, 497-503, 509, 512, 518, 531, 538, 544, 551, 553, 563, 571, 588, 593-94, 601, 608-609, 637, 656
Georgia legislature, 349
Georgia Power Company, 350, 360
Georgia Press Institute, 347
Georgia Tech, 159, 418-21
Gettysburg, 499
ghetto, 416, 596, 621
God, 297, 471, 593, 603, 640
God Wills Us Free, 530-32
Godkin, E. L., 525
Golden, Harry, 267
Goldwater, Barry, 482-83, 489, 497, 542, 602

Goodman, Andrew, 642
Gordon, John B., 57, 78
Gordon, William, 194
Gore, Albert, 249
Gothic Politics in the Deep South, 605
government, centralization of, 204
Grady, Henry W., 30, 38, 65, 183, 303, 566, 635-36
Graham, Billy, 583
Grant, U. S., 13, 16, 182, 254, 396
Great Society, 567
Great Speckled Bird, 649
Greek culture, 336, 597
Green, Sam, 79, 106
Greenback Labor Party, 28-29
Grenier, John, 500
Griffin, Marvin, 187, 269, 499
guilt, national, 472
guilt, Southern, 336-37
Gwinnett, Button, 56

H. L. Hunley, 341
Hagan, Odd, 582
Haiti, 456
Hall, Lyman, 56
Hamilton, Charles, 620
Hamilton, J., 120
Hanberry, Jim, 165-67
Harris, Joel Chandler, 58, 304
Harris, Roy, xvi, 499
Hartford, 342
Hartsfield, William B., 544-46, 658
Harvard University, xi, 526
Hatch, Albert, 422
Hayes, Rutherford B., xl, 25, 193, 285, 439, 525, 597, 613, 623, 635
Hays, Brooks, 260, 292
Hazzard, Liverpool, 6
Headstart program, 653
health, 371
Heery, Harriet, 407
Heflin, Tom, 72
Help Our Public Education (HOPE), 272
Heery, Harriet, 407
Hendricks, Bill, 567
Henry, Aaron, 643
Herberg, Will, 584
High Museum of Art, 159
Hill, Ben, 57, 65

Hill, Lister, 98, 500
Hiroshima, 396
historians, 338
Hitler, Adolf, 85
Hoar, George F., 479
Hodges, Luther H., 251
Holden, William, 19
Holliday, James, 566
Holmes, Hamilton E., 347, 350-51, 554-55
homes, 360
Honest to God, 428, 585
Hood, John, 171
hookworm, 371, 558
Hooper, Ben, 497
Hoover, Herbert, 176, 221
Hoover, J. Edgar, 485
Hornsby, M. A., 81
House, E. M., 39
House of Bishops, Texas, 584
Housing, xxvi, 108-17, 449
Houston, David F., 38-39
Hover, Laura H., 85
Howe, Louis M., 161
Howell, Clark, Sr., 34
Hughes, Robert E., 475
Humphrey, Hubert, 514-16
Humphrey-Durham Drug Act, 515
Hughes, Robert E., 475
Hunter, Charlayne, xxix, 347-53, 554-55 (*see also* Stovall, Charlayne Hunter)
Huntington, Collis P., 36

ideals, 338
illiteracy, 405, 458, 513, 640
In Cold Blood, 581
income, 44
independent electors, 489
India, 211
Indiana, 630
Indians, 355, 358, 395, 492
indigo, 2
individualism, 351
industry, xxii, xxxv, xl, xli, 30, 34, 43, 124, 149, 158, 215, 232, 250, 303, 360, 372, 420, 595, 615, 617
Ingram, Irvine S., 308-11
insecurity, 337
integration, xlii, 251, 590, 613, 620, 657
International Business Machines, 552

International Cotton Exposition, 30
interposition, xxxvii, 248
interracial marriage, xxxix, 224, 378, 386, 432-34
Interstate Commerce Commission, 33
interstate highways, 596, 637
Ivy League, 366
Jackson, Andrew, 10, 174, 395
jail, 475, 517, 646
James, Henry, 335
Jamestown, 371
Japanese, 42, 434
Jeffers, Robinson, 529
Jefferson, Thomas, xix, 120, 199, 487-88, 494
Jenkins, Charles J., 58
Jews, 56, 80, 193, 292, 375, 476, 493, 534
Jim Crow, 242, 478, 560
Jimerson NC, 476
Job Corps, 653
John Birch Society, 501, 542, 566
John Brown's Body, 329
Johns Hopkins University, 142
Johnson, Andrew, 22, 497
Johnson, Mrs. J. H., 436-37
Johnson, John H., 436
Johnson, Lyndon B., 502, 602-603, 649, 655
Johnson, Mrs. J. H., 436-37
Johnston, Joseph, 16, 49, 638
Jones, Bob, 607
Jones, Frank, 80
journalists, xxvii, xxxii, 93, 224, 407, 416, 462, 485, 527, 556, 572, 599, 614
judiciary, 197
justice, xxii

Kaiser Company, 403
Kasper, John, 577
Kefauver, Estes, 396, 549
Keith, Walling, 85
Kennedy, Ethel, 550-51
Kennedy, Jacqueline, 550
Kennedy, John F., xxviii, 364, 402, 427-28, 441, 449, 469, 502, 514, 535-56, 655
Kennedy, Robert F., 377, 379, 415-16, 537, 545, 550-51, 554
Kennedy Library, 547
Kentucky, 12, 250-51, 320, 364, 396, 474

Key, David M., 623
Key, V. O., 141
King, Martin Luther, Jr., 380, 416, 439, 448, 455, 465, 502, 518, 544-45, 583, 633, 642-45
King George's War, 359
Kipling, Rudyard, 479
Knapp, S. A., 30
Korean War, 374
Ku Klux Klan, xiii, xviii, 23, 77, 79, 83, 88, 106, 120, 140, 150, 154, 169, 194, 241, 294, 327, 350, 377, 429, 485-86, 501, 555, 559, 564, 567, 599, 613, 629, 643, 648

labor, 287, 351, 415, 548, 552, 614, 616, 634, 644
Labor in the South, 611
Lake Lanier, 360
Lamar, Lucius, Q. C., 172
Lambert, Gus, 166
Lamont, Thomas W., 163
landlords, 99
Lanier, Sidney, 354
Lash, Joseph P., 164
Lawrence, David, 429
Lawrence, William, 536, 550
laws, xxii-xxiii, 510 (*see* civil rights bills)
leadership, 326, 331, 338, 532
League of Nations, 172
Leckie, George, 302
Lee, Robert E., 14, 22, 57, 78, 103, 182, 254, 419
Lend Lease, 656
Lenk, Arthur, 24, 40
Lewis, Anthony, 507
Lewis, John L., 415, 548, 616, 644
liberalism, 461, 516
Liberation of Lord Byron Jones, 520-24
Library Association, 303
lien system, 31
"Lily White," 483
Lincoln, Abraham, 11, 22, 171, 181, 192, 254, 398, 469, 650
Lippmann, Walter, 321
literacy tests, xxvi
Little Rock AR, 46
Long, Huey, 73, 102
Long, Russell, 489
Loomis, Homer, 80, 84
Los Angeles Times, 652

Louisiana, 40, 184, 192, 236, 324, 330, 345, 366, 398, 471, 509, 512, 559, 576
Louisiana Purchase, 488
Louisiana State University Press, 574
Lovejoy, Hatton, 69
Lovett School (Atlanta), 422
Lowell, Robert, 529
Lucy, Authurine, 474
Lusitania, 655
Lutherans, 55
lynchings, xxiii, 32, 73, 123, 189, 480, 504, 569, 630-31

MacArthur, Douglas, 538
McCallie, Thomas, 396
McCallie School, 393
McCarthy, Joseph, 180, 349, 602
McClellan, George B., 19, 171
McCullers, Carson, 128, 571-72
McKinley, William, 129
McKissick, Roy, 654
McLaurin, John L., 479
McNeill, Robert Blakely, 289, 530-32
McWilliams, Carey, 527
Maddox, James, 611
Maddox, Lester, 432-33, 435, 601, 603, 609, 656, 658
Madison, James, 487
managerial skills, 595
manufacturing, 31, 58
March on Washington, 447
Marshall, Edison, 128
Marshall, F. Ray, 611
Marshall, George, 176, 180
Marshall, Thurgood, 589, 600
Marshall Plan, 204, 438
Martin, Jim, 500
Martin, Joe, 107
Martin, Roscie C., 141
Martin, T. S., 39
Maryland, 127, 320
Maryville College, 497
Mason, Lucy Randolph, 615
Masons, xvi, 547
Massachusetts, 395, 419, 479
Matheson, Jenneth G., 420
Mathis, Rebecca, 394
Maury, Matthew F., 340
Meany, George, 552
media, 452, 475
Melville, Herman, 335
Mencken, H. L. 528, 571

Meredith, James, 388, 390, 392, 407-409, 645
Metropolitan Opera, 301
Mexico, 655
migration, 112, 122, 147, 331, 363, 414, 561, 590, 595, 621, 628, 630, 636, 646
Miles College, 475
military, Southern, 611
Millay, Edna St. Vincent, 348
Miller, William, 499
mills, 2
mine sweepers, 343
ministers, 389-97
Minnesota, 514
Missionary Ridge, 396
Mississippi, xxviii, xxix, 1, 52, 97, 119, 121, 148, 151, 192, 210, 236, 250, 270, 274, 306, 324, 328, 330, 377, 383, 388-92, 396, 398, 407-408, 416, 437, 445, 458, 461, 463, 471, 477, 479, 488, 500, 507, 509, 512, 518, 527-28, 531, 549, 553, 568, 602, 635, 637, 642-43, 645
Mississippi Plan, 479
Mississippi: The Closed Society, 505
Missouri, 12, 223, 251, 320, 399
Mitch, Bill, 615
Mitchell, Broadus, 615
moderates, xi, xiii, xliii, 11, 74, 244, 260, 348, 599
Monitor Tecumseh, 342
Monroe, James, 4
Moore, Ray, 402
moral leadership, 449
moral right, xiv, xix, xxxi, xlii, xliv, 8, 321, 428, 481, 579, 644
Morgan, Charles, 423, 473-76
Morgan, John, 479
Morrissey, Charles T., 535
mortgage foreclosed, 331
Moseley, Hardwick, 1
Murphy, Frank, 161
Murphy, Reg, 652, 656-57
Murray, James, F., 196
Mussolini, Benito, 85
Myrdal, Gunnar, 560
myths, xliv, xxxvii, 2, 219, 230, 352, 385, 453, 596, 599, 614, 635, 637

Nash, Ogden, 558
Nation, 26, 344, 525-29
National Association for the Advancement of Colored People (NAACP), 132, 229, 266, 380, 417, 434, 439, 465, 471, 518
National Banking Act of 1863, 25
National Book Awards, 572
National Broadcasting Company, 173
National Conference of Christians and Jews, 534
National Defense Education Act, 515
National Education Association, xxxv
National Guard, 450
nationalism, 3, 468
Nazis, 81
"Negro," spelling of, 657 (*see* black)
Nelson, Jack, 651
neocolonialism, 403
New Deal, 332, 542, 567
New Departure Democrats, 566
New Jersey, 1
New South, 30, 43, 66, 103
New York, 419
New York Herald Tribune, 512
New York Times, 370, 536, 550, 652
Newman, Ernest, 528
Nichols, James, 361
Niebuhr, Reinhold, 528, 583
Nixon, Richard M., 179, 237, 436, 541-42, 603, 653
Nkrumah, Kwame, 537
Norris, Frank, 77
North, 459
North Carolina, 1, 12, 20, 192, 250, 267, 326, 396, 480, 490, 546
nuclear reactor, 418

Ochs, Adolph, 396
O'Connor, Flannery, 571-72
Odum, Howard, xii, 144, 559, 614, 639
Oglethorpe, James E., 54, 492
Ohio, 177, 547, 589
Ohio Northern University, 582
Okefenokee swamp, 60, 454
Oklahoma, 223, 251, 320, 399, 574, 630
okra, 593

Old South, xxxvii, 336
Old South, 634
Olmsted, Frederick Law, 527
One Hundred Years of the "Nation", 525-29
one-crop system, 558
O'Neill, Eugene, 129
oratory, xxxvii, 646
Oregon, 630
Origins of the New South, 335, 440, 569
Osborne, John 634

Page, Thomas N., 39, 559
Page, Walter Hines, 39
Paige, George, 402
Paine, Tom, 498, 541
Palmer, A. Mitchell, 629
Palmer, John, 402
paper mills, 595
Parent Teacher Association, 220, 452, 522
Parker, Mack Charles, 274
partisanship, 336
passive resistance, 381
paternalism, 3
paternalistic, xlii, 522, 567
Patterson, Eugene, 434, 446, 650-51
Patterson, Hugh, 619
Peace Corps, 407, 515
Pearl Harbor, 42
Pelham, John, 14
Pennsylvania, 1, 362
People's Anti-Bourbon Party, 29
Perez, Leander, 607
Peters, James, 68, 187
Peters, William, 264
Petigru, James Louis, 13, 558
Phi Beta Kappa, 391, 475, 555
Philippines, 479
Phillips, B. J., 650
picket lines, 517
Pickett, George, 13
Pilcher, J. L., 187
pine trees, 593
Pittman, Marvin S., 69
Plaintiff, Mary Ellen, 85-86
plantation, xliv, 5, 189, 331, 414, 495, 628
planters, 3, 8, 634
Plessy v. Ferguson, 35
police brutality, 478
police dogs, 457, 578

politics, xvi, xix, xxxiii, 9, 17, 91, 141, 214, 223, 235, 251, 268, 285, 320, 325, 328, 331, 399, 440, 441, 464, 480, 482, 485, 497-503, 591, 601, 607, 621, 630, 646
poll tax, 123, 134, 275
Pollard, Reuben T., 52
population, 332, 364, 440
Populism, 28, 32, 198, 285, 334, 335, 377, 480, 560, 567
Porter, Katherine A., 528
Portrait of a Decade, 507
ports, 360
Pound, Ezra, 528
poverty, xli, 29, 645
Powers, Francis Gary, 436
prejudice, xl, xxxviii, 348, 380, 414, 477
Presbyterian, 289
Pritchard, J. Carson, 311
private schools, xxxv, 157
propaganda, 452
Protocols of the Elders of Zion, 629
psychological compensation, 570
public accommodations, 509, 599
public education, xxvii, 139, 285
public facilities, 400
public schools, xxiv, xxxii, xxxv, xliii, 198, 206, 209, 251, 271, 306, 320, 327, 331, 365, 378, 448, 495, 599, 602, 612, 620, 641
Pulitzer Prize, 313
pulpwood, 593
Pupil Placement Act, xxix

race, xxii, 145, 191, 200
race problems, 531
race relations, 44
race relations, progress in, 100, 328, 513
race, violence, 33
race-baiters, 102, 250
racial equality, 70, 484
racism, 480, 498
radio, 562
Raffington, A. B., 52
railroads, 15, 31, 206, 598
Rayburn, Sam, 173
Reader's Digest, 584
real estate racket, 82
reapportionment, 400, 441

Reconstruction, 24, 29, 193, 285, 525, 598, 615, 630
Red and Black, 348
Redding, Jay Saunders, 211
Reed, James, 586
Reed, Walter, 165
religion, xxi, xxxii, 9-10, 77, 127, 206, 224, 260, 289-97, 326-27, 331, 352, 375, 382, 384, 386, 396, 399, 422-35, 438, 444-45, 453, 456, 471, 493, 504, 511-13, 530-32, 544, 547-48, 581, 599, 614, 616
Republicans, 4, 25, 99, 101, 136, 142, 170, 178, 183, 196, 215, 235, 248, 285, 332, 482-83, 489, 497, 499, 502, 542, 602, 624
resources, Southern, 595
Reunion and Reaction, 335
Reuther, Walter, 552
Revolt in the South, 344
Reynolds, John, 56
Reynolds, Richard S., Jr., 552
Rhett, Robert B., 10-11
rice, 2, 337, 495
Rise of Cotton Mills in the South, 615
rivers, 356
Robert, L. W., 71
Robins, L. J. J., 339
Robinson, Edwin Arlington, 529
Robinson, John A. T., 428
Rockefeller, John D., 316
Rockefeller, Nelson, 603
Rockefeller, Winthrop, 482
Rockefeller Foundation, 142, 212
Rodgers, William P., 546
Rogers, H. H., 35
Roosevelt, Eleanor, 101, 162, 314, 472
Roosevelt, Franklin Delano, 40, 45, 100, 152, 161, 172, 176, 216, 221, 312, 396, 472, 547, 613
Roosevelt, Theodore, 38
Rotary Club, 430, 501
Rothchild, John H., 563
Ruffin, Edmund, 11
rural conditions, 220, 372, 590, 600
Rural Electrification Administration, 42
Rusk, Dean, 402

Russell, Richard B., 170, 186-87, 325, 364, 441, 481, 528, 538, 553, 595, 642, 645
Saltonstall, Leverett, 535
Sanders, Carl E., 463, 627-33
saw mills, 617
Schardt, Arlie, 650
Schwerner, Michael, 642
segregation, xxiv, xxxiv, xl, 105, 139, 229, 249, 272, 320-21, 327, 336, 345, 349, 365, 367, 368, 374, 389, 438, 443, 458, 477, 485, 502, 522, 558, 574, 577-78, 596, 601, 627, 630, 640, 641, 653
Selective Service Act 656
Selma AL, 587
separate-and-equal, xxi, xliv
separatism, 626
Seward, William H., 19
sharecroppers, xli, 37, 362, 414, 481
Shelby, Evan J., 52
sheriffs, 364, 509
Sherman, William T., 14, 16, 48, 168, 171, 300, 371, 638
Sherrill, Robert, 605
Shingler, Leila E., 94
Shingler, Robert, 94
ships, 341-42, 357
shipyards, 39
Shivers, Allan, 214-15
Sigma Chi, 51
silk, 56
Silver, James, 505
Sims, Cecil, 119
Sinclair, Upton, 528
sit-ins, xliv, 321, 326, 344-46, 380, 485, 489
Skinner, Otis, 312
slavery, xl, 2, 8, 13, 16, 228, 329, 335, 337, 447, 525, 527, 589, 594, 616, 635
slums, 459
Smart, Sue, 394
Smathers, George, 606
Smith, Alfred E., 172, 312
Smith, Ed, 498, 601-602
Smith, Frank E., 503
Smith, Gerald L. K., 499
Smith, Hoke, 172
Smith, Lillian, xii, xxix
SNCC: The New Abolitionists, 517
Snodgrass, Robert, 501

social change, 202
social equality, 105
social inventiveness, xiv
social life, 611
social progress, xviii, 513, 613
social services, xxvi
sociology, 559
soil, 34, 41
solid South, 1, 597
South and the Southerner, 444, 459, 569
South Carolina, 21, 97, 119, 121, 192, 236, 250, 270, 306, 324, 328, 330, 341, 457, 479, 512, 546, 558, 608, 637
South Rejects a Prophet, 623
Southern Bourbons, 146
Southern Christian Leadership Conference, 642
Southern Farmers Alliance, 32
Southern leaders, 38
Southern Legacy, 574
Southern Mystique, 517
Southern Regional Council, xii, 241, 252
Southern Regions, 559, 614
Southern School News Reporting Service, 252
Southern writers, 336
Southerners, 637
Soviet Union, 176, 403, 436, 469, 537, 558
soybeans, 593
space age, 495
Spain, 494
Spanish, 54
Sparkman, John, 98
Spelman College, xxiii
sports, integration of, 600
Sprigle, Ray, 131
Stanford, Henry King, 475
Stassen, Harold, 233
states' rights, xxxvii, 10, 15, 118, 180, 323, 399, 498, 501, 598, 600, 603, 624, 630
stereotypes, 460
Stevens, Thaddeus, 20
Stevenson, Adlai E., 12, 18, 57, 180-81, 183-87, 214, 565
Stovall, Charlayne Hunter, 432-33
Strange Career of Jim Crow, 335, 557-61
Street, James Howell, 168, 335

Stringfellow, William, 581
Stuart, B., 14
Student Nonviolent Coordinating Committee, 439, 455, 478, 517, 620-21, 642, 643, 645
submarines, 15-16
Summerfield, Arthur, 181
Sumner, Charles, 20
Sunday School bombing, xxix, 427, 470, 476, 478, 568
Supreme Court decisions, xxi, xxvii, xxx, 45, 105, 122, 135, 200-201, 215, 218, 222, 229, 244, 252, 262, 274, 306, 317, 344, 365, 386, 448, 457, 477, 498, 511, 518, 531, 576, 598, 603, 641, 645
Survey Graphic, 70

Taft, Howard, 103, 176
Taft, Robert A., 111, 177
Taft-Ellender-Wagner Bill, 117
Talmadge, Eugene, xvi, 68, 74, 87, 90, 102, 567, 601, 610
Talmadge, Herman, xxviii, 89, 142, 187, 539, 607
tariff, 7
taxes, 208, 325, 466, 490, 589, 594
Taylor, Alf, 497
teachers, 272
telegraph, 15
television, 413
tenancy, 37, 364, 441
Tennessee, xxix, 12, 119, 223, 250, 312, 324, 330, 393-97, 497, 521, 563, 576, 594, 615, 623
Tennessee, 342
Tennessee Valley Authority, 41, 163, 181, 394
Texas, xxix, 1, 65, 119, 173, 184, 209, 215, 223
textiles, 153, 548, 615
third party, 489
Thomas, Norman, 528
Thompson, M. E., 187
Thoreau, David, xvi
Thurmond, Strom, 221
Tilden, Samuel J., 25, 285
Tillman, Ben, 32, 223, 480, 602
timber, 62
tobacco, 2, 337, 352, 458, 495
Tom Watson: Agrarian Rebel, 334, 566

Toombs, Robert, 57, 127
torpedoes, 339
Towne, Anthony, 581
towns, 597
transportation, 303
Trappist Monks, 508
Truman, Harry S., 96, 116, 173, 181, 216, 221, 391, 538, 547-48
Tulane University, 37
turnip greens, 593
Tuskegee Institute, 34, 137, 188, 400, 451, 491
two-party politics, xli, 441, 597
Tyre, Nedra, 128

"Ugly American," 406
"Uncle Tom," 644
unemployment, 404 (*see* blacks)
Union, 284, 395, 598
United Automobile Workers, 153
United Mine Workers, 415
United Nations, 163, 310, 374, 405, 412, 466, 502
United Negro College Fund, 316
United States Arms Control, 554
United States Department of Commerce, 44
United States Information Agency, 408
United States marshals, 470
United States Navy Department, 340
University of Alabama, 37, 464
University of Alabama Law School, 475
University of Atlanta, 316
University of Chattanooga, 393
University of Georgia, xxix, 69, 94, 154, 286, 347, 399, 554, 555, 602-603
University of Kentucky, 37, 370
University of Mississippi, xxxvi, 388-92, 470, 505
University of North Carolina, 554, 639
University of South Carolina, 223, 272
University System of Georgia, 309
unskilled workers, 617
Urban League, 380, 439
urbanism, 8, 113, 189, 251, 268, 325, 365, 590, 595, 645
U.S. News and World Report, 429
USS *Housatonic*, 341

values, xiv, xxii, xxxiv, xl, 11, 336-37, 516
Vance, Zebulon, B., 18
Vandenberg, Arthur H., 107
Vanderbilt University, 37, 336, 394, 563, 570-71, 637
Vandiver, Ernest, 249, 554
Vardaman, James, 602
Vietnam War, 655
Villard, Henry, 527
Villard, Oswald, G., 527
Vincent, Haywood, 444
Vinson, Carl, 187, 548
violence, xiii, xx, xxii-xxiii, xxxvi, 225, 328, 331, 373, 383, 415, 441, 471, 476, 478, 489, 508-10, 518, 527, 534, 537, 568, 589, 599, 608, 627, 642, 646, 654
Virginia, xxxvii, 1, 12, 19, 97, 184, 250, 324-25, 327, 330, 366, 396, 448, 492, 559
vocational education, 35
Voter Education Project, 489
voter registration, 277
voting, xxv, 332

Wade, Ben, 23
Wagner Act, 617
Wakefield, Dan, 344
Walden, A. T., 626
Walker, Edwin, 652
Wallace, George, xxxiv
Wallace, Henry, 93, 98, 194
Walton, George, 56, 415, 435, 464, 473, 500, 603, 607-608
Wannamaker, Elliott, 165

War of Jenkins Ear, 359
Warfield, David, 312
Warren, Robert Penn, 228
wars, 374
Washington, Booker T., 34, 45, 150, 277, 304, 491
Washington, George, 210
Washington Post, 652
Watson, Thomas E., 32, 38, 79, 223
Watson, Thomas J., Jr., 552
Watson, Tom, 334
Watts riot, 645
weather, 3
Weaver, Buck, 81
West, Don, 654
West Georgia College, 308, 551
West Virginia, 223, 364, 399, 532
western civilization, 375
white children, 599
White Citizens' Councils, 220, 225, 241, 246, 268, 278, 293, 345, 347, 372, 375, 379, 381, 384, 389-90, 400, 460, 463, 484-86, 499, 505, 565, 599
White House, 553
"White Man's Burden," 479
"white politics," 591
white population, 5
white primary, xli, 324, 374, 441
white supremacy, xxii, xxxix, xl, 71, 617, 640
White, Theodore, 542
white voters, 588
white-collar workers, 331

whites freed too, 598
Whitman, R. L., 81
Whitman, Walt, 109
Whitney, Eli, 495, 593
Wilkie, Wendell, 173
Williams, John Bell, 197-210, 601
Williams, Kathryne, 94
Williams, Malcolm, 395
Williams, Wilson, 107
Willingham, Calder, 128
Wilson, Edmund, 528
Wilson, Woodrow, 38, 172, 221, 629
Winship, Lawrence, 535, 549
women, 362, 569
Wood, Canon M., 422
Woodward, C. Vann, 26, 324, 440, 557-61, 562-73
World Methodist Council, 582
World War I, 42, 62, 148, 191, 286, 351, 363, 527, 602, 617
World War II, xli, 46, 95, 110, 122, 286, 345, 358, 438, 476, 631
Worley, Cade, 191
WSB Television, 187, 402

Yale Daily News, 563
"Yale Reports," 562
Yale University, 562
Yancey, William L., 11
Yeats, William Butler, 529
Yerger, Wert, 500

Zinn, Howard, 517